D1592988

PHILOSOPHICAL ANALYSIS AND HUMAN WELFARE

PHILOSOPHICAL STUDIES SERIES
IN PHILOSOPHY

VOLUME 3

DICKINSON S. MILLER 1868–1963

DICKINSON S. MILLER

PHILOSOPHICAL ANALYSIS
AND HUMAN WELFARE

Selected Essays and Chapters from Six Decades

Edited with an Introduction by Loyd D. Easton

D. REIDEL PUBLISHING COMPANY

DORDRECHT-HOLLAND / BOSTON-U.S.A.

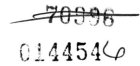

Library of Congress Cataloging in Publication Data

Miller, Dickinson Sergeant, 1868–1963.
    Philosophical analysis and human welfare.

    (Philosophical studies series in philosophy ; v. 3)
    Bibliography: p.
    Includes index.
    1. Analysis (Philosophy)—Collected works. 2. Public wel-
fare—Collected works. 3. James, William, 1842–1910. I. Easton,
Loyd David. II. Title.
B945.M471E2   110   75–4832

ISBN 90 277 0566 6

Published by D. Reidel Publishing Company,
P.O. Box 17, Dordrecht, Holland

Sold and distributed in the U.S.A., Canada, and Mexico
by D. Reidel Publishing Company, Inc.
306 Dartmouth Street, Boston,
Mass. 02116, U.S.A.

CONTENTS

Editor's Preface   IX

Dickinson S. Miller On Analysis, Pragmatism, and Welfare –
   An Introduction, by Loyd D. Easton   1

TEACHERS AND TEACHING

Fullerton and Philosophy   39
A Student's Impressions of William James   47
James and Analysis   52
George Santayana   63
Is Philosophy a Good Training for the Mind?   75

ANALYSIS: THE METHOD OF PHILOSOPHY AT WORK

The Relations of 'Ought' and 'Is'   91
Free Will as Involving Determination and Inconceivable
   Without It [Revised]   104
Is There Not a Clear Solution of the Knowledge-Problem?   132
A Debt to James   146
Universals   156
An Event In Modern Philosophy with Hume   184
Hume's Deathblow to Deductivism   201
Moral Truth   220

CONTENTS

RELIGION AND HUMAN WELFARE

What Religion Has To Do With It   231
The Defense of the Faith Today   236
Heart and Head   241
Democracy and Our Intellectual Plight   252
Matthew Arnold, On the Occasion of His Centenary   263
Conscience and the Bishops   270
James's Doctrine of 'The Right to Believe' [Revised]   281
Morals, Intelligence, and Welfare   312

Published Writings of Dickinson S. Miller   327
Publications about Dickinson S. Miller   330
Index   331

EDITOR'S PREFACE

When I was Dickinson Miller's assistant from 1940 to 1942, I soon realized that I had encountered an unusually powerful, acute, and original mind and a writer whose clear but vivid style matched the high quality of his intelligence. These traits were apparent in his comments about eminent philosophers with whom he had associated – particularly William James but also Santayana, Dewey, Husserl, and Wittgenstein – and in the mutual criticism he demanded of his writing and my first efforts. I was pleased and felt immensely privileged to share in his planning of a book devoted to "analysis, the method of philosophy at work" as in his articles on the knowledge-problem, induction, and free will. In view of the penetration of his articles, such a book seemed long overdue as James had insisted even in 1905.

When Miller's projected book on "analysis at work" did not appear by 1956, I consulted him about putting together a collection of his published essays. Such a collection seemed but slight homage to one who had made such a striking contribution to American philosophy in relation to James and one from whom I had learned so much. He felt, however, that such a collection would be inappropriate and preferred to concentrate on a book, never finished, on "the principles of practical intelligence", the application of intelligence in a "morality of results" for human welfare.

After Miller's death in 1963 I resumed work on a collection of his writings and when my resolution flagged, I was encouraged and substantially supported in my efforts by the late Charles L. Street, Suffragan Bishop of the Episcopal Diocese of Chicago, who had studied under Miller at General Theological Seminary. Dr Street aided me in completing the bibliography, in collecting Miller's writings, and in providing extensive notes on his ideas and teaching. With Dr Street's death I decided to continue the project alone. Mrs Street encouraged and materially aided me in this decision, and I gratefully thank her for her help and the collaborative support of her late husband. I must equally thank Miss Constance Worcester for her encouragement, her provision of biographical details, and for lending me Miller's surviving papers to use as I might see fit. Those papers provided four previously unpublished articles for this volume and revisions of two articles preparing them to serve as chapters.

For encouragement and for information conveyed in letters or conversation about Miller, I gratefully acknowledge indebtedness to M. B. Stokes, J. H. Randall Jr., Hiram McLendon, the late Daniel Cory, Herbert Feigl, Edward Madden, and the late C. J. Ducasse. To the editors of various periodicals in the list of Miller's published articles at the end of this volume I give thanks for permission to republish his writings. Finally, but not least, I am deeply grateful to Ohio Wesleyan University for a Faculty Fellowship that facilitated research and writing, to the staff of Beeghly Library for assistance, and to Shirley Walker and Judith Hershkowitz for help in preparing the manuscript.

The writings chosen for inclusion in the volume proportionately reflect the main themes of Miller's analytical philosophy or in the case of pieces under 'Teachers and Teaching' and 'Religion and Human Welfare' main formative interests in his life. Thus the collection is representative of the scope of Miller's thought. The major section, 'Analysis: The Method of Philosophy At Work', carries out Miller's own plans in title and content for the book he began in 1941 but never finished. For each section the articles have been selected to provide Miller's fullest or maturest conclusions on their theme, and they are presented in their entirety. Main editorial additions are indicated by the customary square brackets.

Delaware, Ohio   LOYD D. EASTON

DICKINSON S. MILLER ON ANALYSIS, PRAGMATISM, AND WELFARE

An Introduction by Loyd D. Easton

From William James's remarks in *The Meaning of Truth* and in correspondence, Dickinson S. Miller has long been known as a formative contributor to pragmatism in its beginnings and also one of its sharpest critics. What has not been generally recognized, however, is that both of these roles were the consequence of Miller's own consistently firm view as to the proper concern and method of philosophy – namely, the logical analysis of terms and statements in relation to facts of ordinary experience. Where Miller could agree with James he could do so on the ground that James had made a trenchant and adequate analysis of 'consciousness', 'idea', or 'oneness'. Where he differed, he gave evidence that James was lacking in "pertinacious analysis". Miller's own independent results in applying his method to the problems of free will, knowledge, and induction – in some cases under the name of R. E. Hobart – have recently been recognized in anthologies and bibliographies as acute examples of analytical philosophy. So in the current "age of analysis" Miller's thought emerges from the shadow of James to be seen as indigenous analytical philosophy making its mark as early as 1893.

I. EDUCATION AND TEACHERS

Miller came to believe that philosophy is centrally and essentially analysis through the teaching of George S. Fullerton at the University of Pennsylvania where he received his A.B. degree in 1889 and where his father was a professor of law. As a result of his family's religious affiliation – his uncle, Bishop Hare, had been the first missionary to the Indians of South Dakota – he had previously attended the Episcopal High School in Philadelphia, his birthplace October 7, 1868, but most of his time after school was spent in the Philadelphia Library rather than at games, a consequence of his slightness of bodily frame and delicate constitution, with difficulties from a curvature of the spine. "From the library", Miller later remarked, "I got ideas. They did not grow in school". The

main idea he got from Fullerton was that the "somewhat startling analyses" of Locke, Berkeley, and Hume could be seen not as destructive or
sceptical but as explanatory, as giving new insight into the nature of what
we assumed to exist all along. Though Fullerton did not overtly formulate
his method, Miller summarized it as *analysis versus scepticism*. Many of
Miller's subsequent applications of the method extended and developed
Fullerton's suggestions about free will, the problem of the external world,
and Hume's 'scepticism'. In important respects Miller himself resembled
his description of Fullerton as man and teacher: "limited in health and
nervous force" yet "strong in command of himself" with a "confident
and contagious smile"; the habit of bringing all abstractions "back to
the concrete", to "daily experience in the matter"; like Socrates, asking
questions to get "judgment on the soundness of each step of the argument".

Miller most pointedly went beyond Fullerton in his insistence that
analytical intelligence be applied to issues of social welfare. In this
respect he differed from some contemporary analysts who hold that the
philosopher *qua* philosopher has no more to do with questions of belief in
religious, moral, or political matters than a mathematician or botanist.
For Miller analysis entailed "a fine accuracy" in observing and reasoning
and hence a "conscience of the mind" to be applied to the achievement of
human welfare. The alternative is to "play metaphysics" while Rome
burns. So he applied the method of analysis in articles and addresses on
religion, education, and politics as well as the technicalities of moral
theory. He had a strong bent toward social reform to enhance human
welfare and hence a strong personal affinity in this respect with James and
Dewey but antipathy to Santayana.

After his years at the University of Pennsylvania under Fullerton, Miller
went to Clark University for a year to study psychology under G. Stanley
Hall and then to Harvard for two more years after which he received
the A.B. and A.M. degrees in 1892. At Harvard he studied under William
James, G. H. Palmer, Josiah Royce, George Santayana, and C. C. Everett,
but of all these teachers he was closest to James. Their relationship developed into a life-long friendship reinforced by close relations with the
James family. After Harvard, Miller went abroad, with James's encourage-
ment, to study at the universities of Berlin and Halle under Dessoir,
Ebbinghaus, Paulsen, and Erdmann. In 1893 he received the Ph.D. from
Halle with a dissertation on *Das Wesen der Erkenntnis und des Irrthums*.

He translated and abridged the dissertation for an article on 'The Meaning of Truth and Error' published in *The Philosophical Review* in 1893, within a few months of his appointment, on James's recommendation, as Associate in Philosophy at Bryn Mawr College.

II. 'THE JAMES–MILLER THEORY' OF COGNITION

At Bryn Mawr Miller published an analytical essay on 'The Relation of "Ought" and "Is"' and one on 'Confusion of Function and Content in Mental Analysis'. The latter was influenced by what he had learned from James and was influential in the formation of James's view of truth that evolved into 'pragmatism'. While at Bryn Mawr, Miller had a crisis in health. He suffered from what he called "crippling neurasthenia" that semi-paralyzed all his activities for the rest of his life. This became a severe limitation on his writing, teaching, and social relations. As a result of his ill-health, a serious courtship could only end in his remaining a bachelor. At Bryn Mawr he developed close, friendly relations with Woodrow Wilson whom he greatly admired. He frequently referred in conversation to Wilson's liberal idealism and in 1912 wrote lengthy letters to *The New York Times* defending Wilson's application for a Carnegie Teacher's Pension against his political detractors.

In 'The Meaning of Truth and Error' Miller made his commitment to analysis clear at the outset. "The philosophical world in our time", he observed, "has discovered that the analysis of terms – which Descartes completely neglected – is the most important business of philosophy".[1] While Descartes wanted to discover the existence or nonexistence of certain supposed facts, modern investigators "seek to analyze facts whose existence is not disputed". Miller specifically intended to analyze how our ideas can know objects external to them. Royce had well formulated the problem but Miller could not accept his conclusion. Miller's "analysis of the states of mind that we call knowledge" led him to reject as logically incoherent the "metaphysical hypothesis" that certain mental states have a self-transcendent power enabling them to report something not of themselves. Our ideas, rather, are simply mental appearances or images before the mind, and 'belief' is not a feeling over and above the ideas but rather their mode of behavior, their spontaneous association and maintenance apart from any effort of will. Such an association may in all cases be accompanied by "the sense of reality" of which James wrote in his *Psychology*, but it never performs any "feats of self-transcendence". On this basis 'truth' is not a thought's correspondence with a transcendent object but with an object in consciousness involving 'belief' in which thought, after development, terminates.

'The Meaning of Truth and Error' was decisive in leading James to abandon Royce's solution of the knowledge-problem in terms of an absolute mind. Royce had argued that our minds can get at their objects and so agree with them as to be 'true' only if our ideas and their objects are both included in an all-embracing universal consciousness. James held this view, with some misgivings, until Miller helped him to see an alternative that dispensed with the absolute mind as intermediary between idea and object. "Largely through the influence of Professor D. S. Miller," said James, "I came to see that any definitely experienceable workings would serve as intermediaries quite as well as the absolute mind's intentions would." James acknowledged this debt to Miller in a note to 'The Function of Cognition', the essay he later called "the *fons et origo* of all *my* pragmatism".[2]

In an article of 1895 on 'Confusion of Content and Function in Mental Analysis', Miller noted that his chief theses were identical with or allied to James's in 'The Function of Cognition' and *Psychology*. Miller argued that an idea not only has a specific content but also a part to play in mental life as it calls up other ideas and influences the future course of thought and action. On this basis an idea can represent a class by its function, "by leading us to behave in action and in thought in the manner required by our desire". It can "do duty as the representative of a class" and by its association prompt the right action toward the members of the class. James was impressed by Miller's analysis of the functioning of ideas and noted in his presidential address to the American Psychological Association, 'The Knowing of Things Together', that Miller had reconfirmed his "sometime wavering opinion" on the subject.[3]

James's acknowledgement of his significant intellectual debt to Miller testified to the wide congruence of their thought during the years when Miller was teaching at Bryn Mawr. At the same time, however, Miller came to differ sharply with James at certain points, and the differences were publicized in 1899 in criticism of James's 'Will to Believe' and in a brief article on James's philosophical method as found in his California address on 'Philosophical Conceptions and Practical Results'. With that address Miller discerned a unity in James's thought but not an indivisible totality that the student or critic must take or leave.

What would Miller take? He would take James's identification of his principle with "the way in which English empiricism from Locke to Mr. Shadworth Hodgson investigates a conception", i.e., by asking in what facts it results, "What is its *cash-value* in experience?" Miller noted James's claim that Hume could be corrected and built out "by using Humian principles exclusively". But while the analysis of British empiricists was genetic, asking whence a conception came, James appealed to "future practical experience". In this respect, Miller observed, James was still empirical and had profoundly applied Darwinian ideas in respect to the testing and winnowing of conceptions by experience. Further, James's address summed into a general formula his previous conclusion that there is no self-transcendency in mental images by themselves and that the pointing of thought to its object is solely a procession of mental associates leading to the object. Such a position, Miller added, is perfectly harmonious with the nominalist view that the meaning of a generic belief is not in the mind's concrete image but in "the mental action, the rejection of false instances and acceptance of true ones, to which its presence, together with that of the 'abstract' term, commits the mind". Miller had already written about such a nominalism in his essay on 'Confusion of Content and Function in Mental Analysis'.

III. CRITICISM OF JAMES'S 'WILL TO BELIEVE' AND 'PRAGMATISM'

What did Miller have to reject from James's view in 1899? First and most forcefully, James's view of "the lawfulness of voluntarily adopted faith" in excess of the evidence. Miller formulated his rejection and the grounds for it in an article entitled 'The Will to Believe and the Duty to Doubt'. With Miller's first reactions to 'The Will to Believe' in mind, James referred to him as "my most penetrating critic and intimate enemy".[4] On the other side, Miller always firmly believed that the first homage one can do a teacher is to take his ideas seriously enough to criticize them analytically.

Miller's objection to 'The Will to Believe' centered on the analysis of 'belief'. Whereas James considered belief to involve inclination, motive,

or will, Miller argued that belief is entirely distinct from will. It is altogether a different thing, so to refer to 'voluntary belief' was, in Miller's
view, virtually a contradiction in terms. Here Miller was substantially
reiterating what he had said about belief in 'The Meaning of Truth and
Error', and there he had argued that belief is not "a feeling over and above
the ideas which form the matter of the belief, but a mode of behaviour
of those ideas themselves", namely, their spontaneous association and
maintenance apart from any effort of our will.[5] So when James merged
the two, Miller saw the very foundations of knowledge, particularly its
claim to objectivity, being radically undermined. We do not accept the
foundations of science, Miller argued, because we have a certain motive
or impulse to do so. On the contrary, "we find them existing for our
minds; an assured belief presents itself without our forth-putting. Nature
to us, and its elementary properties, are simply real: that is what is
meant by saying that we believe in them. Where we have to create a belief
we at first by hypothesis have it not. In that stage the thing is not real
to us." Contrary to James, then, belief is a species of mental presentation,
a spontaneous association of ideas involving the attitude of the mind toward
"the shape the images take of their own accord".

Miller also questioned the view of truth that might be developed from
James's linkage of meaning with practical results. He noted that James
had thus far concerned himself only with the meaning and clearness of
conceptions, but he would be interested in knowing whether James would
be prepared to take the further step of holding that truth as well as
meaning depends on the success and utility of actions. Such a view of
truth had already been suggested by Georg Simmel and Miller found it
in keeping with James's view of the verification of religious hypotheses
in 'The Will To Believe'. If James were to take this further step, "philosophic precision" would require us to note, Miller held, "that belief
enters into a composition of causes with desire, since two sets of desires,
with the same belief, may produce different courses of conduct". Thus
Miller's objection to the theory of truth that James subsequently developed as 'pragmatism' again centered on the analysis of 'belief'. He found
James failing to make the precise distinctions required by ordinary
experience in conduct.

These criticisms of James's thought appeared in 1899, the year that
Miller left Bryn Mawr to become an instructor in philosophy at Harvard.

During his five years at Harvard he maintained close relations with James and served as 'tutor' to James's sons during summers in the Adirondacks. Though Miller later said that his criticism of James's 'Will to Believe' had "strained our friendship",[6] there was no evidence of such a strain on James's side. On the contrary, in a letter of January 18, 1900 expressing appreciation to Miller for his "extraordinary faithfulness to the boys", James wrote: "I always turn to you inwardly as the completest ideal responder whom I have to any strivings of the spirit in myself – and this equally whether the response be agreement or dissent, for you genuinely meet me and others almost always glance side-ways off the surface".[7]

Some of Miller's agreements with James in this period were reflected in James's letters characterizing Royce as "simply magnificent" in class but in his books "a sketcher and popularizer, not a pile-driver, foundation-layer, or wall-builder", one in whom "looseness of thought" is an essential element – an estimate that Miller fully shared.[8] A few years later James wrote to Miller that he was at work "on the infernal old problem of mind and brain, and how to construct the world out of pure experience" but felt foiled again.[9] In other words, James was at work on what he was to call "radical empiricism" involving a new view of the relation of thought and object. A year later he promised to try to meet a difficulty Miller had found in the draft of an article on 'How Two Minds Can Know One Thing' but was glad that Miller could agree with and had anticipated so much of it. "I owe much of my firmness of conviction on some of these points", James wrote to Miller, "to your independent conviction of the same."[10] Miller's specific points of dissent on these issues were crystallized later, but while he was at Harvard areas of agreement with James were most prominent. Hence in 1904 C. A. Strong hailed "the James–Miller theory" of cognition as an original, naturalistic view and traced it to James's essay on 'The Function of Cognition', noting that the "subjective side" of the view had been ably worked out by Miller in 'The Meaning of Truth and Error' and 'The Confusion of Function and Content in Mental Analysis'.[11]

While teaching at Harvard, Miller became more closely acquainted with Santayana, now his senior colleague who had formerly been his teacher along with James, Royce, and others. They were close enough to consider sharing an apartment in Cambridge, but Miller decided against such an arrangement in view of his chronic ill health. With this association, more formal and less intimate than with James, Miller acquired first-hand knowledge of Santayana's ideas, work habits, and social attitudes and was generally out of sympathy with them. He admired Santayana's poetry but saw his philosophical writing as too impressionistic, lacking in persevering analysis. This lack, Miller recalled, was manifest in Santayana's unwillingness to pursue discussion of philosophical issues into their details, his habit of writing on a lapboard and dispensing with references to books for exact quotations if that would interrupt the flow of composition, and his general preference for ease, serenity, and orderliness in life. Miller intended to deal with these dispositions and their results in a book to be called 'George Santayana – A Study in the Effects of a Ruling Passion'. Though he never finished such a book – it was not among his papers after his death – he wrote a detailed article on 'Mr. Santayana and William James' for the *Harvard Graduates' Magazine* of 1921. Some of its major themes reappeared in an essay of 1944, 'George Santayana', intended for publication but only now appearing among the writings to follow under 'Teachers and Teaching'. These essays indicate a direction in Santayana's thought opposed to Miller's own persistent liberalism and preoccupation with human welfare, so in spite of financial need he abruptly terminated arrangements to read and comment on Santayana's writings in Rome in 1926 and 1934.

In 1904 Miller left Harvard to accept appointment as a lecturer in philosophy at Columbia University where he became a professor in 1911 and remained as a full time teacher until 1919. At Harvard he was one of two instructors in the philosophy department being considered for a permanent position, the other being Ralph Barton Perry. After a correspondence between adjacent offices in which Miller conveyed to his chairman his sharp dissent about library orders – and Miller could sometimes be acerbic – the department decided to advance Perry. And thus, said Perry many years later and with characteristic generosity, "Harvard lost the better man."

IV. CRITICISM OF JAMES'S 'RADICAL EMPIRICISM'

During Miller's years at Columbia until James's death in 1910 his thinking was largely focussed on developments in James's 'radical empiricism' that asserted the identity of consciousness and object in perception with 'natural realism' as to the object. In the year that saw the publication of *Pragmatism*, 1907, James took note of Strong's reference to "the James–Miller theory" of cognition but observed that both Miller and Strong had privately assured him that his view was inadequate and left out the gist of real cognition.[12] Miller, it would appear, objected to James's *identification* of truth with an idea's "satisfactory working or leading". He had already indicated serious reservations about such an identification in his article of 1899 on James's method. In his maturest writing on the knowledge-problem and truth in 1937 he held, with specific reference to 'pragmatism', that the tendency of an idea to lead us to behave correctly in relation to the object and bring us out satisfactorily is indeed important and a fact that belongs to knowledge "but it is not the whole of knowledge". Knowledge, rather, means something else as well, namely, "a mental, a conscious acquaintance with the thing, an appearance of it in its true nature," and this relationship, Miller felt, was never adequately analyzed in James's theory of perception as part of his 'radical empiricism'.

James's 'radical empiricism' involved the notion that in "knowledge by acquaintance" our percept "in its wholeness" is a part of the physical world and the object "in its wholeness" is part of the stream of consciousness. The object-matter of the mind and the object-matter composing nature are one, and this single fact he called "pure experience". Hence there is no transcendent reference in perception and no go-between or mediation from consciousness to object. James saw this as asserting with Berkeley that *esse est percipi*, but whereas Berkeley considered that the world was mind-stuff, James affirmed 'natural realism' and held to the continuous existence of the whole physical world in independence of any knower or subject. For James, 'pure experiences', 'phenomena', or 'data' were in themselves neutral. Whether they were to be called 'mental' or 'physical' would depend on how they are associated. If they are part of the physical world, their relations are stable and orderly; if they are in the mental series, the order is loose and unsystematic.[13]

Miller found James's 'radical empiricism' to be seriously defective as an analysis of the relation of consciousness to object, and James in turn recognized the quandaries of his position in view of Miller's criticisms. Miller formulated his criticisms in letters to James, an unpublished manuscript, and an article, 'Naive Realism; What Is It?' in *Essays Philosophical and Psychological* (1908) in honor of William James by his Columbia colleagues. This article was not one of Miller's best in respect to its directness and lucidity. Most of its major theses, however, reappeared in more pointed and pungent form in an address at a commemoration meeting of 1942 under the title, 'A Debt to James'. In a letter of December 6, 1905 responding to one of Miller's criticisms of 'radical empiricism' James expressed his delight in learning that Miller had a considerable amount of manuscript "thunder" in cupboard and urged him not to delay publication, even if some revision were needed. James urged the appearance of "volume one" and insisted that Miller had too long hidden his light under a bushel.[14] This complimentary advice was omitted from the published letter at Miller's request. It reveals much about Miller's persistence in thinking and writing and the demands he made on himself then and later for thoroughness and precision to a degree he never found in James.

The main point of Miller's criticism was that James's conception of consciousness as developed in the chapter on 'The Mind-Stuff Theory' in *Principles of Psychology* was such that it could not be identified with physical objects as James was attempting to do. Consciousness, said Miller in agreement with James, is the "field of experience" or "pool of conjoint phenomenality" in which appearance and reality coincide. In contrast to Hume's position it is a unique and "undecomposable integer". It must be thought of subjectively, never as an object. Consciousness or the field of experience has only one aspect; physical objects have many aspects. Consciousness has "no hidden nature, no underside, no central substance or kernel, no interior recesses to be explored" but physical objects reveal "aspect after aspect to the advancing percipient". In a given case a consciousness may be a spatial content but it is not in space because it is not an object. It is a reality to which location is irrelevant. "In other fields of consciousness it can at best be represented."

With such a view of consciousness in relation to physical objects and other persons Miller could only find difficulties and contradictions in the 'natural realism' that James asserted as a corollary of 'radical empiricism'. James held that one and the same pen may be known by two different knowers. But that would imply, Miller objected, that an identical part can constitute two different fields – a contradiction.[15] Further, James held that the percept "in its wholeness" is a part of the stream of consciousness. But here, Miller objected, there is no provision for the fact that a large part of any percept is interpretation, is subjective, supplied by the records in the brain not by the new object that confronts me. How possibly, Miller puzzled, can the new object be my percept when my percept is largely made out of the past? In view of such difficulties and his own commitment to empiricism, Miller thought it highly unfortunate that James called his view 'radical empiricism' and identified it as his *Weltanschauung* involving a theory of the universe, a view of the nature of physical objects, minds, and their relationship. Before James, empiricism had referred to a way of justifying propositional knowledge on the basis of experience rather than intuitions of reason alone. To swap definitions in the midstream of the history of philosophy, Miller believed, was disservice to philosophy.[16]

Miller's own thinking on these matters was in partial agreement with 'realism', as he first noted in 'The Meaning of Truth and Error', and he saw the impulse to return to natural realism as "healthy and hopeful". But in the end he thought that natural realism would have to be "interpreted and completed" in a direction different from James's. It should move, Miller held, into the neighborhood of Mill's position: "Unperceived objects *are* possibilities of successive experience to us, as they figure in our natural thought, but Mill was mistaken if he meant that we class them as such." Actually most of what belongs to an object in its integrity does not appear in the perception. Strictly speaking, perception is the possession of certain aspects of the object *plus* preparedness for others, and such preparedness is partly the associative function of elements present in consciousness and partly "an element of consciousness answering to motor processes half awakened". "Perception", Miller concluded, "is a step into the world of objects, with the other foot held ready, as it were, for another step."[17]

Miller's "debt to James" as to the nature of consciousness in distinction from physical objects was not only the basis of his criticism of James's 'natural realism', but it also remained a keystone in all his subsequent thinking and was particularly apparent in polemical articles against those who would deny the reality of consciousness or identify it with behavior. In 1911 Miller charged that Professor E. A. Singer's identification of consciousness with "an expectation of probable behavior based on an observation of actual behavior" had missed the crucial feature of consciousness, namely, that it is a special and peculiar manner of objects being together or not being together in "pools of conjoint phenomenality". Forty years later, in the next to last publication of his lifetime, Miller criticized Professor Gilbert Ryle's *Concept of Mind* in similar terms. Miller could grant that much of what is said about 'the mental' is a matter of language and much of what we ordinarily call 'mind' is objective behavior. Nevertheless Ryle missed "the facts that force us to form the conception of consciousness", so his book is "one long *ignoratio elenchi*". The facts, as Miller marshalled them, led to the conclusion he had long held and traced to James – namely, consciousness is the "field of appearance" and not an object. It is invisible, the one realm where appearance and reality coincide, and indubitable as being 'the given'.

Immediately after his criticism of James's 'radical empiricism' and 'natural realism', Miller devoted himself to an extended, appreciative essay on 'Some of the Tendencies of Professor James's Work' that was published a few months before James's death in 1910. Viewing James as "the doctor", Miller found him going further than any psychologist of the time in a physiological interpretation of thought, feeling, emotion, and their abnormalities. As "the artist" – perhaps the most influential factor in Miller's eyes – James was responsive to the uniqueness, individuality, and concreteness of consciousness, to the fact that it is all aspect, "all in a sense surface", and not a compound. Finally, as "the sympathetic human being" James was the great fraternizer and co-operator who read widely and was receptive to what "any youngest fledgling from the graduate school" might contribute to this thinking. He was "an incarnation of the ideal of the democracy of thought". Though there were, Miller concluded, "essential subjects on which I do not share his conclusions as he states them", James gave new direction and impulse to psychology and philosophy, and American philosophy would be fortunate if it ever had an equal contributor.

James's response was warmly grateful. Though he thought Miller may have too much emphasized his psychological phase at the expense of epistemological and metaphysical contributions, he regarded the essay as a "profound analysis of an individual mind". "I have pantingly turned the pages", James wrote, "to find the eulogistic adjectives, and find them in such abundance that my head swims. Glory to God that I have lived to see this day!"[18]

While Miller was teaching at Columbia, his colleagues included John Dewey, C. A. Strong, Arthur Lovejoy, and Wendell Bush with whom he regularly met in a philosophy club to discuss papers presented in turn by the members. While he found these meetings highly stimulating and fruitful he also remembered them as revealing the poor state of philosophical criticism, the failure to analyze ideas openly and rigorously. He remembered how one eminent member absented himself from the meeting when his own views were to be criticized by an acute colleague or how another responded to criticisms each member had offered in turn by saying, without further elaboration, that he had considered all such objections and others as well before writing his paper. For a time Max Eastman was Miller's assistant at Columbia and in addition to the usual duties of an assistant went canoeing with Miller on the Hudson. He "gave me a canoe ride", Eastman wrote in *Enjoyment of Living*, "through the history of ideas and paid me to paddle the canoe". But in a canoe this "brilliantly erudite friend of William James", a discriminating person of precise habits, seemed "as out of his element as a pope on a roller coaster". Eastman also recalled a sharp difference he had with Miller at a meeting of the Columbia Philosophical Society. In response to a criticism from Arthur Lovejoy, whom Miller greatly admired, Eastman said that his scepticism in ethics was "apt to be more fruitful than the tight dogmatic egotism of the professional philosophers". Miller protested to President Butler that Lovejoy had been insulted and there followed a sharp exchange of letters between Eastman and Miller in which Miller again showed that he could be 'acerbic', a trait to which he attributed Lovejoy's subsequent departure from Columbia.

V. RELIGION AND HUMAN WELFARE – CONCERNS OF A SEMINARY PROFESSOR

The year that saw the publication of Miller's article on 'Naive Realism' among the essays from Columbia honoring James also found him delivering the Phi Beta Kappa address at Hobart College and being ordained a deacon in the Episcopal Church. In the following year, 1909, Hobart College awarded him an honorary Sc.D. degree, and he began teaching Christian Apologetics at General Theological Seminary in New York while continuing to teach philosophy at Columbia for another decade.

In his years at General Theological Seminary until 1924 his interest continued in philosophical issues related to knowledge, consciousness, and empiricism but it was overshadowed by his growing concern for social welfare, a concern that was identified in his mind with the essentials of Christian faith and with the processes of education and teaching that might develop truly critical intelligence, a "conscience of the mind".

Miller's continued interest in the problems that had preoccupied him since the 1890's was apparent in his teaching and lecturing at the Seminary. In addition to the usual courses of his chair, he introduced others of a more strictly philosophical bent such as Philosophy of Religion and the Logic of Christian Life. The subject-matter of his Paddock Lectures of 1911, intended for publication but never published as such, was 'The Rational Life and the Religious Life'. His philosophical conclusions and sympathies were particularly apparent in a mimeographed essay he distributed to his classes in 1915 on 'Heart and Head', published among Miller's writings to follow. It might well have been titled 'Emotion and Analysis' for it centrally argued, with reference to Hume, that emotion or 'the heart' is the basis of value to be served, not created, by 'the head' or intellect. The head typically "analyzes while the heart realizes". All science, Miller held, proceeds by analysis, and its very language is the language of analysis just as the language of common sense tells the story of analysis in its reference to classes and causes. Analysis yields us "truth of fact" to serve and be guided by "truth of value", and the genius of the Christian gospel in contrast to Greek philosophy was that it opened a new world of value.

With such an approach to Christian apologetics Miller's students readily detected the analytical philosopher in him. One of them, the late Dr Charles Street, who became a steady and life-long friend, testified that Miller frequently urged his students to develop an overall position that would express their theology and philosophy in such a way that science and other aspects of experience would find their proper place. Another student of the time particularly noted Miller's stress on clear, logical analysis of ideas. Miller's answers to students' questions on pragmatism, truth, cause, and natural order generally sought to resolve problems by analysis of and distinctions among key concepts. With such concerns Miller was hardly a typical theological professor. Charles Street and former colleagues recalled, many years later, that Miller did not speak the same language as other members of the Seminary faculty. "They did not understand him", Street said, "and he did not understand them". He lived in a different world from the faculty, the students, and the Episcopal Church in general. This was undoubtedly difficult for him, Street felt, but potentially very good for the Seminary and the Church as a whole.[19] Nonetheless Miller took his religious commitment very seriously. Starting in 1911 he devoted himself to "considerable preaching", as he put it in a Harvard alumni report, and was "special preacher" at the Episcopal Cathedral on Morningside Heights. Further, he was effective enough in his teaching to be invited to join the faculty of a Summer School of Theology sponsored by the Berkeley Divinity School, Middletown, Connecticut in 1919, his last year at Columbia University. Two years later the Berkeley Divinity School awarded him an honorary S.T.D. degree.

Miller's continued preoccupation with the philosophical issues related to knowledge, empiricism, and analytical method was also apparent in his published writings while he was teaching at the Seminary. As already noted, he wrote a criticism of Singer's view of consciousness and a comparative essay on 'Mr. Santayana and William James'. After considerable study and reflection, he finished an extensive essay on 'M. Bergson's Theories' for *The New Republic* of 1921. Though the essay was occasioned by the publication of Bergson's *Mind–Energy*, it examined all his major writings and ideas. Its criticism of Bergson suggested the outlines of Miller's own position on the role of analysis in philosophy, determinism, and the nature of deity – outlines that were, in some instances, given body in subsequent writings. Though Miller found in Bergson a fineness of observation concerning the immediate data of consciousness and a passion for freshness of thought in numerous original ideas, he was lacking in "intellectual delicacy", *i.e.*, in logic, as he substituted metaphor for definition, carried interpenetration of ideas too far, implausibly argued about the origin of the eye from psychic forces, and failed to see that only determinism is compatible with freedom because it stands for the control of character over action. Above all, Miller charged, Bergson is really asking us to abandon explanation and resort to feelings of things as wholes or the essences of medieval science. Explanation, however, inescapably involves analysis, and "philosophy, like science, is all analysis".

Miller's growing concern for human welfare during his years at the Seminary was manifest in his writings on specifically religious matters, including some published sermons and numerous book reviews on theological publications. In his first year at the Seminary, *Good House-keeping* published extracts from a longer writing on 'What Religion Has To Do With It', part of a course of reading in psychotherapy sponsored by the League of Right Living organized by Dr Samuel Fallows, a Bishop of the Episcopal Church. This first writing on religion appears among Miller's essays and "chapters" to follow as indicating key planks in the platform of his thinking about religious truth. Divine power, in Miller's view, is to be understood as "personified Goodness", a means of controlling the frictions and chaos of appetites and finally a 'presence' to be sought for itself. Such control and harmony in our conscious life also brings strength to the body. Miller had corresponded extensively with James about *The Varieties of Religious Experience*, and his contribution was acknowledged in the preface. In wide agreement with James, Miller saw religion as reinforcement and enrichment of life, a source of human welfare. Its truth, however, was thus "the truth of value" not the "bad science" of unproved metaphysical or theological propositions.[20] Hence Miller could not share James's theism as a view of God in relation to the world. Miller, rather, emphasized the symbolical character of religious terms and statements as focussing on human welfare. Discussing the symbolical character of religious ideas many years later, he remarked that he had been a naturalist in his world-view since childhood. He warmly responded to Dewey's *Common Faith* as the work of a "great man", a boon to our country.

The moral thrust of Miller's religious views was apparent in his address to Pennsylvania clergymen in 1915 on 'The Defense of the Faith Today' – reprinted among Miller's writings to follow – and more fully developed three years later in articles on 'The Problem of Evil'. Miller saw the problem of evil as expressing the contrast between the present state of the world and God's supreme goodness and power. The latter is a matter of faith as 'trust' and in relation to the present state of the world it is 'mysterious', something the logical understanding is not yet in a position to formulate. But Christian duty is nonetheless clear. It is "to subdue evil, and this duty is long prior to any duty to explain it". On analysis Miller found each of the four main 'solutions' of the problem of evil to be no solutions at all. In various ways each perversely denies the facts of experience and cuts the nerve of effort to vanquish evil. To say that pain is not evil, as in the second 'solution', is particularly misleading because it throws away the key to morality, forgetting that morality has an object, benefit to humanity, which is also the purpose of the duties God enjoins upon us. This "consequence-theory of morals", on which even intuitionist ethics must rely, is central to "the entire Christian scheme" and our only clear test of conscience, character, and duty.

In dealing with the "anthropological problem of evil" – namely, why does man permit evil when he has the power to prevent it? – Miller found the answer in the widespread failure to grasp the "consequence-theory of morals" and rigorously attend to its application. Throughout his life he was deeply concerned with the problems of moral theory, though other issues in philosophy, particularly issues related to knowledge, were the center of his attention and writing for longer periods. Thus his second publication at the age of twenty-five, 'The Relation of "Ought" and "Is"', analyzed the relation of 'relativity' in ethical judgments to imperatives and the special meaning of 'oughtness' as expressing the requirement of "a certain ideal arrangement of things, acts and lives", a system forever "relative to the individual that holds it, and yet from his standpoint absolute". This essay is reprinted among Miller's writings to follow as pointedly illustrating "analysis at work" in moral theory. He subsequently devoted himself to kindred problems in ethics with a brief article in 1929 on the union of pleasure and welfare and in 1950 dealt with the subjectivity and objectivity of moral judgments as related to welfare in an article on 'Moral Truth', reprinted among Miller's essays to follow. His conclusion in these articles on moral theory – on what today is commonly but awkwardly called 'meta-ethics' – were fully consonant with what he had to say on the "anthropological problem of evil" in 1918. Then, too, he was concerned with problems in moral theory. He contrasted the 'consequence-theory' with intuitionism. He considered in detail the relation of moral rules to consequences, arguing that established rules – for example, as pertaining to veracity – are not to be set aside or relaxed but rather developed so as to make clear their intent and service to general welfare.

VI. EDUCATION AND SOCIAL WELFARE IN THE FOREGROUND

Miller's overriding concern, however, was the use and application of

morality in the daily affairs of individual life and society, and this particularly involved sharper awareness of the aim of morality, circumspect
attention to consequences instead of evaluation by epithets, and a clear-
headed grasp of the significance of moral rules. In short, the commanding
requirement was more widely exercised good judgment or intelligence as
to means and proven practice in the conduct of life. While the church as
an institution, Miller observed, was already committed to the ground-
principle of morality, the well-being or happiness of all mankind, it also
needed to inculcate the practical virtues of good judgment and intelligence
to control events so that they make for the happiness of mankind. The
institution of education as it is usually carried on, could not be trusted,
Miller held, to give men good judgment and make practical intelligence
habitual. For one thing, schools and colleges have been generally content
to impart "what people ought to know" without asking how good judgment might be taught. Further, logic has been taught with no reference
to the purpose of thinking or its truth and has been confined to mere
correctness of inference.

After a decade of teaching at General Theological Seminary, Miller
noted in his annual report to the faculty and trustees that his experience
had shown more than ever the urgent need to teach students "not merely
to receive but to act upon the material given them, to discriminate, analyze,
reason, and develop a sound critical judgment". Thus he was deeply concerned with the process of education as it might inculcate a "conscience of
the mind" essential to the achievement of human welfare. This interest in
the teaching process was manifest in his description of James as a teacher,
reprinted among the essays to follow, and in such writings as 'The
Shaping of Seminary Education', 'The Great College Illusion', 'Fullerton
and Philosophy,' and 'The Antioch Idea'.

But Miller did not confine 'welfare' to the conduct of individuals. He
had in mind, rather, social or collective welfare as involving the institutions of politics and economic life along with the church and education.
He was preoccupied with "the social idea", to use the phrase he applied to
Matthew Arnold. In book reviews going back to the late 1890s he had
discussed reason as an instrument of social purpose and had criticized
a book on "the social problem" for being too "idealistic" and "spiritual"
as it neglected "the social foundation", *i.e.*, material and economic life.
His ardent commitment to social welfare as the focus of education,

religion, and politics was most apparent in his writings from 1921 to 1925 for *The New Republic*, a journal whose tendencies were largely his own.

In 'Democracy and Our Intellectual Plight' Miller characterized morality as the scheme of ideas and rules existing "for the welfare of society and for that only". As morality reinforces rules by making them sacred and inviolable, so must democracy make the participation of every citizen a sacred duty reinforced by education at all levels. Since democracy is essentially government by discussion, its ideal is that the most reasonable proposal, not force, shall prevail. This requires general education in logic or "the elementary habits of the fair mind", now widely "distorted by that singular excrescence called a text-book of logic". The habit of relying on objective, public tests and rules of evidence must displace "the will to believe", the willingness to believe on insufficient evidence because a belief is attractive. "The will to believe" obstructs mobility of sound ideas and gives a handle to despots and political manipulators. Further, democracy cannot rely on the intellectual class for its progress because that class is not intellectual enough and itself lacks the discipline of "honest thinking, the morals of the mind". A few years later Miller emphasized the social obstructions to wider, more steady exercise of intelligence. Writing on 'Intelligence In Our Time' he summarized those obstructions as the "tradition of passivity" in which social taste restrains destructive criticism, political structure devalues "expert thought and information", and social conscience is indifferent to the duty of careful thinking because "our morality does not see its own aim and reason for existing, the production of welfare in all its kinds, and that we may accomplish this aim only through the use of our wits".

Social welfare was a central theme in Miller's appreciative essay on 'Matthew Arnold, On the Occasion of His Centenary'. Unlike those who saw Arnold as merely "a delicately gloved literary exquisite", Miller found him to be a great sharer, a proponent of "the social idea", viewing men of culture as true apostles of equality and proposing distribution of landed estates and limitation of inheritance to achieve "the equality of all as the true basis of a healthy civilization". In comparison with Arnold, there was in Santayana the want of "a certain fundamental human seriousness" in spite of his "acute and large-minded spectatorship". Though Arnold, in Miller's view, well translated the conceptions of the Christian faith into "the language of human experience and salutary consequence", he was, if anything, too moralistic and failed to take the point of view of religion itself in dealing with God as personal. Further, Arnold failed to see that literature, in addition to educating and forming us for better living, also has the function of being a high and satisfying experience in itself. Miller had already dealt with this double function of literature in a brief essay on 'Beauty and Use', part of a symposium in *The New Republic* of 1921 to which R. M. Lovett, H. L. Mencken, Morris Cohen, and Clive Bell also contributed. There he found Emerson, by common consent the greatest American writer, to be completely wrong in respect to moral judgment. Emerson was preoccupied with behavior, not service. Esteeming and disesteeming the powers and action of men, he forgot that the aim and test of achievement is the welfare of sentient beings and that "all moral judgment of actions, motives, ideas, institutions and men can have but one standard or basis, their practical tendency to promote the collective welfare (except so far as certain ideas and feelings may be constituents of that welfare)".

Such a view of morality in relation to social welfare lay behind Miller's decision to resign his teaching post at General Theological Seminary in 1924 and informed his article for *The New Republic* on 'Conscience and the Bishops', reprinted among the essays to follow. As before, Miller centrally identified the truth of Christianity with "the truth of value". He saw the church as "a deep-seated organ of society, powerful for good", and through the church "Christ, by his principle of love and benefit, which he declared to be the one basis of the whole moral law, and by the identification of his whole personality, acts, teaching, death and spirit with the principle, becomes an object of the Christian's personal worship as an embodiment of the divine". The historic dogmas all aim to exalt and magnify Jesus Christ. To refer to him in the creed as the son of God born of a virgin is to use "a historic and poetic symbol". The Bishops of the Episcopal Church, however, had issued a pastoral letter making clergymen liable for trial for interpreting the words in the creed about Jesus' birth in any other than a literal sense. Miller found this to be contrary to precedent in the church, undercut by one bishop's refusal to apply the ruling, and inimical to growth in new interpretation of the Christian message. While it is not the business of religion to formulate a correct philosophical analysis, it does, Miller held, seek to reveal aspects of reality that create impulse and transform life. Its symbolism is not something trivial but rather "an instrument of knowledge, a means to practical truth". Holding to such views, Miller could not but resign from the Seminary though he retained his membership in the church, was ordained in 1935, and subsequently served as pastor from time to time.

Immediately following his resignation from the Seminary, Miller became professor of philosophy at Smith College, notwithstanding the fact that his essay on 'Conscience and the Bishops' had been pointedly challenged by a professor at that college. Toward the end of his first year at Smith, his article on 'Fullerton and Philosophy' appeared in *The New Republic* indicating his firm commitment to the method of analysis in philosophy and noting suggestions from Fullerton about the application of analysis to questions about free will, the external world, and Hume's scepticism. But Miller went beyond Fullerton to insist that analytic intelligence be applied to issues involving human welfare, the theme of most of his writings in the previous decade. With such affirmation of his intellectual debts and his commitment to analysis, 'Fullerton and Philosophy' is properly the opening piece among all of Miller's writings to follow.

VII. ANALYTICAL WORK IN 'EUROPEAN RETIREMENT', VIENNA AND FLORENCE

After two years at Smith College Miller resigned his position in 1926 and retired from academic work but not from thinking and writing on philosophical problems along lines projected in 'Fullerton and Philosophy'. He first went to Rome where, as already noted, an arrangement to read and comment on Santayana's writings ended abruptly. Then, for the next eight years, he alternated his 'European retirement' between Vienna and Florence.

Miller's long-standing commitment to analysis and empiricism led him to make contact with the 'Vienna Circle', a group of philosophers – Moritz Schlick, Otto Neurath, Rudolph Carnap, Herbert Feigl, and others – with a similar commitment. "Although mostly a silent listener at the Circle's sessions", Feigl recalled, "he was an intensely interesting and challenging discussant in individual conversations."[21] Among the ideas that Miller challenged was the principle that "no sentence can be admitted to philosophical thought as having a meaning unless it is verifiable in experience". Such a principle, Miller argued in his last published writing in 1952, "cuts the ground from under its own feet" because a sentence has to have meaning before you can apply the test. As always, Miller was very critical and independent-minded in his analytic empiricism.

In Vienna Miller also associated with Ludwig Wittgenstein who was later to become the dominant figure among analytic philosophers but was then only casually related to the Vienna Circle through contacts with some of its members. Miller found Wittgenstein with saw in hand at work on a house he had designed for one of his sisters and took some meals and walks with him to discuss philosophical issues. In one conversation, as Miller recalled it, Wittgenstein could see no grounds for believing that pleasure or pain are really good or bad. To be sure, he would try to help an elderly lady from falling and being painfully injured, but that would be habit or instinct, not ethics. Some echoes of this discussion, with Miller's own deflection, appeared very shortly in a brief article in *Mind*, 1929, on 'The Pleasure-quality and Pain-quality Analysable, Not Ultimate'. There he sought to show why pleasure and welfare are conjoined by distinguishing between primary sensations on the one hand and our instinctive reactions seeking benefit on the other, reactions that lead us to classify primary sensations as pleasures or pains because they are attractive or repugnant. Pleasure and benefit (welfare) are joined as "the beneficial becomes the attractive and the attractive *is* the pleasant".

Miller's second year of his European retirement saw the publication of his review of *Religion In the Philosophy of William James* by J. S. Bixler and the beginning of periodic discussions with C. A. Strong in his handsome Villa le Balze near Florence. Miller used Bixler's book for more than a review in the usual sense. It became the occasion for an extended assessment of James's thought, summarizing and reformulating criticisms he had already made and also anticipating his more final assessment a decade later in his review of Perry's biography, a review reprinted among the essays to follow as 'James and Analysis'. Miller saw in James a persistent concern for life, freedom, freshness, relief from pain, and release of energies to secure human welfare. At the same time James was a keen observer and man of science. These tendencies, taken together, made his relation to analysis "peculiar". While there were "masterly examples of analytical triumph" in his *Psychology* and the lecture on 'The One and the Many' in *Pragmatism*, his concern for the richness and freedom of experience led him to accept "chief ideas as ultimate when they could in fact be analyzed and when their analysis would have prevented him from misinterpreting them". That concern even led to a sacrifice of logical conscience as in "the will to believe", "the fountainhead of all fallacy" based on confusion between hypothesis and belief.

Miller found James's treatment of 'free will' to be a particularly striking case of failure to analyze and proceeded to give a brief preview of his own full analysis that appeared in *Mind* in 1934, the year he left Europe to return to America, under the title 'Free Will as Involving Determination and Inconceivable Without It'. That article is reprinted among the essays to follow with Miller's subsequent revisions as he prepared it to serve as a chapter for a book, never finished, on 'Inquiry, Analytical or Sceptical'. Miller sought to show in precise detail how analysis of 'could' or 'can' as implied in choosing and as involving 'self' and 'power' inescapably leads to determination expressing a law of cause and effect. And this result, far from undermining moral 'responsibility' and 'desert', is logically required for those ideas in their ordinary meaning. Thus analysis as "the prosaic process of examining words" reveals that the controversy of free will *vs.* determinism has been a waste of energy over a false antithesis. Determinism is not opposed to free will but turns out to be a feature of its analysis. With the current emphasis on analysis in philosophy – 'analysis' largely as Miller conceived and practiced it – his treatment of free will as involving determination has received increasing attention and has been reprinted twice as an acute example of 'soft determinism' or 'reconciliationism'.

Miller's discussions with C. A. Strong from 1927 to 1929 were interspersed with periods in Vienna that were relevant to another major work of his European retirement, a lengthy study of Hume's thought in relation to analysis, causality, and reason. With Strong the conversation – and it was systematic conversation as revealed in Miller's unpublished notes – focussed on issues in epistemology, particularly perception in relation to space and time. On two occasions Herbert Feigl joined them to explore the significance of Einstein's theory of relativity for perception. Sometimes the conversations between Miller and Strong became "strained", according to Daniel Cory, as a result of "a condition imposed by Miller (and accepted by Strong) ... that the concept of God should not be discussed". Miller's own maturest answer to some of the issues he discussed with Strong appeared a decade later in 'Is There Not A Clear Solution of the Knowledge-Problem?' reprinted among Miller's essays to follow. Miller's writing on Hume was an extensive, two-part article that appeared in *Mind* in 1930 under the title, 'Hume Without Scepticism'. As already noted, he had long admired Hume's analytic empiricism. Even as an undergraduate he had been impressed by Fullerton's suggestion that Hume's analysis of self and causality could be seen not as destructive or sceptical but as explanatory, providing new insight into what we assumed to exist all along. A decade later he quoted with approval James's observation that Hume could be corrected and built out "by using Humian principles exclusively". Now such conjectures could be given precise support as Miller sought to show how Hume's doctrines of induction and causality could be considered "analyses of fact without sceptical consequence". Contrary to the widely held view, Hume did not deny causation and derivation but rather he analyzed them to show that while one proposition may imply another proposition a thing cannot imply another thing, so the connection between cause and effect is not deductive, and it is contradictory to speak of the pre-existence of the effect in the cause. Though one particular may be deduced from another through a previously known law, that law itself rests on the uniformities of experience. Whatever 'necessity' there is in causality depends on such a law but there is no necessity for the law itself which formulates the ultimate order of events. To attempt to go behind it to find its 'ground' is to try to explain why explanation explains.

As against such a position Whitehead never showed, contended Miller, that Hume missed any "fact of derivation" nor did H. W. B. Joseph show that knowledge of cause comes through universals rather than from experience only. Kant's assertion of necessity in the causal relation depended on the assumption that we cannot perceive priority and subsequence, but this assumption, Miller held, is psychologically false. Hume called his results sceptical because, like Bertrand Russell, he held that an inference from experience was not deductive and thus not 'rational'. But we may look on past and present facts of experience, Miller proposed, as *grounds* for our conclusions as indicating other fact. Such a procedure is exactly what we mean, in dealing with facts, by 'rationality', so Hume's analysis does not necessarily lead to scepticism about induction. Subsequently Miller reworked the basic theses of 'Hume Without Scepticism' to express and defend them more pointedly in four separate articles that appeared from 1937 to 1939 during his 'American retirement'.

'Hume Without Scepticism' and the article on 'Freewill as Involving Determination' both appeared in *Mind* under the name R. E. Hobart, though Miller openly acknowledged his authorship in footnotes of subsequent articles on 'James and Analysis' and the knowledge-problem. Further, he travelled to England, Ireland, and Italy from 1932 to 1934 with a passport issued in Frankfurt/Main under the name of Richard Emlen Hobart, the first name being derived from his nickname and the last two from family names. He even corresponded with his brother about a permanent legal change of name but abandoned 'Hobart' on returning to America in 1934. His specific motives for adopting the name of Hobart are obscure because he had an intense sense of privacy and vigilantly guarded it. He did, however, tell one associate that he thought people who knew him would not read his articles because his links with James would make him appear "too old". To another he explained that it is perfectly appropriate to use any name that suits one's private convenience. The content of the articles may have been a factor. His main points in the article on Hume had been dismissed by an eminent British scholar as insubstantial, not worthy of publication.

VIII. CONSOLIDATIONS ON THE KNOWLEDGE-PROBLEM AND JAMES IN 'AMERICAN RETIREMENT'

Miller returned to the United States in 1934 to spend his remaining 29 years in or near Boston in what he called, with some amusement, his 'American retirement'. A year after his return he was ordained to the priesthood by the Right Reverend Henry Sherrill and became rector of St. George's church in Maynard, Massachusetts. After a year as rector he established residence on Boston's Beacon Hill at Louisburg Square and finally on Marlborough Street at the home of Miss Constance Worcester whose father, Dr Elwood Worcester of Emmanuel Church, had been his friend of long standing. From time to time he served as supply pastor for Episcopal churches in or near Boston but most of his time and energy, so far as his continued ill-health permitted, were devoted to philosophical work, chiefly articles for professional journals, chapters of projected books, and addresses at various universities.

Miller's first publication in his American retirement was an extended review of R. B. Perry's biography of James, reprinted among the essays to follow as 'James and Analysis' because it significantly consolidated his criticism of James in relation to his own commitment to analysis.

Contrary to the view that James's achievement reflected his rich environment, Miller found that environment inauspicious because it led James to be satisfied with hasty analysis that prevented him from giving sound formulation to his persistent concern for the richness of experience and openness of life. James was misled because the philosophy of his period did not discern the function of analysis, namely, to clarify meanings in relation to assured facts of experience that were not themselves in question. To be sure, James had been exposed to the method in Shadworth Hodgson, but Hodgson, like Fullerton at a later date, had not generalized it and driven it home. Further, James had well practiced the method of analysis when, in his *Principles of Psychology*, he found "the very 'original' of the notion of personality", *i.e.*, the very meaning of it, in the mental procession itself. But he had lost sight of the method in his treatment of freedom in willing, the basis of his pluralism, and applied it haltingly in his statement of the pragmatic method. James's concern for the richness and thickness of experience enabled him to grasp the specific quality of our consciousness of space and time and our 'meaning' in regard to relations and tendencies but at the same time made him distrust analysis or cut it short with an assumption that certain facts of experience are unanalyzable. Thus what James needed most, in Miller's view, was the intent and inner meaning of the philosophy of Locke and Hume as shown in their treatment of free will, namely, "a more pertinacious analysis – an analysis in just the spirit that, with reference to personality, speaks in James himself".

A year after his exploration of James's relation to analysis, Miller's own alternative analysis of knowledge appeared in *The Journal of Philosophy* of 1937 under the questioning title, 'Is There Not a Clear Solution of the Knowledge-Problem?' The first part of this article is reproduced among the essays and chapters to follow as giving Miller's maturest consolidation of his thought on how the mind gets at its object without any "transcendent reference". The second part of the article dealt with "another department" of the knowledge-problem, namely, the rational basis for inference from past experience through induction. There Miller argued that 'cogency' need not be confined to deductive implication – the needless source of Hume's 'scepticism' – but must also mean corroboration of inference by "a fact which stands as such by itself", by a "basic appearance" for which there is no counter-indication or dependence on anything else, so the repetitions of experience have *de jure* status as a first principle expressing "the cogency of safe conduct to new fact". In subsequent articles on Hume and deductivism Miller more pointedly and fully analyzed the 'cogency' or 'rational justification' of inference from experience.

As already noted, Miller found in James's pragmatism, particularly in his emphasis on the tendency of an idea to lead us to behave correctly in relation to the object, a fact that indisputably belongs to knowledge but is not the whole of it. Pragmatism had never adequately analyzed our "conscious acquaintance with the thing, an appearance of it in its true nature". An adequate analysis, Miller thought, would extend and refine his own view, presented in his first writing on 'The Meaning of Truth and Error', as to how belief involves a mental presentation in "the shape the images take of their own accord". So in 1937 Miller reworked his 'presentationism' to argue that knowledge is consummated by the presence in consciousness of an image precisely similar to the object, and this is made possible by the principle of "the identity of indiscernibles", whereby at the moment of knowing the image, stripped of its external relations, is equivalent to the object or an aspect of it. Such an equivalence excludes any conscious reference of the mind to objects not given to it. Such reference, Miller sought to show, is not only false psychology but is actually meaningless in relation to what 'knowledge' implies, so he proceeded to answer the major objection to his position, particularly the view of G. F. Stout that knowledge consists of "a mental act of assertion or judgment, an act involving reference to an object, the recognition of certain necessary relations". In that answer Miller reasserted his view of belief as involving "spontaneous self-maintenance of the idea" and his view that generic ideas, like propositions, pertain only to the expression of knowledge and the function of consciousness rather than its content.

At the end of the first part of his article on the knowledge-problem Miller characteristically invited criticisms as required by "the spirit of inquiry". A few years later he received them in letters from Professor Edgar Brightman of Boston University who defended the indispensability of 'reference' in knowledge. Miller found Brightman's letters to be "the most interesting and valuable" he ever remembered having received but doggedly defended his own view as published in 1937 and called it 'presentationism'. He was, however, little concerned with labels. The precise meaning of a thesis and its supporting arguments were always the main thing for him. He once observed, with wry irony, that no one can get anywhere in philosophy without having an '-ism' and one has really arrived when he has an '-istic -ism'.

With invitations to participate in commemorative meetings on James in 1942 at Columbia and the Universities of Wisconsin and Minnesota, Miller applied himself to further assessment of James's thought and influence. His address at Wisconsin on 'William James, Man and Philosopher' was largely an appreciation such as he had written in 1910 stressing James's openness to life and to the uniqueness and richness of experience.

At Columbia his paper on 'A Debt to James' dealt more directly with James's ideas and theories. As already noted, Miller shared James's view of consciousness as the "field of experience" or "pool of conjoint phenomenality", a unique and undecomposable integer in which appearance and reality coincide. He could not, however, follow James's 'natural realism' identifying the percept in its entirety with the physical object. Rather, James's view of consciousness implies that "existence, actuality, can have but one aspect", so ultimate and adequate truth in contrast to the provisional truth of Mill's "permanent possibility of experience" would "approximate panpsychism", *i.e.*, would bring "the physical world into kinship with psychic fact". This debt to James in regard to the nature of consciousness was a permanent part of Miller's thinking. It had guided his criticism in 1911 of the view that consciousness is a form of behavior and his subsequent criticism in 1951 of Gilbert Ryle's similar view. With a theme so central to Miller's thought 'A Debt to James' appears among his major philosophical essays to follow.

Another essay occasioned by the James commemorations was a further reckoning with "the will to believe" entitled 'James's Doctrine of 'The Right to Believe'.' Its main points were incorporated in an address to the Boston University Philosophical Club at its annual banquet meeting in April, 1942. In this essay Miller reworked and consolidated his earlier criticisms beginning in 1899 – criticisms already mentioned and described in this introduction – to take account of his controversies on the subject with James and F. C. S. Schiller. Even after the publication of 'James's Doctrine of 'The Right to Believe'' in 1942, however, Miller made further revisions and additions to prepare it to serve as a chapter or appendix of what he called "a book on religion" that he never completed. In a letter of January 20, 1943 Miller wrote that he "must add something on considerations" such as C. J. Ducasse of Brown University had brought up in correspondence. Professor Ducasse had argued that there are cases – such as whether to stay on or jump off a streetcar going down a hill when suddenly the brakes fail – in which we cannot suspend decision because to refuse to decide is automatically to decide, and evidence on one side or the other is wholly lacking or evenly balanced. In such cases decision must be a nonrational gamble. Miller argued that there might be a case requiring us to go solely by impulse, but in the case of the streetcar we could in a flash make an estimate of circumstances and danger of jumping at once. As for choosing to strengthen a religious belief for which there is no evidence, Miller gave as his "best answer" our "central duty" to be as intelligent as we can "because unintelligence bears more fruit of misery, wretchedness, and frustration than any other human weakness or sin" and "in religion the ill consequences of baseless faith are enormous". Our central duty, Miller concluded in a later letter, requires the suspension of judgment where there is no evidence.[22] His answers to the "considerations" Ducasse had brought up were incorporated in 'James's Doctrine of 'The Right to Believe''. Thus revised, it is included among the essays and chapters to follow as Miller's fullest word on the subject.

During the years when he was at work on the knowledge-problem and writings in commemoration of James, Miller had a series of assistants who were graduate students in philosophy at Boston University and Harvard – M. B. Stokes, Sheldon Ackley, Hiram McLendon, and the present writer. They had experiences with Miller comparable to those of Max Eastman two decades earlier except that this time they manned a sailboat on the Charles River instead of a canoe on the Hudson and had no clashes with their mentor over presumed insults. In addition to clerical and research duties, they were given a sail through the history of ideas and were paid to man the tiller. They also tried to respond to Miller's request for critical attacks on his current writing and he, in turn, helpfully criticized theirs.[23]

IX. ACTIVITIES AND PROJECTS OF THE FINAL DECADES IN BOSTON

Following his writings on James, Miller turned to further analytical work on the problem of universals, Hume's view of causality, induction, and empirical rationality. Late in 1943 he completed an extensive, detailed chapter on 'Universals' for a book that was never finished but was to include revisions of his articles on Hume, free will, and the knowledge-problem. To deal with a difficulty remaining in Berkeley's otherwise admirable analysis of universals as abstract ideas, Miller carefully distinguished between the content and function of ideas in order to show, with pointed illustrations, how an idea is general not by virtue of its particular content but the way it leads us to behave in thought and action, the way its content "*can do duty as* the representative of a class" by its associations. In elaborating this distinction Miller used verbatim key paragraphs of his article of 1895 on 'Confusion of Content and Function in Mental Analysis', the article that had reconfirmed James's "sometime wavering opinion" on the subject. To defend and further clarify his position, Miller analyzed confusions in the 'concrete universal' from Hegelian idealism, in Santayana's 'essences' that do not exist, in the neo-realists' doctrine that universals subsist, and in Husserl's claim that universals are 'intentional' objects, a claim that Miller found to be a failure of analysis and resort to a *causa occulta*. With a thesis so central to Miller's analysis of knowledge his chapter on 'Universals', hitherto unpublished, is included among his writings to follow.

Miller further reworked and applied conclusions at which he had arrived during his European retirement in 'Hume Without Scepticism'. His article of 1945 on 'An Event in Modern Philosophy' particularly focussed on Hume's analysis of causality, defended Hume's conclusion against Kant and Blanshard, and concluded with a defense of empirical rationality against Hume's gratuitous identification of reason with deduction. Miller intended to make this article into a chapter of a book on 'Inquiry, Analytical or Sceptical', and it was more pointed and precise than 'Hume Without Scepticism' so it is included among the essays to follow. For similar reasons Miller's piece of 1949 on 'Hume's Deathblow to Deductivism', originally a lecture at Harvard, appears among the essays to follow. It developed at length and in detail what Miller meant by "empirical rationality" in relation to evidence for fact, necessity, significance and association, and empiricism. In connection with empiricism he devoted a paragraph to pragmatism and "the will to believe" as being "at deadly enmity with empiricism." "Pragmatism", Miller concluded, "is an excellent sermon but a confused philosophy". Some years later, in line with this judgment, he remarked that he had reluctantly come to the conclusion that James's influence in philosophy had, on the whole, done more harm than good.

In correspondence with C. J. Ducasse about Hume and causality,[24] Miller was hard pressed in defense of his conclusions. He asked Ducasse how he would refute Hume. Ducasse cited Hume's incompatible and inconsistent statements on causality and then asked Miller which of those statements he had in mind. Ducasse noted that Hume, contrary to Miller, had actually asserted that one sole instance of Single Difference in experiment would establish causation and further that "deductive necessity" in causation was not the issue but rather "physical necessitation" as suggested by Miller's own reference to "factual, not logical compulsion". Though Miller urged and welcomed such criticism for the progress of inquiry, Ducasse's acute and sustained arguments must have suggested to him that his conclusions about Hume and causality were hardly unassailable and that there was more analytical work to be done.

In the last two decades of his 'American retirement' Miller further developed his views on the application of morality to human welfare and education – matters with which he was particularly concerned from 1918 to 1925 in articles on the problem of evil and contributions to *The New Republic*. His views led him to speak out on issues of social and political reform in private conversation and public addresses. He presented two memorial addresses on Mrs Glendower Evans, a close friend of the Jameses. Eulogizing her social conscience and efforts in social reform, he saw her spirit as a dedication "to the belief that essential betterment is feasible and by work and thought must be ceaselessly pursued, that all may have the right to live as decent human beings in a decent world". Mrs Evans had contributed importantly to the defense of Sacco and Vanzetti, and through her Miller had come to know Felix Frankfurter. In November, 1942 he addressed the Boston University Philosophical Club on 'Russian Policy the Past Four Years', particularly in relation to a more clear-headed, realistic American foreign policy. He discussed George Santayana's hostility to "the immense liberal movement of modern

times" in an essay of 1944, published for the first time among the writings
to follow. In this matter Miller was preponderantly opposed to his
former teacher, and this antipathy, as already noted, had abruptly
terminated their association in Rome.

Miller's address to the Clericus Club of Boston in the mid-1940s,
published for the first time as 'Morality, Intelligence, and Welfare' among
the essays and chapters to follow, specifically focussed on the functional
character of morality. With vivid autobiographical illustrations and
reference to James's repudiation of anti-semitism, Miller explored the
relation of intelligence to morality, developing what he had earlier written
about the aim of morality, moral rules, and the moral premises of
Christianity. He thus outlined the major topics of the book on which he
was at work up to the last year of his life and variously thought of titling
'Revolution In Ethics', 'Principles of Practical Intelligence', or 'Intelligence, How and Why It Has Not Been Taught'.

In an article on 'Moral Truth' published in 1950 and reprinted among
Miller's essays to follow, he returned to fundamental issues in moral
theory at the level of his earlier treatment of 'ought' and 'is' and the
"anthropological problem of evil". He was particularly concerned with
the problem of subjectivity and objectivity in moral judgments. He analyzed the relation of feelings and attitudes in moral judgments to statements
of psychological fact with the conclusion that moral truth depends on the
functional character of morality, its purpose to meet human needs, and
hence ultimately on the facts in respect to consequences of action and the
constitution of man.

Miller's last publication in 1952, 'Is Philosophy a Good Training for the
Mind?' concentrated on the process of education, particularly in philosophy, as it might achieve that "conscience of the mind" entailed in
"pertinacious analysis" and "a fine accuracy" in observing and reasoning.
Thus he dealt with a problem that had been at the center of his attention
since 1918 and was inseparable from the practice of philosophy's proper
method, logical analysis of terms and statements in relation to facts of
ordinary experience. He drew extensively on his own experience for
illustrations and incidents – many of which have appeared in this introduction – to show why unsparing criticism, circumspection, and detection
of logical fallacies need to become permanent habits of thought and how
this end might be achieved in teaching.

With such a vital theme, illustrated by his own experiences in American universities and abroad, 'Is Philosophy a Good Training for the Mind?' concludes Miller's writings to follow under 'Teachers and Teaching'. Some of its major points appeared in an address at Brown University in 1950 on the use of philosophy and later in an address at Harvard on 'The Mission of Philosophy in a Dark Age'. He intended it to be "part of a chapter" of a book on which he was working. A decade earlier he had outlined a book whose longest section would show "analysis at work" as in what he had written on free will, Hume, universals, and objectivity of value. The introductory section was to be devoted to "custom and education" with particular reference to criticism and analysis. In spite of his apparent decline in health and vitality after 1955, Miller said that he was still revising that book, tentatively entitled 'Inquiry, Analytical or Sceptical', along with the book on 'Principles of Practical Intelligence' and intensive studies of James and Santayana, but none of them was ever found "substantially completed", as he put it, among the papers that survived his death on November 13, 1963.

X. ACHIEVEMENTS AND GAPS

In distinguishing between "the morality of epithets" and "the morality of results" Miller noted the tendency of biographies to rest on estimable labels but overlook the main thing, namely, what was accomplished in terms of human benefit, results in human service. This introduction has recounted Miller's accomplishments in philosophy and how he thought that philosophy as "conscience of the mind" in analysis decisively serves human welfare. He contributed to the redirection of modern philosophical thought in respect to the function of ideas in knowledge, and this contribution was signalled in references to "the James–Miller theory" of knowledge. His criticism of James's development of that theory into 'pragmatism' and 'radical empiricism' left its mark on James's own accomplishment. Further, Miller espoused and practiced the method of analysis decades before its prominence in 'neo-realism' and recent 'analytical philosophy', and that practice resulted in articles on Hume, free will, and knowledge that have been recognized as outstanding and sometimes characterized as 'remarkable'. His practice of analysis also made itself felt in his teaching, public addresses, and conversation on philosophical and social issues through six decades.

At some points, however, Miller's accomplishment was unfortunately and disappointingly incomplete, and the results of his analyses turned out to be less definitive and unassailable than he wanted. He was painfully aware of this incompleteness. Early and late in his life he said that his "substantially completed" projects needed reworking, and he once pathetically remarked that he had had no career in philosophy because he had never completed a book. As a result he never made a circumspect, probing analysis of his own method though he planned to devote a section to it in his unfinished book on 'Inquiry, Analytical or Sceptical'. In particular, he never made systematically clear the bearing of analysis on concepts and thought as related to language though there were suggestive paragraphs on the subject in some of his writings. This incompleteness was partly a result of his demand for 'definitiveness' and 'finality', a demand that his own liberal temper in social matters and his professed openness to experience should have softened. It was also the result of his chronic ill-health, the "neural insufficiency" that reduced his hours of reflection and writing by one half. His effort to deal with his illness through the medical profession was, in his own report,[25] a tragicomic series of contradictory diagnoses and contradictory prescriptions. While his chronic illness undoubtedly heightened his sensitivity to human suffering and misery, the longevity he achieved through self-prescription could not make up for lack of accomplishment in his years of greatest vitality.

Very likely the criticism that he received of his conclusions, directly through correspondence and discussion and indirectly through continued study, was a factor contributing to the incompleteness and gaps in his "philosophical work", to use his phrase. Criticism from C. J. Ducasse must have shown him that his position on Hume and causality was far from unassailable and needed more work. At least it must have suggested the incongruity of using the title, 'Some Settled Questions In Philosophy', for his projected book to show "analysis at work" as in his articles on Hume, free will, and knowledge. In correspondence of 1944 he wrote of his preoccupation with a puzzle about empiricism – whether our idea of "before and after" involves memory and anticipation and thus "the idea of a relation *a priori*, a possession of the mind not gained from experience" – a puzzle that was certainly "a worm (the only worm) at the heart of empiricism". Apparently he had overlooked this worm in his previously settled strictures against Kant's view of time. To questions in conversation about his view of 'belief' as being entirely distinct from "our forth-putting", a central premise for much of his thinking, he reaffirmed his position from the 1890s but sometimes seemed to waver and may have felt that here too more analysis was needed to take into account the difference in ordinary usage between 'believing' and 'knowing' and the patent element of adoption or abandonment in the former not present in the latter as it involves learning and recognition.

The gaps in Miller's accomplishment, however, diminish in importance when weighed against the originality and penetration of his achievement in "the James–Miller theory" of cognition and the practice of analysis in his essays and teaching. His deficiencies were largely the vices of his outstanding virtue – his unflagging dedication to the clarity, thoroughness, and definiteness of "pertinacious analysis". And the products of that dedication were, in quality if not in quantity, remarkable achievements of an unusual life.

NOTES

[1] Specific bibliographical data for Miller's own writings may be found in the chronological list of his publications at the end of this volume.
[2] W. James, *The Meaning of Truth*, Longmans, Green and Co., New York, 1909, p. 22n. Cf. R. B. Perry, *The Thought and Character of William James*, Little, Brown, and Co., Boston, 1935, I, pp. 797–800.
[3] W. James, 'The Knowing of Things Together', *Psychological Review*, 2 (1895) 109.
[4] To Miller, August 30, 1896, *The Letters of William James* (ed. by Henry James), Atlantic Monthly Press, Boston, 1920, II, p. 48.
[5] Miller noted that he was indebted to Alfred Hodder for this view of belief as a species of mental presentation, "the shape the images take of their own accord". Hodder (1866–1907), a native of Ohio, was a fellow student and friend of Miller at Harvard. He received the Ph.D. from Harvard, taught briefly at Bryn Mawr College, then abandoned academic life for journalism and writing on social problems. In 1901 he published a philosophical treatise, *The Specious Present*.
[6] Letter to Ducasse, September 10, 1952 quoted in Peter Hare and Edward Madden, 'William James, Dickinson Miller and C. J. Ducasse on the Ethics of Belief', *Transactions of the Peirce Society* 4 (1968) 115.
[7] Deleted at Miller's request from *The Letters of William James* (ed. by Henry James), The Atlantic Monthly Press, Boston, 1920, II, p. 115. By permission of the Harvard College Library and Mr Alexander James.
[8] To Miller, January 18, 1900 and January 31, 1899, *ibid.*, II, pp. 116, 86.
[9] To Miller, August 18, 1903, *ibid.*, II, p. 198.
[10] To Miller, December 1, 1904. By permission of the Harvard College Library and Mr Alexander James.

[11] C. A. Strong, 'A Naturalistic Theory of the Reference of Thought to Reality', *Journal of Philosophy* **1** (1904) 253–55.

[12] Cf. W. James, *The Meaning of Truth*, pp. 136–37; *Letters of William James*, II, p. 295.

[13] Cf. W. James, *Essays in Radical Empiricism*, Longmans, Green, and Co., New York, 1912, pp. 13, 21–22, 30–32, 212.

[14] To Miller, December 6, 1905. By permission of the Harvard College Library and Mr Alexander James. Cf. *Letters of William James*, II, pp. 236–37.

[15] Cf. R. B. Perry, *Thought and Character of William James*, II, p. 394, Appendix X; *Letters of William James*, II, p. 236.

[16] The latter of these criticisms were developed by Miller in 1941 in discussions with me about key passages in *Essays In Radical Empiricism*.

[17] 'Naive Realism; What Is It?' *Essays Philosophical and Psychological*, Longmans, Green and Co., New York, 1908, pp. 260–61.

[18] Elizabeth Hardwick, (ed.), *Selected Letters of William James*, Farrar, Strauss, and Cudahy, New York, pp. 256–57.

[19] C. L. Street, 'Notes on Miller's Teaching at General Theological Seminary', typescript, 1968.

[20] Miller told Charles Street that the character Stair in 'Nature's Good: A Conversation' by John Dewey was meant to represent his views on religious knowledge. Stair held that words are but symbols leading us to "the one attitude that reveals truth – an attitude of direct vision" as in the common and convincing "self-impartation of the ultimate good in the scale of goods; the vision of blessedness in God". Such a doctrine is empirical and "mysticism is the heart of all positive empiricism". The sole possible proof of the supremacy of ideal values in the universe is their "direct unhindered realization". (J. Dewey, *The Influence of Darwin on Philosophy and Other Essays*, Henry Holt, New York, 1910, pp. 38–40.)

[21] 'Dickinson S. Miller', *Encyclopedia of Philosophy*, Macmillan Co., New York, 1967, V, p. 323.

[22] Cf. Peter Hare and Edward Madden, 'William James, Dickinson Miller and C. J. Ducasse on the Ethics of Belief', *Transactions of the Peirce Society* **4** (1968) 116–21 supplemented by copies of Miller's full letters kindly supplied by Edward Madden. Hare and Madden find in Miller an "absolute prohibition of belief without evidence", and such a prohibition, they argue in agreement with James and Ducasse, is unjustified. Miller allowed that there might be *decisions* requiring us to go "solely by impulse", but in subsequent additions to 'James's Doctrine of "The Right to Believe"' he insisted that "choices, decisions, commitments are not belief". We can act firmly in a way that seems best at the time without denying our ignorance because "the proprieties of action and the proprieties of belief are not the same".

[23] With characteristic, retiring generosity Miller asked me not to give him credit by name for his great aid in writing 'What Dr. Whitehead Finds in John Locke' (*Philosophical Forum* **1** (1943) 11–18), an article whose main thesis he enthusiastically welcomed as needed criticism in philosophy.

[24] I am indebted to Edward Madden and Peter Hare for permission to see this correspondence, 1943–1959, to be used in their projected book on Ducasse's thought.

[25] The 'moral' of his unpublished essay on 'What I Have Suffered From Doctors' was that the medical profession needed more "free common sense" and thoroughness. Above all, it needed waking up. He was not, he insisted, reproaching individuals but rather "the human mind when it is once set rolling in a professional alleyway".

TEACHERS AND TEACHING

FULLERTON AND PHILOSOPHY

[The following essay, though written in 1925 near the midpoint of Miller's adult life, is deservedly the leading piece of this collection in view of its contents. Here Miller not only describes the method of his most influential teacher and thus indicates his own view of the main aim of teaching, but he also reveals the primary source of his view of the proper method, outcome, and application of philosophy.

Miller himself prominently resembled his description of Fullerton under whom he studied at the University of Pennsylvania from 1885 to 1889: "limited in health and nervous force" yet "strong in command of himself" with a "confident and contagious smile"; the habit of bringing all abstractions "back to the concrete", to "daily experience in the matter"; asking questions like Socrates to get "judgment on the soundness of each step of the argument". Such qualities of mind are apparent in Miller's writings to follow as is also his dedication to that "conscience of the mind" he found in Fullerton.

Further, the more strictly philosophical essays in the next section extensively apply Fullerton's method as Miller formulated it – "analysis versus scepticism" – to develop Fullerton's suggestions on free will, the problem of the external world, and Hume's 'scepticism' about reasoning from past to future. But Miller went beyond Fullerton in ethical philosophy to insist on unrelenting, concrete use of critical intelligence to achieve human well-being, or welfare as he usually called it. This use of "the conscience of the mind", "a fine accuracy" in observing and reasoning, Miller notes, is widely neglected. With the saving exception of John Dewey, ethical philosophy is "playing metaphysics" while Rome burns. Concern for human welfare, its achievement and security, is a pervasive theme in Miller's other writings on education, ethics, religion, and public affairs and was particularly the center of his attention in his last years.]

The tragic death of George Stuart Fullerton brings reflections on his career and brilliant gifts and on the subject of philosophy, as conceived today, which he taught in universities and colleges. Fullerton was a man of extraordinary intellectual and personal power. First of all, as a teacher.

My memory goes back to the evenings when a group of students of the University of Pennsylvania gathered in his study, a group interesting in itself, several of whom bore family names interwoven with the history of Philadelphia and destined in their persons to be further distinguished: William Newbold, James Montgomery, George Wharton Pepper. It was a volunteer class, unofficial, with no seminar-table, no notes. Fullerton sat there by the green lamp (which often figured in his illustrations) a man of medium size or less, crippled in one leg, and limited in health and nervous force, yet always in some sort indescribably strong; strong in his fine Scotch face with its somewhat high cheekbones and trimmed mustache, strong in his fine Scotch voice in spite of its quietness – by no means a nasal or brassy voice but somehow not far from those tones, with a vibrant and resonant quality peculiarly agreeable to the ear – strong in his complete command of himself and his subject, in his confident and contagious smile and laugh.

His method was all his own. When any question or proposition in philosophy was launched he at once took its chief terms one by one and asked where we got that idea, from what experiences, what facts actually presented themselves in our lives to exemplify it. By what had grown to be an instinct of his mind he brought all abstractions back to the concrete. He took hold of any formula, however popular and taken for granted, with the tongs, and, while he held it thus, made us look at our daily experience in the matter with a fresh, awakened observation; and the results were startling and stimulating. He gave a bracing elementary discipline to the mind, and set it free from the slovenly assumptions of popular philosophy.

Disputants are prone to take the terms for granted and question about the things. Fullerton pounced upon the terms; he stood at the entrance of the mind and watched narrowly everything that came in. Just as narrowly he watched logic, and was in his quiet manner one of the keenest of destructive critics. Like Socrates he asked questions, like Socrates he wanted your judgment on the soundness of each step of his argument, like Socrates he sought definitions – in a sense; but unlike Socrates he asked, not "What is so-and-so?" but "What do you *mean* when you say so and so?" "What exactly have you in mind, in point of fact?" "When do we experience facts of that sort?" "What do they consist in as they really come to us?" Over all played his rich humor and anecdotes. There was often a spice of "psychic research", mediums, ghost-stories, and their exposure, choice samples of human credulity, or again hypnotism. On a few occasions he hypnotized men for an object-lesson.

Another scene I recall was at the Chestnut Street Theatre where a well-known mind-reader was giving an afternoon performance, and whither Fullerton with a group of us had gone at our request. He was made one of 'the committee', and of course became its leading member. I see him now, having tied the mind-reader's head in an old-fashioned green cloth 'lawyer's bag', led hastily about the stage, orchestra, and balcony by that wizard, as he darted with his hand on Fullerton's arm to find the object Fullerton had had hidden, which after a little was unearthed, with great applause, in a proscenium-box. Fullerton, thrust into this prominence, lame, throwing back his body a little at each step as always to heave forward the half-paralyzed leg, was none the less cool, keenly observant, master of the situation; and though he spared the performer at the time, afterwards explained the trick to us fully. That was one side of his function in life, to explain tricks, including the unconscious tricks of philosophers and those our own minds play upon us. He was at that time, together with Weir Mitchell and H. H. Furness of the Variorum Shakespeare, one of the Seybert Commission for the investigation of spiritualism.

Again I see him at the Philosophical Club of New York after he came to Columbia, the whole table listening to his brilliant talk, and again hear his laugh, genial but with a touch of unconscious reserve, for Fullerton's enjoyment was always his own and only partly shared. These occasions were few, for owing to his health he took long leaves of absence and was living chiefly at Munich, where he delighted in hospitality and had a large circle of warm friends. There he remained continuously through the War, the privations of which told severely upon him.

He was made for activity and vigor, but at the age of fifteen infantile paralysis had attacked him and deprived him for life of free exercise, a deprivation which more and more undermined his health. Severe illness followed the War and for a time recently he was in a sanitarium. There had always been a pessimistic and tragic undercurrent in his nature. Before the final act he wrote an affectionate letter to his wife, who had been the mainstay of his life for many years, to say that he had just had a hallucination, that his mind was about to give way: "better a dead husband than a mad husband."

Fullerton the author was Fullerton the teacher over again. The exploits of British philosophy, that of Locke, Berkeley, Hume, and the rest, have consisted in somewhat startling analyses of substance, knowledge, abstract ideas, matter, cause, the self, the basis of morals, etc. These philosophers themselves have been in two minds as to how they should regard their own analyses; whether as destructive, proving that what we had assumed did not exist, or as merely analytical, leaving it undisturbed in existence but giving a new insight into its nature. Mr Santayana criticizes this philosophy as though the first of these were the only tendency; he accuses the British philosophers of "malicious psychology", that is, of psychologically explaining human assumptions in order to discredit them. But in fact the other attitude, not sceptical or destructive, but purely explanatory, is all the while there.

Fullerton's importance lay in this, that while he really had his place in the line of the same philosophy, experience-philosophy, he dismisses one of these tendencies and enthrones the other. Turning away from formulas, he did not formulate his own method. But perhaps it could be formulated as *analysis versus scepticism.*

A brilliant example is seen in his treatment of freedom and determination. Of course, we are free in willing, he says, that is a fact of experience; but the analysis of this very fact involves determinism. There has never been any clash between freedom and determination at all. The whole controversy has been based on a failure to analyze thoroughly, on the crudity with which certain formulas have been brandished. Precisely so with the problem of the external world. Fullerton began very near to Berkeleyan idealism, but throwing away more and more its negative or destructive side and dwelling merely upon the analysis of our experience of matter, he stoutly affirms natural realism and pronounces subjectivism the merest crudity. Moreover, he applies a similar analysis to time, with striking results.

Again, I remember as a student encountering him in a corridor and asking what he thought of Hume's 'sceptical doubts' about the validity of reasoning from the past to the future, Hume's idea that we could not *rationally* know or expect that because a thing had happened it would happen in the same circumstances again. Fullerton answered in a sentence or two: "The argument from past experience is what we *mean* by a good argument, a good reason. It's what we *mean* by rationality." I cannot help thinking this a masterly flash. It turns scepticism into analysis. So again as to Hume's destructive treatment of the self or soul which in Taine's rendering caused Michelet to exclaim, "I have lost my *moi!*"

In all such cases Fullerton went deeper. We have the idea, that is plain; from where did we get it, of what elements given to us in our experience is it composed? If the thing in question does not exist how could we ever have come by the idea? Our task then is simply to find out what it means and always has essentially meant to us. Analysis does not destroy the thing analyzed; it only affords us a closer insight into its nature. If after the analysis we feel estranged from the old familiar thing, *that proves a shallowness in the analysis.* The terms have been in some degree too stiff and crude for their subject. He proceeded in these things with independence and originality. His chief positions cannot be set forth here, and have never received the attention they deserve.

Why did they not? Because of his manner of writing. The writer was the teacher over again in mission and contribution, but not in immediate effectiveness. His style was admirable, but, distrusting the formulas of professional controversy, he avoided them. And professionals looking into his pages often hardly knew what to make of him and were tempted to let him alone. It was easy to see what he was so carefully talking about, but not just where he came out on their own maps.

When *A System of Metaphysics* appeared, William James, always ready with intellectual sympathy, wrote (I quote from memory): "I have read it through, but really cannot see whether Fullerton thinks that the external world is *in mente* or *extra mentem.*" Fullerton would have said that he did not place it under either category, for he distrusted them, and the purpose of his book was to go deeper and explain how they arose. He felt that the problem was not being solved because the terms were wrong. Thoroughly characteristic was his early pamphlet 'On Sameness and Identity', devoted to the humble task of noting the several senses in which the words 'same' and 'identical' are legitimately used, and how profound errors arise in philosophy from not noticing the difference. Nothing can be more tonic for philosophy, but such analysis lacks the allurement of innovating and sweeping theory.

In his chief work he was not given to summaries, upon which the reader could fasten, being loath to pin the fortunes of his meaning to a few abstract phrases.

In philosophical meetings he spoke, if at all, in a tone of quiet reason and courtesy, but with some reserve, caring little to intervene in debate. He would have felt it necessary to begin too far back and come forward too cautiously. He did not see his philosophy as one of the contestants in the present arena, and would not do it the injustice of letting it appear so. It was a pity; Fullerton was an unsurpassed controversialist, and could have rendered wider aid to clear thinking in that capacity.

If we ask what was his broadest service, we must answer: to awaken the conscience of the mind, to teach a fine accuracy, that is, a fine truth, whether in observing or in reasoning. Now the most momentous application of this is in the management of life. There it is that we most need the power to see things as they are and foresee them as they will be, to penetrate the tricks of plausible appearance and fancied impossibility by which life perpetually misleads us; the power to steer accurately because we think accurately.

What a strange light is cast upon philosophy as so generally pursued today by a life and death such as Fullerton's! One-half of true philosophy is practical philosophy or ethics (which happened not to be the side of his chief work or interest) whose business is to grapple with the question, how to secure wellbeing for all or as many as possible, how to reach the actual causes of wretchedness and calamity and master them, both in social life and personal life, how to check, for instance, the forces that cripple and plunge in gloom and prematurely end a career such as his. Yet the minds of many authors of ethical treatises would be considerably jolted by the thought that they should focus the general conscience on such tasks as mastering infantile paralysis or teaching its victim how by cleverly adapted arts and games of physical exercise to keep his vitality in spite of fate. To point out our duty in relation to such a situation seems beneath the dignity of their science.

Much of our ethical philosophy is dreaming in the moonlight. What has it to do with the rope, the hook and the closet of that ghastly morning? It is little interested in the actual guidance of life and ministration to it, in what to do and how to live; it leaves that to the feelings and chance thinkings of the individual, while it treats of 'the realm of ends', 'the development of hedonistic theories', 'intention and motive', 'utilitarianism', 'perfectionism', and the rest; honest subjects all for intellectual disentanglement and for philosophic contemplation, but taking us for the purposes of ethics but a very little way. It is playing metaphysics while Rome is burning. Of course there are saving exceptions, such as the philosophic leadership of Mr John Dewey. One may respectfully suggest The Realm of Means, which has also to be scanned before a single duty can be determined. Perhaps the writers look to their reader for that patient and consistent application of their all too abstract formulas to life which they themselves as writers (and it is easier in writing than in life) will not undertake.

There are such maxims as "It is not the business of ethics to make people good". It is not the business of any practical study to make us do something but it is its business to show us how to do it. Or again "Principles will never go all the way; intuition is needed to guide us in life". True, but principles should go as far as they can, and they can render priceless aid; they can often come to our succor. Yet how idle to rest on the abstract word principle, when what we mean is that people should be brought to see what are the real causes of misery and the real causes of wellbeing, and what are therefore the real centres of morality, which unfortunately their 'intuition' does not sufficiently tell them, and on which the ethical teaching of our day has left the student's mind, as regards daily life, in a state of vagueness and disorder, almost abandoned to his ethical likes, dislikes and oblivions. By dint of omission it has left us one and all exposed to a kind of infantile paralysis of our potential faculty for snapping the bonds of mental habit, and grappling vigorously with life.

The student sees the teacher and the treatise-writer fly a kite of philosophic theory far up in a blue sky of idealism, but even if he is fascinated he cannot trace the connection with what he is to do next upon the earth.

What he needs is to be practiced, through cases, in clear-headed moral decision, following cause and effect, and deciding in all previously doubtful instances accordingly. It is because ethical theory is so divorced from action that such deep divergences of view can prevail in it and teachings survive that could not live a day under the test of thoroughly awakened application. The philosopher is too often writing much as he apparently expects his readers to live, by his sympathies and antipathies, his loves and hates, and not by any test of result at all.

Now granted first the aim or objective of ethics, the wellbeing of all, everything else in it is natural science, a study of the consequences of acts. The fixed code of elementary morals is fixed because its unhesitating observance is necessary for the common wellbeing. But, for the same reason, that code must be intelligently extended, because the observance of the present fragmentary code proves not enough to bring that wellbeing. Philosophy, because of its divorce from action, has not succeeded in carrying into general culture even the idea that morality *has* a purpose by which it is to be shaped and measured, and that if it does not accomplish this purpose it has failed in its reason for existing. Much less has philosophy made the cultivated public see the need for the conscience of the mind, the obligation to use the most accurate intelligence as the means of accomplishing this purpose, and hence it has done almost nothing to engage the force of public opinion on behalf of this obligation.

Ethics, as we have seen, was not the sphere of Fullerton's absorbing work and interest. His little *Handbook of Ethical Theory*, published in 1922, is an able and eminently impartial treatment of first principles, which, however, does not depart from the tradition in question. Had his interest turned that way, how brilliantly could his passion for bringing every abstraction back to the concrete have been brought to bear on the philosophy of life!

A STUDENT'S IMPRESSIONS OF WILLIAM JAMES

[The following impressions were based on Miller's observations of James as his teacher at Harvard from 1890 to 1892 and as his close friend and senior colleague thereafter. They refer to James's warmth and humanity as a person, a point that Miller reiterated in other writings, and particularly take note of James's method of teaching. In contrast to Royce's continuous and composed exposition, James's was broken, conversational, and exploratory. For Royce, Miller once remarked, lecturing was always the easiest form of breathing. James's course in psychology using his *Principles*, fresh off the press, began with readings from Sidgwick's 'Lecture against Lecturing' and proceeded thereafter by discussion, with controversy and questions on both sides. Further, James pointedly asked his students for criticism and recommendations for improving his method of conducting the course. Such observations reflected Miller's own mounting interest in methods of effective teaching and the process of education as it might inculcate a "conscience of the mind" essential to human welfare. From 1920 to 1925 he wrote a number of articles on educational method and returned to the subject for his unfinished book on 'Inquiry, Analytical or Sceptical' and his final publication, 'Is Philosophy a Good Training for the Mind?']

I have a vivid recollection of James's lectures, classes, conferences, seminars, laboratory interests, and the side that students saw of him generally. Fellow-manliness seemed to me a good name for his quality. The one thing apparently impossible to him was to speak *ex cathedra* from heights of scientific erudition and attainment. There were not a few 'if's' and 'maybe's' in his remarks. Moreover he seldom followed for long an orderly system of argument or unfolding of a theory, but was always apt to puncture such systematic pretensions when in the midst of them with some entirely unaffected doubt or question that put the matter upon a basis of common sense at once. He had drawn from his laboratory experience in chemistry and his study of medicine a keen sense that the imposing formulas of science that impress laymen are not so 'exact' as they sound. He was not, in my time at least, much of a believer in lecturing in the sense of continuous exposition.

I can well remember the first meeting of the course in psychology in 1890, in a ground-floor room of the old Lawrence Scientific School. He took a considerable part of the hour by reading extracts from Henry Sidgwick's 'Lecture against Lecturing', proceeding to explain that we should use as a textbook his own *Principles of Psychology*, appearing for the first time that very week from the press, and should spend the hours in conference, in which we should discuss and ask questions, on both sides. So during the year's course we read the two volumes through, with some amount of running commentary and controversy. There were four or five men of previous psychological training in a class of (I think) between twenty and thirty, two of whom were disposed to take up cudgels for the British associational psychology and were particularly troubled by the repeated doctrine of the *Principles* that a state of consciousness had no parts or elements, but was one indivisible fact. He bore questions that really were criticisms with inexhaustible patience and what I may call (the subject invites the word often) *human* attention; invited written questions as well, and would often return them with a reply penciled on the back when he thought the discussion too special in interest to be pursued before the class. Moreover, he bore with us with never a sign of impatience if we lingered after class, and even walked up Kirkland Street with him on his way home. Yet he was really not argumentative, not inclined to dialectic or pertinacious debate of any sort. It must always have required an effort of self-control to put up with it. He almost never, even in private conversation, contended for his own opinion. He had a way of often falling back on the language of perception, insight, sensibility, vision of possibilities. I recall how on one occasion after class, as I parted with him at the gate of the Memorial Hall train, his last words were something like these: "Well, Miller, that theory's not a warm reality in me yet – still a cold conception"; and the charm of the comradely smile with which he said it! The disinclination to formal logical system and the more prolonged purely intellectual analyses was felt by some men as a lack in his classroom work, though they recognized that these analyses were present in the *Psychology*. On the other hand, the very tendency to *feel* ideas lent a kind of emotional or aesthetic color which deepened the interest.

In the course of the year he asked the men each to write some word of suggestion, if he were so inclined, for improvement in the method with which the course was conducted; and, if I remember rightly, there were not a few respectful suggestions that too much time was allowed to the few wrangling disputants. In a pretty full and varied experience of lecture-rooms at home and abroad I cannot recall another where the class was asked to criticize the methods of the lecturer.

Another class of twelve or fourteen, in the same year, on Descartes, Spinoza, and Leibnitz, met in one of the "tower rooms" of Sever Hall, sitting around a table. Here we had to do mostly with pure metaphysics. And more striking still was the prominence of humanity and sensibility in his way of taking philosophic problems. I can see him now, sitting at the head of that heavy table of light-colored oak near the bow-window that formed the end of the room. My brother, a visitor at Cambridge, dropping in for an hour and seeing him with his vigorous air, bronzed and sanguine complexion, and brown tweeds, said, "He looks more like a sportsman than a professor." I think that the sporting men in college always felt a certain affinity to themselves on one side in the freshness and manhood that distinguished him in mind, appearance, and diction. It was, by the way, in this latter course that I first heard some of the philosophic phrases now identified with him. There was a great deal about the monist and pluralist views of the universe. The world of the monist was described as a "block-universe" and the monist himself as "wallowing in a sense of unbridled unity", or something of the sort. He always wanted the men to write one or two "theses" in the course of the year and to get to work early on them. He made a great deal of bibliography. He would say, "I am no man for editions and references, no exact bibliographer." But none the less he would put upon the blackboard full lists of books, English, French, German, and Italian, on our subject. His own reading was immense and systematic. No one has ever done justice to it, partly because he spoke with unaffected modesty of that side of his equipment.

Of course this knowledge came to the foreground in his "seminar". In my second year I was with him in one of these for both terms, the first half-year studying the psychology of pleasure and pain, and the second, mental pathology. Here each of us undertook a special topic, the reading for which was suggested by him. The students were an interesting group, including Professor Santayana, then an instructor, Dr. Herbert Nichols, Messrs. Mezes (now President of the City College, New York), Pierce (late Professor at Smith College), Angell (Professor of Psychology at Chicago, and now President of the Carnegie Corporation), Bakewell (Professor at Yale), and Alfred Hodder (who became instructor at Bryn Mawr College, then abandoned academic life for literature and politics). In this seminar I was deeply impressed by his judicious and often judicial quality. His range of intellectual experience, his profound cultivation in literature, in science and in art (has there been in our generation a more cultivated man?), his absolutely unfettered and untrammeled mind, ready to do sympathetic justice to the most unaccredited, audacious, or despised hypotheses, yet always keeping his own sense of proportion and the balance of evidence – merely to know these qualities, as we sat about that council-board, was to receive, so far as we were capable of abstorbing it, in a heightened sense of the good old adjective, 'liberal' education. Of all the services he did us in this seminar perhaps the greatest was his running commentary on the students' reports on such authors as Lombroso and Nordau, and all theories of degeneracy and morbid human types. His thought was that there is no sharp line to be drawn between 'healthy' and 'unhealthy' minds, that all have something of both. Once when we were returning from two insane asylums which he had arranged for the class to visit, and at one of which we had seen a dangerous, almost naked maniac, I remember his saying, "President Eliot might not like to admit that there is no sharp line between himself and the men we have just seen, but it is true." He would emphasize that people who had great nervous burdens to carry, hereditary perhaps, could order their lives fruitfully and perhaps derive some gain from their 'degenerate' sensitiveness, whatever it might be. The doctrine is set forth with regard to religion in an early chapter of his *Varieties of Religious Experience*, but for us it was applied to life at large.

In private conversation he had a mastery of words, a voice, a vigor, a freedom, a dignity, and therefore what one might call an authority, in which he stood quite alone. Yet brilliant man as he was, he never quite outgrew a perceptible shyness or diffidence in the lecture-room, which showed sometimes in a heightened color. Going to lecture in one of the last courses he ever gave at Harvard, he said to a colleague whom he met on the way, "I have lectured so and so many years, and yet here am I on the way to my class in trepidation!"

Professor Royce's style of exposition was continuous, even, unfailing, composed. Professor James was more conversational, varied, broken, at times struggling for expression – in spite of what has been mentioned as his mastery of words. This was natural, for the one was deeply and comfortably installed in a theory (to be sure a great theory), and the other was peering out in quest of something greater which he did not distinctly see. James's method gave us in the classroom more of his own exploration and *aperçu*. We felt his mind at work.

Royce in lecturing sat immovable. James would rise with a peculiar suddenness and make bold and rapid strokes for a diagram on the blackboard – I can remember his abstracted air as he wrestled with some idea, standing by his chair with one foot upon it, elbow on knee, hand to chin. A friend has described a scene at a little class that, in a still earlier year, met in James's own study. In the effort to illustrate he brought out a blackboard. He stood it on a chair and in various other positions, but could not at once write upon it, hold it steady, and keep it in the class's vision. Entirely bent on what he was doing, his efforts resulted at last in his standing it on the floor while he lay down at full length, holding it with one hand, drawing with the other, and continuing the flow of his commentary. I can myself remember how, after one of his lectures on Pragmatism in the Horace Mann Auditorium in New York, being assailed with questions by people who came up to the edge of the platform, he ended by sitting on that edge himself, all in his frock-coat as he was, his feet hanging down, with his usual complete absorption in the subject, and the look of human and mellow consideration which distinguished him at such moments, meeting the thoughts of the inquirers, whose attention also was entirely riveted. If this suggests a lack of dignity, it misleads, for dignity never forsook him, such was the inherent strength of tone and bearing. In one respect these particular lectures (afterwards published as his book on Pragmatism) stand alone in my recollection. An audience may easily be large the first time, but if there is a change it usually falls away more or less on the subsequent occasions. These lectures were announced for one of the larger lecture-halls. This was so crowded before the lecture began, some not being able to gain admittance, that the audience had to be asked to move to the large 'auditorium' I have mentioned. But in it also the numbers grew, till on the last day it presented much the same appearance as the other hall on the first.

JAMES AND ANALYSIS

[Miller's first writing after his return from Europe in 1934 to begin his 'American retirement' in Boston was the following essay occasioned by Perry's two-volume, prize-winning biography tracing the development of James's thought. With Perry's book as a point of departure, Miller makes a comprehensive and fundamental assessment of James's views and sketches out his own alternatives. In particular, Miller finds James lacking at the very point where his earlier teacher, George Fullerton, had most impressed him, namely, discernment of how analysis can base 'free will' and 'knowing' on assured facts of experience to achieve durable results in philosophy. To be sure, James well practiced the method of analysis in his treatment of 'personality' in *Principles of Psychology* but elsewhere applied it haltingly or not at all because his prophetic side, his concern for the richness and openness of experience, made him distrust analysis.

As revealed in other writings, Miller shared James's 'prophecy', his ideal of life, in opposition to Santayana's spirit of renunciation. The motor of Miller's thinking on religion and human welfare was precisely the "sympathy and demanded liberty for all" he found in James, but he firmly believed that this ideal, particularly its theoretic underpinnings, required what James lacked, namely, "pertinacious analysis". Several of Miller's essays to follow systematically fill out the sketches given here of his alternatives to James's thought, alternatives derived from searching analysis of 'free will', 'knowing', and 'reason' as grounded in experience.]

Rumor had said that Professor Perry was preparing a well-documented volume, tracing the development of James's philosophical opinions. If this was the plan it has grown into one far more over-spanning. What we have[1] is an exceptionally complete biography, a wilderness of materials thoroughly subdued to order and structure, a masterpiece of devoted and unerring scholarship, a monument on a great scale to William James. The author has "dared to be voluminous" and the result justifies his judgment. The patience and determination with which in many a case he has dug out just that particular expression of a sentiment on James's part that is the pithiest and most telling, only careful study of the book reveals. It is interesting to see a genius by no means of the constructive, the architectural, order brought out with such effect in a book so admirably built. Moreover the delicate intellectual sympathy of the interpretative work becomes more and more satisfying as one reads. The summings-up at the close are just and felicitous. (There is at first perhaps a doubt whether 'morbid traits' are not a trifle too much emphasized but a closer reading dispels it.)

This book, in which resound the echoes of philosophic controversy, rises none the less above all controversy and portrays an indisputable James. It is a James whose moral and prophetic greatness is independent of the technical formulas he defended. In them his spirit and tendencies found expression, but the spirit and tendencies are greater than the expression, great as that so often is. Such definite formulation in philosophy depends, of course, on two factors, the man and the intellectual environment, the environment of ideas, in which he finds himself and from which his mind must be nourished. Since this book appeared the inevitable remark has been made, "In what a rich environment was this man born and reared; how warmly, indefatigably, did he respond to that environment and increase and multiply its extent and keep responding to the very end!" True indeed, in obvious respects; for range of personality, nationality, ability, reputation, speculative tendency, the human background of his education and of his life was astonishing. But at the one point most vital for James's philosophy it was, strange to say, not a rich but a somewhat poor and inauspicious environment, unworthy of the man, inadequate to minister to the great needs of a great nature. So far as certain of his chief philosophic conceptions go, his environment betrayed him. It permitted and led him to be satisfied with hasty analysis, which gave a form to his teaching that did not do it justice. Inexorably, philosophy is analysis; that is to say, like all science, it views things, processes, and ideas in their composition, so far as they have a composition. On that side, the teachings of the time, those that the man, the temperament, were likely to be arrested by and to fasten upon, were deficient. Of those close to him in early days perhaps Charles Peirce was the one who may be thought best qualified to aid him here. But at the vital point here in question Peirce had nothing to contribute, suffering himself in the same respect.

In point of breadth and largeness James was distinctly the best mind in the known intellectual life of this country. Moreover he had the stature of a prophet. The prophecy he had it in him essentially to deliver was of a commanding power, sweep, and truth. Of a commanding simplicity as well. It needed to be stated in its full sweep, which it never quite was. He lived it, and applied it to this and that question in his writings, more than he preached it at large or even formulated it. It needed too to be embodied in terms which would do it justice, that would not disguise or compromise its truth, terms fit to stand the test of time, unentangled in hasty and dubious technicalities. It needed to be embodied in the language of life and literature. This particular broad prophecy had really nothing to do with technical metaphysics, cosmology, or epistemology. It did not need pragmatism, pluralism, tychism, interactionism, or indeterminism. It was in this respect like the essential leadings of Emerson or of Rousseau. He thought it involved points in analytic theory because he imagined that some of the philosophies of the day contradicted and excluded it, so that his first conflict was with them. Putting aside for our purposes his important doctrine of the religious 'right to believe', he did not see that what he held precious in life was matter of unquestioned experience, assailable in respect of value, if at all, only on broad grounds of that experience, such as all may perceive; that the philosophic theories appearing to bear on the subject were really but rival minute *analyses* of the experience of life, powerless to raise doubts as to the reality of that experience itself. Of this more presently. He did not discern this because the philosophy of his period did not discern it. On the points in question its analysis was superficial. This was where it did him an ill turn. On certain major questions of life and ideal it embroiled him in needless specialistic controversies. This, if it has not obscured, has weakened the force and the effect of what I have called his prophecy.

James made momentous contributions, some conclusive and all suggestive, at other points, to strict philosophic theory. I speak here only of his moral and prophetic significance and its unfortunate entanglement.

What was his ideal of life? For what on this, by him justly deemed the most important side of his thought, did he essentially stand?[2] For life itself, for the fulness and richness and satisfaction of human life; not least its emotional satisfaction. To this end he would have us open our minds to every means, even the most unexpected or unaccredited, to every ray of light bearing upon means. "Open doors and windows" to any idea, mood, attitude, propensity, that might possibly aid toward the great end. Freest suggestion, freest experiment; the test of all being. How do they turn out in experience? Do they durably enrich life, or do they impoverish it? He believed that there was far more in the depths of human nature than our eyes, custom-dulled, see in it and far greater things in life than we mechanical creatures attain. In this spirit he looked at human beings; looked past their defects, blunders, and pettinesses, at the valuable qualities that he was quick to discover in them and to which he gave cordial appreciation. He looked at the character of others as he looked at the thought of others. And what he was in this respect entered into his prophetic temper. William James was the great appreciator, and Professor Perry's book, with its correspondence, shows him to us as such. He was therefore the great encourager, and the effect he thus had in promoting the work of others and the growth of philosophy and psychology in America is beyond the telling. This was not merely the private man. It was his theory of life, and it found written expression in quarters of which space sadly fails me to remind the reader. But it has never stood forth in full expression as it gradually does in this book, which thus presents the attitude of James toward life as it has never been presented before.

This 'prophecy' is untechnical but not uncontroversial. Its spirit is of course the opposite of Mr Santayana's, whose eye is on the maladjustments, disappointments, disenchantments of life, not least of emotional life; who would counsel us to draw in our tentacles and remember "the fatal antiquity of human nature" – that is, that we have learned by now, if we have sense, what is in it and where are its limits, and that caution and renunciation, not experiment and adventure and the following of April hopes, will bring us the only richness attainable. James seeks a richness including that of achieving and loving life, Santayana a richness of understanding, imagination, and peace.

Let us briefly trace how certain of James's ideals and sentiments carried him, though what I can not but think misconception, into theoretic controversy. The craving for freedom, the need to shake off oppressive control, to snap narrow restraints, the note of revolt, the break for liberty – this mingled in him with sympathy and demanded liberty for all. It

mingled with the ideal of fulness of life and demanded an extreme breadth
of mind and openness to unfamiliar, strange suggestions. It was impatient
of straight-laced scientific orthodoxy and snobbery. It mingled with the
love of freshness and variety and the recoil from sameness and tameness.
It would not be fettered even by his own formulas, his own intellectual
past.

If the past is not to hold us in an iron, inescapable control, if life must
have richer possibilities than that, if we are in the last resort free in willing,
if we can break with the moral past and be "authois of novelty", this
must mean, he thought, a break in the causal nexus. The question of free
will thus conceived and decided, there is at once a portentous result for
metaphysics and *Weltanschauung*. That result is 'pluralism' as against
'monism –' his great philosophical cause. We individuals are not each
held in his place in a "block-universe", a world-system that knows no
exceptions, no outbreaks of spontaneity, no moments of real uncertainty
when "fate's scales ... quiver". Pluralism in James's world is the consequence of his indeterminism, of his particular way of conceiving and
deciding the will-problem. His driving motive for pluralism would not
otherwise have existed. (To be sure there is his refusal of monistic *religion*
on the added ground that it makes Deity supreme over the whole world
and hence responsible for evil, an objection that might still have swayed
him had he been a determinist; but against monistic *metaphysics*, the
deeper, the primary enemy, it is his conception of free will that drives him
to battle.)

But that his ideals of life demanded the taking up of these theoretic
positions – that was where he was misled. James himself has in one
place (how like him in his rich wayward variety and unexpected turns!)
put his finger on the key to some of the chief theoretic questions. In *The
Principles of Psychology*, page 226, we read:

A French writer, speaking of our ideas, says somewhere in a fit of antispiritualistic
excitement that, misled by certain peculiarities which they display, we "end by personi-
fying" the procession which they make, – such personification being regarded by him
as a great philosophic blunder on our part. It could only be a blunder if the notion of
personality meant something essentially different from anything to be found in the
mental procession. But *if that procession be itself the very 'original' of the notion* of
personality, to personify it can not possibly be wrong. It is already personified. There
are no marks of personality to be gathered *aliunde*, and then found lacking in the train
of thought. It has them all already.

The emphasis is my own. These are golden words. We should not ask "Does personality exist?" because we mean by personality something 'given' in our experience of ourselves. We should ask, In what does personality consist? And this is a question calling simply for analysis.

But of the principle here involved, in this case so clearly seen, James loses sight again. When he wrote the article entitled 'Does Consciousness Exist' he might, according to his own principle just cited, have approached his subject otherwise. He might rather have asked, and for identically the same reasons: In what does consciousness consist? What is the meaning of the word? From what experiences of self and of others, and inference in terms of those experiences, do we come by the notion? He might by so proceeding have produced a more adequate treatment, embracing more fact, ignoring nothing. The conception of consciousness can not be "a mere echo, the faint rumor left behind by the disappearing 'soul' upon the air of philosophy" – or by anything disappearing – any more than the conception of personality can be; any more than the conception of experience itself can be. And this remark prejudges nothing whatsoever as to what we shall find the notion to consist in when we proceed to analyze it with care.

So is it precisely when we come to freedom in willing. To be sure, he is here asserting, not, as in the case of consciousness, denying. But he permits his opponents to deny it, he declares that they do, and concedes to them therein a tenable and plausible position. He admits what he should not admit, that we can reasonably ask, Does freedom in willing exist? We mean by freedom in this respect something with which experience acquaints us. The question is: In what does it consist? If we did not derive it from our experience we should not have thought of it at all, we should have had no material out of which to fabricate the idea. Just so the question is not: Does moral responsibility exist? but: What is the meaning of moral responsibility? Similarly, what is the meaning of praise and blame, what is the meaning of "I could have done otherwise?" These are questions for analysis of a given situation, a given set of relations and the feelings naturally, usefully, and appropriately responding thereto. Freedom – in its full and usual signification for our life – can be analyzed without being destroyed, and determinism is merely a feature of the analysis of it. This is not to say that determinism is universally true, only that it is true in so far as we have free will. Careful, persistent analysis will disclose that free will implies determination.[3]

At any determinism, however, that claimed to be consistent with free will and to have the right to use the language of free will, James had a missile to throw. He called such a conception "soft determinism", grasping at acceptable terms to which it had no title. Now this reproach is based on the supposition that there is another idea of freedom, not deterministic, which *has* a right to the word, namely, an idea of which James is in possession. But careful, persistent analysis will disclose that there is no such idea, that he was deceiving himself, that at this point he was thinking obscurely because not analytically, because he did not ask himself, and keep asking: Just what in our experience do these terms mean? Indetermination is inconsistent with our idea of freedom, determination is consistent with it and inescapably implied by it.

There is a brilliant passage in 'The Dilemma of Determinism' in which James considers the alternative presented to the will of walking home after the lecture by way of one street or another. "You, as passive spectators, look on and see the two alternative universes – one of them with me walking through Divinity Avenue in it, the other with the same me walking through Oxford Street. Now, if you are determinists, you believe one of these universes to have been from eternity impossible", etc. That is to say, James takes possibility here as a plain term, whose implications are promptly clear, which he need not stop to analyze. He asks: Does the possibility exist?, instead of asking: In what does the possibility consist? What is the meaning in experience of the term 'possibility'? From what experiences do we derive it? And precisely so with the words 'I can' and 'I could'. Analysis discloses that these assertions, so far from involving indetermination, involve the opposite, and would completely lose their meaning if and so far as indeterminism were true.

But if that is the case the whole motive for his prolonged and ardent crusade against 'monism' and for 'pluralism' drops away. Free choice is not an exemption from law but in its inmost essence an embodiment of law. Free individuality, sovereign selfhood, able to renounce past courses, habits, ideas; able to be (in the only sense the words will bear) "the author of novelties", is not handcuffed and bound down by membership in a world-system of cause and effect; – such a confusion is simply the result of refraining from analysis. This is not at all to say that the world *is* such a system, that physical determination, or any determination, has universal reign. It is not to say that there is no such thing as absolute chance. It is not to say anything on that subject. It is merely to say that the utterly free initiative and spontaneity that James justly prized would not profit in the least by the existence of such chance, have in fact nothing whatever to do with chance. They imply a continuing self as a source of action, and a continuity of cause and effect within that self constituting its life, moral individuality and election, which can not be conceived without such continuity. James was thinking in terms of that continuity at the very moment that he denied it. For there are no other terms in which to think his thoughts. His remarkable declaration for 'tychism' at a period long before its present scientific vogue remains as interesting as ever, but it has not the moral significance that he imagined. And it was the moral significance, once more, that was the chief driving motive for his own interest and advocacy.

So it was when James, in the discussion of pragmatism and earlier, professed 'irrationalism', opposed himself to intellectualism and declared his independence of logic. The helpful question (once again, if the reader will bear with me) is not: Is there really any obligation to submit to reason or intellect? It is: Just what is reason and what does it do for us? What is its place in our experience? What, precisely, in a specified instance would submitting or not submitting to it mean? Define reason in the light of our experience of it. Define logic in the same light. We should then see that independence of logic, fearless rebellion against reason, are phrases that appear to have a philosophic meaning only so long as we do not thus analyze. James conceded too much, he made the fatal concession, when he admitted by his phrases that reason can offer obstruction to any empirical thinking, or that experience can present anything opposed to logic, or that there is any rationality not based upon experience or the meaning of symbols. And if he meant reason and logic as superficially and improperly conceived, then it was conceding far too much for lucidity and sound guidance to use the words without adding 'falsely so called'.

In these questions the illuminating method, that of analyzing the familiar ideas, that of analysis versus scepticism, is the method toward which British philosophy kept pointing and moving. It pointed to this method all the while, so to speak, as its own goal and consummation, though it seldom or never arrived there. We see the method approximated in the treatment of free will, for instance, by Hobbes, Locke, and Hume – but never entirely reached. It was the secret, the inner meaning, of their whole treatment that complete freedom and determination are united in the facts; they all but realize this. In its completeness the method is indeed proclaimed by Berkeley as regards 'body' (his equivalent for our term 'matter', in the everyday sense, – a word that he used for another idea). He "agrees with the vulgar" about the outer world, he is merely telling you the nature of the thought that all alike share. We can not, however, call this reaching the goal, since "the vulgar" and he were not really in perfect accord, and further analysis of the natural notion of the outer world was required. But the true plan of the classic British philosophy was not that of 'malicious psychology' destroying the validity of the fundamental beliefs of common sense by a pitiless psychological dissection that exposed their hollowness; that was the phase that if often showed because it was only on the way, because it lingered in its crude stage, and had not come to the ripest understanding of what its proceedings really meant.

Thus in the period of James's development the analytic method had never come to its own. He, with his roving philosophic eye and flashes of insight, saw the principle in the case of personality. But when he turned to other cases the same principle did not leap to view. It was often the way of his genius to "philosophize in spots". The insight was not sufficiently generalized to be abiding and trusty. It could not save him from the influence of his environment. It could not intervene to qualify the effect of Renouvier. Shadworth Hodgson indeed had hold of the general principle and James had read his work.[4] But Hodgson was far from driving it home. Especially he did not drive it home for a mind like James's, whose great psychological gift tended another way. That gift was to see whatever in an experience was unique and unanalysable in quality, to catch the 'peculiar effect', as we say of a picture. To assert that some impression in *sui generis*, indescribable, indivisible, that is what we find him doing in chapter after chapter of his *Psychology*; as to the consciousness of space, of time, of "our meaning" ("an altogether special bit of consciousness *ad hoc*") of the taste of lemonade (*not* the taste of lemon and that of sugar combined but a new and unique taste), of relations, of tendency, etc. etc. I am not arguing that these views were wrong or that their presentation was not a profound service to psychology; merely that this psychologist's special vocation did not help to fit him for perceiving the principle with which this article has to do. Analysis, to our imagination, often seems to take the life out of a thing, and James was most of all jealously tenacious of whatever tastes of life. But not all psychological facts are unanalysable, and analysis does not destroy, else it is false analysis. The true analytical imagination is able to perceive the identity of the parts, taken conjointly, with the living whole.

About pragmatism too what James had to teach or preach for life in his whole dealings with the subject was not bound up with any technical propositions. That we should hold our beliefs or most of them as hypotheses liable to modification in the light of experience, that we should be open and receptive to all hypotheses until experience confirms or rejects them, that we should not forget that knowledge is instrumental to action and life, that any beliefs that lastingly deepen, strengthen, enrich life and render it on the whole more satisfactory must in some sort have truth in them; these are theses that may be conveyed straight to the public at large without any abstruse analysis or controversy. The soundness of the last can readily be shown by examples and common sense. Any further and more difficult thoughts could have been separately discussed. But on this subject too he conceived that his truths required or would be helped by disputable philosophic reasoning. In fact, as in the case of pluralism they are weakened and imperiled by this connection. After what we have seen, however, it is an interesting fact that the two chief doctrines of his pragmatism, that of 'the pragmatic method' and 'pragmatism's theory of truth' do profess in some passages to be pure analyses of the meaning of terms. There is emphasis upon their being so. The battleground lies quite otherwise than in the case of pluralism. Here it is *by means of* an ingenious analysis that he undertakes to justify his conclusion. But these analyses are injured by being mingled with the more practical teaching, and the practical teaching here too is weakened in effect by having its fortunes pinned to very disputable analyses. 'The pragmatic method' is not stated and illustrated with sufficient exactness, and in the analysis of the reference of thought to its object the line is not drawn sharply enough between the cases where we believe ourselves to perceive the intrinsic nature of the object and those where our knowledge is only indirect, virtual, and practical.

So we may conclude as we began. It is worth while to study the effect of an intellectual environment on a gifted thinker, all whose chief tendencies are sound and even inspired. In philosophy James's environment did not give him the assistance he most needed. Hence he remained greater in himself than in his purely philosophic product, though that was a great product. Matthew Arnold long ago said, in effect, that the function of criticism was to purify the springs in which original thought must arise. In James's time they sadly needed purifying. The classic British philosophy had not succeeded in bringing out its own inner meaning. Thus the German, Oxford, and French philosophies opposed to it had still a towering plausibility. The master-key to understanding the position was a more pertinacious analysis – an analysis in just the spirit that, with reference to personality, speaks in James himself.

NOTES

[1] Ralph Barton Perry, *The Thought and Character of William James*. As revealed in unpublished correspondence and notes, together with his published writings. Vol. I. Inheritance and Vocation. Vol. II. Philosophy and Psychology. Atlantic Monthly Press, Boston, 1935. xxxviii + 826 pp.; xxii + 786 pp.

[2] I have used in part in this paragraph phraseology already employed elsewhere. [Review of J. S. Bixler, 'Religion in the Philosophy of William James', *Journal of Philosophy* 24 (1927) 204-205.]

[3] I have endeavored to make this clear in detail in an article, 'Free Will as Involving Determination and Inconceivable Without It', *Mind*, 43 (1934) 1–27.

[4] So also at a later date had G. S. Fullerton in his *System of Metaphysic*, though he never, like Hodgson, gave it general formulation. Too late and too obscurely to influence James. Fullerton derived it from Berkeley and employed it very effectively, as regards the external world, in his classroom teaching. There is no space here to comment on James's correspondence with Hodgson and Renouvier.

GEORGE SANTAYANA

[Like James and Royce, Santayana was one of Miller's teachers at Harvard and his senior colleague thereafter. Miller became an intimate friend of James but could not claim to know Santayana well though they were close enough at one time to consider sharing an apartment in Cambridge.

The following essay, written for publication in 1944 but only now appearing in print, explores Santayana's temperament in relation to the tendencies of his thought. At a number of points it extends what Miller had to say in a longer essay of 1921 on 'Mr. Santayana and William James'. There Miller saw Santayana as being essentially "a poet teaching philosophy" who lectured "like an artist painting a picture". Facing a class, Santayana was always the same composed, "frictionless being". Preferring "the easiest thing", he had little use for the apparatus of scholarship and a "distaste for painstaking analysis", so his opinions tended to be unsupported and oracular. His temperament led him to miss the central thing in Christianity, love, so he had a "strange deficiency of interest in the welfare of *others*", the proper fruition of his own ideal of the perfect Good.

In the pages to follow, Miller seems to be more sympathetic and balanced in his appraisal. He notes with approval Santayana's criticism of the confusion of means and ends in modern life but cannot fully sympathize with his detachment and "contentment in limitation", traits that kept him alien to the broad liberal movement of modern times "to make humanity and reason prevail in human affairs". This assessment was very likely a part of sketch of the "thick manuscript" that Miller said he had completed in 1960 and entitled 'George Santayana – A Study in the Effects of a Ruling Passion', but such a manuscript was not among his posthumous papers.]

In Rome Mr Santayana has been living serenely through Fascism, its downfall, and the taking of the city, but Mr Herbert Matthews' brief interview with him in the *New York Times* of June 14 [1944] suggests far too much the Rip Van Winkle. He "lives in the eternal" within the Eternal City, but he remains one of the most wideawake of minds.

Those few words from Rome sent my mind back to a scene many years ago. During that year at Harvard there was a series of social meetings of graduate students and professors of philosophy at the houses of the latter, at which the order of the evening was for one professor or "instructor" and several students to tell how their interest in philosophy began and developed. On one of these occasions, at the house of Professor Francis Peabody in Kirkland Street, Mr Santayana, then an instructor in his upper twenties, told this story. He was a handsome young man, with black hair, brown eyes, fine and pallid complexion, and an agreeable voice. He had then, as always, the gift of the accurate and apt word. Amongst other things he said that in early days at college he had felt that either the faith of the Roman Catholic Church was true or – pessimism; and he had come to believe that the former was impossible. But later, with his study in Europe, especially with his stay at Oxford, he came to see that, even on the basis of the pessimist's negations and disillusionment, a not unhappy life could be lived, the life of a man of the world, a life of understanding. Very notable were the perfect simplicity and sincerity and the absence of any instinctive attuning of what he said to the tone of teaching in the Department of Philosophy, or of any impulse to guard himself. Professor Palmer (Hegel-inspired) asked him if each stage of his progress in philosophy had brought him into a larger, a richer world. By this was meant a friendly stricture on what had been said. No, said Santayana, he could not say that. Peabody, Professor of Christian Morals, put in satirically, alluding to Santayana's artistic interests, that he would like his world to be "pretty", wouldn't he? An earnest graduate of Oberlin College asked, "Mr Santayana, have you ever experienced conversion?" "No", was the reply, in all simplicity.

There was an impression that "the Department" was somewhat disturbed over this confession of attitude by one of their own members. I took this to be at the want of religious belief. "No, no", said William James a day of two afterwards (he had come in late and heard only what his colleagues had told him) "it was the want of moral seriousness." Yet it was James who in later years when Santayana was first thinking of quitting Harvard (as he afterwards did) exerted himself successfully to secure his remaining. And who afterward exclaimed, "just suppose we had let him go!" As for the young man himself, he said in one of those years: "If they won't take me as God made me they can't have me at all."

And now we find him in his autobiography accusing Harvard of "spiritual penury and moral confusion" – a shaft at which we must presently look again.

Meanwhile it is interesting that the man his older colleagues thus shook their heads over has evinced in a surpassing degree one great trait of moral seriousness, the control, ordering, and discipline of a life. Never did a life better answer the helm. There are clever and 'brilliant' young men in a college generation, but, good heavens, what usually comes of them? It was a grave question about this young man, was he sufficiently productive? He has eclipsed them all, except James, in production. He very deliberately planned, and what he planned he has with precision brought fully forth. He conceived a systematic philosophy, on one side of the subject, in five volumes, and completed it; then another systematic philosophy, on another side, in five volumes, and has completed it also. (Can this be an instance of the well-known biological tendency to a pentadactylic or pentactinal forthputting?) He always intended to write a novel, did something at one even in his early days, and there it is, eventually, a unique product for an adept in technical philosophy. For many years he has meant to write in the end his memoirs, and now one notable instalment has appeared. And then there are the volumes of essays, such as *Soliloquies in England* which contain some of his finest work. How many planners in youth can show such fulfilment? He has "kept the law in calmness made and *seen* what he foresaw."

And this has come largely through resolutely ridding himself of distractions and obstructions. He always had a powerful bent toward simplifying life – nothing is more characteristic. In electing studies at Harvard he said, "First I took only classics and then I took only philosophy." (Barrett Wendell, Professor of English, remarked sadly that the best writer who had in his time emerged from Harvard had taken no courses of instruction in the English Department at all.) Once I mentioned that packing for a summer in Europe was such a bother – picking out just what to take with you. "That is no bother to me," he said. "I take all the clothes I have (he was always very well, and in those days fashionably, dressed) and put them in a trunk." "Oh," I answered, "it is not the clothes but the books, for instance." "That is no trouble to me; I don't take any books."

I cannot interpret this quite literally, but it did mean that no apparatus of books accompanied him, only the fewest and simplest. One year he was to begin in the autumn a course of instruction on Kant, one of the most difficult topics in the range of the Department. He was taking with him for the summer Kant's three Critiques: "That will be my preparation." No commentaries, analyses, or critical literature, nothing from the world of footnotes, no complications. If this suggests that he is not a conscientious and exact scholar, the impression is totally false. Of course he had read Kant a few years before. But attempting too much was a thing he detested; he preferred to attempt a little and finish it thoroughly without haste or perturbation. Contentment in limitation, that was his choice – in the whole of life, for that matter. He liked to do his writing in an easy chair and, to make it simpler, wrote in a blankbook with a pencil. In useless friction and waste of force he did not believe, and he thought they abounded in America.

Santayana lived for some years at 7 Stoughton Hall, afterwards occupied by Professor Copeland, and there was something very attractive about the old study with its glowing coal fire in the high grate. There one evening, a little after the meeting I have mentioned, William James read to a small club of students a paper on 'The Moral Philosopher and the Moral Life' which in after-years he thought the best of his essays. In it occurs a comparison of the strenuous and the easy-going moods – a passage that I have always believed suggested to Theodore Roosevelt his address on 'The Strenuous Life'. Santayana asked, "Don't you think that the philosophic temper is of the easy-going kind?" No, decidedly James did not think that. We can see what easy-goingness for Santayana meant. It meant deliberation and freedom from turmoil, calm and peace, moderate expectations in the interest of settled equilibrium and satisfaction. He himself looked fearlessly into the future, said he might lose his health, etc., and was fully prepared in mind for reversals of fortune. The absence of sanguine optimism in general has certainly made for the canny management of life.

In all this it was striking how definite and final were the decisions. If something was not essential and was cumbering to life out it went for good. One felt the power of the character underneath. He understood himself. There was no vagueness and therefore no confusion.

The true order of life, he once said playfully, was that of a monk who took the same walk under a row of plane-trees every day. James once found him staying at Athens and told me afterwards with great relish that Santayana had been but once up to the Parthenon and but once at the Museum, and that he took every day the same walk toward the Piraeus. No doubt he had been there before. Nothing could be more antithetical than the temperaments of these two, though James had a delighted appreciation of Santayana's abilities and Santayana a high personal appreciation of James. One was more for richness of experience, the other more for order and serenity. When I said to the younger man, "Why don't you try to see more of James?," his answer was, "I don't know which way he'll jump." At another time, quite apart from this question: "I don't want geniuses for my friends." As Norman Hapgood wrote of him, "he liked a small mind, simple and harmonious, more than a large one distorted or turbulent" – not that the last words would apply to James.

James needed variety and one of his chief works is entitled, *Varieties* –. He loved the woods, the mountains, the wilderness – indeed the wilderness of life, with its varied wealth of persons and its unexpectedness. In one passage he speaks of life as "this delicious mess". No mess could be delicious to Santayana. As for the wilderness, when he was invited to the 'camp' of the Putnam and Bowditch families in the Adirondacks, the mountains that James so loved, he very politely declined, and was tickled at the mere suggestion of such an incongruity. He was too wedded to civilization, too fastidious as to its appointments, too enamored of its elegances, to be drawn to anything half-way or quarter-way 'back to nature'. On this theme how he would have appreciated one exceptional remark of James's! When in later life he was urged to spend the night with others on top of Mount Chocorua his answer was, "If we were primitive men all the romance would lie in having a roof over our heads, clean sheets, and a comfortable bed." It was just in that remoteness from sordid savagery, that assured escape to things ordered by human taste and sense of fitness, that Santayana took satisfaction. He has loved civilization, its continuities, its refinements, its reasonable conventions, and disliked outbreaks, revolutions and revolutionists, as much as Edmund Burke.

The temperament of James was of the romantic type while Santayana's is distinctly classic. When the former's *Varieties of Religious Experience* was published Santayana, meeting him in the street, said, "You have done the religious slumming for all time." "What! all that is of the slums, is it?"

asked James genially. "Yes, all." In telling of it he chuckled to himself: "Santayana's white marble mind!"

He was certainly not a monk in those days. He enjoyed society, went out good deal in Boston and was a dinner-guest at the houses of Mrs Gardner, Mrs Whitman, Mrs Dorr, and not a few others. He was said to have a very happy way with debutantes, and in general, took pleasure in the society of the young. A good deal of social grace was characteristic of him, without exactly social cordiality – he condemns 'heartiness' in his last book. But the marked thing socially was his wit. It is a pity that there is not freer scope for this in his printed work. Not many years ago, in Italy, some one was praising Mussolini and made the extra-ordinary remark, "He doesn't put himself forward." "Well", said Santayana, "at any rate he doesn't put his wife forward". Earlier, in Cambridge, Josiah Royce, speaking of the Dean of the Faculty, said meditatively, "I wish I could feel as *good* as Briggs is." When this was repeated to Santayana he added, "Or be as good as X feels." There was no rancor or venom in such mockery, but just a constant playing with the humors of things. As I once wrote long ago, "How exquisite was Santayana's laugh, soft but uncontrollable – the sense of the ludicrous and delicious could have no acuter edge. It began to vibrate almost as the electric fan begins to revolve, so subtly and intensely did it catch him. It seemed to go down into a depth of perception and delight beyond the reach of others. Yet it irresistibly increased the enjoyment of the rest and made the fortune of his jest, whether they could wholly appreciate it or not. He was far from the affectation of keeping a grave face over his own pleasantries – could not think it a duty, as Lamb puts it, to sit fasting before the refreshment he provided for others."[1] Indeed in his manifest pleasure in the sympathy of humor, the keen enjoyment of a joke in common, whether his or another's, he was very human and social.

I think his volume of autobiography, *Persons and Places*, valuable as it is, does him some injustice on this side. His constitutional propensity to look through the large end of the telescope, which has something to do with the 'pessimism', has laid a stronger hold on him than usual. Looking back at those early times, he describes them not wholly as they were then but as they seem to him now. The coldness of view is overdone. He tells that his mother, when asked how she occupied herself, replied, "In winter I try to keep warm and in summer I try to keep cool." A propos, one reader of the book has said, "When he is talking of those who were nearest and dearest to him I try to keep warm, and when he criticizes people I knew myself I try to keep cool." Reviewing critics have said that there is little sign of affection. In fact, the observer could see that he both gave and received affection. There was a humanity of courtesy too that, seeing the impression his book has left, it may not be amiss to recall. An elderly Swedenborgian minister in whom he could have had no personal interest whatever but who had occasion now and again to consult him said, with some feeling, "Santayana is always the same, always very pleasant and kind." At a Ph.D. examination when the candidate who entered the room was an older man than usual with gray hair Santayana rose (we heard) and gave him his more comfortable chair. He was a considerate and polite examiner.

There was indeed of course a certain detachment that belonged to the man. I seem to see him looking down from high places on human life below him. Looking for instance out of his window in Stoughton Hall in the autumn the day before college began and watching the students in the Yard as they came back and met. He was amused by the enthusiasm with which they greeted each other and shook hands. "They knew that they were going to see each other again!" Or I see him looking down from the window of his high apartment in the Hotel Bristol at Rome on the people swarming in the Piazza Barberini below. Or standing at the low parapet of a garden at Fiesole from which the hillside fell abruptly away and looking down at the city of Florence. And, finally, looking down in thought and contemplation from the heights of his philosophy at the human race in its plight. It was written of Goethe:

> And he was happy, if to know
> Causes of things, and far below
> His feet to see the lurid flow
> Of passion and insane distress
> And headlong fate, be happiness.

This is equally true of Santayana, so far as the causes at work are concerned; there is not the smallest ground to accuse him of drawing happiness from the spectacle of distress.

If you wish to understand his life and his writings remember that he is a poet and has the immediate, exacting sense of atmosphere, of tone and taste, of congruity and harmony, that should belong to a poet. That is the secret of the consistent elevation of his style in prose, a rare quality. And it is the key to the fastidiousness that marks him so essentially. He wants to introduce such congruity and harmony and worthiness of content into the life of every day. Here is the poet *plus* the Greek philosopher. Who that has read his poems, could imagine him without deep human feeling? Or who that heard him read Racine aloud? I give myself the pleasure of printing two of his youthful sonnets here. I choose them however as examples, not of this human feeling, but simply of the exquisite in poetry.

> Sleep hath composed the anguish of my brain,
> And ere the dawn I will arise and pray.
> Strengthen me, Heaven, and attune my lay
> Unto my better angel's clear refrain.
> For I can hear him in the night again,
> The breathless night, snow-smothered, happy, grey,
> With premonition of the jocund day,
> Singing a quiet carol to my pain.
> Slowly, saith he, the April buds are growing
> In the chill core of twigs all leafless now;
> Gently, beneath the weight of last night's snowing,
> Patient of winter's hand, the branches bow.
> Each buried seed lacks light as much as thou.
> Wait for the spring, brave heart; there is no knowing.

The second (with introductory lines from the sonnet that precedes) describes his descent to pure Nature from the faith that had become impossible to him.

> So came I down from Golgotha to thee,
> Eternal Mother; let the sun and sea
> Heal me, and keep me in thy dwelling-place.
>
> Slow and reluctant was the long descent,
> With many farewell pious looks behind,
> And sad misgivings where the path might wind,

And questionings of nature, as I went.
The greener branches that above me bent,
The broadening valleys, quieted my mind,
To the fair reasons of the Spring inclined
And to the Summer's tender argument.
But sometimes, as revolving night descended,
And in my childish heart the new song ended,
I lay down, full of longing, on the steep;
And, haunting still the lonely way I wended,
Into my dreams the ancient sorrow blended,
And with its holy echoes charmed my sleep.[2]

Another poet has said that "the lyrical cry" was not to be heard in Santayana's poems except in that called 'Cape Cod'. This it soo narrow. It is unmistakably heard, for example, in the verses that appear near the end of the novel, *The Last Puritan*.

His older colleague, Josiah Royce, told an Arabian tale of a spirit that lived under a cool spring, away from the scorching sun. But when evening came he would rise through the air to the walls of heaven, and listen long to the singing of the angels within; then return to his cool abiding-place under the spring. That, said Royce, is Santayana.

But the moment one thinks of him as a poet there comes back to mind that other side, the purely intellectual penetration, the astonishingly quick grasp, the fine edge of the mind. Once in a college lecture he had occasion to refer to the doctrine of John Stuart Mill that all our knowledge comes from our experience. Mill carried this so far as to say that only from experience do we know that two and two make four; if on another planet whenever two and two came together a fifth thing came into being the people there would all believe, and it would be true, that two and two make five. The lecturer seemed to consider this a moment and then said: "Yes, in such a fertile world two and two would make five; but it would still *be* four." No more exact answer could have been excogitated in a year. "His mind works perfectly," said Mr George Rublee, "where it works at all" – for there are subjects he undertakes and other, even closely neighboring subjects, from which he definitely stands aside. It may as well be said at once: there has been no more powerful mind at any time in American philosophy. This I say though his conclusions are largely shaped by temperament, and though there is no one with whom I myself have deeper differences, whether it be in literary criticism or in metaphysical, moral, and religious philosophy.

If I were asked what is the most impressive quality of his life and of his work I should say, independence. He struck out this own individual way, and that a strangely instructive way, and he stands alone amongst the philosophers of his period. He always sought to lift himself above the prevailing assumptions and influences of his time and place.

What is his philosophy? It is in the main a philosophy of life. It says, whether it be for others, or whether it be for self, the thing to secure is happiness – a life that from day to day gives satisfactory consciousness, something good for itself and not for the sake of anything else. That is the kind of consciousness that men have sought to depict in describing heaven – a life good in itself and for its own sake. Do not forget the end in running after the means. Else you will find yourself doing everything you do for the sake of something else, and never coming to what is to be done or lived for its own sake; you will always be struggling and never satisfactorily attaining – for anyone.

This he holds, is the great blunder and blindness of modern thought and modern idealism; they do not look to the end; they tend to idolize what properly is only means to the end. Hence a disquieted, troubled, hurried, frustrated, confused life, without clearness of goal or true self-possession; a life that is cheated out of the serene fruition it might enjoy. And here is the superiority of the Greeks, that they saw clearly what was fruition and what was not.

And to gain this fruition we must distinguish between the surely and satisfactorily attainable and what is not so, and deliberately cultivate the former. This offers a richness of fruition of which modern life knows little. It means making such of the satisfactions that are, as nearly as possible, independent of circumstance and therefore unfailing.

Such are possible for everyone. They call for peace of mind, contentment in limitation. For the more thoughtful what is essential is the power of the mind to understand and accept the limitations of life, to frame, out of the golden fragments supplied by experience, the ideal in all its forms, and to live in its presence. Just what this specifically means in terms of every day I do not find that Mr Santayana sets forth to us.

How does this author stand related to the broad immense liberal movement of modern times – immense in one view, yet so sorely delayed, baffled, crippled – the movement in politics, in literature, in thought at large, to make humanity and reason prevail in human affairs? It would seem that the writer of an eminent work on reason in life must be a powerful forwarder of the movement. And such in principal effect he is. But there are traits that tend to stand between and keep him alien to it.

(1) He is not a missionary, not an advocate. He is not seeking to win you over to his ideas; you may take them or leave them. The endeavor to propagate ideas, which he designates as propaganda, he detests; "it is an insult to human nature". His works are a contemplation, not an appeal. This is a disposition rather natural to one by temperament a poet, for most poetry is a seeking of beauty of thought and form for its own sake, and not an effort to convince. Just so can one seek truth.

(2) Reason for him gradually takes form in custom, conventions, tradition, morals, institutions. The progress he contemplates is chiefly what may be called a natural process, not one consciously shaped and directed by society. The idea of society's seeking to master its own fate figures with him but little. Indeed such ideas and their advocates usually call forth his delicious raillery. From his pen 'liberal' is by no means a term of favor. But "while we wait for the sentiments, customs, and laws which should embody perfect humanity and perfect justice, we may observe the germinal principle of these ideal things; we may sketch the ground-plan of a true commonwealth". Meanwhile in politics he sits on the right.

(3) This attitude toward reform and advance is intelligible, for in life and the philosophy of it his great interest has been, as we saw, to separate the attainable from what he deems the unattainable; to shun the rash, troubled, and baffling struggles and to confine effort to labors that shall be quietly, steadily, and surely productive. He once said, "There the world is; the thing to do is to change oneself so that one can live in harmony with it". "What about changing the world?" I asked. "Yes", he answered, "change the world as much as you can, then for the rest change yourself". Evidently there was to be a good deal of the rest; the changing of the world would not go very far.

Look now at his remarks on Harvard, which could, it would appear, as well apply to almost any American University. "– at Harvard a wealth of books and much generous intellectual sincerity went with such spiritual penury and moral confusion as to offer nothing but a lottery ticket or a

chance at the grab-bag to the orphan mind. You had to bring a firm soul
to this World's Fair; you had to escape from this merry-go-round, if you
would make sense of anything or come to know your own mind." The
moral confusion was just that same confusion of means with end. It
consisted in his opinion in not knowing what you were really after, in
pursuing a medley of objects without the discipline that would lead you to
look at life as a whole and reject what was incompatible with equilibrium
and tranquility of spirit. It consisted in not putting your ideas in order and
possessing your own soul. The spiritual penury lay in the want of that living
in the presence of the ideal which is for him the chief answer to the pre-
dicament of life.

These pages would not have entered so far into personal detail had not
his book set the example. It may be added that I do not consider that
personally I have known him well, rather I have had numerous brief
contacts.

I do not here enter into criticism or reply. My aim has been to describe;
and therewith to express the appreciation of one who in early years
encountered a mind and personality of singular power and grace, and
received therefrom, then and later, much that he prizes. "Happy the man
who in the susceptible season of youth hears such voices; they are a possession to him forever."

NOTES

[1 'Mr. Santayana and William James', *Harvard Graduates' Magazine* **29** (1921) 353.]
[2 *The Works of George Santayana*, Triton Edition, Charles Scribner's Sons, New York,
1936, Vol. I, pp. 228, 215. With permission.]

IS PHILOSOPHY A GOOD TRAINING FOR THE MIND?

[Miller's final publication, the following essay of 1952, crystallizes in fifty forceful points what a lifetime devoted to philosophy had convinced him about its mission and its teaching. He was so strongly convinced of the mission of philosophy that he made it the subject of special addresses at Harvard and Brown Universities. Further, he intended this essay to be "part of a chapter" of a book, never finished, whose subsequent main section would show "analysis at work" in chapters on free will, Hume and causality, knowledge, and universals. Miller is here centrally concerned to show how the teaching of philosophy might develop a "conscience of the mind", to use his phrase from other writings, a sensitivity to slips in reasoning and circumspection in thinking through "co-operation by mutual criticism". The study of philosophy, in short, should make the student habitually "a connoisseur of snares" and thus "a good citizen of the republic of thought". From wide acquaintance with leading philosophers and teachers of philosophy Miller recounts snares and slips that had particularly impressed him – in Carnap's theory of meaning propounded in Vienna, in Royce's treatment of knowledge and infinity, and in reactions of colleagues to probing criticism. If teachers and students of philosophy can become intellectually serious, co-operatively critical, and persistently circumspect in thought, philosophy may yet, Miller concludes, discern its opportunity for service, "its power to lead us out of the dark age in which we find ourselves".]

This article is addressed to students who are going out to teach philosophy and write upon it.

A grave and rather mature graduate student once summed up to me thus his experience with our subject: "I have made up my mind that philosophy is of no use except as a training for the mind." I repeated this to a teacher of law, now a distinguished professor in a law school. He replied: "I never thought philosophy was of any use except as a training for the mind."

I do not share their opinion. So far from doing so, I believe it to be the mission of philosophy to lead us out of the dark age we are in, and to begin by showing that a dark age it is. By this I mean something specific and definite. But also I must be so ungracious as not to accept their one tribute to the study; I must confess that I cannot think it, as it stands and has stood, a good training for the mind. The latter is my topic here.

Let me draw attention to the following considerations.

(1) A good training for the mind is one that enables it to detect unreliable reasoning and recognize reliable.

(2) A study that keeps bringing men to irreconcilably different conclusions cannot be such a training.

(3) The mark of a genuine science is what is called a consensus of the competent, extending over at least a considerable subject-matter. In philosophy this does not exist.

(4) Such a consensus is rendered possibly by the fact that there are recognized tests of correct inference (for example, laboratory experiment) which are applied to professed discoveries of importance. In philosophy the regular or habitual application of recognized tests to important new theses or theories does not exist.

(5) In other words, what we regard as a genuine science is on a high critical level; philosophy remains on a low critical level.

(6) Nevertheless there are tests in philosophy that are unquestioned: such as the consistency of a doctrine with itself and its consistency with admitted fact – to go no further where it is very possible to go further. If these two unpretending tests were searchingly applied I think it is not sufficiently realized what carnage there would be amongst philosophic theories.

(7) The point is that the unquestioned tests are not searchingly applied. There is a considerable amount of highly valuable criticism, but its forthcoming when needed cannot be counted on. Nor is it sufficiently addicted to quoting the very words of the text in question and meeting them with comment direct, explicit, and precise. Some of the grossest fallacies in conspicuous and influential doctrine go permanently unexposed. (What shall we think of a training that can produce the well-intentioned perpetrators of these fallacies?)

(8) Why has philosophy, as a common, a co-operative pursuit, never brought itself to a higher critical level? Why has it not developed as far in

that direction as it can? Why has it not made that its first concern? Because, speaking generally, it has never been characterized by the deepest intellectual seriousness. Its subject has been of the deepest, but the mood or spirit in which it has pursued its reflections on that subject and put them forth, its attitude in relation to the seductions and snares in the subject and in human nature, in relation to the imminent danger of mistake, has wanted something of possible depth.

(9) The test of the deepest intellectual seriousness is simple. Those who have it *desire the refutation of their views* if that is in any wise possible. For if a view of theirs is refutable it is not true, and *what interests them*, what they care about – what they are diving into the depths for and wholly intent on bringing up – is the *fact* of the matter, and not a mere laudable 'contribution to the discussion', nor even an impressive doctrine that will attract many followers. If the critic points out just where they have been led off their road he has forwarded them on their way, helped them toward their chosen destination.

(10) That is, the test of the deepest intellectual seriousness is whether there is a single-minded demand for the test of truth – the most searching and unsparing tests that can be found. The question is whether we are serious ENOUGH to keep subordinating everything else to that.

(11) Such seriousness, then, will not only tolerate adverse criticism but welcome it, and not only welcome it but seek it, and not only seek it but try to extract from it every grain of truth or sound suggestion that may be in it.

(12) Apart from the mind's seriousness there is a question of duty. It is the duty of a writer or speaker on philosophy not to deceive the public, or such portion of it as may give heed to him. He has a function to perform in which there is the deepest need for honest workmanship. Every teacher, by book or by word of mouth, undertakes to be a leader, in however modest a degree, and the first commandment for a leader is: Thou shalt not mislead.

(13) These considerations, I say, go to the spot where the malady resides that keeps philosphy low – as a common, a co-operative pursuit – keeps it from genuine scientific life. Please remember that 'scientific' means knowledge-making. Laboratories hold a science up; human nature, unassisted by laboratories or other decisive tangibilities, lets it down. To hold itself up despite the temptations of human nature philosophy as a

would-be science must summon up a complete intellectual seriousness and keep insisting on its standards.

(14) But who is 'philosophy'? 'Philosophy' is individuals. Good intention may summon, but will the serious temper required answer to the summons, will it come and stay? Only if embodied in objective institutions, in college education, periodical publications and philosophical associations, large and small. Only if the training and functioning of the critical faculty, the care for right reason, be given a central place in these three organs of philosophy.

(15) I owe foundation-laying thoughts to my teachers; I often count them over as received from this man and from that; but my undertaken topic obliges me to say that as a student I never heard the above principles of intellectual honor, so painfully needed, impressed upon us or even mentioned in any class or seminar.

(16) The individual teacher is tempted to think: "If my own reasoning presented to students is sound, then I am making my proper contribution to the training of the mind." In this he overlooks a formidable fact: No student can recognize reliable reasoning reliably unless he can detect unreliable reasoning. You will find, on carefully investigating, that most students are taking your reasoning on authority or on its plausible sound and are unable to gauge the decisiveness of its clinch. They have lacked adequate exercise in judging and discriminating philosophic arguments. They have lacked the critical exercise that makes critical perception. Their minds are not on a sufficiently high critical level to measure the cogency of your own arguments.

(17) An idea or inference that has always been presented as sound, impressive and authoritative, as though no question of it could reasonably arise, tends to be accepted as a matter of course. Witness Descartes and Spinoza on 'the ontological argument", which no lucid mind of their era that happened to turn critical attention full upon it could possibly trust. Descartes rests his weight upon it in the second positive step of his philosophy, Spinoza in the first positive step. An example of the innocence so common among philosophers.

(18) To lift the student's mind to as high a level in this respect as may be possible has to become a prime object in itself, for without it philosophic teaching does not become knowledge-making.

(19) The study of logic by itself does not provide such a training, since

plenty of its devotes have been amongst our most distinguished fallacists.

(20) A peculiarly unhappy result of the lack of a bracing critical atmosphere is that it has affected even the reforming movements, even those thinkers who have come forward in this century to propose severe tests of truth and meaning. I remember hearing in the days of the Vienna Circle a paper read by Professor Carnap in that city. He said that no sentence can be admitted to philosophic thought as having a meaning unless it is verifiable in experience. Now this pronouncement cuts the ground from under its own feet. A sentence has to have a meaning before you can apply the test. It is to the meaning that you apply it. It is the meaning that you verify or cannot verify. If you apply the test and decide that the sentence is not verifiable, you can say that you do not like it; you can say that we should be shy of such propositions; you can say that they are unprofitable; but you cannot say that it has no meaning. You have conceded that it has a meaning. What you are trying to do is to base on its meaning your verdict that it has no meaning. And it does not mend matters in the least if for 'verifiable' you substitute the formula 'of a kind or order that is verifiable', You cannot decide whether it is of that kind or order except in so far as it has a meaning. And this applies to any formula whatever that would make meaning depend on a relation to confirmation in experience. The idea of confirmation implies the idea of a meaning already given. So it is with "The meaning of a proposition is the method of its verification" (a statement of Moritz Schlick's) or Professor Carnap's later form "If you knew what it would be for a sentence to be *found* true [the emphasis is mine], then we would know what its meaning is." The plausibility of this last arises perhaps from its approach to the truism "If we knew what it would be for a sentence to *be* true, then we would know what its meaning is." (Professor Carnap appears to have moved away from these doctrines, but not all Logical Positivists have done so.) So it is also with "If and only if assertion and denial of a sentence imply a difference capable of observational (experiential, operational or experimental) test, does the sentence have factual meaning."[1] Once more, there is nothing to assert, deny, or imply unless the sentence already has a factual meaning, so the 'test' unhappily arrives too late.

What these formulas appear to be reaching toward – or shall I say leaning upon? – is the very old familiar doctrine that the terms of all significant sentences, as conceived by the mind, have been derived without exception from experience, and that the sentences accordingly have no other content than that of possible *or conceivable* experience. All that is new in the formulas is fallacious. It is a pity that what claims to be a great clarification should be introduced with a confusion of elementary ideas at the very threshold. If you lay down the law about meaning it is quite important to be sure that you know what you mean.

(21) Now will you tell me, reader, that this specimen of the inevitable effects of the low critical level upon our minds is due to the peculiar difficulty and elusiveness of the subject-matter of philosophy? Is it so difficult to detect what is called 'an Irish bull'? Is it so difficult to detect a slip of the tongue and of the wits, such as we are all liable to? In point of fact the gullibility of philosophy, which (quite apart from the necessary limitations of each century) has played so enormous a part in its history, is the gullibility of human nature when not taught to keep a sharp enough lookout for pitfalls. Those who speak of the peculiar difficulties of our subject forget the peculiar and stubborn difficulties that other sciences have had so patiently to overcome. The 'peculiar difficulty' of philosophy has been the difficulty of self-discipline when unassisted by objective circumstances.

(22) Thinking is a process that has to be conducted within the mind. The tremendous fact that speaks out to us from the history of philosophy is that there is no safety in the solitary mind. It may be magnificent, it may do magnificent service, but it is never safe. Hence the necessity for co-operation by mutual criticism.

(23) Suppose there were a vigilant and responsible criticism in print, respected as a necessary and chief instrument of philosophy and forthcoming on occasion of any new and considerable work. Suppose, for example, that Hobbes had written a close, extended, careful critical examination of Descartes's *Discourse, Meditations and Principles*, and it had fallen into the hands of Spinoza, Leibniz and those who followed. Descartes was methodically skeptical as to matters of fact, but not of his terms; Hobbes was skeptical of terms. How perceptible would have been the advantage to the philosophy of these last three centuries. Suppose it were felt to be a responsibility of the profession to see that its critical resources on such an occasion and not a few lesser occasions were mobilized.

(24) This affects the background, the general conditions, the state of

intellectual life in the profession as it influences the student; and it influences him fundamentally.

(25) But it is widely felt that adversely critical work in philosophy is to be deprecated. For, it is said, if your positive work is sound, it supersedes the false ideas on the topic, and the destructive work becomes unnecessary. This is indeed the pious traditional tenet on the matter. Ah! what a relief and reassurance it would be were it so. But we have only to open our eyes to see countless doctrines glaringly inconsistent but cheerfully co-existing side by side in the philosophic world. The sound ones do *not* of themselves exorcise the spurious ones – precisely because of the low critical level. Critical work has to exist for the sake of the constructive work, to make and keep it genuine construction. The one is an indispensable accessory of the other.

(26) Indeed if you keep your eyes open you will find glaringly inconsistent ideas cheerfully co-existing side by side in the same wind. Already this has appeared in the case of Logical Positivists. But the instances are countless. As a student I read a book by Josiah Royce, entitled *The Religious Aspect of Philosophy*. Its most important chapter is called 'The Possibility of Error'. Most of that chapter is the statement of a problem, the ultimate problem of knowledge; then follows the proposed solution. The statement of the problem is in my deliberate opinion a work of genius, and should be regarded as a masterpiece of thoroughgoing exposition. On page 422 he begins his solution. What is startling is that it proceeds as if the difficulty just set forth so tellingly did not exist. The difficulty is that there can apparently be no such thing as the mind's 'referring to' or 'meaning' or thinking 'about' anything beyond its own content, what is immediately 'given' to it. How can the mind refer to something that does not 'heave in sight' for it at all, something 'out of sight and mind'? How can it 'mean' to designate as the object of its thought what in the nature of the case does not present itself to its thought, does not figure in the world of its thought in any form whatever? Having an idea *similar in fact* to the object of one's though is not enough, one must intend one's idea to represent that object; a similarity might be accidental. How can our thought 'get at' such an object or fact even to refer to or intend it? Berkeley had dealt of course with a like difficulty in regard to sense-perception, the perception of material objects; he had not dealt with the problem as relating to thought, one's thought for instance of another man's conscious-

ness, of one's own past consciousness, or of the consciousness of God; of these he speaks quite freely; it seems not to have occurred to Berkeley that a similar course of reasoning would disclose here too a similar difficulty. Royce carries over a comparable line of reasoning with determined tenacity to all thought of what is absent from consciousness. And the resultant difficulty is: How is knowledge possible? How is even error possible, since we apparently cannot frame any mental assertion *about* what is not given in the content of consciousness?

(27) Then comes the solution. Suppose there is a world-consciousness that includes in its content that of my consciousness and also all facts outside it. The existence of this world-consciousness solves the problem, for it can compare my thought with the real object and judge whether my thought is true or false. Truth and falsity become an entirely clear affair.

Now this supposed solution wholly depends on one's power to do what he has just elaborately demonstrated that one cannot by any possibility do. For the world-consciousness is mainly quite outside and beyond the content of one's own consciousness. How can we conceive such a world-mind? In other words the statement of the problem strictly excludes the solution he offers. Yet the solution embodies and is the support for the chief and essential idea of the book. If ever a man carefully and in the most workmanlike fashion sawed off the bough he was sitting on it is Royce. (In fact the problem can be solved as he first states it.)

(28) How a man of his intellectual capacity, his logical power, could in the same chapter so suddenly become oblivious of his own trenchant reasoning and fatally contradict himself is a riddle. Yet scholars of ability have read the chapter without noticing the contradiction. Why? Because they have never had the training that calls sufficient attention to the sort or errors that may lurk in a plausible stream of exposition.

(29) I have a memory of an evening in Sanders Theatre, Royce lecturing in full evening dress, the president of the university present in his central and commanding seat, and a distinguished audience. Philosophy is to the front. Royce is explaining that our world is merely a "show-world", not a reality. The President of the British Association has declared it evident that the atoms of the universe are gradually through the ages approaching each other. Well then, says Royce, look back in time. At each past moment any two atoms will tend to be further apart. Now "pass to the limit"; at an infinitely remote moment of the past two atoms would be infinitely far

apart. But that means they could be connected by a line infinitely long. But a line infinitely long with two ends is a contradiction in terms, an impossibility. So our physical conception of the world goes to pieces, is an illusion.[2]

But Royce has manufactured the entire difficulty out of nothing, by committing himself the self-contradiction he ascribes to the physicist's universe. *There is no point of past time infinitely remote.* That would be a point between which and the present there would be an infinite interval – with two ends. There are points of time more and more remote as you go back in thought, but no one point infinitely remote. The whole difficulty is a soap-bubble that bursts. Yet the error was not remarked at the time either in private (so far as I know, and I knew much talk about it) or in any review of the book whatever. Such is the state of philosophy. If I err in the above comment I certainly should be unsparingly exposed.

(30) I cannot but think always of that evening scene in the Theatre as symbolic exhibit of a great portion of philosophy – a most impressive front and no solid substance behind. (Oh! There is solid substance in philosophy, but if it is asked what or which it is, then begins the confusion of tongues, and we see controversalists "charging spiritedly down parallel lanes at each other and never meeting".)

(31) Was Royce in these two instances exceptionally rash, exceptionally uncircumspect? Not in the least. To cite one out of numberless examples, in the same decade appeared a book that aroused wide interest and is still cited in some quarters as a sort of classic, Bradley's *Appearance and Reality*, the aim of which was to prove Royce's own thesis that the world as it appears is not real. The book is a museum of fallacies.

It was impossible for a deeply interested student to know Royce as a teacher without respect, admiration and affection. And I cannot contemplate without bitterness the deficient training of the mind in early years that has betrayed so many men of obvious power whom I have known into so much tragic waste of their power. Such waste has marked philosophy from the outset, mainly because of the relative absence or inaction of the critical "arm of the service". Yet there is no acute and aroused consciousness of this waste on the part of the profession. There philosophy sleeps the great sleep.

It is with reluctance that I 'turn upon' one of my former teachers. A student owes (within certain limits) a loyalty to his professor. But I assert that first of all a teacher owes to his pupils a sense of responsibility for teaching the truth. And I assert that the claim of philosophy upon every one of its followers alike as a quest for truth is the highest of all claims in the matter, and should be so announced in the classroom. There is nothing more important that a teacher can teach.

(32) The decade mentioned is far behind us. Well, is all the better known writing of the most recent years on a higher critical level? I am afraid not.

It is today entirely possible to put forth a book maintaining in all sincerity some thesis that is abjectly indefensible, hiding its weakness in what is usually the most effective way by the elaborateness of the presentation – hiding it persistently from the reader because it is first hidden from the writer himself. Space here forbidding further detail, I select for mention a book which I have already sought elsewhere to examine with some closeness: Professor Gilbert Ryle's *The Concept of Mind*.[3]

(33) What intellectual seriousness demands is decision. And this as soon as decision is possible. A state in which everything is 'a matter of opinion', in which nothing is recognized as decided, in which tests veritably exist but general acknowledgment of their results is neither expected nor demanded, in which nothing is pushed to finality, in which through custom we are all agreed *not* to go to the point and keep to the point till we settle the point, is a state in which the quest for truth is slack, a state of needless inefficiency therein. What we have is not the courage of our question, the will to bring it to a conclusive and undeniable test, but a tendency to indefinite postponement. This is true not only of the philosophic community but, in a measure, even of the individual mind.

(34) As we read books or essays in our subject do we ask ourselves as we go, and decide the question, "Is this argument valid or invalid, and exactly wherein?" Pretty often no. The reader contents himself with impressions *pro* and *contra*, perhaps half consciously thinking, "This is just preliminary; some day I must really grapple with the matter." With many, wide reading is intellectual sight-seeing; they wish to be acquainted with the country; they are tourists, viewing, remembering, becoming familiar, with the world of their study, becoming properly learned, but not keen as might be on the scent of right reason and wrong, not gaining daily the priceless practice of scanning and judging the soundness of inference, a practice which steadily strengthens the grip of the kind. This the reader

tends to postpone. Here is the most deep-seated weakness of our philosophic habits.

(35) I was sitting one summer evening in a delightful country spot talking with a professor of philosophy. We touched on a point with which his own work was concerned and I threw out a doubt whether a common opinion which he accepted was well-founded. At this he made the friendly and kindly remark, "Why don't you write an article on that?" We should hardly in our lives have a moment of more complete leisure to exchange ideas upon it, and the point was one that lent itself to the briefest statement, but he instinctively postponed it to a possible future. Not only in reading but in opportunities for uninterrupted conversation do we tend to postpone grappling with our questions.

(36) Strange to say, not only in reading books but in reviewing them is the same tendency to be seen. I recall a review by Mr Bertrand Russell and his remark to the effect "Mr X will find it hard to persuade his readers that so-and-so is the case". He did not stop to put his finger on the mistake in reasoning, as he was so qualified to do. He contented himself with stating an impression or attitude. Again I recall a review of a book containing an elaborate theory; the reviewer referred to it as the author's 'solution'. The quotation-marks meant that it was very doubtfully or not at all a solution but the reason for this judgment was not given. Many reviewers deem it their sufficient function to express in one form or another a favorable or unfavorable judgment and pass on. It is easier, but they miss their opportunity for service.

(37) I shall certainly never forget a conversation with a respected and beloved professor whom I one day met and walked with a short distance in my youth. I spoke of a problem that was on my mind. "Are you writing something on that?" he asked. "No", I said, "but it is interesting and I want to find the answer." "Oh!" said he, with a very kind smile, "you will get over that. When I was your age I used to do that automatic thinking [such was his expression], but now my mind works on a question only when I am writing a book or an article about it." He made it clear that this was meant for advice as to the most economical plan. He postponed grappling with the problem till he should have occasion to write about it. His books then did not express the thought of his life, but this thought was called into action for the books of his life. They certainly show it.

(38) A young instructor in this subject remarked to me long ago, "People may say that philosophers should not resent adverse criticism, but the fact is they often do resent it." Yes; I cannot help recalling the deliverer of a presidential address turning white with mortification and annoyance when it was critically discussed; how a very eminent philosopher absented himself from a club-meeting at which his own philosophy was to be the subject of a critical paper by an acute member; how another read a paper at the same club and, after each member in turn according to custom had offered criticism, and it fell to him to comment, told us in his brief remarks "I considered all these objections *and others* before writing my paper", and made no further reply. Another eminent philosopher deemed it undignified to reply to criticism at all; the truth was, less important than what he conceived to be the demands of dignity. But these cases are not typical; there is much patient and good-humored treatment of objections when they are put forward.

(39) There is such a thing as being a good citizen of the republic of thought, and remembering its needs even under grim trial. Students in our classes have been sent, not by any wish of their own, into combat, where hardships, wounds, pain, crippling, or death might well lie in wait for them. A very young soldier, boyish and excited, broke out "I don't want to die, doctor. Can't you save me? Can't you save me? I don't want to die." The doctor could not save him. If many who have studied with us have to face possible death, their instructors can surely face the wounds or scratches of intellectual discussion.

(40) Training of the mind in this subject can do two things: (1) Teach the student to keep a keenly watchful lookout for slips in reasoning, and (2) show him by interesting and curious examples out of philosophical literature what sort of slips to look out for. It must give him *circumspection,* which means looking all round. It must make him a connoisseur of snares. Without that, history has overwhelmingly shown that there is no safety whatever. An excellent field, but by no means the only one to practice with, is passages from the works of the great philosophers.

(41) It has been said that the 'normal introduction' is the history of philosophy. This is of course indispensable and invaluable but hardly a good first course. It offers little training of the mind and it tends to leave the impression that everything in the subject is a matter of opinion, that philosophy is a literature, not a science.

(42) The best thing that could happen to a graduate student embarking in the subject is that he should give his unreserved belief to some attractive system of thought and then see it cogently ripped up from top to bottom. But instruction cannot provide this 'treatment'.

(43) Lectures, however, can do much by putting (or reading) a train of argument briefly and plausibly, questioning the students on its validity, then pointing out with a pointer where it slips.

(44) A page or two of well-disguised bad reasoning might be commended to the student with the advice that he should shut himself up in a room till he finds out whether the reasoning is sound, or just where and what is the error.

(45) Another method is to hold an hour-examination in which dealing with such a specimen is the whole task.

(46) It is an excellent device to have single sheets printed or mimeographed with the word 'Proposition' at the top, 'Reason' below, below that 'Possible Objection', then 'Answer', the student to fill out with some proposition in philosophy that he believes or deems probable, and the rest of it. Specimens of such papers would be read in class and commented upon, possibly without the name of the writer. To prepare many such papers is far more useful than a long paper reporting on a book or a subject.

(47) It is of importance to take examples sometimes that will throw into relief the inherent tragedy of the matter, how a greatly endowed mind can insensibly go astray and waste its efforts.

(48) Very possibly others will devise further or better methods.

(49) Emphatically advisable is a course of instruction devoted to the training of the mind for this subject.

(50) To see a need is to see a chance for fruitful work. I have tried to indicate a certain need. In my college days a graduate student (he became a college president) told me he regretted that he had been born so late; all the great work in philosophy had been done. I would suggest that there has never been a greater opportunity for service than today – in which philosophy has not as yet even discerned its power to lead us out of the dark age in which we find ourselves.

NOTES

[1] H. Feigl, *Readings in Philosophical Analysis*, (ed. by Feigl and Sellars), p. 9.
[2] You will find this argument in J. Royce, *The Spirit of Modern Philosophy*, Chap. X, 331–333: it is the argumentative substance of the whole chapter.
[3] *Journal of Philosophy*, 1951, p. 270.

ANALYSIS: THE METHOD OF PHILOSOPHY AT WORK

THE RELATIONS OF 'OUGHT' AND 'IS'

[In 1941 Miller began work on a book, never finished, whose main part would show "analysis at work" as in his articles in this section on free will, knowledge, Hume and causality, universals, and objectivity of value. This section, then, carries out Miller's own plans in title and content.

With his first publication in 1893, his translation of his doctoral dissertation at Halle on 'The Meaning of Truth and Error', Miller expressed his commitment to "analysis of terms" as the main business of philosophy and applied it to "the states of mind we call knowledge" in relation to 'belief' and 'error'. He was not much concerned, he remarked to a fellow-student at Halle, with the *Geschichte* of the problem but rather, characteristically, with its *Lösung*. The results of his analysis led William James to see that "any definitely experienceable workings" would serve as intermediaries between ideas and object quite as well as the intentions of Royce's 'Absolute Mind', and this conclusion, James later remarked, belonged to "the *fons et origo* of all *my* pragmatism". Many years later Miller referred to 'The Meaning of Truth and Error' as "a poor business", thus suggesting that it was well superseded by the more pointed and circumspect analysis in his article of 1937, 'Is There Not a Clear Solution of the Knowledge-Problem?'

'The Relations of "Ought" and "Is"' appeared in 1894, shortly after Miller became an Associate in Philosophy at Bryn Mawr College, his first teaching position. It applies the method of analysis to ethics with a view to 'definiteness' and assured progress in philosophy and indicates that for Miller 'analysis' was primarily "logical analysis" as currently prominent in American and British philosophy, i.e., dissection of and distinction among concepts and statements in relation to ordinary "facts of consciousness" and ordinary sentences expressing those facts. Miller explicates the relation of 'reason' to 'relativity' in ethics, analyzes arguments denying relativism, refutes the view that statements of obligation are imperatives, and then proceeds to analyze 'oughtness' as the requirement of a system, "a certain ideal arrangement of things, acts, and lives".

Utilizing a distinction between specificatory and indicative propositions, which Plato's "interminable puzzles" confused, Miller concludes that 'ought' and the system it involves is forever "relative to the individual that holds it, and yet, from his standpoint, absolute". Seeking greater precision and currency, Miller returned to some of these points, with different formulation, in the essay of 1950 on 'Moral Truth.']

The fact, as it is freely asserted to be, that metaphysics – including, we may suppose, the theoretical part of ethics – is "the most contentious of all the sciences", has not brought with it all the results that an observer of the effects of chronic war might have expected. Repelling, on the one hand, all those minds which value intellectual peace above intellectual conquest, it has not, on the other, given to the remainder those stern satisfactions of discipline and of definite victory or defeat which belong to a developed state of militancy. Philosophic dispute lingers in the guerilla stage of warfare. The infinite relief of seeing controversies decided is denied to us. "Definiteness", Cardinal Newman has said, "is the life of preaching". Definiteness is also the life of philosophic thinking; not, indeed, its bare vital spark (for, if only the definite in this sphere survived, the overcrowded condition of the theoretic world had been immensely relieved), but certainly its healthy life. Definite premises if not definite conclusions, definite ignorance if not definite knowledge, – these form the only sure preparative for progress. It is the misfortune of philosophy, not that like all true science it is contentious, but that it does not duly profit by its contention; that it is not sufficiently organized as a science to take stock of its advance and to prevent old controversies that have performed their appointed part in the historical development from living on in the midst of our proper present controversies to confuse and retard them. The need of demanding recognition for cogent argument, of extorting admission for established results, and of executing justice on condemned theories – the need, in a word, of discipline – may profitably at the present juncture be insisted on.

No topic of speculation suggests this need more forcibly than the rational basis of ethics. There is no common consciousness here either of tasks or of achievements. Yet the problems in themselves are both pressing and distinct. How can one moral end or moral order logically be proved supreme? If it cannot be so proved at all, if there is in the last resort no rational standard in ethics, then are we to say that ethical preferences are relative only to the mind that prefers, that they are due to the organization of that mind, and, save to other minds in this respect similarly organized, are without authority beyond it? In that case we have not, as it has been phrased, a single moral universe, but rather as many moral worlds as there are different minds. No one of these worlds can be esteemed superior to another, except by standard of value itself relative to one world and invalid for the others.

These propositions strike at the root of every ethical system purporting to establish its universal validity by reasoning. They have often been asserted more or less completely, either explicitly or by implication, in one or other of their numerous forms, during the course of ethical thought. To recognize wholesale principles in general terms and to pass on is not necessarily a difficult or a significant performance. And the few thinkers, such as Hume and Schopenhauer, who have laid especial stress on the principle that reason of itself has no purchase on the will, have proceeded to fortify an ethical system in part at least by an appeal to reason.[1] Not, I think, until Mr Arthur Balfour's 'Note on the Idea of a Philosophy of Ethics', contained in his 'Defense of Philosophic Doubt', has the principle at once been thoroughly stated and brought to bear on the mass of current moral controversy. That by no artifice can an ethical proposition, a proposition, that is, asserting obligation, be extracted from a proposition expressing matter of fact or existence – this is his thesis; and it is pressed to its final consequence in the logical relativity of ethical judgment in general. Since the appearance of this piece of reasoning new ethical systems and new forms of the old have sprung up in their usual plenty; exhibiting the usual endeavor to prove the rational supremacy of this standard or of that; and exhibiting too, as a rule, the completest oblivion of the principle of relativity, thus recently set forth, which, if sound, would utterly discredit and supersede them.

It may be worth while, as a slight step towards defining the situation and eliciting discussion of it, to ask here what manner of answer could be given on behalf of ethical systems claiming to be universally valid, to the arguments for ethical relativity. These arguments are of the simplest. To say a thing ought to be is not to say that it or anything else is, was or will be. Obligation is thus something specifically different from existence, and

a proposition asserting obligation can never follow by logical consequence from premises asserting nothing but existence. Hence a proposition asserting obligation, if capable of proof at all, can be proved only
from some other proposition asserting obligation and that from another
of the same sort, until a fundamental proposition in this kind is reached
for which no proof is possible. But if the fundamental proposition of a
moral code or system is in all cases indemonstrable, then there is no
standard of decision between inconsistent codes or systems, and it follows
that each has validity only for the mind that holds it.

In face of this demonstration there are three ways, broadly speaking, by
which the universal validity of an ethical code may be defended. First, the
logical relativity may be admitted, but it may be maintained that mankind,
however divided against itself in the estimation of particular acts, is in its
ultimate moral instincts at one; that nature thus has obviated the difficulty and left us in a real ethical unity. This seems to be the position of
most utilitarians (though their expressions on this head are seldom free
from obscurity), as also of certain determined foes of utilitarianism; a
circumstance from which it appears that these ultimate and uniform
moral instincts are extremely hard to identify. In this first form of the
defense the logical argument for relativity is fully admitted. But the
second form takes issue with the argument. According to it obligation is
indeed concerned with matter of fact. To say that a given act or event
ought to take place is to describe certain objective relations of the act or
event, to assert its actual conduciveness to something – let us say, to the
greatest happiness. This is part of the actual meaning and definition of the
word. Some utilitarians seem tempted to take this view, though they are
apt to fall back upon the first without recognizing its distinctness. This
view is allied with such psychological theories as that of James Mill, by
which desire and (with some complications) approval are simply the
discernment of a quality of the object in regard – namely, its pleasur-
ableness. The view is, however, so hard to reconcile with the deliverance
of consciousness when we use the words 'ought' and 'obligation', that I
have mentioned it mainly for the sake of completeness.

The third possible mode of defense if of a very different kind, and to it,
passing by the first two as irrelevant or improbable, I shall confine my
remarks here. Like the second mode, it bases itself on the nature of the
idea of obligation, asserting, however, not that that idea refers at bottom

to matter of fact and is therefore in each case right or wrong independently of personal preference; but that, although referring to something essentially distinct from matter of fact, its purports in its nature to be 'objective' and superpersonal.

Putting ourselves for purposes of exposition at this point of view, we should comment on the theory of relativity as follows: We should say that it *takes for granted* precisely what most requires proof, that the object of moral conduct is merely an end personally preferred by the moral agent. It does, to be sure, point out that individuals may differ in such preferences; nay, undeniably do, and challenges the moralist to show how one such ideal can be proved superior to others. This makes a plausible case enough, but it in no wise touches the facts of the moral life. It neglects the import of the most significant symptom of that life, the idea of obligation. Thus, Mr Balfour, after seeming to catch the real sense of the word 'ought', proceeds to call it merely "an imperative", one of a class of 'imperatives', and so clean forgets its distinct character. Consider the words he uses at the outset of his discussion. Contrasting an 'ethical' with a 'scientific' proposition, he says:

An ethical proposition, on the other hand, though, like every other proposition, it states a relation, does not state a relation of space or time. 'I ought to speak the truth', for instance, does not imply that I have spoken, do speak, or shall speak the truth; it asserts no bond of causation between subject and predicate, nor any coexistence, nor any sequence. It does not announce an event; and if some people would say that it stated a fact, it is not certainly a fact of the 'external' or 'internal' world.

In this passage (speaking as believers in a super-personal moral law, we should say,) Mr Balfour grasps the unique character of moral obligation. Why, then, does he confound it with mere commands, and call it one of the class of statements which "prescribe an action with reference to an end"? How can he fail to see the error of asserting that no philosophical difference exists between propositions containing 'ought', and non-moral or immoral imperatives which a man may address to himself or his fellows? An imperative is not a proposition at all. The words, "hand me my stick", for example, form no declarative sentence; they do not include a subject and a predicate (save by a fiction of grammarians); they do not even express a judgment; they are a combination of words uttered with the design of producing a certain useful motor effect in the hearer. Propositions do not 'prescribe', they assert.[2] "I ought to speak the truth", however, is incontestably a proposition. It is not merely to say "speak the truth", that injunction, indeed, shares its form with all manner of evil and indifferent commands. "I ought to speak the truth" is assertive; it asserts *something*, though we may not be able to tell more analytically what. It has a subject, and affirms of it a predicate. What is the essential quality of that predicate?

We cannot (the argument might go on) tell what? The reason is that we have touched bottom. All analysis must leave us in the end with irreducible elements. Obligation is such an element. What do you mean, one might as well ask, by existence; what is the analysis of that term? Existence is an ultimate, and so is obligation, duty, desert, – the conception we employ when we say "It ought to be". "It ought to be" has just as much standing-ground in the region of intelligibility as "It is". The two are separate but co-ordinate categories. The one can be resolved into component elements as little as the other.

If, now, you ask how we shall ascertain with assurance what ought to be; whether by the revelations of the faculty of conscience, or by reasoning from self-evident axioms like those of geometry, or by some other such direct informations; or whether we have now no means of assured knowledge, but, knowing that *some* truth there is, must await a future enlightenment; – if these questions are pressed, the answer is that, whichever be the true solution, the questions do not touch the present issue. That issue is, Does 'ought' express a mere personal preference? We answer no. In the very first suggestion of its meaning, it is objective and independent of tastes. It implies an essentially valid standard which is no respecter of persons. Somewhat in this way, on grounds of introspection, the relativity of moral judgments might be denied.

Though I cannot cast the responsibility of the reply thus worded upon anybody but myself, it surely expresses in the main the more or less explicit views of many. Thus, Mr Sidgwick, in the chapter on 'Reason and Feeling' of his *Methods of Ethics*, institutes an extended examination of the attempts to explain obligation, and concludes:

It seems, then, that the notion of 'ought' or 'moral obligation', as used in our common moral judgments, does not merely import (I) that there exists in the mind of the person judging a specific emotion (whether complicated or not by sympathetic representation of similar emotions in other minds); nor (2) that certain rules of conduct are supported by penalties which will follow on their violation (whether such penalties result from the general liking or aversion felt for the conduct prescribed or forbidden, or from some other source). What then, it may be asked, does it import? What definition can we give of 'ought', 'right', and other terms representing the same fundamental notion. To this it may be answered that the notion is too elementary to admit of any formal definition.

And again:

This fundamental notion must, I conceive, be taken as ultimate and unanalyzable.

As against this position, I shall argue that the notion expressed by the word 'ought', if sufficiently scrutinized, will appear to be neither ultimate nor unanalyzable; that, further, it will itself, when analyzed, supply the most conclusive evidence, and the final statement, of the relativity of ethical knowledge.

Perhaps, however, a certain method of analyzing it, which will to many appear obvious, and which is insufficiently treated, I think, by Mr Sidgwick, should first for a moment be noticed. It will be said that the seeming objective character of obligation arises merely from the fact that our approval of the conduct in question is instinctively supposed by us to be shared by others. The super-personal 'ought' is the social 'ought'. Man is a social animal; social elements are worked into the very structure of his mind. Moral rules, in especial, have been impressed upon him from infancy as things about which all are agreed. In consequence, his approvals and disapprovals bear with them in some sort a social reminder. Precisely as Mr Shadworth Hodgson ascribes the objective and independent aspect of our sense-perceptions to our feeling that they or their copies are "objects for consciousness in general" – that other men do or can see the same things – so this analysis ascribes the 'objective' character of our sense of obligation to our feeling that moral acts, colored with their appropriate praise or blame, are objects for ethical consciousness in general.

To this the answer is that introspection promptly discredits it. Whether our sense of obligation had its *origin* or its *antecedents* in a sense of the social judgment or not, – an indifferent matter to us in the present inquiry, – it does not now at all events necessarily contain a social reference. Quite the contrary. I do not here rely upon the fact that the feeling of a subtle moral pressure, of an exigent moral law, may be felt in the absence of social support, nay, in the teeth of it; that the mandate of duty may be hurled in rebuke by some intrepid prophet against the solid front of the people; for I cannot stop to discuss the obvious retort that the rebuker's conscience would draw sustenance from the thought of the ratifying judgment of deity or posterity. I can only call to witness what is to my perception the unambiguous fact of consciousness, that the idea of obligation may be present in full force without the smallest recognition of any one else's moral judgment whatever, without even, as I shall presently show, a self-conscious recognition of the thinker's own.

Another reply sometimes made to the view that the moral law is by its own evidence 'objective' is equally beside the mark. It is said that the feeling of an obligation emanating from some source not dependent on our own natures is simply an illusion. But it has to be asked, How can the illusion be? How is such a super-personal moral law so much as conceivable? Where do we find a mental term for it? That is to say, we are confronted afresh with the question, What is the analysis of it? An absolute moral law that can be conceived, that can be intelligibly rendered in thought, is at least a supposable thing; and, this granted, it will go hard but some ethical philosopher will discover a proof for its existence.

I will now proceed to explain what suggests itself to me as the secret of the 'objective' and 'absolute' character of propositions containing the term 'ought'. What is the most conspicuous fact of my mental state when I am insisting that a certain deed *ought* to be done? First, there is the notion of a system, more or less complex, which needs the deed in question to be perfect. If this particular deed is not in place, is out of line, is not performed, the system is broken. There is a certain feeling of pressure upon the deed, that it may be performed and the system thus be perfect. There is always, I assert with some confidence, a reference to what may loosely be called a system, when the word 'ought' is used otherwise than mechanically. "You ought not to think of such things", – I quickly and perhaps vaguely picture a certain consistent purity of mind upon which such thoughts are a blot. "You ought to lift your hat", – I see in a flash an orderly and polite world, or some dim fragment thereof, uniformly uncovering its head at the proper moment; and so on to the end of the chapter. A thousand cases of the use of 'ought' apart from men and morals attest the presence of this element in the conception. "This tree ought not to be placed here"; – it spoils a certain imagined effect. "That fruit-dish ought to go in the middle of the table", – otherwise it shatters the housewifely ideal of a neat symmetry. "That piece ought to go here", – when the children are putting together their puzzle-mosaic of blocks.

In moral cases, the conceived system may consist simply of a certain ideal arrangement of things, acts, and lives, or of these viewed as subserving some dominant end. For the common run of men and also for philosophers in their irreflective moments, it is the former; no Highest Good is conceived. In the more premeditated philosophical usage it is apt to be the latter; the system is crowned and sanctioned by a supreme end. Thus the utilitarian holds that we ought punctually to perform our duties as citizens, because thus only does our conduct subserve the greatest possible happiness; for in his mind a system in which all hands contribute as much as possible to the greatest happiness is the ascendant thought. The like may be said of those who make self-realization the greatest good, and of those who prefer the harmonious fulfilment of all demands. Each and all of these moralists have in mind a system, consisting of an end and of acts subservient to that end. We may then interpret the proposition, "*A*. ought to tell the truth", thus: only by telling the truth can *A*. perform his part in the true system of the world.

'The *true* system"; at this objectors will not be slow to protest. How *true*, and why true? Which system is true? And how does this definition consist with the relativity of ethical judgment? The answer is at hand. I have chosen the word 'true' because it seems least inadequately to express the attitude of each mind towards the system to which it cleaves. Instead of "the true system", I might have written "*the* system", – that is, the system which is dominant and undisputed in the subject's mind, to which he looks with a single eye. Those who would urge that since the 'ought' appears as 'absolute' it cannot refer merely to the chosen ends of individuals, forget that one does not always contemplate the furniture of one's mind as that of an individual, – of one in a multitude. Our attention is often absorbed by its primary objects. When the thing before the mind is a conceived supreme end or normal order of action, it may command our full and instant heed and deference, and so far and so long as it is present hold uncontested sway in thought. When this is so, the thinker does not take stock of himself as desiring or approving; rather he simply sees the object in what is for him its native and natural attractiveness or commendability. What the psychologist calls his desire or approval is for him the fact that the object is in itself commanding, its achievement self-evidently the true course.[3] For he absolutely desires it. He absolutely favors its attainment. It is for him *the* object, and its attainment *the* advisable conduct. This conduct as subserving this end is, within his purview, *the* system. Whatever mars the system *ought* not to be done. The absoluteness of the 'ought' is a measure of the exclusiveness of the desire or approval.

This grows abundantly clear when we consider again that it is not only moral ends so-called that beget an 'ought'. "I *ought* to take greater pains", for my aim is to dazzle the room with the brilliancy of my playing. The thief *ought* to have brought his tools, or to have walked more softly; for the ascendent aim with him was to effect his theft. These illustrations might be multiplied at pleasure.

It will, I know, be said by some of those who have followed this analysis, that it still leaves a gap. Try as I could, they will say, to translate the statement, "*A* ought to tell the truth", into an equally categorical statement in more elementary terms, not involving rectitude or obligation over again, I was unsuccessful. My paraphrase contained the words "the true system", thus making an almost undisguised use of the notion of rectitude in the attempt to define its next of kin, obligation. If the analysis were correct, it will be insisted, an unambiguous equivalent, not containing the term to be defined, would be producible.

To meet this criticism, which I admit to be a fair one, the general nature of propositions must be considered. Propositions may for our purposes be divided into two classes, which we may distinguish as specificatory and indicative propositions. By specificatory propositions, or propositions at large, I mean those which reveal the identity of their terms by referring to their qualities. Indicative propositions or propositions of standpoint are those in which the identity of the terms is assumed to be known, – the objects are, as it were, merely pointed to. As an instance of the latter, suppose I look out of my window and say, "The lake is unruffled by the wind". The lake? What lake? *This* lake. If I were to transform my sentence into a specificatory proposition, I should say, not "this lake", but "a lake of such and such dimensions and character, situated in mountains of such and such character and locality", etc. 'This', 'that', 'the other', 'to-morrow', 'next week', 'you', 'I', are all indicative terms; terms, that is, that have meaning only *from a standpoint*, – to wit, to a person particularly circumstanced. It was a confusion between indicative and specificatory terms that led to Plato's interminable puzzles about 'the one' and 'the other'.

The most obvious remark to make about indicative terms and propositions is, that they are 'relative'. 'This lake' might mean a dozen different bodies of water, according as one was situated in Geneva, in Westmoreland, in Chicago, etc. The content of 'this' changes with the speaker. But in another sense the term is especially 'absolute'. Nothing could signify a more absolute identity than 'this lake', 'this house', 'this mountain'. A generally descriptive term might fail to hit the mark; another object might in some cases duplicate the assigned qualities. But I could pitch upon no more absolutely designating term than 'this' or 'that'. There is precisely one particular thing in the wide world to which I am referring. We may say, then, that, *to the speaker*, no terms have more of absoluteness than indicative terms.

A further peculiarity of indicative propositions is that they are untranslatable. They cannot be turned into specificatory propositions without altering their content. To say "This lake is calm" is not equivalent to saying "A lake of such and such a description", or "a lake perceived at such and such a moment by such and such a person, is calm", for in uttering the first sentence I had not all these circumstances in mind; I had in mind '*this* lake', the lake I might point to, the lake in its immediacy, in its unmistakable identity. The proposition, if cast into a genuinely specificatory form, would indeed refer to the same lake, but it would not embody the same content; the connotation would be different. And this is a typical case. "I shall do so-and-so to-morrow" can never be transformed into "I shall do so-and-so on the 30th of March, 1894", without introducing the thought of relations not previously conceived, and dropping the thought of some that were. That propositions of standpoint can never, without violence, be translated into propositions at large is thus seen to be an invariable law.

The bearing of these facts upon our problem is plain. "*A*. ought to speak the truth" is an indicative proposition. It means, "Only by speaking the truth can *A*. perform his part in *the* system of the world", – in *this* system; in the system upon which my attention is riveted, which exclusively possesses my approbation. Its absoluteness consists in the absolutely exclusive tenure of my mind, or at least of my approbation by the truthful system. It cannot be translated into a specificatory proposition without the loss of some of its essential traits. The specificatory proposition would run, "Only by speaking the truth can *A*. perform his part in the world which such and such an individual [namely, the speaker] approves?" In this the 'ought' has let go its absoluteness; just as the phrase 'this lake' loses its absoluteness when transformed into "the lake now seen by so-and-so".[4]

"So you admit, after all, that obligation is an illusion?" it will be said. "As soon as the individual gets out of the circle of his own pretty likes and dislikes, he sees the 'ought' to be baseless". The admission is not necessary. In its own sphere, the personal sphere, the 'ought' has force and is no illusion. Where we know that others cherish the same ultimate ends as we, it has force between different persons. Where we are assured that the ultimate likes and dislikes of another are irreconcilably diverse from our own, the 'ought' still has significance to ourselves as describing for us the other's proper conduct; as addressed to him, except for impressive purposes it is a mere *flatus vocis*.

We have here reached, it might seem, the ultimate statement of the relativity of ethical knowledge. If this be so, every moral system is, speaking at large, relative to the individual that holds it; and yet, from his standpoint, absolute; for indicative propositions can never be translated into specificatory propositions without the loss of an essential part of their significance. Because indicative propositions are incommunicable, except by a coincidence in the point of view, ethical statements are forever relative, and derive their authority from no source but the breast of the speaker or hearer. And it is this view I have wished to develop.

NOTES

[1] It is perhaps worth noting that the term 'reason' is used by ethical writers in two widely different senses; in the sense, first (as above), of the faculty of reasoning, and second (as by Professors Windelband and Sidgwick, following the practice of Kant), of the consciousness of a universally valid moral standard, 'das Normalbewusstsein'. In the latter sense it may be said to involve a denial of the relativity of ethical judgments.

[2] Though I am elaborating here a view that is not my own, this particular assertion that mere 'imperatives' have no place in the logic of ethics seems to me both well founded and important. Compare Locke: "'Parents, preserve your children', is so far from an innate truth, that it is no truth at all, – it being a command and not a proposition, and so not capable of truth or falsehood. To make it capable of being assented to as true, it must be reduced to some such proposition as this: 'It is the duty of parents to preserve their children'". *Essay*, Bk. I., Chap. iii., Section 12.

[3] The psychology of desire and of those admirations and approvals which are allied though not identical with it, is not sufficiently advanced to supply us with an unquestioned account of the light in which the moral order or the moral end appears to the mind. To use definite descriptive terms in the absence of a definite consensus would

involve an argument for which I have no space; and I therefore confine myself to general and untechnical terms throughout.

4 The distinction here dwelt upon is ignored, I think, in the important argument by which Professor Windelband (*Präludien*, essays on Kant and on 'Normen und Natur-gesetze') and Dr Heinrich Rickert ('Der Gegenstand der Erkenntnis') seek to prove that obligation (*das Sollen*) is not merely co-ordinate with but ulterior to reality (*das Sein*). Reality, I understand them to say, is for me the mode in which I *ought* to arrange my ideas or form my judgments; it is in the last resort a rule for the mind's thought. Hence reality involves obligation. Is there not here a confusion between psychologic self-knowledge and the original outlook of simple consciousness? Is it not an instance of "the psychologist's fancy"? In arriving at a belief I am not consciously arranging my ideas; rather the objects are arranging themselves to my mental vision. Professor Windelband and Dr Rickert would say that the objects thus arranging themselves are really my ideas; to which I should agree: but they are not *classed* as my ideas, not thought of as subject to the active 'I' of which obligation may be asserted.

FREE WILL AS INVOLVING DETERMINATION
AND INCONCEIVABLE WITHOUT IT

(Revised)

[Near the beginning of his 'European retirement', which lasted from 1926 to 1934, Miller sketched out his analysis of free will in a review of a book on James's philosophy of religion. The sketch amplified the suggestion of his teacher, George Fullerton, that analysis of our experience of freedom in willing yields determinism, so there has never been any clash between freedom and determination. What is required is simply a probing analysis of 'could' and 'power'. Toward the end of his 'European retirement' Miller undertook such an analysis, and the result was an article in *Mind* with the above title and under the name of 'R. E. Hobart', a name he assumed for private convenience and to make his argument stand on its merits.

With the current emphasis on analysis in philosophy – analysis largely as Miller conceived and practiced it – his article in *Mind* has received increasing attention and has been reprinted twice as an acute example of 'soft determinism' or 'reconciliationism' akin to the position of John Stuart Mill. As reprinted here, however, 'Free Will as Involving Determination' includes Miller's revisions in the 1940s as he prepared it to serve as a chapter in a book, never finished, on 'Inquiry, Analytical or Sceptical'.

In what follows Miller seeks to show precisely how analysis of 'could' or 'can' as implied in choosing and as involving 'self' and 'power' inescapably leads to determination expressing a law of cause and effect. This result, far from undermining moral 'responsibility' and 'desert', is logically required by those terms in their ordinary meaning. So "the prosaic process of examining words" reveals the controversy of free will *vs.* determinism to have been a waste of energy over a false antithesis. Determinism is not opposed to free will but turns out to be a feature of its analysis.]

The thesis of this article is that there has never been any ground for the controversy between the doctrine of free will and determinism, that it is

based upon a misapprehension, that the two assertions are entirely consistent, that one of them strictly implies the other, that they have been opposed only because of our natural want of the analytical imagination. In
so saying I do not tamper with the meaning of either phrase. That would
be unpardonable. I mean free will in the natural and usual sense, in the
fullest, the most absolute sense in which for the purposes of the personal
and moral life the term is ever employed. I mean it as implying responsibility, merit and demerit, guilt and desert. I mean it as implying, after an
act has been performed, that one "could have done otherwise" than one
did. I mean it as conveying these things also, not in any subtly modified
sense but in exactly the sense in which we conceive them in life and in law
and in ethics. These two doctrines have been opposed because we have not
realized that free will can be analysed without being destroyed, and that
determinism is merely a feature of the analysis of it. And if we are tempted
to take refuge in the thought of an 'ultimate', an 'innermost' liberty that
eludes the analysis, then we have implied a deterministic basis and constitution for this liberty as well. For such a basis and constitution lie in the
idea of liberty.

The thesis is not, like that of Green or Bradley, that the contending
opinions are reconciled if we adopt a certain metaphysic of the ego, as
that it is timeless, and identifies itself with a desire by a 'timeless act'. This
is to say that the two are irreconcilable, as they are popularly supposed
to be, except by a theory that delivers us from the conflict by taking us out
of time. Our view on the contrary is that from the natural and temporal
point of view itself there never was any need of a reconciliation but only
of a comprehension of the meaning of terms. (The metaphysical nature
of the self and its identity through time is a problem for all who confront
memory, anticipation, etc.; it has no peculiar difficulties arising from the
present problem.)

I am not maintaining that determinism is true; only that it is true in so
far as we have free will. That we are free in willing is, broadly speaking, a
fact of experience. That broad fact is more assured than any philosophical
analysis. It is therefore surer than the deterministic analysis of it, entirely
adequate as that in the end appears to be. But it is not here affirmed that
there are no small exceptions, no slight undetermined swervings, no ingredient of absolute chance. All that is here said is that such absence of
determination, if and so far as it exists, is no gain to freedom, but sheer

loss of it; no advantage to the moral life, but blank subtraction from it. – When I speak below of 'the indeterminist' I mean the libertarian indeterminist, that is, him who believes in free will and holds that it involves indetermination.

By the analytical imagination is meant, of course, the power we have, not by nature but by training, of realizing that the component parts of a thing or process, taken together, each in its place, with their relations, are identical with the thing or process itself. If it is 'more than its parts', then this 'more' will appear in the analysis. It is not true, of course, that all facts are susceptible of analysis, but so far as they are, there is occasion for the analytical imagination. We have been accustomed to think of a thing or a person as a whole, not as a combination of parts. We have been accustomed to think of its activities as the way in which, as a whole, it naturally and obviously behaves. It is a new, an unfamiliar and an awkward act on the mind's part to consider it, not as one thing acting in its natural manner, but as a system of parts that work together in a complicated process. Analysis often seems at first to have taken away the individuality of the thing, its unity, the impression of the familiar identity. The reader may recall Paulsen's ever significant story about the introduction of the railway into Germany. When it reached the village of a certain enlightened pastor, he took his people to where a locomotive engine was standing and in the clearest words explained of what parts it consisted and how it worked. He was much pleased by their eager nods of intelligence as he proceeded. But on his finishing they said: "Yes, yes, Herr Pastor, but there's a horse inside, isn't there?" They could not *realize* the analysis. They were wanting in the analytical imagination. Why not? They had never been trained to it. It is in the first instance a great effort to think of all the parts working together to produce the simple result that the engine glides down the track. It is easy to think of a horse inside doing all the work. A horse is a familiar totality that does familiar things. They could no better have grasped the physiological analysis of a horse's movements had it been set forth to them because they are differently inclined. They would have been tempted to say, "But there's *a horse* inside that does it all, isn't there?"

The reason for thinking that there is no occasion for the controversy lies exclusively in the analysis of its terms.

Self and Character. – Let us consider these in succession. It is clear that 'the self' merely as knower (irrespective of just what particulars it knows) is similar in all men. The relation of subject to object, whatever it may be, is the same with you and with me. But 'the self' as it interests ethics is not the same in different persons. It is the concrete, active self. This is the first vital fact: that we are not ordinarily supposing, when we talk of morals, that, completely similar selves deliberately do different acts. Different selves do different acts. With that proviso we may set about considering our question. The whole stress of morality arises because moral selves are not alike, because there is need of influencing some moral selves to make them behave otherwise, that is, in order to make them better moral selves. How do we express the difference? We call it a difference of moral qualities, traits, or character – what acts will come from these selves. By character we mean, do we not? the sum of a man's tendencies to action, considered in their relative strength; or that sum in so far as it bears upon morals.

Now the position of the indeterminist is that a free act of will is the act of self. The self becomes through it the author of the physical act that ensues. This volition of the self causes the physical act but it is not in its turn caused, it is 'spontaneous'. To regard it as caused would be determinism. The causing self to which the indeterminist here refers is under the circumstances to be conceived as distinct from character; distinct from temperament, wishes, habits, impulses. He emphasizes two things equally: the physical act springs from the self through its volition, and it does not spring merely from character, it is not simply the result of character and circumstances. If we ask, "Was there anything that induced the self thus to act?" we are answered in effect, "Not definitively. The self feels motives but its act is not determined by them. It can choose between them".

The next thing to notice is that this position of the indeterminist is taken in defence of moral conceptions. There would be no fitness, he says, in our reproaching ourselves, in our feeling remorse, in our holding ourselves or anyone guilty, if the act in question were not the free act of the self instead of a product of character.

We have here one of the most remarkable and instructive examples of something in which the history of philosophy abounds – of a persistent, an age-long deadlock due solely to the indisposition of the human mind to look closely into the meaning of its terms.

How do we reproach ourselves? We say to ourselves, "How negligent

of me!" "How thoughtless!" "How selfish!" "How hasty and unre-
strained!" "That I should have been capable even for a moment of taking
such a petty, irritated view!" etc. In other words, we are attributing to
ourselves at the time of the act, in some respect and measure, a bad character, and regretting it. We are assuming, as a matter of course, that the
bad act was a result of the bad character. Of course we chose freely
(without interference) and so showed what our character under the circumstances of the moment really was. And that is the entire point of our
self-reproach. We are turning upon ourselves with disapproval and it may
be with disgust; we wish we could undo what we did in the past, and,
helpless to do that, feel a peculiar thwarted poignant anger and shame at
ourselves that we *had it in us* to perpetrate the thing we now condemn. It
is self we are reproaching, i.e., self that we are viewing as bad in that it
produced bad actions. Except in so far as what-it-is produced these bad
actions, there is no ground for reproaching it (calling it bad) and no
meaning whatever in doing so. All self-reproach is self-judging, and all
judging is imputing a character. We are blaming ourselves. If spoken,
what we are thinking would be dispraise. And what are praise and dispraise? Always, everywhere, they are *descriptions* of a person (more or less
explicit) with favorable or unfavorable feeling at what is described, – descriptions in terms of value comporting fact, or of fact comporting value,
or of both fact and value. In moral instances they are descriptions of his
character. We are morally characterizing him in our minds (as above) with
appropriate feelings. We are attributing to him the character that we approve and like and wish to see more of, or the contrary. All the most intimate terms of the moral life imply that the act has proceeded from *me*,
the distinctive me, from the manner of man I am or was. And this is the very
thing on which the indeterminist lays stress. What he prizes with all his
heart, what he stoutly affirms and insists upon, is precisely what he denies,
namely, that I, the concrete and specific moral being, am the author, the
source of my acts. For that, of course, is determinism. To say that they
come from the self is to say that they are determined by the self – the
moral self, the self with a moral quality.

When he maintains that the self at the moment of decision may act to
some extent independently of character, *and is good or bad according as it
acts in this direction or that*, he is simply setting up one character within
another, he is separating the self from what he understands by the person's

character as at first mentioned, only thereupon to attribute to it a character of its own, *in that he judges it good or bad.*

The whole controversy is maintained by the indeterminist in order to defend the validity of the terms in which we morally judge, – for example, ourselves. But the very essence of all judgment, just so far as it extends, asserts determination.

If in conceiving the self you detach it entirely from motives or tendencies, what you have is not a morally admirable or condemnable, not a morally characterizable self at all. Hence it is not subject to reproach. You cannot call a self good because of its courageous free action, and then deny that its action was determined by its character. In calling it good because of that action you have implied that the action came from its goodness (which means its good character) and was a sign thereof. By their fruits ye shall know them. The indeterminist appears to imagine that he can distinguish the moral 'I' from all its propensities, regard its act as arising in the self undetermined by them, and yet can then (for the first time, in his opinion, with propriety!) ascribe to this 'I' an admirable quality. At the very root of his doctrine he contradicts himself. How odd that he never catches sight of that contradiction! He fights for his doctrine in order that he may call a man morally good, on account of his acts, with some real meaning; and his doctrine is that a man's acts (precisely so far as 'free' or undetermined) do not come from his goodness. So they do not entitle us to call him good. He has taken his position in defence of moral conceptions, and it is fatal to all moral conceptions.

We are told, however, that it is under determinism that we should have no right any more to praise or to blame. At least we could not do so in the old sense of the terms. We might throw words of praise to a man, or throw words of blame at him, because we know from observation that they will affect his action; but the old light of meaning in the terms has gone out. Well, all we have to do is to keep asking what this old meaning was. We praise a man by saying that he is a good friend, or a hard worker, or a competent man of business, or a trusty assistant, or a judicious minister, or a gifted poet, or one of the noblest of men – one of the noblest of characters! In other words, he is a being with such and such tendencies to bring forth good acts. If we describe a single act, saying, for instance: "Well done!" we mean to praise the person for the act as being the author of it. It is he who has done well and proved himself capable of doing so. If the happy act is accidental we say that no praise is deserved for it; it did not come from his character. If a person is gratified by praise, it is because of the estimate of him, in some respect or in general, that is conveyed. Praise (once again) means description, with expressed or implied admiration. If any instance of it can be found which does not consist in these elements our analysis fails. "Praise the Lord, O my soul, *and forget not all His benefits*", – and the Psalm goes on to tell His loving and guarding acts toward human-kind. Praise Him, remember these acts and how worthy of worship must be the character that brought them forth. To praise the Lord is to tell His perfections, especially the perfection of His character. This is the old light that has always been in words of praise and there appears no reason for its going out.

Indeterminism maintains that we need not be impelled to action by our wishes, that our active will need not be determined by them. Motives "incline without necessitating". We choose amongst the ideas of action before us, but need not choose solely according to the attraction of desire, in however wide a sense that word is used. Our inmost self may rise up in its autonomy and moral dignity, independently of motives, and register its sovereign decree.

Now, *in so far* as this "interposition of the self" is undetermined, the act is not *its* act, it does not issue from any concrete continuing self; it is born within the self at the moment, of nothing, hence it expresses no quality; it bursts into being from no source. The self does not register *its* decree, for the decree is not the product of just that *it*. The self does not rise up in *its* moral dignity, for dignity is the quality of an enduring being, influencing its actions, and therefore expressed by them, and that would be determination. *In proportion* as an act of volition starts of itself within the self without cause it is exactly, so far as the freedom of the individual is concerned, as if it had been thrown into his mind from without – 'suggested' to him – by a freakish demon. It is exactly like it in this respect, that in neither case does the volition arise from what the man is, cares for or feels allegiance to; it does not come out of him. *In proportion* as it is undetermined, it is just as if his legs should suddenly spring up and carry him off where he did not prefer to go. Far from constituting freedom, that would mean, in the exact measure in which it took place, the loss of freedom. It would be an interference, and an utterly uncontrollable interference, with his power of acting as he prefers. In fine, then, *just so far* as the volition is undetermined, the self can neither be praised nor blamed for it, since it is not the act of the self.

The principle of free will says: "*I* produce my volitions". Determinism says: "My volitions are produced by *me*". Determinism is free will expressed in the passive voice.

After all, it is plain what the indeterminists have done. It has not occurred to them that our free will may be resolved into its component elements. (Thus far a portion only of this resolution has been considered.) When it is thus resolved they do not recognise it. The analytical imagination is considerably taxed to perceive the identity of the free power that we feel with the component parts that analysis shows us. We are gratified by their nods of intelligence and their bright, eager faces as the analysis proceeds, but at the close are a little disheartened to find them falling back on the innocent supposition of a horse inside that does all the essential work. They forget that they may be called upon to analyze the horse. They solve the problem by forgetting analysis. The solution they offer is merely: "There is a self inside which does the deciding". Or, let us say, it is as if the *Pfarrer* had been explaining the physiology of a horse's motion. They take the whole thing to be analyzed, imagine a duplicate of it reduced in size, so to speak, and place this duplicate-self inside as an explanation – making it the elusive source of the 'free decisions'. They do not see that they are merely pushing the question a little further back, since the process of deciding, with its constituent factors, must have taken place within that inner self. Either it decided in a particular way because, on the whole, it preferred to decide in that way, or the decision was an underived event, a rootless and sourceless event. It is the same story over again. In neither case is there any gain in imagining a second self inside, however wonderful and elusive. Of course, it is the first alternative that the indeterminist is really imagining. If you tacitly and obscurely conceive the self as deciding *its own way*, i.e., according to its preference, but never admit or recognise this, then you can happily remain a libertarian indeterminist; but upon no other terms. In your theory there is a heart of darkness.

Freedom. – In accordance with the genius of language, free will means freedom of persons in willing, just as 'free trade' means freedom of persons (in a certain respect) in trading. The freedom of anyone surely always implies his possession of a power, and means the absence of any interference (whether taking the form of restraint or constraint) with his exercise of that power. Let us consider this in relation to freedom in willing.

'*Can*', – We say, "I can will this or I can will that, whichever I choose". Two courses of action present themselves to my mind. I think of their consequences, I look on this picture and on that, one of them commends itself more than the other, and I will an act that brings it about. I knew that I could choose either. That means that I had the power to choose either.

What is the meaning of 'power'? A person has a power if it is a fact that when he sets himself in the appropriate manner to produce a certain event that event will actually follow. I have the power to lift the lamp; that is, if I grasp it and exert an upward pressure with my arm, *it will rise*. I have the power to will so and so; that is, if I wish, if I definitively so incline, that act of will will take place. That and none other is the meaning of power, is it not? A man's being in the proper active posture of body or of mind is the cause, and the sequel in question will be the effect. (Of course, it may be held that the sequel not only does but must follow, in a sense opposed to Hume's doctrine of cause. Very well; the question does not here concern us.)

Thus power depends upon, or rather consists in, a law. The law in question takes the familiar form that if something happens a certain something else will ensue. If A happens then B will happen. The law in this case is that if the man definitively so desires then volition will come to pass. There is a series, wish–will–act. The act follows according to the will (that is a law, – I do not mean an underived law) and the will follows according to the wish (that is another law). A man has the power (sometimes) to act as he wishes. He has the power (whenever he is not physically bound or held) to act as he will. He has the power always (except in certain morbid states) to will as he wishes. All this depends upon the laws of his being. Wherever there is a power there is a law. In it the power wholly consists. A man's power to will as he wishes is simply the law that his will follows his wish.

What, again, dees freedom mean? It means the absence of any interference with all this. Nothing steps in to prevent my exercising my power.[1]

All turns on the meaning of 'can'. "I can will either this or that" means, I am so constituted that if I definitively incline to this, the appropriate act of will will take place, and if I definitively incline to that, the appropriate act of will will take place. The law connecting preference and will exists, and there is nothing to interfere with it. My free power, then, *is not an exemption from law but in its inmost essence an embodiment of law.*

Thus it is true, after the act of will, that I could have willed otherwise. It is most natural to add, "if I had wanted to"; but the addition is not required. The point is the meaning of 'could'. I could have willed whichever way I pleased. I had the power to will otherwise, there was nothing to prevent my doing so, and I should have done so if I had wanted. If someone says that the wish I actually had prevented by willing otherwise, so that I could not have done it, he is merely making a slip in the use of the word 'could'. He means, that wish could not have produced anything but this volition. But 'could' is asserted not of the wish (a transient fact to which power in this sense is not and should not be ascribed) but of the person. And the person *could* have produced something else than that volition. He could have produced any volition he wanted; he had the power to do so.

But the objector will say, "The person as he was at the moment – the person as animated by that wish – could not have produced any other volition". Oh, yes, he could. 'Could' has meaning not as applied to a momentary actual phase of a person's life, but to the person himself of whose life that is but a phase; and it means that (even at that moment) he had the power to will just as he preferred. *The idea of power, because it is the idea of a law, is hypothetical, carries in itself hypothesis as part of its very intent and meaning – "if he should prefer this, if he should prefer that", – and therefore can be truly applied to a person irrespective of what at the moment he does prefer. It remains hypothetical even when applied.*[2] This very peculiarity of its meaning is the whole point of the idea of power. It is just because determinism is true, because a law obtains, that one "could have done otherwise".

Sidgwick set over against "the formidable array of cumulative evidence" offered for determinism the "affirmation of consciousness" "that I can now choose to do" what is right and reasonable, "however strong may be my inclination to act unreasonably". But it is not against determinism. It is a true affirmation (surely not of immediate consciousness but of experience), the affirmation of my power to will what I deem right, however intense and insistent my desire for the wrong. I can will anything, and can will effectively anything that my body will enact. I can will it despite an inclination to the contrary of any strength you please – strength as felt by me before decision. We all know cases where we have resisted impulses of great strength in this sense and we can imagine them still stronger. I have the power to do it, and shall do it, shall exercise that power, if I prefer. Obviously in that case (be it psychologically remarked) my solicitude to do what is right will have proved itself even stronger (as measured by ultimate tendency to prevail, though not of necessity by sensible vividness or intensity) than the inclination to the contrary, for that is what is meant by my preferring to do it. I am conscious that the field for willing is open; I can will anything that I elect to will. Sidgwick did not analyse the meaning of 'can', that is all. He did not precisely catch the outlook of consciousness when it says, 'I can'. He did not distinguish the function of the word, which is to express the availability of the alternatives I see when, before I have willed, and perhaps before my preference is decided, I look out on the field of conceivable volition. He did not recognise that I must have a word to express my power to will as I please, quite irrespective of what I shall please, and that 'can' is that word. It is no proof that I cannot do something to point out that I shall not do it if I do not prefer. A man, let us say, can turn on the electric light; but he will not turn it on if he walks away from it; though it is still true that he can turn it on. When we attribute power to a man we do not mean that something will accomplish itself without his wanting it to. That would never suggest the idea of power. We mean that if he makes the requisite move the thing will be accomplished. It is part of the idea that the initiative shall rest with him. The initiative for an act of will is a precedent phase of consciousness that we call the definitive inclination, or, in case of conflict, the definitive preference for it. If someone in the throes of struggle with temptation says to himself, "I can put this behind me", he is saying truth and precisely the pertinent truth. He is bringing before his mind the act of will, quite unexcluded, open to him, that would deliver him from what he deems noxious. It may still happen that the noxiousness of the temptation does no affect him so powerfully as its allurement, and that he succumbs. It is no whit less true, according to determinism, that he could have willed otherwise. To analyse the fact expressed by 'could' is not to destroy it.

But it may be asked, "Can I will in opposition to my strongest desire at the moment when it is strongest?" If the words "at the moment when it is strongest" qualify 'can', the answer has already been given. It is Yes. If they qualify 'will', the suggestion is a contradiction in terms. Can I turn-on-the-electric-light-at-a-moment-when-I-am-not-trying-to-do-so? This means, if I try to turn on the light at a moment when I am not trying to, will it be turned on? A possible willing as I do not prefer to will is not a power on my part, hence not to be expressed by 'I can'.

Everybody knows that we often will what we do not want to will, what we do not prefer. But when we say this we are using words in another sense than that in which I have just used them. In *one* sense of the words, whenever we act we are doing what we prefer, on the whole, in view of all the circumstances. We are acting for the greatest good or the least evil or a mixture of these. In the *other* and more usual sense of the words, we are very often doing what we do not wish to do, i.e., doing some particular thing we do not wish because we are afraid of the consequences or dis-approve of the moral complexion of the particular thing we do wish. We do the thing that we do not like because the other thing has aspects that we dislike yet more. We are still doing what we like best on the whole. It is again a question of the meaning of words.

If the initiative for volition is not a wish, what is it? Indeterminism says that a moral agent sometimes decides against the more tempting course. He does so, let us say, because it is wrong, the other course is the right one. In other words, the desire to do right is at the critical moment stronger within him than the temptation. No, no, replies indeterminism, it is not that; he sometimes decides against the stronger desire. Very well; 'can' meaning what it does, tell us what is the leaning or favourable disposition on the part of the ego, in a case of undetermined willing, toward the voli-tion it adopts; what is that which constitutes the ego's initiative in that direction, – since it is not a wish? Shall we say it is an approval or con-scientious acceptance? Does this approval or acceptance arise from the agent's distinctive moral being? That is determinism, quite as mush as if you called the initiative a wish. But the indeterminist has already answered in effect that there is no such initiative, or no effectual initiative. The act of will causes the physical act but is not itself caused. *This is to deny the presence of power*, according to its definition. How has it a meaning to say in advance that 'I can' will this way or that? The self, considering the alternatives beforehand, is not in a position to say, "If I feel thus about it, this volition will take place, or if I feel otherwise the contrary will take place; I know very well how I shall feel, so I know how I shall will". The self now existing has not control over the future 'free' volition, since that may be undetermined, nor will the self's future feelings, whatever they may be, control it. Hence the sense expressed by 'I can', the sense of power inhering in one's continuous self to sway the volition as it feels disposed, is denied to it. All it is in a position to mean by 'I can' is, "I do not know which will happen", which is not 'I can' at all. Nay, even looking backward, it is unable to say: "I could have willed otherwise", for that clearly implies, "Had been I so disposed the other volition would have taken place", which is just what cannot, according to indeterminism, be said. Surely, to paraphrase a historic remark, our 'liberty' does not seem to be of very much use to us. The indeterminist is in a peculiarly hapless position. The two things that he is most deeply moved to aver, that the free volition is the act of the self, and that the self can will one way or the other – these two things on his own theory fall utterly to pieces, and can be maintained only on the view that he opposes.[4]

Compulsion. – The indeterminist conceives that according to determinism the self is carried along by wishes to acts which it is thus necessitated to perform. This mode of speaking distinguishes the self from the wishes and represents it as under their dominion. This is the initial error. This is what leads the indeterminist wrong on all the topics of his problem, the point with which I *began* in *Self and Character*. The error persists even in the most recent writings. In fact, the moral self is the wishing self. The wishes are its own. It cannot be described as under their dominion, for it has no separate predilections to be overborne by them; they themselves are its predilections. To fancy that because the person acts according to them he is compelled a slave, the victim of a power from whose clutches he cannot extricate himself, is a confusion of ideas, a mere slip of the mind. The answer that has ordinarily been given is surely correct; all compulsion is causation, but not all causation is compulsion. Seize a man and violently force him to do something, and he is compelled – also caused – to do it. But induce him to do it by giving reasons him and his doing it is caused but not compelled.

Passivity. – We have to be on our guard even against conceiving the inducement as a cause acting like the impact of a billiard ball, by which the self is precipitated into action like a second billiard ball, as an effect. The case is not so simple. Your reasons have shown him that his own preferences require the action. He does it of his own choice; he acts from his own motives in the light of your reasons. The sequence of cause and effect goes on within the self, with contributory information from without.

It is not clarifying to ask, "Is a volition free or determined?" It is the person who is free, and his particular volition that is determined. Freedom is something that we can attribute only to a continuing being, and he can have it only so far as the particular transient volitions within him are determined. (According to the strict proprieties of language, it is surely events that are caused, not things or persons; a person or thing can be caused or determined only in the sense that its beginning to be, or changes in it, are caused or determined.)

It is fancied that, owing to the 'necessity' with which an effect follows upon its cause, if my acts of will are caused I am not free in thus acting. Consider an analogous matter. When I move I make use of the ligaments of the body. 'Ligament' means that which binds, and a ligament does bind bones together. But I am not bound. I (so far as my organism is concerned) am rendered possible by the fact that my bones are bound to one another; that is part of the secret of my being able to act, to move about and work my will. If my bones ceased to be bound one to another I should be undone indeed. The human organism is detached, but it is distinctly important that its component parts shall not be detached. Just so my free power of willing is built up of tight cause-and-effect connections. The point is that when I employ the power thus constituted nothing determines the particular employment of it but *me*. Each particular act of mine is determined from outside itself, i.e., by a cause, a prior event. But not from outside myself. I, the possessor of the power, am not in my acts passively played upon by causes outside me, but am enacting my own determinate preferences in virtue of a chain of causation within me.

What makes the other party uncontrollably reject all this – let us never forget – is the words. They smell of sordid detail, of unwinsome psychological machinery. They are not bathed in moral value, not elevated and glowing. In this the opponents' instinct is wholly right; only when they look for the value they fail to focus their eyes aright. It is in the whole act and the whole trait and the whole being that excellence and preciousness inhere; analysis must needs show us elements which, taken severally, are without moral expressiveness; as would be even the celestial anatomy of an angel appearing on earth. The analytic imagination, however, enables us to see the identity of the fact in its composition with the fact in its living unity and integrity. Hence we can resume the thought of it as a unit and the appropriate feelings without fancying that analysis threatens them or is in any wise at enmity with them.

Spontaneity. – The conception of spontaneity in an act or an utterance is the conception of its springing straight from the being himself, from his individuality, with naught to cause it but the freest impulse, the sheerest inclination, of that being. The term implies and requires but one causation, that from within. If we deny all causation behind the volition itself, even that from within his nature, we deny spontaneity on his part. We have emptied our formula of all human meaning.

Source. – The indeterminist declares a man to be "the absolute source" of his acts. Let us scrutinise the term. The source of a stream is not a point where the water constituting the stream comes suddenly into existence, but on the contrary that from which it issues, that which supplies it because it has contained it. The stream – that particular stream – begins there, just as the action begins at its source, though the active energy flows from within that source. The word 'absolute' must mean true, genuine, complete, without reservation or qualification. Now such a genuine source a man in fact is; he knowingly and deliberately creates an act; the act issues forth from his chosen purpose, from his moral individuality. What the indeterminist, however, must mean by 'absolute source' is a source that has in turn no source; a source, he thinks, cannot in the fullest and truest sense be such if it derives what it emits. This, as we see, certainly receives no support from the natural uses of the word, but is flatly incompatible with them. But the final objection is deeper. Will the indeterminist point out anything in the definition of the word 'source' which implies that the thing defined is itself sourceless, or is imperfectly realised if it has a source? If he cannot, then the addition of the word 'absolute' does not import that sourcelessness into the idea. Obviously 'the man', as figuring in the indeterminist's conception here, would have to be the momentary man, not the enduring moral being. The truth clearly is that the indeterminist is confusing the idea of *flowing from this source and previously from another* with the quite distinct idea of *not flowing from this source but from another*. He feels that they cannot both be sources of the same act. And this is part of his confusion between causation and compulsion. If the agent were compelled to act as he does by the previous source, not he but the compeller would be the moral source of the act.[5]

Prediction. – If we knew a man's character thoroughly and the circumstances that he would encounter, determinism (which we are not here completely asserting) says that we could foretell his conduct. This is a thought that repels many libertarians. Yet to predict a person's conduct need not be repellent. If you are to be alone in a room with $ 1000 belonging to another on the table and can pocket it without anyone knowing the fact, and if I predict that you will surely *not* pocket it, that is not an insult. I say, I know you, I know your character; you will not do it. But if I say that you are "a free being" and that I really do not know whether you will pocket it or not, that is rather an insult. On the other hand, there are cases where prediction is really disparaging. If I say when you make a remark, "I knew you were going to say that", the impression is not agreeable. My exclamation seems to say that your mind is so small and simple that one can predict its ideas. That is the real reason why people resent in such cases our predicting their conduct; that if present human knowledge, which is known to be so limited, can foresee their conduct, it must be more naive and stereotyped than they like to think it. It is no reflection upon the human mind or its freedom to say that one who knew it through and through (a human possibility) could foreknow its preferences and its spontaneous choice, what it would wish. We would not be denying that it chooses freely; we would only be framing expectations as to what it *will* freely choose. If it lost that freedom to do as on the whole it preferred, then we could no longer foretell from knowledge of the mind in question what it would do. It is of even the very best men that we say, "I am sure of him". It has perhaps hardly been observed how much at this point is involved, how far the question of prediction reaches. The word 'reliable' or 'trustworthy' is a prediction of behavior. Indeed, all judgment of persons whatever, in the measure of its definitude, is such prediction.

Material Fate. – The sage in the old story, gazing at the stars, falls into a pit. We have to notice the pitfall in our subject to which, similarly occupied, Prof. Eddington has succumbed.

"What significance is there in my mental struggle to-night whether I shall or shall not give up smoking, if the laws which govern the matter of the physical universe already pre-ordain for the morrow a configuration of matter consisting of pipe, tobacco, and smoke connected with my lips?"[6]

No laws, according to determinism, pre-ordain such a configuration, unless I give up the struggle. Let us put the physical question aside for the moment, to return to it. Fatalism says that my morrow is determined no matter how I struggle. That is of course a superstition. Determinism says that my morrow is determined through my struggle. There is this significance in my mental effort, that it is deciding the event. The stream of causation runs through my deliberations and decision, and, if it did not run as it does run, the event would be different. The past cannot determine the event except throught the present. And no past moment determined it any more truly than does the present moment. In other words, each of the links in the causal chain must be in its place. Determinism, (which, the reader will remember, we have not here taken in all detail for necessarily true) says that the coming result is 'pre-ordained' (literally, caused) at each stage, and therefore the whole following series for tomorrow may be described as already determined; so that did we know all about the struggler, how strong of purpose he was and how he was influenced (which is humanly impossible) we could tell what he would do. But for the struggler this fact (supposing it to be such) is not pertinent. If, believing it, he ceases to struggle, he is merely revealing that the forces within him have brought about that cessation. If on the other hand he struggles manfully he will reveal the fact that they have brought about his success. Since the causation of the outcome works through his struggle in either case equally, it cannot become for him a moving consideration in the struggle. In it the question is, "Shall I do this or that?" It must be answered in the light of what there is to recommend to him this or that. To this question the scientific truth (according to determinism) that the deliberation itself is a play of causation is completely irrelevant; it merely draws the mind delusively away from the only considerations that concern it.

Now as regards the role of matter in the affair. Prof. Eddington, on behalf of the determinists, is here supposing that the behavior of all matter, including the human organism, takes place according to physical law. In that case we must conceive, according to the familiar formula, that the mental process is paralleled in the brain by a physical process. The whole psycho-physical occurrence would then be the cause of what followed, and the psychic side of it, the mental struggle proper, a concause or side of the cause. To-morrow's configuration of matter will have been brought about by a material process with which the mental process was inseparably conjoined. I make this supposition merely to show this: that supposing the existence of a physically complete mechanism through which all human action is caused and carried out has no tendency to turn determinism into fatalism. For the mental struggle must in that case be paralleled by a physical struggle which, so to speak, represents it and is in a manner its agent in the physical world; and upon this struggle the physical outcome will depend. (The determinist need not, but may of course, hold this doctrine of automatism, of a physically complete mechanism in human action.)

Self as Product and Producer. – We can at this stage clearly see the position when a certain very familiar objection is raised. "How can any one be praised or blamed if he was framed by nature as he is, if heredity and circumstance have given him his qualities? A man can surely be blamed only for what he does himself, and he did not make his original character; he simply found it on his hands." He did not make his character; no, but he made his acts. He is not blamed for making his character; he is blamed for what his character makes – namely, bad acts; and to blame him for that is to describe his character. Are we to be told that we may not recognize what he is, with appropriate feelings for its quality, because he did not create himself – a mere contortion and intussusception of ideas? The moral self cannot be *causa sui*. To cause his original self a man must have existed before his original self. Is there something humiliating to him in the fact that he is not a contradiction in terms? If there were a being who made his 'original character', and made a fine one, and we proceeded to praise him for it, our language would turn out to be a warm ascription to him of a still earlier character, so that the other would not have been original at all. To be praised or blamed you have to be; and be a particular person; and the praise or blame is telling what kind of a person you are. There is no other meaning to be extracted from it. Of course, a man does exist before his later self, and in that other sense he can be a moral *causa sui*. If by unflagging moral effort he achieves for himself better subsequent qualities, what can merit praise but the ingredient in him of aspiration and resolution that was behind the effort? If he should even remake almost his whole character, still there would be a valiant remnant that had done it. These are commonplaces, precisely of the moral outlook upon life. When we come to the moral fountainhead we come to what the man is, at a particular time, as measured by what he does or is disposed to do with his power of volition. It is fantastic to say that he finds his character on his hands. It is nothing but the moral description of himself. It is that self alone that wields his hands.

The indeterminist is disquieted (through a mental confusion) by the discovery that the nature antedates the act, that virtue antedates the virtuous decision. (For that contains in itself the whole logical essence of the difficulty about origin.) And that lies in the signification of the terms. If we fancy that there would be any gain (or any meaning) in circumventing this order, we delude ourselves. The final fact we esteem or disesteem in a man is some subsisting moral quality. Morality has its eye upon acts, but an act is fleeting, it cannot be treasured and cherished. A quality can be, it lasts. And the reason why it is treasured and cherished is that it is the source of acts. Our treasuring and cherishing of it is (in part) our praise. It is the stuff certain people are made of that commands our admiration and affection. Where it came from with what spiritual dignity is another question; it is precious in its own nature; let us be thankful when it is here. Its origin cannot take away its value, and it is its value we are recognizing when we praise.

The peculiar importance that attaches to this 'stuff' lies in its peculiar properties, so to speak. It is not a fixed 'article of value', but lives, moves about in "this raging and confounding universe", this maze of unstable circumstances, yet can acquit itself with some fitness in face of all of them; reveals itself by choosing and rejecting with open eyes; steers its way through the dangers and complications, able to compare acts in advance, conscious of good and evil, allured to do otherwise but electing to do thus; good in a very special manner, in that it consciously cleaves to the good. A reliable character in the midst of unreliable circumstances. Consciousness, foresight, intelligence, moral consciousness, and sound choice. A unique 'stuff'.

The indeterminist, we noticed, requires a man to be "an absolute moral source" if we are to commend him. Well, if he were so, what could we say about him but what kind of a source he was? And he is so in fact. Suppose now that this source has in turn a source – or that it has not! Does that (either way) change what it is?

"But moral severity! How can we justly be severe toward a mere fact in nature – in human nature?" Because it is evil; because it must be checked. If somebody takes pleasure in torturing an innocent person, we spring to stop the act; to hold back the perpetrator, if need be with violence; to deter him from doing it again, if need be with violence; to warn any other possible perpetrators: "This shall not be done; we are the enemies of this conduct; this is evil conduct". At what could we be indignant but at a fact in somebody's human nature? Our severity and enmity are an active enmity to the evil; they are all part of that first spring to stop the act. "Society is opposed in every possible manner to such cruelty. You shall be made to feel that society is so, supposing that you cannot be made to feel yourself the vileness of the act." It does not remove our sense of its vileness to re-flect that he was acting according to his nature. That is very precisely why we are indignant at him. We intend to make him feel that his nature is in that respect evil and its expression insufferable. We intend to interfere with the expression of his nature. That what he did proceeded from it is not a disturbing and pause-giving consideration in the midst of our con-duct, but the entire basis of it. The very epiphet 'vile' assumes that his behavior arose from an intention and a moral quality in the man. How can we justly be severe? Because he *ought* to be checked and deterred, made to feel the moral estimate of what he has been doing. This we con-sider more fully under the topic of *Desert*.

Compare a case where the wrongdoing, whatever it be, is one's own. Catch a man in a moment of fierce self-reproach, and bring the objection above before him. Would it relieve him of his feeling? It would be an ir-relevant frivolity to him. He is shocked at a wrong that was done and at himself for doing it; he repents of the acts of will that brought it about; he would gladly so change himself as never to do the like again; he is ready to "beat himself with rods". With all that the metaphysical entangle-ment has simply nothing to do.

It would follow from the objector's way of thinking that if a man's moral state at one time was produced by himself through previous efforts, then our praise or blame must shift back to the earlier moral state and be applied to that alone; or, if that again was such a product, must shift still further back and be confined to the state that began the process. This is a vital misconception. The man in each of the moral states in the series may justly be characterised as good or bad, in this respect or that, in proportion as we truly know him; according to his decisions and intentions, or tendencies thereto, as compared with his then situation and knowledge of what he confronts, and of the effects that may fairly be expected from acts. This is implied whenever we make the remark that someone has deteriorated or improved in character; in other words, he is less or more to be praised than he was now formerly.

I say, "as compared with his then situation", for of course, in seeking to know what the forces of his character in themselves really are, we must take full account of the hardships, the exasperations, provocations to passion, causes of fatigue, etc., that enter into that situation. As regards the source of any moral degeneration, we cannot and do not call a person good because we can see that it is evil circumstances that have made him bad; nor do we refrain from deeming him bad, since he is so; but we may have gained thereby a better insight into the hidden potential forces of his character, and see, in view of the previous circumstances, that it is at root less bad than we might have supposed. And while deeming him bad we may profoundly pity him in his wretched fortune.

"Still, does not determinism force us to face a fact in some sort new to us, that the offending person came to act so from natural causes; and does not that of necessity alter somewhat our attitude or state of mind about moral judgment?" Why, the fact is not new at all. In daily life we are all determinists, just as we are all libertarians. We are constantly attributing behavior to the character, the temperament, the peculiarities of the person and expecting him to behave in certain fashions. The very words of our daily converse, as we have so amply observed, are full of determinism. And we see nothing inconsistent in being aware at the same time that he is free in choosing his course, as we know ourselves to be. We merely form expectations as to what he *will* freely choose. Nor do we see anything inconsistent in blaming him. At the very moment when we do so we often shake our heads over the environment or mode of life or ill-omened pursuits that have brought him to such ways and to being a blameworthy person. To be sure, in our rigid economy of thought which is one of the salient traits of humanity, we seldom trouble ourselves to trace back with any attempt at thoroughness another's life, education, early temperament, etc. We do not go far back, but we are attentive, as we have to be, to his disposition and spirit in the present, at least as objectively expressed and thence imputed. And that is sufficient to include the whole point at issue.

We recognise the one essential fact, that the nature precedes the act, and that the nature is simply a 'given' fact in the world (not originally created by the agent himself – a would-be notion that visits the mind only in an attack of logical vertigo). Indeed, since blame is in itself the assertion of a particular nature existent in the world and father to an act, blame has contained in itself the truth in question from the beginning.

To be sure, determinism as a philosophic doctrine, determinism so named, may come as a new and repellent idea to us. We have been thinking in the right terms of thought all the while, but we did not identify them with terms of causation; when the philosophical names are put upon them we recoil, not because we have a false conception of the facts, but a false conception of the import of the philosophical terms. When we feel that somebody could have done otherwise but[7] chose to do a wrong act knowingly, then we one and all feel that he is culpable and a proper object of disapproval, as we ought to feel. We merely have not been schooled enough in the application of general terms to call the course of mental events within him causation. So again, goodness consists in qualities, but the qualities express themselves in choosing, which is unfettered and so often trembles in the balance; when we are suddenly confronted with the abstract question, "Can we be blamed for a quality we did not choose?" the colours run and the outlines swim a little; some disentanglement of abstract propositions is required, though we think aright in practice on the concrete cases. So all that philosophic determinism "forces us to face" is the meaning of our terms.

No, it is the opposite doctrine that must revolutionize our attitude toward moral judgments. If it is true, we must come to see that no moral severity toward the helpless subject of an act of will that he suddenly finds discharging itself within him, though not emanating from what he is or prefers, can be deserved or relevant. To comprehend all is to pardon all – so far as it is undetermined. Or, rather, not to pardon but to acquit of all.

However, in face of the actual facts, there is something that does bring us to a larger than the usual frame of mind about indignation and punishment and the mood of severity. And that is thought, sympathetic thought, any thought that enters with humane interest into the inner lives of others and pursues in imagination the course of them. In an outbreak of moral indignation we are prone to take little cognizance of that inner life. We are simply outraged by a noxious act and a noxious trait (conceived rather objectively and as it concerns the persons affected) and feel that such act should not be and that such a trait should be put down. The supervening of a sympathetic mental insight upon moral indigation is not a displacement, but the turning of attention upon facts that call out other feelings too. To comprehend all is neither to pardon all nor to acquit of all; overlooking the disvalue of acts and intentions would not be comprehension; but it is to appreciate the human plight; the capacity for suffering, the poor contracted outlook, the plausibilities that entice the will. This elicits a sympathy or concern co-existing with disapproval. That which is moral in moral indignation and behind it, if we faithfully turn to it and listen, will not let us entirely wash our hands even of the torturer, his feelings and his fate; certainly will not permit us to take satisfaction in seeing him in turn tortured, merely for the torture's sake. His act was execrable because of its effect on sentient beings, but he also is a sentient being. The humanity that made us reprobate his crime has not ceased to have jurisdiction. The morality that hates the sin has in that very fact the secret of its undiscourageable interest in the sinner. We come, not to discredit indignation and penalty, nor to tamper with their meaning, but to see their office and place in life and the implications wrapped up in their very fitness. Of this more presently.

Amongst qualities none, of course, is higher than that which masters strong impulsive tendencies within ourselves that we decide not to tolerate. It is the possibility of this desperate inner struggle of self-overcoming, the genuine possibility of defying habit and weakness and asserting new life, which has caught and held the indeterminist's mind; but which he formulates loosely. He wishes to conceive of a self that need have no capital stock of qualities at all on which its volition depends. He thinks, or imagines that he thinks, of virtue as a thing nobly arising in the moment. In fact it is a thing nobly manifested in the moment; roused perhaps, brought to active life through it seemed dead, but still in some form pre-existing. What he admires is admirable, but he does not stop to think out its nature. To be "the author of novelty" is as possible, as fruitful for society, as challenging to the spirit as he deems it; but that author must exist as author, must have it in him to make a break for the new. The indeterminist would promptly retort that this is evidently not the sort of novelty he has in mind, that he means a moral act which is not an effect of anything pre-existing in the person. To which I answer: The novelty interesting to morality and to humanity is the escape from the spell of habit or ease or a straitened mental outlook, the leap of the soul with all its strength in a new direction; the question of causal nexus is of interest only to the philosophical analyst. The determinist's analysis leaves the escape from habit, etc., entirely possible and as creditable as it seems. On the indeterminist's account it would be a cosmological accident without moral significance.

Responsibility. – Again, it is said that determinism takes from man all responsibility. As regards the origin of the term, a man is responsible when he is the person to respond to the question why the act was performed, how it is to be explained or justified. That is what he must answer; he is answerable for the act. It is the subject of which he must give an account; he is accountable for the act. The act proceeded from him. He is to say whether it proceeded consciously. He is to give evidence that he did or did not know the moral nature of the act and that he did or did not intend the result. He is to say how he justifies it or if he can justify it. If the act proceeded from him by pure accident, if he can show that he did the damage (if damage it was) by brushing against something by inadvertence, for example, then he has not to respond to the question what he did it for – he is not consciously responsible – nor how it is justified – he is not morally responsible, though of course he may have been responsible in these respects for a habit of carelessness.

But why does the peculiar moral stain of guilt or ennoblement of merit belong to responsibility? If an act proceeds from a man and not merely from his accidental motion but from his mind and moral nature, we judge at once that like acts may be expected from him in the future. The colour of the act for good or bad is reflected on the man. We see him now as a living source of possible acts of the same kind. If we must be on our guard against such acts we must be on our guard against such men. If we must take steps to defend ourselves against such acts we must take steps to defend ourselves against such men. If we detest such acts, we must detest that tendency in such men which produced them. He is guilty in that he knowingly did evil, in that the intentional authorship of evil is in him. Because the act proceeded in every sense from him, for that reason he is (so far) to be accounted bad or good according as the act is bad or good, and he is the one to be punished if punishment is required. And that is moral responsibility.

But how, it is asked, can I be responsible for what I will if a long train of past causes has made me will it – the old query asked anew in relation to another category, responsibility, which must be considered separately. Is it not these causes that are 'responsible' for my act – to use the word in the only sense, says the objector, that seems to remain for it?

The parent past produced the man, none the less the man is responsible for his acts. We can truly say that the earth bears apples, but quite as truly that trees bear apples. The earth bears the apples by bearing trees. It does not resent the claim of the trees to bear the apples, or try to take the business out of the trees' hands. Nor need the trees feel their claim nullified by the earth's part in the matter. There is no rivalry between them. A man is a being with free will and responsibility; where this being came from, I repeat, is another story. The past finished its functions in the business when it generated him as he is. So far from interfering with him and coercing him the past does not even exist. If we could imagine it as lingering on into the present, standing over against him and stretching out a ghostly hand to stay his arm, then indeed the past would be interfering with his liberty and responsibility. But so long as it and he are never on the scene together they cannot wrestle; the past cannot overpower him. The whole alarm is an evil dream, a nightmare due to the indigestion of words. The past has created, and left extant, a free-willed being.

Desert. – But we have not come to any final clearness until we see how a man can be said to *deserve* anything when his acts flow from his wishes, and his wishes flow from other facts further up the stream of his life. There is a peculiar element in the idea of deserving. This is the element expressed by the word 'ought'. A man deserves punishment or reward if society ought to give it to him; he deserves the punishment or reward that he ought to receive. (We cannot say universally that he deserves what he ought to receive, but only when it is a question of reward or punishment.)

What treatment a man should receive from society as a result of wrong-doing is a question of ethics. It is widely held that an evildoer deserves punishment, not only for the defence of society but because there is an ultimate fitness in inflicting natural evil for moral evil. This, as we know, has been maintained by determinists. Since the idea of desert collapses altogether on the indeterminists' conception of conduct, this theory of the ground of desert cannot be said to be logically bound up with indeterminism. For my own part, however, owing to reasons for which I have no space here, I cannot hold the theory. I believe that the ideal ends of the administration of justice are (1) to see that all possible restitution is made, (2) to see as far as possible that the malefactor does not repeat the act, and (3) so far as possible to render the act less likely on the part of others. And these ends should be sought by means that will accomplish them. Morality is humane. It is animated by good-will toward humanity. Our instinctive impulse to retaliation must be interpreted with a view to its function in society, and so employed and regulated to the best purpose. Being a part of the defensive and fighting instinct, its functional aim is evidently to destroy or check the threatening source of evil – to destroy the culprit or change his temper. Our common and natural notion of desert is in harmony with either of these views; only on the second it receives a supplement, a purposive interpretation.

We discover punishment not only in combat but in nature at large. If a child puts its hand into flames it is burnt. After that it puts its hand into flames no more. Nature teaches us to respect her by punishments that deter. Society, to preserve itself, must find deterrents to administer to men. It must say, "I'll teach you not to do that." Already nature has taught it such deterrents. Society must shape men's actions or at least rough-hew them, to the extent of striking off certain jagged and dangerous edges, and the most obvious way to do so is by penalties. A secondary way is by rewards, and these nature has taught also.

When a man needlessly injures others, society by punishment injures him. It administers to him a specimen of what he has given to others. "This", it says, "is the nature of your act; to give men suffering like this. They rebel at it as you rebel at this. You have to be made more acutely conscious of the other side; the side of the feelings and the forces that you have outraged. You have to be made to feel them recoil upon you, that you may know that they are there. You have to be made to respect them in advance. And others like-minded to respect them in some degree better by seeing how they recoil upon you."

But this is only a method of working upon him and them; it is justified by effectiveness alone. It supposes two things; that society has been just in the first instance to these men themselves, that is, that they were not drawn by unjust conditions of life into the acts for which they are made to suffer; and that the suffering will in fact improve their conduct or that of others. The truth is that society often punishes when it is itself the greater malefactor, and that the penalty, instead of reforming, often confirms the criminality. It is due to nothing but the crude state of civilization that we have added so little of a more sagacious and effectual mode of influencing criminals and preventing crime than the original and natural method of hitting back.

Out of this situation arises a subsidiary sense of deserving. A man may be said to deserve a punishment in the sense that, in view of the offence, it is not too severe to give him *if* it would work as above conceived; though if we believe it will not so work it ought not to be given him.

It is here that we confront the school that would sweep away all notions of desert, all indignation, whether against public or private offenders, on the ground that free will and responsibility are illusions, and would substitute the moral hospital for the prison. Tietjens, for example, would have us apply 'de-suggestion' to rid ourselves of the heartburnings and disquiet that imputing moral responsibility brings upon us. It is a pity that a teaching which speaks to us in the name of advanced psychology should be founded on a hasty and crude analysis. If we did not acquire the idea of free will from our experience of the conditions of our own volition, how did we come by it at all? Under the laws of origin of our conceptions, how were we able to conceive an elementary type of volition that has no counterpart in real life? How could we fabricate the idea without any material for it? What these determinists do is, first, to make the unthinking concession to the indeterminists that they have a coherent theory and that it is one with the naive belief in free choice; having hastily conceded so much, they are constrained to call the native notion an illusion. They do not see the strength of their own fundamental position.

Honor and dishonor will never be withdrawn from morals. We shall not cease to look upon our world with appropriate emotions. But it behooves us to take care that they are appropriate. The moral emotions are often barbarously and with terrible effect misapplied; it shows what they could do if intelligence guarded their appllication. The Christian principle of hating the sin because it is in fact noxious, but bearing good-will to the sinner and preferring his reformation with a minimum of suffering to his punishment, is surely the root-principle. And here it is that the school of cool realism, of the medical, educational, and environmental treatment, brings fresh air and aid. It wants to discover effectual means to what is in truth a chief part of the moral end. We shall not be troubled by its shallow philosophy in so far as it can help to that end.

If the general view here taken, which seems forced upon us in the prosaic process of examining words, is correct, then as we look back over the long course of this controversy and the false antithesis that has kept it alive, how can we help exclaiming, "What waste!" Waste is surely the tragic fact above all in life; we contrast it with the narrow areas where reason and its economy of means to ends in some measure reign. But here is huge waste in the region of reasoning itself, the enemy in the citadel. What ingenuity, what resource in fresh shifts of defence, what unshaken loyalty to inward repugnances, what devotion to ideal values, have here been expended in blind opposition instead of analysis. The cause of determinism, seeming to deny freedom, has appeared as the cause of reason, of intelligence itself, and the cause of free will, seeming to exclude determination, has appeared that of morals. The worst waste is the clash of best things. In our subject it is time this waste should end. Just as we find that morality requires intelligence to give it effect and remains rudimentary and largely abortive till it places the conscience of the mind in the foreground, so we find that determinism and the faith in freedom meet and are united in the facts, and that the long enmity has been a bad dream.

NOTES

[1] A word as to the relation of power and freedom. Strictly power cannot exist without freedom, since the result does not follow without it. Freedom on the other hand is a negative term, meaning the absence of something, and implies a power only because that whose absence it signifies is interference, which implies something to be interfered with. Apart from this peculiarity of the term itself, there might be freedom without any power. Absence of interference (of what would be interference if there were a power) might exist in the absence of a power; a man might be free to do something because there was nothing to interfere with his doing it, but might have no power to do it. Similarly and conveniently we may speak of a power as existing though interfered with; that is, the law may exist that would constitute a power if the interference were away.

[2] I am encouraged by finding in effect the same remark in Prof. G. E. Moore's *Ethics*, Chap. vi., at least as regards what he terms one sense of the word 'could'. I should hazard saying, the only sense in this context.

[3] *Methods of Ethics*, 7th ed., 65.

[4] [In the margin beside the central parts of this paragraph Miller wrote 'unfortunate', perhaps indicating that he intended further revision.]

[5] [Beside this paragraph Miller wrote 'unfortunate', perhaps again indicating that he intended further revision.]

[6] *Philosophy*, Jan., 1933, p. 41.

[7] [Prominent pencilled question mark in margin at this point.]

IS THERE NOT A CLEAR SOLUTION OF THE KNOWLEDGE-PROBLEM?

[In 1937, the third year of his 'American retirement', Miller published the following analysis of how the mind gets at its object without some kind of transcendent reference to what is not already given to it. A year earlier he had noted that James's pragmatism never met this problem squarely, the very problem on which he had centered his attention in his doctoral dissertation and first publication, 'The Meaning of Truth and Error'. So in what follows Miller reworks and refines the main point of his dissertation to argue that knowledge is consummated by the presence in consciousness of an image precisely similar to the object, and this is made possible by the principle of "identity of indiscernibles" whereby at the moment of knowing the image, stripped of its external relations, is equivalent to the object or an aspect of it. Such equivalence excludes any conscious reference of the mind to objects not given to it, so a position like that of G. F. Stout asserting such reference is groundless, and generic ideas, like propositions, pertain only to the expression of knowledge rather than its content.

Miller intended to convert this article into a chapter of his book on 'Inquiry, Analytical or Sceptical', begun in 1941 but never completed. A second part of the article dealt with "another department" of the knowledge problem, namely, the rational basis for inference from past experience through induction. There Miller argued that 'cogency' need not be confined to deductive implication – the needless source of Hume's 'scepticism' – but should include corroboration by "a fact which stands as such by itself", by a "basic appearance" in experience. Miller analyzed the 'cogency' and 'corroboration' of induction more fully in subsequent articles on Hume and deductivism, also to be used in his book on 'Inquiry', so the second part of the article to follow has been omitted.]

Let us consider, first, the difficulty; second, an apparent solution; third, a fundamental objection.

I. THE DIFFICULTY

How can we know or think about the past, for instance, or the minds of others, since these objects of our thought are not 'given', not present to our consciousness. (Those that hold that they *are* given will find their view presently considered.) If it is answered, by means of mental images, then how does our thought get beyond these mental images to its objects themselves? That the image should resemble the object of thought is not enough. "One egg resembles another egg but does not therefore know it." How do we know that the latter *is* the object of our thought? How does our thought lay hold of our object in its numerical identity, as distinguished from anything else, however similar? If it is said, We intend our image to represent our object, we *mean* the object though it is only the image that is before us, then at once the question takes the form, How can we mean something of which by the nature of the situation we are wholly oblivious? How can we *get at* the object even to mean it or in any wise refer to it?

This is the ultimate problem of knowledge. This is the dragon at the last bridge. Familiar as it now is, it is a problem that Berkeley, for example, never faced at all. In referring to the past and to other minds he assumed that it was possible to think of them, never felt the difficulty, kept his attention on the perception of the material world. It was reserved for Hume to push Berkeley's idea further and profess himself helpless before the apparent breakdown of all knowledge beyond the consciousness of the moment.[1]

The view taken in recent decades that the object itself (the past or other minds, for instance) is immediately present to our consciousness, like a sensation, is a fascinating conception, in which one would greatly like to believe. But it is tenable only so long as our thought is supposed true. This view cannot explain imagination and false belief. It is indeed ingeniously suggested that the content or object-matter of these is in a manner real, consists of object-stuff in the real world, twisted by the mind into new shapes; that nothing is there before it but such objective material, which we have experienced on former occasions and now redate and recombine. But where is the escape from the difficulty? Suppose I imagine somebody I know with his own body but with the hoofs and shaggy legs of a satyr. In the real world his body is connected with its veritable legs; in my imagination it is connected with a satyr's legs. But, upon the theory, it is the real body that is present to my imagination. How can the real body be connected with a satyr's legs and not connected with them? In physical fact the body has not the strange legs; in the imaginary version it has not the normal legs. Is it said that in one sphere it stands in the one relation and in another sphere in the other? But upon the theory there are not two spheres but only one. Where, then, in what realm, is the body with this imaginary complement to it existent? Where, in what realm, are the hoofed and furry legs, which are in animals and in pictures, attached to this man's body? On the terms of the theory, nowhere. The materials are to be in the real world, but the relations between the materials are not to be in the real world. Again, where are they? Or suppose I imagine a friend's mind in the past as hearing a remark, which he did hear, and feeling violent anger at it, which he did not at all. The same question. What we call the imagination must on this view work its magic on realities, dropping some out (what does that mean? – out of what?) and putting some together (but they are not together – they are far apart). All the admirable ingenuity lavished on the attempt to meet this difficulty has not even tended to do so. The cases supposed analogous are not really analogous. They are not really cases of a relation which does and does not exist. Grant mental images and there is no difficulty about imagination and false belief. Deny mental images and the difficulty is adamant. The so-called doctrine of images is the inevitable result of comparing thought with experience and finding that thought can be error. It is not a theory of certain philosophers merely; it is the theory of the human race. The discovery of human illusion is the discovery of mental images.

It will be found that those undiscouraged thinkers who seem to meet with some success in explaining at least physical perception without images have really come out in some form of the image-conception; merely adding that the images are an appurtenance, effluence, or physical effect of the object and are part of the physical world, – a point that does not concern us here.[2] (It would be interesting to see a corresponding theory applied to the case of the imagined anger.)

Another resort has been to regard the object-matter of imagination and false belief as eternally subsistent universals. We must remember that the false belief may contain no mark of its falsity. So it would follow that when we believe at a given moment in some concrete reality, let us say another person's consciousness, which is actual, and also believe in something else which is a fiction, the object of the first belief is a concrete existent and the object of the second a universal; we not knowing which is which until we investigate objective facts. This theory depends on an imperfect distinction and definition of the universal.

We come back then to our unrelieved problem: how can the mind, in thinking of the past or of other minds, for instance, get at its object even to intend it, even to designate it as the object of thought? The mind seems to possess no means of doing so but its images, and these will at best resemble the object. If that be so the only thing before the mind in thinking seems to be the image itself and no object beyond such images will ever come within its ken.

Yet this, with regard to the past and to foreign consciousness, is an impossible conclusion. The past that we do mean and are thinking about is, we know full well, distinct from any image of ours.

That the idea of a conscious *reference* on the part of the mind to objects not directly given to it should so long have been employed to explain how knowledge can be effected is one of the curiosities of the history of thought. The explanation is not tenable for a moment. Reference to an object can not be that which enables an image to serve for knowledge of that object, because reference to an object implies that we have knowledge of it already. I can not intend my image to represent so-and-so unless I have an identifying thought of so-and-so.

Moreover, the idea is false psychology. I do not ordinarily distinguish the image from the object. It was said long ago: That there is an object distinct from my perception (and the same would apply to my thought) is not merely a theory about perception, it is the theory of the perception itself. This is surely an error of observation. In perception and thought alike I am not for ordinary purposes conscious of any perception, thought, or image apart from the object. And as for 'my', I am not often conscious at the moment of myself as a mental individual at all.

Another explanation has been offered in the name of pragmatism. According to this we need not mentally get at the object itself but our idea leads us to behave correctly in relation to the object and thus brings us out satisfactorily. Now this tendency of the image to make us behave aright is indeed real and vital. We must fully recognise it. But we need not here consider it further. It is a fact that belongs to knowledge but it is not the whole of knowledge. It may by itself in certain common instances be called knowledge, but the awakened human mind is aware that by its term 'knowledge', in the full sense, it means something else as well, a mental, a conscious acquaintance with the thing, an appearance of it in its true nature. And it is to *that side*, the side of conscious envisagement, that our whole present question relates.

II. PROPOSED SOLUTION

And is there not a clear answer to the question? Knowledge (on this side of it) is presence of the object to consciousness. But whether the object is present in its own being or through a correct image of it is immaterial. *From the point of view of consciousness there would be no difference whatever* between the immediate presence of the object itself and the presence of a precisely similar image. It would be the same experience. This is the decisive fact. Hence knowledge is consummated by the presence of a precisely similar image. How far it is so is not our question here: it can be thus consummated. Knowledge can thus exist as truly as, in view of its nature, it conceivably could exist. The numerical identity of the object is fixed by its objective relations. What or which object the mind is seeking to know can always be rendered clear by the further specifications it stands ready to add. It adds these of course by the addition of further image-stuff. If and when it becomes pertinent to recognize that the image and the object are two distinct things, then these two are both presented to thought in the content of consciousness, the object being presented afresh through an image. The first image of the object is now seen *as* image, i.e., placed in a psychological setting, one's own mental history; the fresh image appears with an objective setting. That is the only way of knowing (on this side of knowing), to have the object present by its *quale* (in the inclusive and complex sense) in the content of consciousness. And when the mind perceives that it knows only through images it perceives also that this is a genuine means of knowledge.

The object is in fact a concrete *quale*, having its place in nature and history, that is, existing in certain relations. To envisage that *quale* and those relations is the conscious side of knowledge in its most successful state. I am not speaking of how it is verified but of what it is in itself when it exists.

What has been overlooked in statements of the difficulty is the peculiar significance that mere similarity assumes so soon as we recognize that knowledge (on this side of it) is simply the appearance of the object to consciousness.

To speak of mentally 'referring' the image-content of knowledge to some object or situation beyond consciousness can mean nothing. The object as known must be "within the picture", and all relations that are to figure with respect to it must there appear. I can not refer the whole picture because any location or status to which I am said to refer it must be a part of the picture itself. In fact I "get at" the object by means of the picture itself, since it can be extended to include all identifying relations.

Thus the principle that renders knowledge possible is the identity of indiscernibles. To be sure, the image and the object, taken as facts in the open cosmos, are broadly discernible, their respective settings or relations being obviously different. One exists as a fleeting phenomenon in one's own mental life; the other exists in a physical setting or in that of a foreign mind. But in knowledge an essential part is played by the narrow limits of the knowing consciousness, the restricted area of the mental field. This fact, in other respects our great humiliation, becomes a part of the secret of our cognitive power. The relations of the image that are irrelevant are shut off from view and only that *quale* which renders the object is admitted. Seen not in the open cosmos but by the mind in the moment of knowing, the correct image, thus stripped of its external relations, is equivalent to the object or to an aspect of it. If an aspect of the object itself were substituted for the image, were made immediately present instead, it would not by the mind be discernible from the image. This equivalence may be called identity for the mind or noetic identity. By virtue of it the image becomes the medium of knowledge.[3]

Accordingly, where true transcendent knowledge exists there may be reckoned (1) the object, (2) the image, (3) the appearance, which might indifferently be presented by either image or object. The first two are concrete and similar. (The quality they share is of course a universal.) The appearance is also concrete, not a universal. If we said otherwise we should have to say that the mind could know only universals, since for every impression an exact similar could conceivably be substituted. The appearance is concrete, its existence in the cosmos being that of the image, but its reach (that is, the range of objects that may appear through it) extends to anything that perfectly resembles it and whose identifying situation in the real world of space-time might be exhibited by addition to the image.

To those who do not admit mental images we may at least say: If there were mental images they could quite evidently be the media of knowledge.

It has very generally been conceived – notably by Kant – that a great gulf is fixed between what is given to consciousness and the dark *Ding an sich* beyond. But there is no metaphysical reason to suppose that the same natures that are given to consciousness may not exist apart from it. For memory the very image that has been present becomes when it is past a *Ding an sich* – an entity external to the knowing consciousness, not a phenomenon. This is not in accordance with Kant's terminology or opinion; I am merely pointing it out as a fact.

Lastly: Of course we mostly do not and need not stop to make our images accurate or in any sense complete; we take them as cues for action and pass on. And there are other such remarks that might be made as bearing on the above. We are dealing here with one question alone, how conscious knowledge gets at the object in its individual identity, when it does get at it. The language used is adapted to the needs of that question, and not of the innumerable other questions that crowd about it. And brevity compels the omission of much vital detail.

III. THE OBJECTION

But to all this a large school of opinion would raise the most radical of objections: the mere presence of mental images, or of any existent whatsoever, – even of the object in its own being – is not knowledge. In the year 1874 there appeared two works, in Vienna and Oxford respectively, that have powerfully influenced opinion to that effect. Brentano's *Psychologie vom empirischen Standpunkt,* and Green's *General Introduction* to Hume's *Treatise on Human Nature,* included in his edition of Hume's philosophical works, both maintain, as is well known, that knowledge can not consist in the mere presence to consciousness of images or ideas but requires something irreducibly different from this, a mental act of assertion or judgment, an act involving reference to an object, the recognition of certain necessary relations. But perhaps no other statement of the essential position is to be found so admirably lucid and to the point

as that of Professor G. F. Stout in his *Studies in Philosophy and Psychology*
(pp. 369–370).

> The most general reason why a bare feeling [or bare experience, as he has previously
> said], as it is being felt, can not by itself be a complete object of knowledge is that it is
> not a proposition, and that all knowledge is of propositions, and of other things only
> as forming constituents of propositions. To know is always to know "that..."; it is to
> know, for instance, "that something is or exists or occurs", or "that something is of
> such and such a nature", or "that it is so and so related to something else". Now a
> proposition, understood in this sense, is never a particular existence or occurrence, and
> it can not therefore be a feeling, which is always a particular existence or occurrence....
> As, therefore, a particular existent is only known in knowing the proposition that it
> exists, it can only be known by a thought which transcends it.

To this definite argument there is an equally definite reply.

(1) Existence is not a proposition. To know it we do not have to know
a proposition but to know existence. We do so in every sensation we experience. That is existence in the concrete. We are concerned in this article
with the knowledge of concrete objects of knowledge, in perception or
representation. All the inherent characters of a mental image are known
in the concrete by the fact of its presentation. That is what presentation
means.

(2) I look out of the window and see a beautiful old elm. According to
the theory there should be a perceptual act of judgment or assertion that
the elm exists. But all I find is the elm; no act of assertion on my part
whatsoever. (That my past experience modifies and enriches my present
perception is of course well-known; but this has taken place automatically
when the elm appears to me.) If I open my eyes and look, the elm is there
of itself, so to speak. And if I know an absent object or another person's
feelings, the case in this respect is just the same: they are there existent
before the mind (in whatever guise or symbolism – depending on one's
type of imagination); I am not in any wise *affirming* their existence.
Professor Stout himself, speaking of the 'acts' here in question, tells us:
"... the word act must not be taken to signify activity" (p. 357). If 'act' is
not to mean act I would respectfully suggest that the word should not be
used. But not all those who take the position make this disclaimer, and
there lingers the notion of an activity in the matter.

(3) "All knowledge is of propositions; to know is always to know
that...", "that something is or exists or occurs..." etc. Now knowledge
is one thing; language expressing knowledge is another. A sentence with

its words in train is the result of the form of the human mouth, tongue, etc.: not of the form of knowledge. If I say "There is an elm out there on the lawn", the sentence is consecutive and prolonged but the thought is instantaneous, its parts concomitant. If we were hydra-headed, if we had a number of mouths our at disposal, all the words of such a sentence might be discharged simultaneously (and ears be trained to take them in), and correspond more closely to the form of consciousness than now. To express knowledge or belief is to speak or write or make other signs. That is an action. It does not follow that the knowledge or belief is an action. Just so, to tell what I know or believe, employing those verbs, is to say "I know or believe *that* – ". It does not follow that the form of the sentence is a key to the form of the consciousness expressed. We may say truly that in all knowledge we know "that...", but we may quite as fitly say that we know *something*, some *reality*.

(4) What is belief? It is independent reality appearing to the mind or seeming to appear. And it has just the same character in thought as in the perception of the external world. If I open my eyes and look at an object, the object is there, and remains there or changes, of itself, quite independently of my will. There is an 'if', namely, *if* I look at it. Just so in the case of thought. When my thought is a belief, then *if* I think of the matter, the object presents itself, constituted in a particular manner, of itself, independently of my will, and persists in so doing. Belief is the spontaneous self-maintenance of the idea before the mind in its own fashion and configuration. It involves nothing but image; it is the way the images behave. In so far as I tamper with the idea, in so far as I shape and reshape it according to my will, what we have is imagination and not belief. (Of course, too, I *act* as if the object were constituted as it appears and in imagination I do not. But the purely mental difference remains.) In other words, belief is an involuntary conception. If I transform the image, if I tear it apart, reconstruct it, play with it, then as soon as I let it alone again it comes back of itself to its former conformation.

Of course the images of my fancy are just as real as the images of my belief. But they do not make up into a world to which I find I have to conform. I have no reason to hold them responsible for revealing *qualia* that persist when they, the images, have ceased to be. But experience tells me that my perceptions do reveal such *qualia*, and my elementary beliefs, beyond perception, carry on the work of my perceptions. A world that is not under the fiat of my volition thus appears to me. The fact that whenever I turn my mind to the subject things present themselves in their own obstinate manner, and not according to my wishes, is my only safety. I need images that behave like the objective world and in my beliefs I have them. Belief is thus by function and in ideal our means of experiencing the object in thought as if it were our sensation, as if its existence were presented directly.[4]

(5) Since Mr Stout, so far as he is concerned, does not wish judgment or belief to be understood as literally an act of mental assertion, just what remains of his thesis? Apparently that in judgment there is a state of consciousness such that *its purport can be expressed* only by a proposition. Well, there is such a state of consciousness in the cases we are considering. And it is the mere presence of concrete *qualia* to the mind.

By what logical right can a mere experience or presentation be *expressed as* an assertive sentence? The answer is very simple. It might seem as if a mere datum before the mind were equivalent to a term, not a proposition. But this impression would be a mistake. The datum is an existent and its existence is given. A term by itself is not intended to express existence. The expression of the datum as datum must be an expression of existence and in the established forms of language that can only be a proposition.

By way of bringing out this relation, which Mr Stout will not allow, of a presentation to a proposition, perhaps the reader will indulge me if I play for a few moments a somewhat whimsical technical game. Suppose somebody meditating philosophically on a sensation he is experiencing says, "This sensation is real, it exists". (The peculiar logical or extra-logical character of the word 'this' is well known, but it has a clear and unquestionable significance.) His logical warrant for uttering a proposition lies in the fact that for him it is (to use Kant's inadequate and unfortunate term) an analytic proposition. Existence *means* nothing but that of which he has a specimen immediately given in the sensation he feels. The subject of his proposition, 'this sensation', standing for a present experience, *already for him contains all that is asserted in the predicate*. An analytic proposition is self-evident; its 'logical warrant' will not be disputed. He has a right to say it since the sensation is present to him. All this is merely a formal way of showing that the proposition expresses only what is contained in the datum; that there is nothing in the proposition which is not already in the presentation.

Nothing, that is, of the nature of concrete knowledge. Of course in the words 'exist' and 'sensation' he is using generic terms, and there were no generic ideas in the sensation. But that is not due to the deficiency of a sensation as an object of knowledge but to the deficiency of the language at his disposal. He has to resort to a common noun and to a verb (all verbs are of course common). There can not be a proper name for everything. If *per impossibile* there were proper terms naming his particular present experience and nothing else and conveying their meaning to the hearer, he could have used them instead. And it would then have been just as true that his language conveyed the realization of a concrete existence and that it truly rendered what was given in a mere presentation. To enable other people to perceive or feel the sensation as that of another is impossible, but would be an ideally complete communication. Moreover, to use class-terms does not make the mind's original object a proposition. It is not knowledge as such (not all knowledge) but the expression of knowledge that involves generic terms, as also it involves proposition. The sole point of the last paragraph is that the non-propositional form of the datum does not prevent its giving birth to a proposition as its legitimate expression or partial expression in language.

'Generic ideas' have just been mentioned. We must remember that, speaking from a strictly psychological, not a logical, standpoint, the content presented to the mind when we have such ideas is always concrete, however vague or fragmentary; there is no other kind of content to be presented. The generic character of the idea, psychologically, lies not in its presented content but in its associations and its results in action; in the subsequent discrimination, in thought and practice, to which its presence commits the mind; in the function of what is presented, not in its content. (This principle explains 'imageless thought'). Or, to put it in terms of the physical mechanism instead of the mental, in dispositions of the brain. When I say that the sensation 'exists' I have brought into consciousness that word with its possible associations, and perhaps the nascent idea of a possible consciousness in which that sensation is *not* present, with which consciousness I contrast the actual one. But the great danger is to suppose already existent in a state of thought those features that readily and instantly would be added to it if the thought paused to render itself more explicit. The only purpose of using the word 'exists' is to convey that the concrete experience is there, and (possibly also) *not* not there; in other words to convey, so far as possible, *this experience,* and not permit it to be disbelieved in.

Thus there is nothing in a proposition to which there corresponds any mental content or thought-stuff but images or 'feelings'.

Professor Stout tells us " ... the present feeling [by itself] cannot be apprehended as present; for this involves the thought of its relation to a before and after" not included in the feeling itself. But presence to consciousness does not mean presentness in time; it is a distinct and elementary fact, otherwise expressed as appearance, phenomenality, the being experienced. From the point of view of the consciousness itself presence or non-presence does not involve a reference to the time-system beyond the passing experience. Moreover, the feeling does not have to be apprehended *as* present, it only has to *be* present, that is, be apprehended.

Again, it may be said that 'exists' expresses present time and this involves a reference to the time-system, which transcends the datum itself. But it is quite a mistake to suppose that the experience of reality that we communicate in such a case involves looking before and after. We can do so instantly at need but very commonly are absorbed in the present experience. 'Exists' or 'is real' is the term at hand to use, but it must not be supposed that all its formal implications are present to the mind of the user. Once again the difficulty lies in the limited resources of language. Our conception of the time-system is something we build up. As was long ago remarked, the Kantian doctrine would have its bricks built of houses.

So far we have been instancing only a sensation of one's own. Continuing our game, let us turn to the case of a belief in objects or minds as remote as you will. The assertion, "These things exist". is *for the believer* an analytic proposition, for 'these things' appear in his consciousness as existent. Here too what he affirms in his predicate is already *for him* a character of his subject. (Of course this would not be true for an impersonal logic but only from his point of view; the very idea expressed by the word 'these' would not be admissible for an impersonal logic.) That is, the passage in this case from the presence of the images (behaving beliefwise) or, in other words, the presence of the *qualia* that he contemplates, to the propositional expression has *for him* a complete logical warrant. Whether he *should* believe, whether his proposition can be verified, is quite another question. It is not the justification of his belief that is given, *but the justification for his expressing it in the form of a proposition.* Once

more, existence *means only* that of which for him 'these things' are specimens. For him the logical case for expressing a presence to his mind as a
proposition is the same as with his sensation. This again is only a way of
pointing out that the proposition says no more, so far as conveying concrete existence is concerned, than is in the *quale* given. What Professor
Stout misses in the image and finds in the proposition is present in the
image.

The game is over. By throwing 'this', 'these', or certain kindred words
into the proposition we happen to be enabled to illustrate the universal
relation between the datum for a mind and the assertion which expresses
this datum or some feature of it; the relation by which, independently of
such words of peculiar status, the one logically authorizes the other. The
word makes the relation easily seen; but it is there whether easily seen or
not. If we insist on calling the datum equivalent to a mere term then it is
such a term that it generates a proposition; as the "egg of Pharoah's ser-
pent", when we apply to match to it, sends out of itself the crawling ser-
pent. By the nature of knowledge on the one hand and language on the
other, that which appears to the mind is simply the existent itself, while
that which is uttered is required to be assertion.

(6) A proposition, we are told, "is never a particular existence or occurrence". Certainly, that something once happened is an 'eternal truth'. We
have to reckon forever with "the fact that" it happened. But this impressive statement only means that it did happen, and that anyone, at any
time, who says it didn't is making a mistake. To cognize the fact the mind
has only to have the event presented as happening, – in just the right
cosmic and historic place and relations. To believe in 'facts' or 'eternal
truths' we do not have to superadd a ghostly realm of 'propositions' to
our world of existence, we have only to cognize and recognize our world
of existence and each of its items as they really are or were.

(7) Universals, including a variety of logical entities – what they are in
themselves, – there is no space here to discuss. But the subject offers no
difficulty to the solution here proposed of the problem of knowledge.
Certainly that solution does not in any respect confound the logical point
of view with the psychological.

The title of this article is in the form of a question and though it has had
to be briefly and hence positively expressed, the title correctly represents
the spirit of inquiry behind most of it. Any reader of this JOURNAL who

will, either in its pages or privately, point out to the writer flaws in the reasoning above, will be most gratefully regarded as helping him toward his objective.

NOTES

[1] The problem, however, was first completely and compellingly stated, so far as my knowledge goes, by Josiah Royce in his earliest philosophical work, *The Religious Aspect of Philosophy*. Royce's own proposed solution I can not find solvent or even pertinent. But his extended statement of the problem itself is a model of lucidity and point, indeed a work of genius. His service in discerning and setting forth the difficulty should be acknowledged in the history of philosophy.

Professor Lovejoy's book, *The Revolt Against Dualism*, which is just such a searching critical examination of current theory as philosophy most needs, deals at the close with our present question. His account of the matter, which is psychological description, seems true and irrefutable. But does he quite meet Royce's philosophical difficulty? He tells us the content of our images, but leaves us confronting them; he does not tell us how we get at an object distinct from all images. Royce would, I think, have felt that Professor Lovejoy did not face the final problem. Yet all that he does say seems in accord with what is here suggested, which only attempts one step further.

[2] The word 'consciousness' as used in this article assumes nothing beyond those 'fields' of inclusion and exclusion in momentary experience which can not be denied.

[3] I am not assuming the identity of indiscernibles to be ideally or universally a true principle, only true for all purposes here in question.

[4] James Mill said that belief was "an inseparable association of ideas". The late Alfred Hodder in an unpublished manuscript said No, "a spontaneous association". I have taken over the latter conception (with change of terms) and compared it with the case of sense-perception.

A DEBT TO JAMES

[Among the several papers that Miller read at commemorative meetings for James in 1942 the following, presented at Columbia University, was the briefest but also the most probing in respect to theory of mind and knowledge. Like his contribution in 1908 to a volume of essays from Columbia honoring James, this one concentrates on implications of James's view of consciousness as an undecomposable "field of experience", a field that is not an object since it has only one aspect and no hidden components, is not in space, and is itself the identity of appearance and reality.

In 1908 Miller sought to show that such a view of consciousness was incompatible with 'natural realism', the thesis that consciousness and physical object are identical in perception as James held in his 'radical empiricism'. Rather, natural realism must be interpreted and completed in the direction of Mill's position, namely, that "unperceived objects *are* possibilities of successive experience to us" but not classed as such. Now, in what follows, Miller concludes from James's view of consciousness that "existence, actuality, can have but one aspect", so ultimate truth in contrast to the provisional truth Mill had formulated would "approximate panpsychism" and bring "the physical world into kinship with psychic fact".

Miller's "debt to James" as to the nature of consciousness was a permanent part of his thinking. It guided his criticism in 1911 of E. A. Singer's view that consciousness is observed or probable behavior and his subsequent criticism in 1951 of Gilbert Ryle's similar view based on linguistic analysis.]

What I here describe and state is but one of many intellectual debts to James, but it stands out to my own mind as a very notable one. When I went to study in the Department of Philosophy in which James was a professor, I had already for several years been interested in the subject. My invaluable teacher at the University of Pennsylvania, Professor

George Fullerton, had referred to the possibility of there being what he called "a dark chamber of the mind" underlying and influencing the consciousness we know. We did not settle for ourselves or much discuss the question.

Further, in my reading I found W. K. Clifford setting forth that our feelings are compounded of units of which we are not aware: I have a sensation which in reality is made up perhaps of thousands of elementary bits of "mind-stuff". To speak thus was to regard experiences such as sensations as in this respect comparable to matter: that what we know is made up of a multitude of parts that we do not directly know. And oı course such conceptions appeared in other literature as well.

I began as a pupil of James in a course of instruction in which, throughout the college year, the class read his *Principles of Psychology* and discussed it with him. We soon came to the chapter in the first volume entitled 'The Mind-Stuff Theory'. I have always regarded the twelve pages of this chapter, 163–175, as a masterpiece of exact thought and exposition. It had the precision that I for one miss in his *Pragmatism*, in *The Will to Believe*, and in some other quarters. James was a man of many sides; his organ had many stops. Here was drawn the stop of pure intellectual penetration. These pages cleared up completely and for good, so far as I was concerned, the possibilities of "a dark chamber of the mind" and of unfelt bits of mind-stuff. This, I believe, was one of those distinct and decisive steps forward in philosophy, not to be retraced or successfully disputed, which are so rare, so clarifying, so ordering, and so inspiriting.

James meets acutely each of the arguments for "unconscious consciousness", but what helped me most signally were his remarks on what the nature of consciousness permits. "The essence of a feeling", he said, "is to be felt, and as a psychic existent *feels*, so it must *be*". There cannot be any unfelt fact of feeling. Thus he swept away at one stroke the whole dream of mental molecules and also that of a dark cellarage of the mind. This single remark of his, gathering up and giving force to his extended arguments, reverberated in my own mind and has remained with me ever since. I gained a new conception: that consciousness is the realm where appearance and reality coincide.

Let me try to state what this thought seems to involve.

(1) A hasty critic, renewing a train of ideas that was in vogue some years ago, might object that the essence of a feeling is, not to be felt, but to feel;

that it is the 'content' or object-matter or sensatoin-*quale* which is felt. In strictness of speech this is correct, but it does not detract from James's thought. The defect is in our language, not in his principle. The phrase he used expresses the pith of the matter more briefly than any other at his disposal. The word 'consciousness' and much more the word 'feeling' are often employed as including the 'content'. It is, I repeat, correct to draw a distinction between the consciousness and the content, but this does not impair the force of James's principle. The content or object-matter of the consciousness *as such*, in other words, just so far as we are conscious of it, just so far as it is an affair of mind, is subject to all he says. It *is* just so far as we are conscious of it, and it *is not* just so far as we are not conscious of it. To be sure, it is quite conceivable that something of which we are conscious should continue to exist when we are no longer conscious of it. But as an object of consciousness it does not then exist. It is no longer a mental fact. It is important to form a clear conception of the mental, of the field of experience, of just what appears and what does not appear in it, and of the absurdity of saying that appearances can exist and still be called appearances, or the equivalent, when they do not appear. It is the category of the mental or psychic, the subject of psychology, which is in question, and what notions about it are permissible. Putting James's principle in other words, the being of a field of consciousness is to be experienced. The conclusion follows from the meaning of the terms and from the constantly experienced facts to which they refer us.

(2) It has been imagined that James was inconsistent with his own principle here stated when he took up the belief in a "subliminal consciousness" or "unconscious mind". This is to misconceive his principle. To say that I cannot have unfelt feelings is not to deny that somebody else has feelings unfelt by me. The meaning of the saying is that, from the force of the term, there can be nothing in a being's consciousness of which he is not conscious. But of another person's consciousness he is not conscious at all. And toward his "subliminal consciousness" or "unconscious mind" or what is sometimes called in execrable English "his unconscious" his relation will be exactly the same as that toward another mind. His "unconscious mind", if it exists, is not unconscious at all; but he is unconscious of it. It is 'his' only in the sense that it is connected with his brain, not another man's. It is often somewhat hastily inferred that there must be such another consciousness connected with our organism,

from evidence that might rather indicate unconscious cerebration in that organism itself. In any case, if there is, it need be a consciousness no more dark or dim than our own familiar one; it is merely separated from our own like another mind.

(3) The material thing has many aspects. I can look at its other sides. I can pry it apart and look into it. I can almost without end carry on the process of detecting smaller and smaller parts within it. But the field of consciousness as such has *only one aspect*, that which is experienced, just to the extent to which it is experienced. It is idle to look for the underside or hidden components or interior recesses of the field of consciousness; it has none. These expressions carry no meaning as applied to it. It has not even a finer grain – what we perceive if we look closer and sharper at a surface before us – for the moment the finer grain discloses itself we have not the same field, but a new one.

(4) The field of consciousness is *not an object*. If you want to know what its nature is, what its being is, what its substance is, you must look at it *from the subjective point of view alone*. The moment you step aside from the purely subjective point of view, the point of view of the experient, and regard the fact as an objective entity that may, like a material thing, keep secrets from the experient, have unknown features subsisting within it, you err, you are wandering. If its nature puzzles you, go back to the subjective point of view, try to regard the fact as the experient regards it, and remind yourself that the view of it you take there is the one, the only one, that reveals to you its nature; it has no other nature or being than that. An object is a continuing existence that offers a plurality of aspects and can be investigated from without. A field of consciousness cannot be regarded from without at all. It is desperately difficult for our minds to learn to confine themselves about anything to this subjective mode of conception, for our life makes us constantly move among the varying aspects of things, turn things over, advance further into things, and our habit of doing so in thought is inveterate. Nevertheless, the abstinence from this habit must in this case be learned if we would grasp what a field of conciousness really is.

(5) In saying that it cannot be known from without, we do not mean that it might not be known by a representative image. We may know the thoughts and experiences of others by representation, and in the wider sense of the word 'objects' they thus become objects of our thought.

But our representation of them must be governed by the knowledge and rule that there is nothing of them to be known but what is presented to the possessor – in which respect they differ absolutely from objects in the narrower sense.

(6) A field of consciousness is not in space. It cannot be treated as a thing of which we say "Lo, here!" or "Lo, there!" Of course, the field presented may be in parts or as a whole a spatial field, may have extension, in some sense perhaps always has it. But it does not follow that the field as a whole is "in space". What we mean by the space of our objective world is a thing penetrable, traversable, investigable; it is its very nature to permit transition, different positions, at least for thought; to involve that system of complex relative perspective in which each point offers itself as a possible center. This space is divisible and yields ceaselessly new aspects to the investigator, just like the material object; the material object does so because it is in space. Since the field of consciousness has but one aspect, which aspect is to be known from the subjective point of view only, and is divisible, if at all, not in the same manner or degree, such a field cannot be coincident with a portion of objective space.

(7) James's insight on this subject was typical of him as a psychologist, indeed as a thinker in general; he is so often pointing out to us a peculiar impression of some sort, a special quality of experience, and declining to allow it to be conceived as built up of units. He had, as it were, an individual mission in psychology, to insist on the unique, the *sui generis*, the undecomposable integer. Consider, for example, the doctrine of space. According to Hume any spatial field of view consists of *minima visibilia* placed beside each other. This was the very natural assumption of the psychologist at an early stage, who proceeded to deal with mental facts as we do with matter. To this naïve notion James opposed impressively the thought of a sense of bigness, a sense of extensiveness, a sense of depth, a sense of volume, as ultimate unitary experiences that could not be resolved into parts at all. The transition from Hume's visual space, with its component points in rows, so to speak, to James's ultimate sense of spatial quality is one of the most striking steps in the history of psychology and philosophy. And it concerns us when we come to consider in what sense a 'content' is divisible.

(8) A field of consciousness is divisible only in the sense that there may be in it two or more parts that can be conceived, just as they are, indepen-

dently of each other. In that case the subtraction of one need not alter the nature of the other. Be it noticed that I speak of what is conceivable, not of what for physiological reasons is practically possible or impossible.

(9) It is correct, I said, to draw a distinction between consciousness and its object-matter or content. But what of the consciousness as thus distinguished, what of the experiencing, or the cognitive ego that experiences? I think we are forced to regard this as a relation between the parts of the content (if there are parts), which relation does not exist between one's own content and another man's content, a relation that may be called co-experience and which is not capable of further analysis, but is an ultimate idea like that of time-relation. There is no conscious entity or pure ego or subject of consciousness or of feeling not resolvable into this co-experience and nonco-experience of the content. If the content of consciousness is not in any sense plural, if there are no really distinct parts, then the sole fact in point is that this content stands in a relation of non-co-experience toward what we call the content of another man's consciousness. This view agrees, at least on the negative side, with that of Hume; also with that of James when he declares that "the passing thought is the thinker" and when in his later days he asked, "Does 'Consciousness' Exist?" and answered (in his own sense) "No".

When we say that our alleged "unconscious mind" would be separated from the consciousness we know just as another mind is separated, what we mean may be expressed thus: the relation of co-experience which exists between different parts of the content (when there are different parts) in the consciousness we know does not exist as between the contents of that consiousness and those of the subliminal consciousness. Its not existing between them makes them, properly speaking, two minds, not one.

(10) But, it may be said, if the physical world has many aspects, why cannot a field of consciousness be one of them? Granted that physical nature is such that we are constantly making the transition from one phase to another, granted that it reveals one aspect after another to the investigator – well, each one of the these in the investigator's perception is a field of consciousness.

I think the answer is that if we say this we are simply altering our idea of space for the purpose, or simply promising ourselves to alter it in any respect that may be required, in order to accommodate all mental facts.

We are changing our idea of space into an obscure, a not-all-specified idea. We are holding it indeterminate, because we do not know what have to go into it. We are calling an aggregate spatial because we desire to do so, though we do not as yet see in detail just how it is or can be spatial.

First, we have introduced into physical nature a totally new kind of fact, a fact previously in our thought totally alien to it, namely, an indivisible 'field' or one divisible in a manner utterly different from that on which known objective entities in space are divisible. Secondly, we have introduced into physical nature a kind of rift or fissure that we had certainly not conceived as being there at all, the relation of nonco-experience, the relation that constitutes the isolation of a man's consciousness, the fact that it is cut off from anyone's experiences but his own, hence from all the rest of the world outside of them. In saying this I am not assuming any theory, I am referring to one of the most familiar realities of life. It becomes now a feature, here and there, of the world in space. Thirdly, in our naïve notion of a physical world a merely perceptual field (which is only part of the field of consciousness) fits perfectly as an aspect of that world; that is exactly what in daily life we take it to be: but when we find out that this perceptual field cannot come into existence except when radiations from the object have reached eye, nerve, and brain, when we find out that the object might cease to be before the field comes into existence, when we find that we must locate it with the perceiving organism, not with the object, then it does not fit at all. It is a fact superadded to the known physical attributes of eye, nerve, and brain and sustaining a very peculiar relation to them. Fourthly, in the field of consciousness, together with percepts, are ideas – for instance, of the future, imaginations, intentions, and so forth – that we cannot conceive as located in the physical world.[1] If, recognizing all this, you still place mental fields in objective space as amongst its aspects, are you not simply altering your idea of objective space in an unspecified way in order to force their admission? What is the difference between your assertion and what was thought before, namely, that mental facts are a kind of fact arising when the brain works in a particular way? You have not really added to your idea of the field of consciousness or made any change regarding it whatever; nor can you, for all you know about it you get from an ultimate source of information, the subjective point of view, which cannot be superseded by ulterior knowledge or in any wise tampered with.

Minds are in nature, which may be defined as consisting of matter
(physical reality, whatever it may be) and the minds of animals. But this
does not oblige us to say that they are in space or in physical nature.

(11) James's notion has an interesting relation to Descartes' (who,
despite his gesture of rejecting all past philosophy, appears to have derived
it from Augustine). When Descartes says, "I think, therefore I am", he
explains in effect that he means, " I am conscious, therefore I am". This
which is present to me in a moment of consciousness indisputably exists
to the extent that it is present. What is behind his "clear and distinct"
discernment of this truth is that it is from such phenomena that I gain the
very idea of an existent. I cannot question their existence, because they
are what I mean by 'existents'.

Descartes is here engaged in forming the very difficult notion of consciousness, difficult because it so abruptly contrasts with the notion of
anything else. When he says that the soul is a substance whose only attribute is *cogitatio*, having explained that by *cogitatio* he means consciousness, he is approximately asserting James's doctrine. He holds that
the soul always exists, even during sleep, since then it is continuously
dreaming. He goes on to say that it has no need of a place to exist in and
has no local motion.[2] It would be unmeaning to speak of something that
is not an object as if it could go from place to place. But Locke holds
otherwise. A man's soul, he says, being united to his body, "constantly
changes place all the whole journey between Oxford and London, as the
coach or horse does that carries him, and I think may be said to be truly
all that while in motion".

The coach as well as the horse in those days being subject to a good deal
of jolting, it would be interesting to describe the geometrical locus of the
soul during "all the whole journey between Oxford and London". We
have to say, however, that though the soul or consciousness perceives in
succession the scenes between Oxford and London, it has no meaning to
say that it changes place along with the body, for it is nothing but that
succession of scenes, sensations, thoughts, and so forth, that present
themselves during the journey, and these as mental facts have no qualities
but those that are experienced.

(12) F. H. Bradley's work, *Appearance and Reality*, has for its thesis, as
we know, that appearance cannot be reality. James's principle shows us
at once the error here. The being of appearance is to appear. It is from

appearances, once again, that we gain the idea of reality. They are thus for our thought the original standard realities. We may learn of other realities of the greatest importance, but we can never unlearn that appearances are real, even if they are illusions in reference to realities beyond themselves. If so, they are real illusions. Bradley argues that appearance is self-contradictory, hence must be unreal. But appearance cannot contradict itself, for it does not say anything. We may make assertions about it that contradict themselves, but that is another matter.

(13) Thus far I have been speaking, for clearness' sake, with a reserve which I ask the reader to forgive me. I have spoken as though, while a psychic existent had only one aspect, an objective existent had many. It is now time to note perhaps the most momentous of all the results at which James's admirable perception helps us to arrive. Existence, actuality, can have but one aspect. All its constituent parts and features must in such wise co-exist that a thought which perfectly knew them would contemplate them all at once in their whole nature. No system of exchangeabilities can be literally the real world. 'Aspects', in the plural, arise from the superficiality of our physical perception. Any view of the objective world which regards it as consisting of or revealing itself in aspect after aspect presented to the advancing percipient is really regarding it as merely "a permanent possibility of experience", or regarding it in a provisional, a temporary, a superficial manner, without for the moment troubling itself to ask what the adequate and ultimate truth would be. Now this provisional, not final, way of thinking of it is really our established human way and also our established scientific way, for a most radical species of physics; and even such furthest-going physical theory is prone to forget the requirement we now see.

A field of consciousness cannot be an aspect of the physical world because in the last analysis it has no mere aspects. And it cannot be a constituent part of physical world unless that world ceases in our conception to be 'physical', as the term was previously understood. Meanwhile, the character that all reality is seen to possess, of having only one aspect, brings the physical world into kinship with psychic fact. To that extent we may approximate panpsychism, though not in Clifford's form of a molecular mind-stuff.

NOTES

[1] James himself, in 'A World of Pure Experience', suggests that such part of the content of consciousness as is personal and private, not a part of the objective world, bears a spatial relation to that world which he symbolizes by the decorations hanging about the skull of a Dyak of Borneo. What this spatial relation literally is, however, and how and why one portion of space is public and another private I do not understand him to explain.

[2] This is, of course, inconsistent with his statement in *The Passions of the Soul* that its "principal seat" is the pineal gland, if we are to take the latter literally.

UNIVERSALS

[As indicated by references in the text, the following piece was written as a chapter for a book, never published, that would show the method of analysis at work. It was completed, Miller reported, late in 1943 and was intended to accompany revisions of his articles on the knowledge-problem, free will, and Hume.

Miller proposes to deal with the difficulty remaining in Berkeley's otherwise admirable analysis of abstract ideas or universals by distinguishing between the content and function of ideas, by showing with pointed illustrations – a red book, the number forty, and 'all' or 'nothing' – how an idea is general not by virtue of its particular content but the way it leads us to behave in thought and action, the way its content "can *do duty* as the representative of a class" by its associations. In explaining this distinction Miller reproduces verbatim key paragraphs of his article of 1895, the article that had reconfirmed James's "sometime wavering opinion" on the subject and thus provided an important ingredient of pragmatism.

To clarify and defend his view of universals as functions, Miller analyzes confusions in the 'concrete universal' from Hegelian idealism as held by Royce, in Santayana's 'essences' that do not exist, in the neo-realists' doctrine that universals 'subsist', and in Husserl's claim that universals are 'intentional' objects, a claim that Miller finds to be a failure of analysis and resort to a *causa occulta*. During his European retirement Miller had attended Husserl's lectures in Germany and also his Sunday evening conversations, renamed 'adversations' by those who attended since Husserl did all the talking. Husserl once told Miller that his 'phenomenology' must be taken as it stands, not mixed with Heidegger's ideas or Miller's own. The caution was gratuitous for Miller as shown in what follows.]

Philosophic writers, notably Mr Bertrand Russell, raise a question whether there really are universals. The reader of this book will not be in the least doubt as to what is its position on the matter. Of course there are universals; the question is, in what do they consist? Of course our minds have cognizance of universals. The question is, in what does this cognizance consist?[1]

Since Berkeley's 'Introduction' to his *Principles of Human Knowledge* this has been treated in the main as a bye-problem, of secondary or tertiary importance. It is astonishing how little, comparatively, it has been faced, for in the consequences at stake it is surely of the first importance.

Berkeley believed, it will be remembered, that he had "shown the impossibility of Abstract Ideas". What he in effect did was to offer an analysis of abstract ideas, which was substantially, so far as it went, a true analysis. His 'Introduction' itself as a matter of course abounds in them and proceeds by means of them; but he wished to show us just what happens in the mind when we employ either abstract or generic terms of thought – such a term as 'humanity' or such a term as 'a man'. But this particular analysis brought paradoxical conclusions and we must do justice to them in their first paradoxical seeming before we remind ourselves in detail just how they really harmonize with our daily certainty that we can and do think in the abstract.[2]

PROPOSITION 1.   *We never in any single thought confront or perceive the abstract or the generic, any more than we do so in sense-perception; what is before the mind at any one moment is invariably concrete; the abstract or the generic cannot be presented in a 'content' or in any one consciousness.*

Locke asked, "Since all things that exist are only particulars, how come we by general terms?" His answer is: "Words become general by being made the signs of general ideas". No, says Berkeley, "a word becomes general by being made a sign, not of an abstract general idea, but of several particular ideas, any one of which it indifferently suggests to the mind".

Familiar as the passage is, it will be convenient to have before us Berkeley's statement both of the view the rejects and of his own view:

We are told, the mind, being able to consider each quality singly, or abstracted from those other qualities with which it is united, does by that means frame to itself *abstract ideas*. For example, there is conceived by sight an object extended, coloured, and moved:

this mixed or compound idea the mind resolving into its simple, constituent parts, and viewing each by itself, exclusive of the rest, does frame the abstract ideas of extension, colour, and motion. Not that it is possible for colour or motion to exist without extension; but only that the mind can frame to itself by abstraction the idea of colour exclusive of extension, and of motion exclusive of both colour and extension.

Again, the mind having observed that in the particular extensions perceived by sense there is something common and alike in all, and some other things peculiar, as this or that figure or magnitude, which distinguish them one from another, it considers apart, or singles out by itself, that which is common; making thereof a most abstract idea of extension; which is neither line, surface, nor solid, nor has any figure or magnitude, but is an idea entirely prescinded from all these. So likewise the mind, by leaving out of the particular colours perceived by sense that which distinguishes them one from another, and retaining only that which is common to all, makes an idea of colour in abstract; which is neither red, nor blue, nor white, nor any other determinate colour. And, in like manner, by considering motion abstractedly, not only from the body moved but likewise from the figure it describes, and all particular directions and velocities, the abstract idea of motion is framed; which equally corresponds to all particular motions whatsoever that may be perceived by sense.

And as the mind frames to itself abstract ideas of *qualities* or *modes*, so does it, by the same precision, or mental separation, attain abstract ideas of the more compounded beings which include several co-existent qualities. For example, the mind having observed that Peter, James, and John resemble each other in certain common agreements of shape and other qualities, leaves out of the complex or compound idea it has of Peter, James, and any other particular man, that which is peculiar to each, retaining only what is common to all, and so makes an abstract idea, wherein all the particulars equally partake; abstracting entirely from and cutting off all those circumstances and differences which might determine it to any particular existence. And after this manner it is said we come by the abstract idea of *man*, or, if you please, humanity, or human nature; wherein it is true there is included colour, because there is no man but has some colour, but then it can be neither white, nor black, nor any particular colour, because there is no one particular colour wherein all men partake. So likewise there is included stature, but then it is neither tall stature, nor low stature, nor yet middle stature, but something abstracted from all these. And so of the rest....

Whether others have this wonderful faculty of abstracting their ideas, they best can tell. For myself, I dare be confident I have it not. I find indeed I have a faculty of imagining, or representing to myself, the ideas of those particular things I have perceived, and of variously compounding and dividing them. I can imagine a man with two heads; or the upper parts of a man joined to the body of a horse. I can consider the hand, the eye, the nose, each by itself abstracted or separated from the rest of the body. But then whatever hand or eye I imagine, it must have some particular shape and colour.[3] Likewise the idea of man that I frame to myself must be either of a white, or a black, or a tawny, a straight, or a crooked, a tall, or a low, or a middle-sized man. I cannot by an effort of thought conceive the abstract idea above described. And it is equally impossible for me to form the abstract idea of motion distinct from the body moving, and which is neither swift nor slow, curvilinear nor rectilinear; and the like may be said of all other abstract general ideas whatsoever. To be plain, I own myself able to abstract in one sense, as when I consider some particular parts or qualities separated from others, with which, though they are united in some object, yet it is possible they may really exist without them. But I deny that I can abstract from one another, or conceive separately, those qualities which it is impossible should exist so separated; or that I can frame a general notion, by abstracting from particulars in the manner aforesaid – which last are the two proper accepations of abstraction.[4]

This Leaves a Difficulty

Now at once the question arises, Do we know at the moment of generic thought that the particular image or name will suggest the right particulars, Do we mean it to do so? Berkeley further writes, "the particular triangle I consider, whether of this sort or that it matters not, doth equally stand for and represent all rectilinear triangles whatsoever, and is in that sense universal". Do I know at the moment that it stands for and represents them? If not, why do I appear to myself to be thinking of the universal? If so, then I seem to have present in my mind an idea representing all rectilinear triangles in respect of their rectilinear triangularity, and hence to be thinking of the latter. "It must be acknowledged that a man may *consider* a figure merely as triangular; without attending to the particular qualities of the angles, or relations of the sides. *So far he may abstract.*" If a man may *consider* a figure merely as triangular, he is apparently considering its triangularity; in which case we do, after all, confront and envisage the abstract: we do have a content before the mind in which the universal presents itself in its universal nature, pure and simple, to a single consciousness. This, however, is the very thing that Berkeley has denied. For the careful reader, therefore, he leaves his doctrine with a frayed edge, a lingering puzzle, a want of satisfying clearness as to how this theory can be consistently carried through to the end. It seems as if at this point there were something like an unintended evasion, or failure to meet quite the entire difficulty. This then is our problem, which he leaves with us, and it is the whole problem over again.[5]

There have been purely verbal attempts to meet Berkeley's objection as to abstract thinking. It has been said that the 'content' before the mind may be concrete but we nevertheless *mean* the abstract or generic. A "sense of our meaning" which is "an altogether special bit of consciousness *ad hoc*" is what makes our thought cognizant of the universal. This gets rid of the problem by using another word and calling it an explanation. All the difficulties that Berkeley saw in the *idea* of the abstract or generic exist equally for a "bit of conciousness" of the abstract or generic, a 'meaning' whose 'object' is the abstract or generic. *How* can we mean it? How can such an object be in any wise before the mind? How can our meaning be distinguished from all mental content and yet be a form of consciousness with something to be conscious of? If it *has* a content of its own, that content must be concrete, since nothing else than the concrete appears in experience or in existence. If it has no content, that is, no object-matter before it, how under heaven can it mean or intend or refer to anything? A supposed perception or discernment, all in a moment, is attributed to that bit of consciousness which for the plainest reason, set forth by Berkeley above, may not be attributed to any consciousness. With the word 'meaning' we are taking the feat of knowledge on our part which our universal terms seem to us to imply, and ascribing it to a magical capacity in the mind that conveniently o'erleaps all the difficulties, we know not how. In this vein James Ward remarks that our cognition of the universal depends not so much on the content-side of our thought as on the 'intentional' side. And this remark actually appears to satisfy him. A like unconscious evasion of the whole difficulty vitiates Husserl's treatment of the topic. In comparison Berkeley's evasion was but slight and casual. What right have we to let our ungrudging recognition that we do in a true sense mean universals excuse us from attention to the psychological problem in what our meaning consists?

Symbols with Functions

To meet the puzzle we must take a further step. We repeat and also move forward.

PROPOSITION 2.   *Our cognizance of the universal (the abstract or generic) lies not in an intellectual vision of it, consummated in the moment, but in the fact our minds deal correctly with questions and instances as they come before us; it lies in our being so constituted as to make with mind and body the right reactions.*

In the affairs of the mind there is a clear distinction between content and function; between what an idea is in itself as a presence before the mind and what it results in or brings about in the operations of the mind. An idea has not only a particular content, it has a part to play in the mental life. It calls up other ideas; it influences the future course of thought and action. Now there tends to be a confusion in our psychology, a most natural confusion, between these two. It consists in taking for granted that if an idea works in a certain way it must consciously mean to work in that way, it must be aware at each step of its function and the logical considerations involved. The secret of its function must reside in its content. When we glide naturally forward from "a general idea" to dealing appropriately with relevant things and thoughts, that dealing must be simply a conscious logical carrying out of what lay in the idea.

It would be hard to imagine any assumption, in the first stages of inquiry, more easy and inevitable than this. It is suggested by our words. Yet it is unfounded. An idea may introduce another or lead to action, not through a purpose or plan contained in its own nature, but just by its connections, its associations.

The question before us is, how can we employ our minds about "any of a class" of things or about a pure attribute, if we are not in possession of an express idea of the generic or the abstract, distinct from any idea whatever of concrete particulars? How can we disengage those abstract elements, common as we say to a class, from the irrelevant particulars in which they are embodied in individuals and with which alone they exist?

The answer lies in this: there is another sense in which a mental state can represent a class. It can do so by its function, by the consequences it produces, by leading us to behave in action and in thought in the manner required by our desire. An image or other form of particular content can *do duty as* the representative of a class. By its associations it can prompt the right action toward the members of the class and inhibit any false thoughts about them.

Consider some of the typical cases. If we are giving practical instructions and must describe an object, the listener, if he have visual images, may form quite a false image on hearing our words, but will be correctly guided by these words to identify the object. If I tell a child to fetch a certain red book he may imagine at first quite a wrong shade of red; none the less the word 'red' he has heard serves him as a guide and, arrived at the spot, he picks up the right book, because, though it is not as he imagined it, its color is one of those called red.

When, as Berkeley says, we treat the triangle before us simply as a triangle, ignoring its differences from other triangles, we do this without there coming before the mind anything but concrete conceptions. The word 'triangle' (in the most deliberate case) leads us to note its three corners and straight sides and therewith to take it as one for which the word 'triangle' is a name; just as the word 'red book' made the child feel authorized to pick up a particular book although he might not have anticipated that shade of red. The idea of 'three' involves no content other than concrete. 'One, two, three' as applied to any object exhaustively will plainly give us what the word 'three' stands for. We do not for so small a number explicitly carry out the counting; as soon as we gain a perception that we recognize as answering to the name we are satisfied. In our geometrical reasoning we see that we can apply the words to the triangle before us and that any figure we could apply them to, large or small, is to be called 'triangle'. And 'same' and 'any', 'figure' and 'sides', etc., are terms, like 'red', (so far as they come to mind) that guide us when we come to act upon them, and therefore satisfy us now whenever we begin to think in advance of further cases – as in the present instances. In the light of experience nothing unsatisfactory suggests itself.

When a man says 'forty' he usually has not in his mind in any form even the precise number of units denoted by 'forty'. We deceive ourselves if we fancy he has. But he has a word, and in each case the appearance of a word 'forty' will call up all the proper specifications as they are needed. He can draw accurate conclusions about matters that turn upon the sum of forty, without having even that specification of just how many it is, for the same reason; at each turn where he has to recall the fact, or words standing for it and serving to guide others, he can do so.

(Even when I say a precise realization of forty units, my words may stand for any one of a variety of quite different mental contents or object-matters of consciousness; they would be alike only in this, that they would be nearer to the sense-perception of forty units set out before us in neat apprehensible order by tens and fives than is our ordinary verbal idea.)

To take a further instance, suppose we generalize in words, either in the affirmative or the negative. In the ancient proposition of the primers of logic, "All men are mortal", it is interesting to consider with reference to content and function the decisive word 'all'. In connection with its use in this case the mind has, and can have, no specific content whatever beyond the word itself, which has acquired psychological properties that are not at the moment a matter of complete consciousness. We could conceivably picture all the people in a room or all the food in a larder or all the money in a purse, just as we could conceivably see them. Seeing that they are 'all' means seeing the enclosing background and these things in it, and seeing nothing else of the sort there. But when in this general proposition we use the words about a class of beings scattered over all the world, its force is merely to make the mind reject the thought of any member of the class not characterized by the quality in question – that is, not adopt such a thought as a belief. The word 'all' is there for its function and not for its content. Similarly with the word 'no' or 'none'; for example, in "No men are immortal" its force is to make us reject any suggestion of a man who is immortal.

So it is with the idea of 'nothing'. If I am told, for instance, that a room has nothing in it and I accept the information, my mind is so *set*, as we say of a trap, that any thought of an object in the room is promptly dismissed so soon as it presents itself. Suppose we were told, to make a fantastic supposition, that before a certain date in the past nothing whatsoever existed. This is entirely conceivable – I do not mean credible. But the 'conception' while it lasted would consist of an attitude of the mind by which it stood ready to down any rising suggestion of existent things at that time. Our belief in it, if it became a belief, would be a standing indisposition on the mind's part to entertain any ideas of a certain character. Here the verbal sign has (save its sight, sound or articulation) no content, no corresponsive idea at all. Its content is swallowed up in its function. Do not tell me that this is "the grin without the cat" of popular fable. In truth it is comparable to the "potential energy" of the physicist. It is such a state of tendency in the mind as insures the prompt suppression of any intruding thoughts of a certain order. Thus our recognition of the *dictum de omni et nullo* depends wholly on function.

In all deduction the element of necessity depends upon this, that the process is a mere explication of what is already contained in the definable meaning of our premises. And the meaning, as thus followed out, makes itself effective through the function of the symbols employed. The necessity could not be secured by any conceivable images. A belief as to particulars could be constituted by images, if images were present, in so far as a sense-perception is so, but a general belief could not be so constituted. For 'all' and 'none' are not matters of imagery, or of any possible content. We are proceeding according to the established mode of dealing with words or other symbols. We are like one who has signed a contract the provisions of which, however, are not all present to his mind together at

any one time, but by which at any time he confesses himself bound. Such
is the psychological description of the mind's relation to its logical responsibilities.

Notice in all this how far one goes astray when one assumes that language in its structure is in any sort whatever the copy or the homologue
of thought. In language the predicate comes after the subject; in thought
they come together. In language they are connected by a copula; but
there is no copula in thought. In thought there is but content-stuff painted
in the pigments of the different sense, external and internal; content sup-
planting content in endless substitution. 'Action' and 'activity' are but
the names we give to certain sequences in the melting and merging contents as they pass. To say this is not to slight the idea of activity, which is
quite as momentous as it has been supposed to be; but only to take the
first step toward analyzing its mental side. To speak of an action of the
mind or the ego, of an activity of consciousness itself, and to leave the
matter there, when attempting the language of analytic psychology, is to
confess bankruptcy in analysis. In what successive elements of content
does the 'action' consist? Psychological study impresses us ever afresh
with the lesson that language is a mere system of signals, dependent for
its form and order on the structure and convenience of bodily organs.
Were we Hydra-headed or had we a hundred tongues, words might go
abreast, might group themselves in a thousand new fashions, and thus in
some respects more nearly take the shape of thought. But the broadest
disparities – such as those which this discussion has made prominent –
would still remain.

Confusions

Let us turn now from psychology to ask what universals are, and to guard
our thought from confusion respecting them.

PROPOSITION 3.   *Such is the power of words in the working of the mind
that they have even bred in the present subject a deceptive verbalism in
philosophy, semi-popular philosophy included.*

We say of a thing, "It has such and such qualities". Here the thing itself designated by the pronoun 'it' is one fact and the qualities which it
'has' are another. This is a natural form of words because commonly we
know something of the object already; when we say 'it' we mean it as we

already know it, and when we say "has" we affix to the object thus known the further quality mentioned. But this mode of speaking led, as we are aware, to the philosophical doctrine that every existent thing consisted of a substance possessing qualities, to which latter were reckoned *all* the attributes by which we know it. What then was the substance that possessed them?

From this ancient and familiar piece of self-deception we escape by our maxim "A thing is the sum of its qualities", which by comparison seems wholesome common sense. But alas! this maxim too, through the infection of verbalism, became a breeding-spot of fallacy. There is a sense in which a thing is the sum of its qualities and a sense in which it is emphatically not so. If by a quality is meant a universal such as greenness in general, that could be thought of without reference to particular things, then a thing is not the sum of its qualities. They would not sum up to thin air. You cannot make up a real thing out of mere natures or qualities as distinguished from particular existents. It cannot be composed of what does not exist. *But if by a quality on the other hand* is meant a *quale*[6] such as the actual concrete green presented by a particular surface then a thing is truly the sum of its qualities. It is the sum of its concrete *qualia*. The *quale* is not a universal, it is a particular reality. A universal, that is, a nature in general, is present in real things in the sense that there are real things whose nature, in the respect in question, as distinguished from their existence, is identical with it. It is of course indispensable for thought and life to consider a quality by itself, irrespective of its existence anywhere. But when we thus distinguish it as a universal it is important not to forget our distinction and fall to fancying that it is stuff to make things out of.

Mr Bertrand Russell remarks, both early and late in his writing, that it may seem possible to get rid of universals by reducing them all to the similarity of things, but that similarity itself is a universal, so since we must admit that universal we might as well admit all the rest. Now we cannot and need have no wish to "get rid of universals", but one may be permitted to express the conviction that the actual similarity of two or more actual things is not a universal but a concrete and particular fact.

The principle is simple. If something is existent it is not a universal. If it is a universal it is not existent. (The subtler question as to its logical 'subsistence' will be considered presently.)

I said above "irrespective of *its existence* anywhere".[7] Greenness exists in the world: yes, that is of course a proper way of expressing ourselves. Greenness means *being green* – an object's being green – and there are numberless objects that are green. Thus being green exists in the world. Greenness means having a *quale* that belongs to a certain class of *qualia*. When we say, speaking generally, that greenness exists we mean that particulars of this class exist. We do not mean that greenness in the abstract exists. To say that the universal is in this sense found in the particular is not to say that its universality is found in the particular. It keeps that all to itself. The universal makes its appearance when the quality is distinguished from the particular existent.

The confusion between quality in general and in particular arose naturally, for five reasons: (1) they are both called quality; (2) the more specific terms, color, solidity, shape, weight, also greenness and roundness etc. – all the terms however specific, – are used for both; (3) neither one exists apart from the object in which it is found; (4) they are separated from that object by processes called in both cases abstraction; (5) when we describe to others a concrete object we must use adjectives and common nouns, which are general terms, for there is nothing else to use; the limited resources of language oblige us to describe *qualia* in terms of abstract qualities. But in fact the union in objective space of concrete color, solidity, etc., the union of each with the remainder of the whole (profoundly interesting subject of study) is not the same relation as that of a mere nature to the different objects in which it is exemplified.[8]

The objection, by the way, might be raised that shape or figure, considered by itself, is a "geometrical ghost" which defies us to call it concrete. However, though like the other *qualia* it does not exist apart from the object, our whole experience of it is an experience of concrete peculiarities of the structure and quantity of the object. It consists of integral features of the object and if it did not would not be an actual attribute of it. The thing with another shape would have a different concrete constitution. That decides the point; I need not linger upon the important questions that arise here of exact analysis and expression.

It has been imagined that a thing itself with its *qualia*, because it continues to exist and is thus present in different times and relations, is a universal. The argument is that here is "the same" in different settings, just as universal is the same in different embodiments. They are alike, we are told, cases of "identity in difference". Yes, they are alike in that respect but flagrantly unlike in the relevant respect. The continuance of the same concrete group of *qualia* with changing relations, – or the continuance of part of the same concrete group of *qualia* with changing *qualia* and changing relations – does not make an existent into a bare nature that merely might exist. True, the existent as it was in one moment and as it is in another moment has a nature that is the same amidst differences, and that nature (considered independently of its particular embodiment and as possibly to be found in various embodiments) is a universal. But the thing itself is not a universal, and to call it so is to have lost one's bearings.

Again: we are often told that in the life of animals, including ourselves, the generic comes before the particular, that we respond in action to the type of phenomenon we meet, before we look sharply enough to single out the individual thing, and that we therefore know the universal before we know the particular. Without discussing the premise or raising any question about it, we may see at once that it does not mean that the animal is perceiving a universal, but only that he is failing to discriminate one object of perception or one sensation from another. Despite this omission, the content of each experience as it presents itself is in fact a concrete and particular phenomenon, being an instance of what we mean when we use those words – what gives them their meaning.

It is by distinction from the particular, and with reference to a possible realization in the particular, that the universal is defined and secures its entire significance. Any subsequent flights of theory that abandon or forget this distinction are flights into an intellectual chaos. When Professor Brand Blanshard tells us that there are no particulars but only universals I am afraid that he is in the mid-exaltation of such a flight.

Yet again: interminable confusion has been wrought by calling a single thing, or a section of concrete reality taken by itself, that is, without the remainder that influences it and which it influences, 'abstract'. The notion is that it is arbitrarily detached in thought from a whole, without which it could not live, so to speak, could not be what it is, somewhat as a single abstract quality is detached in thought from the objects in which it inheres. But to recognize a thing as a concrete existent, on the one hand, and to explain it or note causal influences upon or from it, on the other, are two matters, not one. To prove that it would not be in existence or be such as it is, unless numberless other factors were at work does not nullify the fact that it *is* in existence, is such as it is, and can be conceived as such, and therefore can be taken cognizance of in itself and be the subject of remarks about its existence, qualities and inner relations. Such cognizance is not explanatory but it is cognizance. The causal dependence of the thing's existence does not take away the existence itself; and the only reason we ascribe existence to any of the other and omitted things, or to the whole is the reason why we ascribe it to the single thing, namely, the ultimate fact that it appears, offers itself, in our experience. It has *what we mean by* concreteness and is therefore not abstract. And to call it 'abstract' in another and topical sense of the same word is not convenient, since it breeds inextricable confusion.

But, it is said, the relations to other things are constitutive of the thing itself, insomuch that we *cannot* take cognizance of the thing as it really is without taking cognizance of these relations. They are necessary to its concrete reality. The answer to this has already been given where we considered the principle of William James that "the essence of feeling is to be felt and as a psychic existent *seems* so it must *be*". In other words, any matter of experience of ours is certified as phenomenally existent by the fact we experience it and hence may be conceived as existent without reference to anything not given. Thus there are existents that obviously do not depend for their due conceivability as such on the thought of anything else whatever. At once we see that the question of separate conceivability and the question of explicability are two questions, not one. Obviously, particular things or their activities cannot be explained without reference to things beyond them. But they can be conceived in their concrete reality without reference to anything beyond them. Unending entanglement has been produced in the whole subject of abstract and concrete by confusing the quite different ideas of conception and explanation.

Calling 'abstract' a particular fact considered by itself is a part of what was suggested "the concrete universal"; fruitful and admirable conception indeed but burdened with a name that is a contradiction in terms. The whole as an organism in which a part has its place and function is not a universal but a concrete reality. Such a whole is not identical with the generic nature that characterizes each of the class to which its parts may belong; that is indeed a universal. Nor with the generic nature that characterizes a class of wholes to which the whole in question belongs, which is also a universal and not concrete.

We are admonished that such a way of classifying and of using terms as ours, which is characteristic of "the old logic" – and also of the newest logic – is sterile. Of course it is sterile. If it were not so, it would have to be sterilized, like the instruments for a surgical operation. It is the facts to which we should look for a rich fertility of suggestion, not our terms. Their virtue is to remain in meaning unaltered and exact – not to germinate on the way, in mid-reasoning, lest the infection of illicit conclusion creep in. And the writings that today magnify "the concrete universal" are typical 'cases' of just this peccant spontaneous germination of terms while reasoning is under way.

There appears to lurk in this topic of the particular and the general a peculiar seduction. Mr Santayana in his beautiful and deeply interesting work *Scepticism and Animal Faith* puts in the foreground the conception of 'essence'. If we use this term in the sense that has historically attached to it, it means what has just been called a nature. Mr Santayana appears to reach his conception as follows. Let us consider a perception and let us suppose it an illusion. Now let us

entertain the illusion without succumbing to it, accepting it openly as an illusion, and forbidding it to claim any sort of being but that which it obviously has .... It is no illusion now, but an idea.... It will appear dwelling in its own world, and shining by its own light, however brief may be my glimpse of it: for no date will be written on it, no frame of full or of empty time will shut it in.... It will be merely the quality which it inherently, logically and inalienably is. It will be an ESSENCE.

When the author tells us that it does not exist he is making the term essence conform to its traditional definition. But he adds that it is not abstract; and certainly an illusion of sense-perception such as he describes is not abstract, it is a concrete existence. Mr Santayana's assumption appears to be that when we detach any experience from its connections in our world, when we drop away its relations to time an space at large, when we take it for itself and look at it simply as it is in itself, we have converted it into an essence. If this be the proper construction to put upon his language, and it seems to permit of no other, an essence in his sense is not an essence in the historic sense of the term. It is not a mere nature, it is a concrete fact, perceived or imagined by itself. Every particular *quale* presented in our experience is a concrete existent, for it is an example of what we mean by an existent. According to the author, once again, an essence is not abstract, so it is apparently concrete, nevertheless it does not 'exist'.

"Nothing given exists", and the essence as just described is given.

Here there is no doubt a special sense attached by the author for convenience is attained. To detach an experience from its position in the history of the world and of our life, to consider it by itself, does not make of it a universal, and Mr Santayana's language in the book does seem to make an 'essence' according to usage, a universal. If such detachment did convert the concrete into the universal then most of our experiences would be such. For it is continually happening that what we at the moment experience, the little corner of the world that we have before us – as when we watch a game or look at a rippling stream or when in the midst of business our attention is wholly taken by present objects and small ideas – is not by us punctiliously read into its place in the great world or the stream of history. It is sufficiently absorbing in itself. Why should we be at the pains of such orientation? At all events we ordinarily are not so, but recall the connections of our passing experiences only when there is some need of doing it or some reminder. But such a scene of every day, undated by us and unlocalized in the world, does not thereby become a universal. It remains particular.

Do Universals Subsist?

A well-known school of thought that has raised its head again very confidently in the last half-century or so maintains that universals, being objects of thought, are independent objects and have a 'subsistence' apart from the mind that thinks about them. Thus length, height, wickedness, "the horse", humanity, divisibility, etc., have all in their opinion this subsistence distinct from our throught of them. They are not mere "abstract ideas", for that would mean that they are only in the mind, and hence when we do not think them they do not in any wise subsist. "No", says this school of thought, "when I am thinking about divisibility I am not thinking about an idea, I am thinking about something in itself as to which general propositions can be and must be maintained. I am thinking about a logical entity, so to speak". At different times I can think of one and the same universal, proving that it has an identity distinct from my transient thoughts. Divisibility does not *mean* an idea in the mind subsisting only when it is there, it means something in the realm of objectivities. It has reality, says Lotze, though not being. It has being, says Husserl, though not reality. If you deny this, if you speak as though universals were mere mental phenomena that come and go, you are substituting psychology for logic, you are committing the fallacy of 'psychologism'. You are blinding yourself to the intent and purport of your own thought. You are ignoring the realm of logic and its validities. Psychologism, as we know, is by this school declared to have been a great prevailing fallacy in British empirical philosophy.

Nevertheless, at this doctrine that universals 'subsist' there is something deep within us that says, "That is over the line. That is an extravagance. That does violence to the sober sense of fact". Let us see if this inner voice is confirmed by further thought.

(1) Universals disclose their relation to reality when we remember that they are qualities. That is what profess to be. A quality makes no profession to be subsistent apart from that of which it is the quality. Our propositions about them are propositions about what they are or would be as exemplified in things.

(2) A universal fortunately can be held in suspension in the mind by itself apart (for the time) from that in which alone it lives, but this is professedly a mere convenience a hand resort by the way, not a finality and resting-place. A universal is "something we can think of", but we think of it as subsisting only in particulars. Men at large would shake their heads incredulously at the idea that 'color' or 'shape' in the abstract had any being of its own.

(3) For this reason it is quite true that our ideas about it refer to the objective world, for they are ideas of the attributes of objects, of attributes that do or might attach to them. That is they refer to a world independent of the ideas themselves. How we are able to think of things of any sort with a status independent of the mind is a question already considered in the chapter on Knowledge. With universals we are employing the 'reference' there dwelt upon. In that respect no peculiar difficulty awaited us in the subject of abstract ideas.

(4) Our experience supplies us with the particular and it supplies us with semblance – a semblance that may be the same or prevailingly the same from particular to particular. We are able to consider the semblance, dropping the question what particular presents it. The character of our experience and of our reactions to it renders this inevitable as well as convenient. We are so constructed as to react to semblance. But there is

nothing to suggest that the semblance has any sort of reality except as presented by a particular. It is merely that explicitly conceiving a particular's individuality in the sequence of one's history, or in time and space, is one thing, and just contemplating its semblance and letting the rest alone is another thing. When we do the latter we are not assuming that the semblance is independent of the particulars; we are only taking advantage of the opportunity to consider it without particularizing.

Every semblance as at any time presented is in itself of course particular. But a semblance (or equally a symbol representing it) can be employed as standing for similar features in particulars. It does duty in this manner, as we have seen, through a mental function devolving upon it. Thinking of particulars and thinking thus of kinds are fundamentally different modes of thinking.

(5) Likeness is an ultimate fact, that is, it cannot be analyzed, cannot be resolved any further. The universal, which is built on it, is also ultimate, it cannot be resolved into a combination of simpler elements. That is, the character of the mind's outlook in thinking of it, what it is attending to and looking for, what it is on the scent of is peculiar to this species of thinking, is not found in any other. From this it does not follow that a universal is subsistent in itself. What is involved is not a mode of being but a mode of regarding – a fixing of attention on a semblance as common to particulars instead of the particulars as such. Quality thus detached becomes an ultimate term of category of thought. The mind can detach it through the exercise of the function of its ideas and by so doing it creates the unique category; or (it is equally correct to say) evokes and reveals the unique category.

(6) A universal is a subject of thought. But an immediate subject of thought need not always be in itself an existent, or a subsistent, or a reality of any sort. Hypotheses, purposes, plans, day dreams, conceptions of possible events, hopes, fears, doubts, fiction, etc., involve forms of thought partly or wholly concerned with that which is not deemed to be reality nor deemed surely destined to be such. But they are all connected with reality, make a reference to it, have a bearing on it. There is in abstract thought a 'content' or subject-matter of some sort before the mind, just as there is in pure imagination of the concrete order. But it may be a pertinent instrument of thought without being a case of immediate belief in the real. It is in fact the mind's means of reaching out after partic-

ulars and roping them off wholesale in certain segregations without counting or specifying the units.

(7) The moment a quality is conceived as a subsistent in itself, its career is ended as a universal. For here is something that in such wise has reality that it is to be conceived as real independently of a possible realization in some concrete existent. It ceases to be *an attributable* and becomes something on its own account. Greenness ceases to mean merely a thing's state of being green – anything's state of being green. Hence the whole need out of which universals arose is left out of sight. They have become so valued by an intellectual school that they are deprived of their only value. They are so petted and caressed by it that they are 'spoiled'.

(8) A historic illustration lies at hand of how the universal so treated at once becomes a particular. The conception of it as a mystic store of a certain kind of quality drawn upon and participated in by every particular thing that has the quality – a primal source which communicates its peculiar nature to each and every member of a worldwide class – this is a conception of fine and high imaginative value, by no means to be surrendered. But is is not philosophy, it is not analysis, it is vivid and felicitous poetry and quasi-folklore. It turns the universal into a material, and therefore into a particular. It is excellent metaphor, it is not comprehension.

(9) Let us repeat, all the peculiarity of a universal lies in its being a quality, nature, or genus as distinguished from a particular existent. Try to keep it a nature or a quality and yet make it some kind of reality and you contradict yourself. For instance, consider the universal, personality. It is present in any individual. It is present entire in him. But it is at the same time present entire in other individuals. "Present entire" involves "nothing of it absent", "nothing of it not there". But something of it *is* not there. The personality which is present in another individual, and which is equally subsistent, is not there. To describe the first fully is not to mention the second, it is to omit something that is just as truly personality as the first. If you say "But it is the peculiarity of this subsistent that it can be entire in each embodiment at once" you are saying it is its peculiarity to contradict itself. If, on the other hand, it is not a subsistent but a quality or nature expressly distinguished from all things subsistent, there is no contradiction. The quality is present entire in both instances simply because it is only a quality, that is, a kind, that we are talking about, and to say that it is equally in each means that each is of that kind,

that in each the quality is found exemplified. I say, the subtle, extraordinary and mystical properties of the universal arise and prevail precisely because we are distinguishing it from all entities and thinking only of the type. Play with the notion of an entity in the matter and you have coarsened the delicacy of the relation; you have lost the right to that magic by which a universal can dwell entire in many different things at once.

(10) The broadest error of the doctrine is to conceive that there can be more than one kind of reality, that there can be a subsistent which is not existent. Reality is a term of thought is simple and ultimate. It has no degrees and no kinds. A thing or thinkable of any sort whatever either is or is not. There is no half-way station, no twilight region. There are many kinds of existents but only one kind of existence. And this indeed is a token of weakness in the doctrine, that it fears to say 'existence' outright, that it edges back and retreats into the shadows with another and dubious word.

(11) The doctrine declares that it belongs to the nature of any universal, such as individuality or indivisibility or angularity or what you will, to have subsistence. The propounder does not notice that he is performing a feat of the same character as the famed "ontological argument" for the existence of the Deity. He is saying that a *term* in itself involves subsistence. According to the ontological argument the conception of the most perfect being proves that He exists. "His essence involves existence". But as we saw (and it was but barely necessary for our purposes to see over again what had been seen so often) this will not do. No essence or nature can possibly involve reality. If we hold that a universal is a subsistent, that is a belief on our part, and a belief as always is expressed by a proposition, not a term. For this proposition we should have to bring evidence. A mere term cannot possibly by its own nature prove the thing signified to be subsistent or to have any species of reality at all.

(12) Calling universals "ideal objects", Husserl writes:

Manifestly every attempt whatever to resolve the being of the ideal into a possible being of the real is wrecked on the fact that possibilities themselves are ideal objects. Just as little as numbers in general or triangles in number are to be found in the real world, just so little are possibilities to be found there.

It is not absolutely clear what the argument here is. The author apparently may mean either one of two objections. First, he may mean that those who try to reduce all universals somehow to facts of the plain prosaic world of existent things cannot succeed because they have to employ the idea of *possible* things, and that is not the idea of an existent, but of a universal; thus they have got no nearer to their goal. This is an effectual argument, but there is no one, so far as I know, upon whom it takes effect, no one who tries to reduce universals simply to features of the existent world; unless it be the late J. B. Watson. Therefore we may not accuse Husserl of intending so to argue.

Otherwise I can take the argument only as meaning that universals cannot be resolved into possible attributes of particulars because that involves a circle in definition – using as part of the definition the idea to be defined. We say universals are actual or possible attributes of things; but 'possible' is itself a universal; we are defining the universal in terms of itself, and thus getting no further, not defining it at all.

Now 'possible' is a universal, but 'possible' does not mean universal. If it did, there would be a circle in definition. Since it does not there is no circle. If the objection were well taken we could not define knowledge in the terms of our intellectual knowledge, nor 'idea' in terms of ideas, nor 'sentence' in a sentence, nor 'word' in words. But we can do all these things, just as we can write the definition of 'pen' with a pen. We could not make any definition without using universals. A circle in definition is a pretended analysis that still leaves the concept on our hands unanalyzed. A true definition is one that genuinely resolves the concept into its component concepts. That they also are concepts is no defect in the analysis, even when one of them is a case, a specimen, of the concept to be analysed – even when we are analysing 'concept' itself.

(13) The view here taken rejects scholastic 'realism' and rejects also conceptualism. In respect of psychology this view may be called nominalism, since it regards the universal as existing, in the mind, only in a name or word (or similar purely symbolic representative) coupled with its associative function. The *object* of thought, however, is not a name or word but that direction in which the mind looks, that exchangeability or equal relevancy of similar *qualia*, that potentiality of exemplification which corresponds to the mind's forward-looking attitude and preparedness. These phrases are of the nature of description however, not definition, since the universal as an object of consideration is an ultimate term of thought.

What Abstract Ideas We Do Have

PROPOSITION 4.   *While we have, complete in the moment, no intellectual vision of the abstract or generic, yet that phrase justly seems to describe what we do have: namely that which effectually stands for all that an abstract nature can mean to us, and which serves to guide our thought in relation to it.*

It looks at first as if getting at universals only through a function of our ideas and not through their content were an artful and systematic dodging of the real thing, the universal in its own intrinsic essence. But the fact is, nothing could be more appropriate. There is no such entity to be known as a universal, there are only particular things, and the whole affair of the universal is an affair of steering aright amongst those particular things – both in action and in thought. When we find that the mind's abstraction is a matter of successive right discrimination, and of symbols that encourage it, we find just what was to be expected.

When we employ an abstract term or similar symbol, we take up a familiar tool and proceed to wield it without mistrust. This is what constitutes our sense of the abstract or generic. In seizing the tool we do not represent in thought all that we shall do with it nor yet all that it could by its nature do, but we are ready to connect it in thought with various things to be done with it, anything we need to do with it. And that is enough. The sight and grasp of it are satisfying, for, owing to the results in our mind of experience, we are free from doubts and misgivings as to its duly serving us.

Or, to take another comparison, when driving in a car we start in a certain 'direction'. What for us at that moment is the direction? A road, perhaps a signpost, – the road running off to the first bend. We do not see or try to imagine its whole course, it would be no aid to see it, but we have been over it, or over many another road and we give ourselves to it in a state of confidence. A general term is the beginning of our road, it opens a direction of thought, and we avail ourselves of it with no sense of insecurity.

Or let us suppose we are going on a voyage. What is present to us? The ship in which we embark. That stands now to us for the voyage, though at any call of circumstance we are ready to think of this or that further feature of what the experience will be. The ship typifies the voyage and we confide ourselves to it. In deliberate abstract thinking the term or other symbol is our ship and the committal is equally complete. (It is hardly necessary to say that for all minds the ship is a needlessly large metaphor, and for a vast number, namely the relatively imageless minds, it is flagrantly inappropriate, save in the one vital respect of sturdy reliability; the all but submerged spar to which they cling is quite as satisfactory and supporting – and, strange to say, it crosses the sea as swiftly and well.)

It might be replied, "But your doctrine really does result in this, that we never have any real immediate grasp of the universal; as we think and act in matters apparently requiring such a grasp, what you say is that we are blindly falling forward". But a grasp in one true sense is just what we have. When a human being grasps an object and lifts it, his hand does not completely envelop and contain the object. The fingers lay hold of it on different sides, and the object can be lifted only because its parts cohere of themselves. We control and move it partly by pressure and partly by its own cohesion – partly by what we do and partly by what it does of itself. We cannot grasp a handful of sand. So is it with our mental grasp of the universal. It is consummated partly by the hold we have upon it through the specimen or symbol that is actually in the mind, and partly by the fact that what ensures will go right of itself. All human safeties, controls and powers are thus constituted. We have a just sense of command arising from experience, our hold upon our procedure is sufficient, our mental *Begriff* at the moment is all that is required. We are grasping our tool. We know no other sort control, hence in such a case are properly persuaded that we possess what alone control means for us.

Escape to the Occult Cause

PROPOSITION 5. *We cannot escape the forgoing psychological conclusions by falling back on the supposition of occult mental powers beyond the reach of psychological analysis.*

Husserl's treatment of this subject is in one respect refreshing in that he does undertake to face the position and arguments of Berkeley and Hume and meet them at close quarters, which by those who reject them has too seldom been done. What is his position? In one sense he admits the whole or Berkeley's thesis: we cannot think of the abstract or generic in the sense of forming an image or portrayal or representative 'content', as many can of an individual object. When we think abstractly or generically we have, so far as 'psychic contents' go, at best an image of a concrete specimen or a word. But although thus on one side going all the way, he none the less wholly rejects the conclusion that we cannot in any one moment think the abstract or generic; he preserves what he regards as the necessity of the logical situation by holding that we think it by means of an intellectual intention (*Denkintention*). If we ask in wonder what a *Denkintention* without any portrayal whatsoever of the subject can be, he replies with what is for him the open secret, the last word, namely that this kind of consciousness is "a way of meaning or signifying behind which we must seek absolutely nothing that would be other, or could be other, than just meaning or signifying. What meaning is, that we know as immediately as we know what color and sound are. It admits of no further definition, it is an ultimate in description. As often as we *understand* an expression, as often as it *means* something to us, we realize (*vollziehen*) the sense of it. And this understanding, meaning, realizing the sense of it, is not the hearing of the word, or the experiencing of any simultaneous imagination. And just as the differences between sounds are evidently *given*, just so are the differences between meanings." How many would say in chorus that this is just how the matter lies?

This 'intention', not consisting in imagery nor in any 'psychic content', will not be discovered at all if we look within our consciousness for these. It eludes that kind of introspection. It eludes also the difficulties pointed out by Berkeley in conceiving the abstract or generic, which apply, Husserl evidently thinks, only to representative 'pictures'.

This position of Husserl's, elaborately entrenched, gives almost incredibly happy point to our argument. There could not, says Berkeley, be a thought of the abstract because the content would have to be something or other particular. But, says Husserl in effect, we have a wondrous thought of it without any content, a thought with nothing that any analyzing psychologist can pounce upon and catch at all. Aha!!, Berkeley, we have escaped your net.

Nothing else, I say, could so aptly illustrate our thesis. This cognizance of the abstract which is thus privileged, which is exempt from the inconvenient requirements that attend upon portrayal or representation, this form of knowledge is invisible to ordinary introspection for a very simple reason; it is not there. It is so marvelously indescribable and invisible because it is – nothing. The function and not the intrinsic character of the terms of thought we use is what enables us in our thinking to deal triumphantly with universals.

Our meaning, says Husserl, is not the hearing of the word, nor the imagining of it. No, he is right for it is only the suggestive power that lies in that word, a power that depends on, or rather consists in, a law of the mind's working and therefore is a matter of what will ensue and not a presented piece of thought-stuff. It is "the fact that" instances will come to mind at need and the subject be followed up as we desire; a potentiality not yet realized, a potentiality like that which is the basis of the freedom from anxiety of a vigorous walker who, unconsciously counting on the vital mechanism of his body, can quite reliably take the next steps to his satisfaction.

The philosopher looks for a pure generic image or picture and finds it could not be. But somehow we do know genera. What more natural and plausible than to infer that there is a super-sensuous, a disembodied concept of the pure abstraction? This concept must not only be abstracted from the concrete instance, but from sense and imagination altogether. It is pure thought.

But notice that it cannot in the nature of the case elude examination entirely. There is an object of our thought, he tells us, we mean that object, it is an *intentionaler Gegenstand*. This object then is before the mind, indeed he expressly says that it is 'given'. Suppose we are thinking of greenness; what, exactly, is before the mind as its *allgemeiner Gegenstand*? No particular green, that would not be greenness in general, which equally well fits different shades of green, being their common attribute. No vague or dimly lighted green, for that would be only a peculiar specimen of a concrete green. Such remarks indeed would surely have given Husserl reason to be impatient, for he has already swept aside all notions of imaginative representation. But still we do mean an object, we *vollziehen* the sense of it; in some cases as it were "we grasp it; we behold it". (*Wir erfassen es; wir erschauen es.*) No, what is before the mind is just greenness in general, the pure species in intension, just its logical nature, so to speak. Such is his position.

Now 'greenness' is a word. Put this word aside, and tell us precisely what is the 'object' before the mind, something which is not to be any appearance of empirical green at all. Is it not evident that any 'object' that is wholly distinct from experienceable green would be *irrelevant*? It is not clear that something that left out the color green as we see it in daily life could be nothing other than a clue, a token, a symbol, utterly distinct from the nature that we call greenness? In point of fact the term is most often used of the color of some well-known thing, the grass, a tree, a material, etc. and then what is before the mind, if any image is before it, is the particular shade or tint of that thing. Greenness in the abstract as we have seen is *being green*, that is, being one or other of certain concrete colors that bear a recognizable resemblance to each other, a resemblance which is in each comparison concrete. (Any color as imagined is concrete.) We do not think of all these colors; they are too many and not all so immediately to be remembered; but we could identify them all as green. What may be asserted of all of them is this striking likeness. Since the above is what greenness is, there is nothing else to be known in connection with the term. The way to be acutely cognizant of greenness in genral is to be attentive to the resemblance, to be poised in readiness to keep recognizing it accurately. It is a cognizance that has its most pronounced life and being amongst alternative specimens, in our competent preparedness for the decisive admission of certain concrete colors and our rejection of all others.

In saying that "as often as we *understand* an expression, as often as it *means* something to us" we *vollziehen* or carry out in our minds the sense of it, Husserl does not seem close enough to the facts. As already mentioned, the word 'forty' for example is ordinarily 'understood' and may be intelligently used without our realizing in detail just how many units it stands for. The saving fact, once more, it that we *can* realize it in so far as we may be called upon to do so.

The pathetic aspect of his account, in great part so exactly and admirably reasoned, is that for his solution he rests his whole weight on something that does not exist at all, on pure myth. A meaning, an intention of the mind, consummated in the moment, distinct from all symbols, and without imagery or 'psychic content' – there could be no such thing. If the mind has an object in some sort before it, this signifies that it has 'content' before it; just so far as the object makes its appearance to the intellect or in any wise whatever heaves in sight, so far there is something, not nothing, given to consciousness, and that is what we mean by 'psychic content', which the psychologist may consider and study. We mean object-matter. What we find in Husserl's solution is that the momentary 'object' is somehow elusive and uncapturable, the wraith melts away into nothingness, and the alleged mode of consciousness is a self-contradictory form of words. It is all exactly as he says, so far as the logic of thought goes. It is all exactly as he says psychologically too, (putting aside the word "*vollziehen*") except that what is there is a word or other slightest clue which can be counted on to perform a handy office. It is a link by which we can at once draw into consiousness whatever serves our turn in the matter. We have in his account one more attempt to escape by a sacredly traditional incantation from the stubborn realities of the problem. By insisting that we cannot go behind the word *meinung*, or the word *intention*, that what it conveys is unmistakable and ultimate, he has simply "stamped his iron heel" and said, "Thus far and no further shall psychological analysis go".

He gives the prettiest demonstration of the temptations of verbalism. It is as if we had entreated him to supply us with a striking episode in speculation that against the speculator's will should expose to us how a mere function may be mistaken for a bit of thought-stuff.

From its dawn philosophy, including semi-popular philosophy, has had of course a tendency to assume the existence of 'pure thought'. Even today we see it quite often assumed that a person found to be thinking in imaginative terms drawn from one of the senses is thereby detected in an *uneigentlich* form of thought, a dangerous substitute for true and unmixed thinking. As if we could do our abstract thinking in terms of anything else than symbols, which must be taken from one or other of the senses. The situation is such as absolutely to compel, so to speak, this fallacy. The abstract words are there, the sense of perfect security in manipulating them is there, the phenomena of sense are often slight and all but vanishing, and would not, if amply present, be what is supposed to be required; accordingly we must have some (marvelously intangible and potent) 'higher' mode of intellection, we must be able to get at the soul or vital principle of what we mean without any gross earthy embodiment. This higher thought is a mental quintessence, whose property it is to know effectually what has to be known, and that is all that needs to be said. There you have it; we are dealing in alchemic essences, in the *causa occulta*, and in this subject Husserl has found it too ready to his hand. We may remember that he was a logical rather than a psychological analyst. But it is unfortunate that he missed the force, even the logical force, of Berkeley's argument. 'Phenomenology', excellent method as it is, is in danger of being entrapped by terminology.

NOTES

[1] The subject of universals involves the class-idea, the quality-idea and the relation-idea. But the class is determined by the possession of quality or relation, and a relation, since it is attributable as a characteristic to the entity that sustains it, may be reckoned as a quality. In this wide sense the whole subject of universals is the subject of quality in general, and in this chapter it is so treated.

[2] Berkeley writes, "I do not deny absolutely that there are *general ideas*, but only that there are any *abstract general ideas....* An idea which, considered in itself, is particular becomes general by being made to represent or stand for all other particular ideas of the same sort". By 'abstract' he means having an abstract content, being in and by itself a perception of the abstract. What he professes to offer, then, is an analysis of "general ideas". But it is unfortunate suddenly to use the common phrase "abstract ideas", universally taken as the name for ideas that we obviously possess, as signifying something that does not exist. For my own part I return to the ordinary sense of the term.

[3] Had the objection been advanced that the shape, color, etc. might be vague and misty, Berkeley would probably (to judge by his general view and approach) have answered that this would be just as concrete and particular an appearance as any other; that a vague and misty scene or picture is perfectly concrete, though he had not thought to mention it as an example; that vagueness is in no wise identifiable with abstractness.

[4] This argument of Berkeley's was in effect another step forward, after Locke, toward a philosophy that makes experience the source and test of our knowledge and our thoughts. Universals by themselves are not found in experience, naturally therefore they are not found amongst the contents of the mind. When in the course of the *Principles* he condemns certain alleged ideas as 'abstract', the virtual point of his objection is that what they profess to represent is not to be found in experience; we have no materials for such ideas; – in this following Locke's principle as to the source of our ideas. That is, his attack on what he called abstraction was one forward step toward a thorough empiricism.

[5] Berkeley's use in the *Principles* of the term 'notion' (a use that seems incompatible with his doctrine as to abstract ideas) and his apparent drift with the years toward conceptualism do not here concern us.

[6] The word *quale* is not used here to indicate necessarily one pure undiversified concrete quality but concrete quality of any kind whatsoever including the complex.

[7] Of course the mind cannot literally represent the nature without the existence – not in any picture or image. You cannot conceive greenness except by conceiving an existent green or some symbol standing for it. You cannot in representation tear apart the greenness and the existence. There is no quality except as existing and no existence except of quality. To conceive a thing and to conceive it as existing are two expressions for the same thing, though to believe in its existence is another matter. What, then, do we do? Here enters function. To whatever representative content is before the mind a working proviso is attached that it shall not of itself become a belief in any existent, that it shall have the function of enabling us to discriminate the right color wherever

it may appear or be in question. It is function alone that enables us to make in the practice of thought a distinction that could not be made by mere imagination.

[8] Those who adopt an empirical idealism and hold that the color, shape, solidity, etc., are nothing but "permanent possibilities of experience", do make them universals. And, of course, the 'properties' of an object in the sense usual in physical science, namely, what it will do and effect under hypothetical conditions, are universals. – What is said above applies also to relations so long as they are literally existent. Edinburgh's being 'north of' London is (on the assumption of natural realism) not a universal, though 'north of' taken in general is such.

AN EVENT IN MODERN PHILOSOPHY WITH HUME

[The following article appeared in 1945 at the beginning of the second decade of Miller's 'American retirement' in Boston. It was intended to serve as a chapter, or the main part of a chapter, of a book that would also deal with the knowledge-problem, free will, and universals to show the method of analysis at work.

In what follows, Miller condenses and freshly applies major conclusions of his two-part article of 1930, 'Hume Without Scepticism', that had appeared in *Mind* under the name of Hobart. There he pursued in detail the suggestion of his undergraduate teacher, George Fullerton, that Hume's analysis of causality should be seen not as destructive or sceptical but simply as explanatory. Hume analyzed causation to show that while one proposition may imply another, a thing cannot, so the connection between cause and effective is not deductive and there is ultimately no 'necessity' for a law that formulates the uniformities of experience. Miller defended these conclusions by criticism of opposing views in Whitehead, H. W. B. Joseph, Kant, and Bertrand Russell. Now in what follows, Miller sharpens his major conclusions about Hume and causality and particularly defends them against Brand Blanshard and Kant to conclude, as before, that induction or inference from experience may indeed be rational because rationality, contrary to Hume, is not confined to deduction.

In correspondence with C. J. Ducasse, 1946–1950, Miller was hard pressed in defense of his conclusions about Hume and causality, particularly in regard to "physical necessity". He invited and welcomed such criticism for "the progress of inquiry", but it may have shown him that further analytical work was needed in this area.]

The feeling of surprise is apt to be sudden; it seems as if by its nature it must be so. But there can be a surprise that arises gradually and slowly through the years, as we turn fuller attention upon the state of a matter, rises to a genuine astonishment, and stays with us the rest of our days.

Such is the surprise I cannot help feeling at the actual total effect in the circle of philosophers of the launching of a great and startling idea amongst them two centuries ago – Hume's analysis of the relation of cause and effect; an idea that may be regarded as a logical discovery of the first magnitude, in its consequences even more momentous than in itself.

Hume was one of the clearest heads and writers that have figured in the history of philosophy at all. In general he is clearer than his interpreters and commentators, who so obligingly explain to us his meaning. Never was he clearer, *upon the whole*, than when treating of cause and effect. He had hold of a subject and an idea that peculiarly lent themselves to lucidity; he came to a conclusion that was refreshingly simple and clean-cut, whatever our judgment of its truth. Yet not only is he today, after two hundred years, persistently misunderstood by learned individuals to an extent that would have seemed incredible, but it has to be said that the general understanding of his conclusions is strangely without basis in his text. What can be hoped for anyone else if that is the fate of Hume?

Moreover, the misapprehension prevents our catching the full importance of his thought and its unanswerable cogency.

Let us look at his conception of causation, and then at what he conceives to be the consequence for reasoning from experience.

I

That Hume "denied causation" is a remark that may be heard in more languages than one. And many who would not quite say that still regard him as mutilating the idea – nay, taking the heart out of it – by denying the necessary connection of cause and effect.

First, for his intention and conscious position. He was not intending to mutilate our idea or deprive it of any of its features, not to modify but to analyse it. He did not mean that it was wrong; he wished to point out what it was. What he denied was something that he believed never occurs to the ordinary man at all but was an assumption of philosophers, namely, that the cause *implied* its effect in the strict deductive sense, so that if you could clearly read the whole nature of the cause you could deduce from it alone that the effect would ensue. That is not the case, he held, even if you include in the cause all the factors in the world that in any wise influence or condition the result. No concrete fact *implies* in the strict deductive sense any other concrete fact. He thought that his idea of causation was the idea common to mankind. Such is the view he takes and such is the view that his theory, by its very basis, obliges him to take.

The only necessity in causation that he seeks to disprove is a deductive necessity. The only energy that he seeks to disprove is an energy in the cause that strictly implies the effect; no energy that has ever been imagined as exerted by the cause could do that. The only connection he seeks to disprove is a deducible connection. We cannot, he holds, frame the idea of such a deducible connection, and are only deceiving ourselves with words when we fancy that we do. Critics and commentators, unable entirely to overlook this last assertion of his, have nevertheless failed fully to consider its bearing upon his whole position. The prevailing interpretation of Hume attributes to him at one and the same time the opinion that all mankind have a certain erroneous conception and that nobody could possibly have that conception.

His essential language is perfectly clear. In citing it the emphasis is my own. "...the constant conjunction of objects constitutes the very essence of cause and effect."[1] "*We have no other notion of cause and effect,* but that of certain objects which have been always conjoined together...."[2] "This multiplicity of resembling instances, therefore, constitutes the very essence of power or connexion, and *is the source from which the idea of it arises.*"[3] "For as our idea of efficiency *is derived from* the constant conjunction of two objects, wherever this is observed, the cause is efficient...."[4] "...we must reject the distinction betwixt *cause* and *occasion,* when supposed to signify anything essentially different from each other. If constant conjunction be implied in what we call occasion, 'tis a real cause."[5] Now for the opinion he rejects. "There is no object which *implies* the existence of any other if we consider these objects in themselves, and never look beyond the ideas which we form of them."[6] This indicates what *kind* of 'connexion' he denies. "Such a connexion would amount to a demonstration, and would imply the absolute impossibility for the one object not to follow, or to be conceived not to follow, upon the other; which *kind of* connexion has already been rejected in all cases."[7] "Now nothing is more evident than that the human mind cannot form such an idea of two objects as to conceive any connexion betwixt them...."[8]

"...we deceive ourselves in imagining we can form any such general idea." [9]

Recognise a law in the case, a law according to which a certain event will always be succeeded by a certain other event, and then indeed it will follow of necessity that the second event will take place. This necessity Hume had no thought of questioning. What he assails is only the idea that you can infer the second event from the nature of the first event taken by itself. Take the first event *plus* a law, and the necessity of the second event plainly follows. To cause a thing is to make it happen, and to make it happen is so to act that it cannot but happen – according to the order of nature, of which we learn from experience. "Making", says Hume, in effect, could not mean anything else to anybody. Given the cause the effect is a matter of course, it has to happen. This practical necessity, this inevitableness *de facto*, has been mistaken by philosophers for a deductive necessity, with which it has nothing to do. In taking cognisance of everyday causes and effects people do not bother their heads about deduction. [10]

The notion of a compulsive force in the cause comparable to the muscular exertion we feel in our own action, does often (not always) play a part in the common conception of particular causes. But this notion (right or wrong) is in no wise inconsistent with Hume's view; such an indwelling force does not logically imply the sequel any more than would a forceless antecedent. Owing to the inevitableness of the sequel, impressed upon us by experience, we call the force quite properly compulsive, for the inevitable sequence of the looked-for event upon the application of force constitutes the meaning of the word compulsion.

I have said above, "The only necessity in causation that he seeks to disprove is a deductive necessity". Yes, his *argument* is directed against that assumption only. But his *conclusion* is that causation is purely a relation of uniform sequence, and therein he denies also any other necessity as distinguishing causation, as entering into its definition, than uniform sequence, what I have called practical necessity. Might there not be an ultimate, unanalysable necessity, not involving deducibility and yet something more than inevitable sequence *de facto?* Why does he conclude, after refuting only the deductive view, that the relation is one sequence only?

He does so because his attention is on just one inquiry: What reason have we for our apparent knowledge of the sequences of nature? From what do we draw that knowledge? Is there any good logic behind it? His thought is that if effects are not deducible, even for one who knows the causes perfectly, then there is no good logic behind it. A necessity other than deducibility would not aid in this difficulty, would not provide any reason for our expectation of effects, since they could not rationally be inferred from their causes any more than on the conception of mere uniform sequence. There would be no means of *proving* a necessary connection in any given situation or in general. He does not even consider the possibility of any other kind of necessity, because (probably) that particular subtlety has never occurred to him and because it would not help him if it had. In his logical problem there are only two alternatives: rationally inferring and not being able to do so. If there is no deductive bond in the relation by which the one 'logically' has to arise out of the other, then there is, first, simply the event we term the cause and, second, simply the event we term the effect, and that is what we mean by a simple se-sequence. Thus it is that his mind naturally proceeds.

And he is right, so far as the idea of necessity is concerned. It is not an unanalysable idea. A necessary sequel means an inescapably certain sequel because the only possible one. A necessary inference means an inescapably certain inference because the only possible one. In each case there is a determinant of impossibility, in the light of which alone the impossibility appears. In the latter case it is the relation of content in premises and conclusion. In the former case it is an order of nature accepted as actual (Why it is accepted is a matter to be taken up in the final section.) Unless there is such a determinant apparent no impossibility appears and hence no necessity appears. Hume was right in recognising no alternatives but deducibility on the one hand and mere sequence on the other, because there is no other determinant of impossibility in a sequence than the intrinsic natures of the events concerned or what is believed to be the known order of such events in space and time.

II

Such, essentially, was Hume's intention and conscious position. But, it may be said, he was wrong; his analysis is mistaken. Granted that many interpretations miss his point, granted that he does not mean to mutilate the idea, his conception does multilate it. There is something else in the relation of cause and effect, something that he excludes.

Well, the only thing his reasoning excludes is deducibility. Those who reject his reasoning will have to show (1) that the ordinary man's idea of an effect includes deducibility and (2) that an effect, if all were known, *would* be deducible from its cause.

Here we come to the proof of Hume's main thesis, which proof I shall state in my own way. In essence it may be briefly put. A proposition may imply another proposition but a thing cannot imply another thing. No concrete fact implies any other concrete fact. Implication is a matter of language and concepts; it is not an attribute of things. Furthermore, a proposition stating that a concrete fact occurs – let us say an event – and specifying its entire nature, does not imply, does not render deducible, that any other event will follow. How can you deduce one particular from another? You cannot. The effect is a particular and the cause is a particular. That is where Hume has an absolute hold upon us. Those who maintain that the nature of a cause, truly known, implies its effect, are maintaining something that the very theory of logic itself peremptorily rejects. We could not even fabricate or imagine any event from whose intrinsic nature any other event could be inferred.[11]

It has been held by psychologists of a certain school, and others, that cause is an idea *sui generis,* not to be analysed. Please observe that if this were true Hume's main thesis would remain unshaken; the cause would not imply its effect.

Suppose we say with Kant that we can not have experience of an objective order of events at all without presupposing the law of cause and effect. In other words, suppose we say that we know the law not from experience but because it is presupposed in all experience. Hume of course would not accept this, but it is important to notice that if it were true his main thesis would not be in the least disturbed. This view, if correct, would not even tend to prove that we can infer the effect from the intrinsic character of the cause alone. Indeed it starts, so to speak, by conceding to Hume that we can not; though unwilling to concede to him also that there is no other way by which we can gain assurance of the law save that of having it impressed upon us by experience. For that way of coming by the belief, Kant felt (here too agreeing with Hume), would be irrational, and he was not willing, like Hume, to put up with an irrational position. It is the initial concession of Hume's main point that forces Kant to find this other, this new and ingenious way of basing our knowledge of the law.

You could conceive a concrete fact completely, says Hume, without conceiving any other fact. There is a theory respecting "internal relations", as they are called, which would indeed be inconsistent with this, the theory that an existent's relation to other existents enters into its very constitution and character. This does not mean merely the familiar truth that a thing is constantly in fact affected by environing things, which is a matter of empirical investigation. From that empirical fact it does not follow that the thing, though thus causally modified by other things, cannot just as it is (while thus modified) be conceived by itself without logically implying anything else. Though its nature is modified this modified nature can be conceived alone – without thinking of that which in fact modifies it. The theory, on the contrary, is that the intrinsic nature of an existent involves and implies its relations to others – that the existent cannot be known in its true being without reference to them. This is indeed what Hume denied. With regard to it consider an axiom from James's *Psychology*: "The essence of a feeling is to be felt, and as a psychic existent *seems* so it must *be*". So far as a phenomenon of consciousness, an experience – a pain, a percept, an idea, a whole field of consciousness – is truly such, is actually given, its nature is given and its existence is given. And yet we experience it without experiencing or conceiving the rest of the universe. Therefore its nature and existence do not imply the rest of the universe, nor any other concrete thing whatsoever. How can the doctrine of "internal relations" stand up against this fact? Here are existents whose relation to other existents does not enter into their constitution and character.

III

The greatest obstacle to our acceptance of the proof of Hume's thesis is our misconception of the immediate consequences of that thesis for our view of the world. If mankind at large and men of science in particular conceive their world without that element of deductive implication that he excludes, then the exclusion in no wise damages their world. In *The Nature of Thought* by Professor Blanshard, a work the philosophical stature of which we all recognise, we read that according to those who hold that cause and effect mean invariable sequence "... the question *why* what followed did follow is one on which we are, and must remain, in total darkness; the connection between the events is not more intelligible than the connection of lightning and thunder for the savage". Now this touches the very pith and heart of our subject. Essentially, Hume is not making the why unknowable, he is analysing what is meant by 'why'. The essential upshot of his analysis is that 'why' as applied to events asks for the facts that occasion, or are the occasion of, the event. 'Why' presupposes a law, an order of nature; it is entirely relative to that. Hume means that there is no other 'why' than this and never has been. The word demands simply what it is in the order of nature that turns on, and the absence of which turns off, the event in question – upon what its occurrence temporally depends. Accept the order of nature and at once our 'whys' have their meaning. Apart from an order of nature they have no meaning at all. Hume's philosophic discovery was that the why and wherefore of an event was not to be found inside the cause, taken strictly alone, but lay in the order of events, which we accept from experience.

Just so with Professor Blanshard's word 'intelligible'. Essentially Hume is not robbing us of the intelligibility of the connection between events. He is analysing it. To make the connection intelligible in the particular case is to reduce it to an instance of that familiar order of things that we regard as constant and reliable. To explain an event is to show that it had to happen according to that order. In the case of thunder and lightning there are underlying processes that the savage does not know, processes that reduce the connection to a fundamental and continuous type familiar to the investigator. If we knew all the sequences connected with them there would be nothing more in the matter to know. The very idea of the intelligibility of events rests upon there being an order under which a particular event can be traced to that which occasions it, in other words, can be explained.

The stuff of things, whatever it be, the kind of existent we come upon in experience, we all take humbly as a given fact that we simply accept; we do not try to deduce it from the Absolute or from the nature of Reason. Thus we accept the stuff of the whole universe. Hume declares in effect that the order or process of things is likewise an ultimate datum. His great proposition is that you can not deduce the process from the stuff; you can not deduce events from the nature of the constituent elements taking part in them, as those elements would present themselves to an all-seeing mind in a just previous cross-section of the events. Precisely as the stuff of nature is an ultimate fact, so the order of nature is an ultimate fact. He says virtually: "Above all, do not make your 'why' depend on deducibility, for then indeed you will find yourself without any 'why' at all."

Another able writer remarks:

Touching the nature of causation in general the upshot of the matter is that we do not know at all the nexus between a cause and its effect: we only view the sequence and its constancy. That there *is* a nexus, we have, from that constancy of sequence, good grounds for surmising; and if we knew its nature we should be in possession of the inmost secret of the universe.[12]

This is an absolutely typical and, so to speak, normal expression of the mind that has never been led to regard the whole matter as a call for analysis – analysis of the meaning of terms and how we came by that meaning. The thing to fasten on is this: the innermost nexus we can imagine or dream of would still be a matter of sequence, of series in time, and the last state of that series could never be inferred from the first. You can not escape this metaphysical ground-truth by taking refuge behind phenomena. It is just as true behind them as it is manifest *in* them ... for the demonstrable falsity of the contradictory proposition has nothing to do with phenomenality, but only with distinct concrete existents. You do not help yourself in the least by going behind the scenes. The idea of a compulsive nexus that you project under phenomena is derived from phenomena themselves, is derived from your experience of the indissoluble conjunction of events in fact, of what we quite properly call their connectedness. I say, the nexus you conceive in your 'surmise', and the only nexus you could conceive, is a matter of experience. To call it a sequence seems to miss the vital thing – because we are very much accustomed to the drive of causation, which is the connectedness of events, and not at all accustomed to analysis. The true but frigid analytical formula of an unvarying sequence seems for the imagination not at all a graphic or telling description of the irresistible impetus of causation, and indeed it is not. Analysis seems to destroy the lump-idea because we have not learned to analyse. Briefly, you can not infer or 'surmise' a nexus as the explanation of all constant sequence because the nexus itself could be nothing other than a constant sequence. As to "the inmost secret of the universe", that is our old friend the alchemic essence, which is dead in chemistry but in philosophy remains alive and of mighty influence.

IV

There have been two historic forms of direct reply to Hume's argument. Their peculiarity has been that they have both assumed the point at issue, in other words, begged the question.

(1) "Same cause, same effect" Taine, Bosanquet and others have urged. If the cause that has produced a given effect is in a fresh case really the same, then it must produce the same effect again. We can know this in advance and predict it with certainty from the nature of the cause; not from an ascertained law, but simply because the cause is the same.

True, but purely an unconscious verbal trick. If the event is a cause then it must have the same effect, for that is involved in the definition of the word 'cause'. The question would be, How do we know that the event is a cause? As soon as we so call it we are assuming the point at issue. Hume had seen this. A husband, he says, must have a wife, for that is involved in the definition of the word; it does not follow that a man must have a wife. So a cause must always have the same effect, but it does not follow that an event will always have the same sequel.

However, the argument is sometimes stated with the verbal trick less obvious. If the event occurs again, it is said, and its nature is genuinely and exactly the same, then of course it will produce the same. If its nature is identical how can it produce something different? But the word 'produces' means causes, and this alleges that the event was the cause of the sequel in question. Hence the same answer. Besides, the wording suggests that the subsequent event comes out of the nature of the precedent event in the sense that Hume denied, namely, could be necessarily inferred from it alone. The argument assumes this, taking no step to prove it. (The subsequent event does come out of the precedent in the natural sense of those words, in the only conceivable sense, in the sense given them by experience. The very words 'event' and 'outcome' indicate as much.)

(2) It is contended that we know from direct experience that there is more in causation than mere succession, that we have a sense of compulsion in it that inevitable succession would not account for. If relevant to Hume's argument, this must mean that we have direct experience, when-

ever we perceive cause and effect, that the latter is deducible from the former. Who will maintain this? At all events it begs the question, for Hume denies the conclusion, and what we have in reply is mere assertion; nothing has been done to prove it. This reply rests in fact upon that somewhat vague misunderstanding of his argument that has been so widespread.

As we saw, Kant's doctrine is not to be reckoned with replies to Hume's argument, for it does not dispute the argument. But it is of interest to note that Kant also, in two of his contentions, is found assuming a point at issue. He assumes that necessity, in a sense which cannot be derived from experience, is present in the category of causation. And he assumes that we cannot cognise pure time or succession. The latter proposition might be taken in either of two senses. It might conceivably mean that we cannot cognise time in a pure vacuum, without any phenomena to be related by it. That of course is true and unquestioned; time is a relation, not a stuff. What the proposition does mean however is that we cannot cognise two phenomena as standing in a relation of priority and subsequence – notes of music heard at a distance, for instance – without connecting them in our mind with some machinery of causation. A causal process in the objective world must be conceived as the clock, so to speak, that marks and embodies time for us. Now the truth must really be maintained, in spite of the high and transcendental ground so jealously guarded by some of Kant's defenders, that this in the end is a psychological proposition, and that established psychology finds it untrue to experience. It greatly concerned Kant's position to prove it, and he does not do so.

So much for the chief historic forms of argument on the subject. Almost all the replies have supposed that Hume meant to take away from us a vital part of our familiar idea of causation. With this misconception they could hardly be expected to meet his real reasoning. As regards certain recent discussion perhaps I may be permitted to say in passing that you cannot confute Hume by solemnly repeating the word 'categorial'.

V

Apart from all these there is what I have long felt to be the strongest reply to Hume, strongest because it meets him squarely on his own ground. It is also a singularly interesting reply because of the considerations into which it leads us and because it supplies a testing case than which none could be more searching. It is contained in Professor Blanshard's work already mentioned. There is one case at least, he holds, in which logical necessity enters palpably into causation, a case of mental causation, namely reasoning, where premises entertained in the mind produce a conclusion. If in this case logical necessity is inherent in causation it may conceivably be so elsewhere – everywhere. I quote a small part of the passage.

That necessity does enter into causality is easier to see in some cases than in others. ... Consider any instances of reasoning, for example, our old case of the abbé and the squire. "Ladies", says the abbé, "do you know that my first penitent was a murderer?" "Ladies", says the squire entering shortly afterward, "do you know that I was the abbé's first penitent?" A conclusion was of course produced in the ladies' minds and our question is as to the nature of the causation that produced it. ... If the ladies were asked how they came to have the belief with which they ended they would say that it was because this belief was obviously implied by what they were thinking the moment before... Not that no other causes contributed to the result; we are not suggesting of course that causality *reduces* to logical necessity. What we hold is that when one passes in reasoning from ground to consequence the fact that the ground entails the consequent is one of the conditions determining the appearance of this consequent rather than something else in the thinker's mind.

This has great apparent force. I cannot do justice here to all the details of Professor Blanshard's argument. I can only offer certain broad comments.

Suppose that at exactly the apt instant, with the end of the squire's sentence, the ceiling had fallen in and killed the whole company. The conclusion would never have followed. Or suppose that a violent alarm of fire had been heard even while the squire was speaking; again, possibly, no conclusion. Logical thought may or may not continue; its continuance is not a matter of logical necessity, but of continued human life and attention. That alone is enough to establish for this case Hume's thesis that no thought or thing implies the coming of anything else, which is all he contends for. The occurrence of a particular thought in a particular mind at a particular moment is an event. What Hume says of all events is emphatically true of it: you could not tell from its nature, even if you knew it all, what will follow.

Professor Blanshard speaks of "more or less" necessity, "some degree of compulsion". Is necessity a thing that admits of degrees? He argues yes. But a necessary consequence surely means the only possible consequence. If it is not the only one possible how can it be necessary?

In the example he cites, what took place in the minds of the listeners? When they heard the squire they *remembered* what the abbé had said shortly before. Thus the two remarks were now in their minds together: the squire was the abbé's first penitent who was a murderer. This *was* the 'conclusion', this *was* the shocking realization; what happened was not that two ideas produced a further and subsequent idea but that two thoughts were put together. The idea of "the abbé's first penitent" (the middle term) now naturally became a less interesting and conspicuous part of the combination; the one detonating fact was that the squire had murdered somebody. How have they arrived at this? By the action of their ears, their memory, and the association of words with their meanings.

"...this belief was obviously implied by what they were thinking before...." It was not implied by what the abbé had said, and it was not implied by what the squire said, and as soon as the two are together in the mind no implication is needed, the startling fact is there staring them in the face. So it was not that two thoughts generated a third thought but that two pieces of information when combined formed a piece of information that happened to possess an extraordinary interest.

Of course we can write down or say "His first penitent was a murderer", "The squire was his first penitent", "Therefore the squire was a murderer", and the third proposition truly follows from the others. What I am saying is that the actual mental process in the case narrated would be as just described. Part of the detail may fade out or fall into shadow, but no third and new proposition is required. You may say that with part of the detail ("his first penitent") forgotten for the moment it *is* a new proposition. In that case I need only add that *that* proposition or thought is not generated by the previous thoughts (psychologically speaking) but is a part of them left over, because attention concentrates on that part.

Suppose however it had been a case where the mind firmly believed a certain generalisation, then encountered an instance that fell under it and applied the generalisation accordingly. Here also there is an absolutely typical implication in the deductive sense. And yet, if it is psychology we are considering, that is, how the mind passes from one idea to another, we have to say that what leads one to apply the generalisation to the instance is what is commonly called the association of ideas. Conjoining in mind the thought of the class in question with the thought of the attribute in question leads one to conjoin the instance with the attribute. The logical implication is there, but it is not the logical implication that actually carries the mind from the one thought to the other. And the mind need not be so carried unless it is sufficiently interested, remembers well, and is not diverted to other objects of attention.

Thus far I have been speaking of processes of spontaneous and progressive thought, lending themselves to outward expression by the verbal or other symbolic forms of premise and deductive conclusion. But there is another case to be considered, where we are engaged in logical study, contemplating propositions already given and their relation of meaning to each other. Here we may note a relation of implication and thenceforward respect its truth and think accordingly. In this case does logical compulsion govern and shape our subsequent thought? How in the human mind is the thing done? Each term calls up its meaning by association, and the comparison of these meanings takes place like the comparison of any other pair of facts whose relation we are led to note. Though not a case of the comparison of objects it is a case of comparison. In conforming our thought subsequently to this perception we are proceeding no otherwise than, for example, a person remembering the disposition of things in a place he has seen, and planning for work to be done there; he is recalling the relations involved and proceeding with due regard to them. Here is the recognised fact: we perceive an implication and our perception as a psychological fact often governs the thought that follows and thus is a cause or part of a cause. The perception affects further thought through memory, association, attention, interest, desire. The forces are psychological, not logical. Logic is not a propulsive force in the mind, or anywhere else; it is not a force at all. It would make a great change in psychology if we decided that the stream of thought was carried forward, even in part, by relations of deductive logic instead of such factors as those mentioned.

We are creatures equipped with psychological 'mechanisms' that *enable us* to follow up logical relations and other relations, and thus to act and live. When we think of the rooms in a familiar house they are not held together in the mind in their right relations by the cohesions of a frame structure, but by the association of ideas. Just so when we think of logical relations and follow them up correctly this is not effected by means of logical proprieties but by the association of ideas.

And we must *learn* to do so. A conclusion may follow in logic and yet not follow in the mind's actual thought. The word 'follow' in the two cases has different meanings. In the one it means "is to be inferred", in the other it means "comes in fact immediately after" – in the same mind. The logical necessity of the former is absolute. The logical necessity of the latter does not exist.

It is one thing to say that a thought perceives that one proposition follows from others, and another thing to say that a thought as a psychic event logically necessitates another psychic event as its sequel. Premises may imply a conclusion but they do not imply that we shall reach it. They say nothing about that. Our minds may stray off into fallacy or into another subject. It is one thing for a thought to perceive an implication and another for a thought to exert an implication. The latter seems to me, I must candidly say, a fairy-tale; an implication is not a thing that can be exerted.

A cause is always an event, a group of conditions occurring in time. An implication is not an event, hence it cannot be a cause. Nor even part of a cause.

VI

I have been taking Hume's analysis on one side only, namely, as it concerns the nature of causation. But, as we all know, it has another side, namely its logical bearing upon reasoning from experience. He is not sceptical about the nature of causation, but he is sceptical about reasoning from experience; here we come to what he calls in an oddly tautological phrase his "sceptical doubts". He doubts, or more properly speaking, he denies, the validity of inference from experience. Here he was governed by the traditional modes of thought of his time – which are the traditional modes of thought of our time as well; he took deduction as the standard of rational inference.[13] Taking his stand upon deduction, he turns upon empirical inference and applies the deductive standard to it. It does not meet this standard, so he pronounces it logically invalid, irrational. Our reasoning from experience, according to him, can be psychologically explained but not rationally justified. This result may naturally provoke a wry smile. The whole of natural science and the whole of practical life are denied rational warrant. Is there really nothing they can say for themselves? Poor science! Poor life!

But now suppose we turn upon deduction, and scrutinise its pretensions precisely as he did those of empirical thought. Suppose we ask, what does it lie in the nature of deduction to prove? What can it do? When we ask this question we see, in relation to science and life, a deficiency at its very root. Deduction, pure deduction, never yields any fact; it shows us only the implication of propositions. If we arrive at facts in our conclusion we have at some point assumed facts, or learned of them by processes not deductive. Deduction takes its start from propositions and cannot supply the basic propositions. They must come from some other source.

Therefore Hume, in pronouncing induction irrational, was judging by a false standard, one which had no relevance to evidence for fact. His criticism of empirical inference was that it never rationally yields fact. Now we are seeing that mere deduction never does so. If we are looking for the evidence of a thing deduction always refers us to the propositions with which it set out, and we still have the whole question before us, How were they proved to be true? How was the element of fact introduced into our reasoning? So that if empirical inference fails to prove fact, as he thinks, he would have had to admit that deduction fails to prove it quite as lamentably.

If Hume had only applied to empirical reasoning the same method, not sceptical but analytical, that he applied to cause and effect! If he had only analyzed what we mean by evidence!

The ground for regarding as rational the evidence for fact found in experience is this: it is what we *mean* by rational evidence; it is what we mean by evidence for fact; there is no other evidence for fact; if it were not for the evidence of experience we should never have formed the idea of evidence for fact at all; no other is even conceivable. It is an elementary, an ultimate, category of thought. We cannot say that something is not evidence if it is what the word evidence means. We cannot say it is poor evidence if it is itself the standard of evidence. Hume was looking for his spectacles when they were on his nose.

When we speak of good evidence we mean simply evidence, that which is really such. When we speak of bad evidence we mean that which pretends to be such when it is not.

In the sphere of logical philosophy, Hume dismissed empirical intelligence on a complaint lodged by deduction. We have to reverse this action, reinstate empirical intelligence, and dismiss deduction (a trusty and mighty agent in its own place) from the office of supplying us with new fact. The stone that the builder rejected becomes the headstone of the corner.

NOTES

[1] *Treatise*, ed. by Green and Grose, I. 532,
[2] *Ibid.* 394.
[3] 457.
[4] 464.
[5] 465.
[6] 389.
[7] 456.
[8] 456.
[9] 457.
[10] Take the first event *plus* a law and the effect is indeed deducible, though not from the cause taken by itself. But in life we do not ordinarily think of the generalisation but of the particular events before us and the expected particular outcome. We believe the outcome to be inevitable but do not deduce it.
[11] Professor Brand Blanshard holds, unlike others, if I understand him, that there are no particulars. In that case a cause and an effect cannot be such. But I do not see how saying this in words, uttering the incantation, leaves us any forwarder in the task of inferring one from the other. For the impossibility of such inference lies not in the name but in the things, whose distinct individuality the name is only an effort to express. Professor Blanshard recognizes apparently that relations of deductive logic are not temporal, but holds that they "have something to do" in a causal sense with the production of conclusions in the mind. This is the basis of his argument.
[12] R. Briffault, *The Making of Humanity* 40. It is a curious thing that Hume sometimes falls into something like this language himself. He is writing a treatise of immense scope before he is twenty-five, and he occasionally writes hastily, forgetting for the moment the all-inclusiveness of his own analysis, and falling back upon ordinary and less uncompromising forms of expression. Hence my word 'essentially'.
[13] In our time even those who break away from these standards continue for the most part to do them the homage of identifying them with reason, and are content to reserve the term 'rationalist' for their philosophic enemies.

HUME'S DEATHBLOW TO DEDUCTIVISM

[Complementing and extending the conclusions of the preceding article on Hume and causality, the following essay appeared in 1949, shortly after its presentation as a special lecture at Harvard. With palpable clarity it organizes Miller's maturest thought and conclusions as what is involved in reasoning from experience, indicating along the way how analysis of 'cause', 'self', and 'free will' clarifies ordinary meanings without challenging ordinary facts.

Miller particularly attends to 'significance', a unique relation between facts and the probability of further facts, as the ground of induction and "the bottom of our logical world". Hence reason is more than deductive implication to which Hume mistakenly confined it. Reason also includes, as testified by ordinary experience, 'indication' rooted in the relation of significance.

Such a position is inseparable from 'empiricism', the view that our knowledge and all generic truths are inferred from data of experience. Kant's view, Miller argues, is the antithesis of empiricism at a central point and hence poisonous to its moral purpose. Similarly, "the will to believe" in pragmatism – "an excellent sermon but a confused philosophy" – is at deadly enmity with empiricism as a result of its misleading identification of belief and hypothesis. Some years later, with this aspect of pragmatism in mind, Miller remarked that he had reluctantly come to the conclusion that James's influence in philosophy had, on the whole, done more harm than good.]

The thesis I am submitting to the reader in this article is that Hume's analysis of cause and effect deals a deathblow to deductivism.

He lays down in substance two propositions.

(1)   Inference from experience is not deductive.

(2)   It is therefore a purely irrational process (being due in fact to the association of ideas).

The first of these is irrefutable. No one has ever been able to make the slightest breach in it. A proposition may imply another proposition, but a thing can not imply another thing. An event can not imply another event. An experience can not imply another experience. Nor can many of them imply another any better than one. You can not deduce one particular from another or from many others.

(Some deductivists feel undisturbed by this reasoning, though true, because they presuppose as self-evident "the uniformity of nature" or the law of causation, with the addition of which as a major premise they can indeed make deductions from experience. This principle, however, we shall find, is not self-evident and can not be deduced from anything self-evident.)

But though Hume's first proposition is irrefutable his second is untenable. Being a deductivist through and through, his first proposition forces him to the second: If inference from experience is not deductive it can not be rational, for (this is the tacit premise) all rational inference is deductive. As we shall see, the conclusion is impossible. Hence it exposes the falsity of the tacit premise. That is the deathblow. To be sure, deductivism has been walking about ever since exactly as before, looking quite unconscious of the tragedy, but it carries a fatal wound and must in the end succumb.

The deductive method and system are the one product of philosophy on which all are agreed. There are, of course, many controversies in and about deduction but virtually no controversy about this, that when it follows the strict rules it proves its point. It gives us certainty and it gives us a peculiar type of insight. Not the certainty that the conclusion is true, for that depends upon whether the premises are true, but the certainty that the conclusion follows from the premises. And it gives us the insight, all its own, that the conclusion arises *out of* the content of the premises by a peculiar and completely satisfying necessity. Indeed the deductive process as set forth by logicians is like a perfect mechanism in a glass case, with the whole action visible; so that we see not only how it works but why it must work as it does.

So it was entirely natural that philosophy should be enamoured of deduction and should insensibly have fallen into deductivism. This is the assumption that the only rational inference, the only inference convincing and satisfying to the reason, is deductive inference: that in which the entire content of the conclusion is found in the premises taken jointly, that in which there is no advance to new fact, to any fact beyond what is there found. On this view induction can be rationally justified only if its principles can be deduced from self-evident propositions. Thus logic is ultimately concerned with deduction only, and reason becomes the deductive faculty, the perception of implication.

This assumption, so deep as to be often unrecognized, because so utterly taken for granted, has reigned for many centuries. In our time those who are alienated in spirit from the old tradition, pragmatists, for example, none the less make the fatal concession of calling it rationalism, thus verbally submitting to the assumption that inference from experience is not rational, that it does not satisfy the demands of reason. And long before pragmatism the same concession was made by the false antithesis, so widely current, between rationalism and empiricism.

It must not be forgotten that many philosophers since Hume have accepted both of his two propositions and have saved the situation (as they thought) only by 'postulating' without logical support the uniformity of Nature or the empirical method of procedure.

To say of the crucial inferences of our lives and of the lives of institutions and of nations that they are not deductive is to say, for any sane and sober thought, that there is some other kind of sound inference than the deductive kind. You can not unfeignedly regard it as practically the wisest thing you can do to go by experience, you can not hold that your best wits warrant you in taking good care not to step off a roof or walk into a fire, and yet regard reason as withholding its approval. *For the faculty of discerning warrant for conclusions is what we mean by reason.* This consideration is final. Your professed philosophy does not annul your belief that uniform experience is a good reason. *You can not believe and not believe at the same time.* You cannot make the most responsible decisions on grounds of experience for yourself, for your family, for the stockholders whom you serve as a director, for your country which you serve as a statesman, you can not as a judge solemnly condemn a prisoner to execution as proved guilty by the evidence, and yet believe that the highest insight of your intellect refuses sanction or countenance to your proceeding. What you say is your philosophy is not your philosophy. These deductivists are entertaining a certain theoretic view and are not even aware that they are doing so on terms of insincerity.

Accordingly our main and well-tried use of the word 'reason' ignores deductivism. When a court pronounces something established "beyond a reasonable doubt" it is consummately indifferent to Hume's contention that at just such a point doubt is reasonable and belief irrational. When in practical affairs we speak of "the appeal to reason" we all with one accord mean the appeal to the inexorable teaching of experience, which we disregard at our peril. When we consider whether or how far the inferior animals possess reason we mean the power to infer intelligently from experience. When we say "Be reasonable" we mean, Bring your mind to face the facts, which are the facts of experience, showing what would be the effects of a certain course of action.

How the walls of philosophic tradition shut us in! Could we not make our escape, and confess that in this assumption of deductivism we have been under the influence of one of the oddest, quaintest forms of pedantry that have ever betrayed the human mind into a ridiculous position?

Then we shall be free to see that the trail reason chiefly and primarily follows is not that of Proposition and Implication but that of Fact and Significance. By facts here is meant existents and their beginning, ceasing, and changing, which we call events.

I ask the reader's close attention to the nature of what is here maintained to be the rational basis of the inferences of life and natural science, which, simple as it is, seems unfamiliar and peculiar so long as we are under the spell of the tradition. The type of thinking required must be rendered clear by other examples before we apply it to learning from experience.

I. THE METHOD

In each of the following cases, in which we feel that we are in sure possession of some knowledge or faculty, somebody arises who says "No, it is an illusion; no such thing exists". In each case the answer is: "What we confessedly have, what is given in experience, is what the term in question means". Hence there is no room for denial or doubt. What is required is not scepticism but analysis.

(1) In the first example the denial or doubt is fantastic and absurd. Yet historically it has in words been propounded. In Hindu religion and in an American cult certain immediate human experiences, such as pain, that

seem to "stain the white radiance of eternity", have been declared to be non-existent. But what is immediately given to consciousness can not be doubted, must exist, just so far as it is given. Why cannot the data of consciousness be doubted? Why must they exist? Because that which they exemplify and present *is what we mean by existence*. The idea of existence is derived from such as they. It would have no meaning to deny it of them. It would be saying, "These phenomena, which are examples of what I mean and have ever meant by existents, do not exist". (That they do exist is an explicative or 'analytic' judgment, in Kant's sense – not indeed for formal logic when written out as a proposition but for the consiousness in question. This – namely, an analytic proposition about the content of immediate consciousness – is the only case where such a proposition makes assertion about reality, because the only case where reality is given in the subject of the assertion.)

(2) Another instance is causation. Hume has been erroneously taken to mean that it is not what we have supposed it to be, that the universal human idea of it is an illusion. In fact he was not denying the idea but analyzing it. What he was denying was an assumption of philosophers, that an effect could be deduced from the nature of its cause. Thus in this case the imaginary Hume was the sceptic who arises, and the real Hume was the analyst who gives the answer. For human beings at large (who do not bother themselves in the least about deduction in the matter!) to cause a thing means to make it happen, and to make it happen means so to act that it will inevitably happen – according to the actual order of Nature, of which we learn from experience. We can not deny or doubt that this is causation, for *it is what we mean by causation*.

(3) It has been many a time asserted that Hume in his chapter on Personal Identity had denied the existence of the mind, or the self, or the ego. Michelet, after reading Taine 'On Intelligence', is said to have exclaimed that he had lost his 'moi'. Here the reader will see at once how our principle applies. A true analysis can not destroy. The self is given in experience and can not be doubted, and any investigator who, like Hume, offers an analysis thereof is saying in effect: "*This* is what is given in experience". By its agreement with that datum his account stands or falls. This, he says, *is what we mean by the self*.

(4) There are numerous further examples that might be cited; let us take but one more, the denial of free will. Man, it is said is not really free

in willing; he has to choose as he does because of the desires, the motive forces, that operate in his mind; he can not escape from the stream of cause and effect that flows within him. Against the assertion of free will has thus been set up determinism. But here again we have a false antithesis. Free will is the fact, and determinism is the analysis of that fact. We can not doubt or deny our freedom in willing because what we experience in the matter is *what we mean by freedom*. Our idea of freedom is derived from that experience. From where else could it be derived? It cannot be an illusion, because all the tests of freedom that we know may be applied to it, and we are still found willing as we elect to will. It is a misunderstanding to set the man over against his own desires and preferences and to picture him as compelled or fated by them. For when we say 'compelled', or 'fated', we mean against his preference or possible preference. We act for a reason. This means that the reason determines our act. We say as much. We say, "What finally determined me was" so and so. Moral praise and blame are descriptions of a person or his act, with the feeling appropriate to the kind of person he has shown himself to be. Moral responsibility means that the person was the conscious author of his act, so that his character, good or bad, may to that extent be inferred from it. His deserving punishment means that he *ought* to be punished – and the reason is the protection of society. "He could have done otherwise" is wholly true, according to the fullest import of the words, and means that he truly had the power to do otherwise. Closely examined, these terms one and all imply the truth of determinism, which merely provides an analysis of their meaning, without (if it be carried through with scrupulous accuracy) in the slightest degree altering it. The principle of free will says "*I* produce my volitions". Determinism says "My volitions are produced by *me*" – that is, by the man I am. Determinism is free will expressed in the passive voice. The 'liberty' of the indeterminist – there is no such idea; the thing he asserts and defines in words does not make liberty at all but the deprivation of it; yet in his own mind he is none the less conceiving real liberty. The point is that the indeterminist is thinking all the while in terms of determinism without knowing it, there being no other terms in which to think his thoughts. But he is resisting the analysis because he does not understand it, being unaccustomed to the discriminations on which all depends. Hence he is violently repelled by its language, which he misconstrues, and will not even try to trace its coincidence with his own thoughts.

He is insisting upon finding the whole of liberty as one of its parts (an unanalyzable part) because he stubbornly shrinks back from analyzing the whole. On the other hand, many determinists have insisted upon denying the whole because it can not be found as one of the parts. The entire controversy has been due to a confusion of ideas and the natural human balking at analysis.

II. EVIDENCE FOR FACT

It is the situation seen in these four cases that we find in the case of *evidence for fact*.

We think it very highly probable that the floor or the pavement will bear us, will not give way when we step upon it, and we think this because of our uniform experience. We can not deduce that it will do so. What it will do the next moment is a quite distinct matter from what it has done, and is not to be found, like a deduced conclusion, contained in the past facts. It will be a new fact. But we find a *significance* in the past facts. They shed the light of probability on the future. Probability is born of experience alone, and of uniformity alone in that experience. The past facts are of the nature of evidence. *This is what we mean by evidence for fact*; data possessing significance; it is what is meant by it in natural science, in courts of law, and in daily life. Significance is an elementary term of thought, that is, it is not to be further resolved. It is a relation, given in our mental experience, a unique relation between the facts in hand and the probability inferred. We are here at the bottom of our logical world.

There is no other evidence for fact than this, and no idea of any other evidence.

Deduction does not profess to prove any new fact. It expressly bases its whole claim to cogency on there being no new fact in the conclusion, on the conclusion's being already completely contained in the premises taken in their mutual relation.

Hence evidence for fact is never deductive. We may infer a particular fact from an accepted law *plus* the data before us, because the law by implication asserts it, but why do we accept that law; what is the evidence for it? Any assertion of a law must itself have evidence to support it. If the support offered is a wider law which implies the one in question, then what is the evidence for that wider law? No generalization can halt the quest for evidence, for we must always ask for the credentials of the generalization. Deduction is a process that may convey or transmit a truth about existent things or events but can never prove it to be such. The question whether propositions imply another proposition can be answered from their content without the least reference to whether the facts are as they declare or not. Thus deduction has nothing to do with truth, except the truth of deductive consequence, that is, implication.[1]

III. 'SELF-EVIDENT'

"But a self-evident law of things – suppose we start with that. Then will not all the rest follow by strict implication, and deductivism after all prove practicable? For instance, the law of cause and effect."

What is meant by 'self-evident'? That it is evident from the purport of the proposition itself that it is true. An explicative or analytic proposition, one for instance in which the predicate only repeats what is already contained in the subject, is deductively self-proving, it is self-evident according to the mere meaning of its terms, it carries its evidentness in its intrinsic import, the opposite would be self-contradictory. But no facts whatever about the real world can be inferred from it, and it would therefore be of no use for our purpose. However, a proposition not of this nature, an ampliative or synthetic proposition, is sometimes called self-evident. This will mean that without any reason to support it outside itself it appears true. Its opposite is not self-contradictory. In this case the fact is simply that our proposition is one that we find ourselves most firmly believing. A mathematician once said that anyone familiar with examination-papers knew that "It is evident" means "I do not know how to prove". If you can point to something in the proposition which makes its truth evident we are dealing with an explicative proposition. If you can not you have shown nothing in the matter but irresistible belief, and the term 'self-evident' is a misnomer. *In neither case have we evidence for fact.* That is found in experience alone.

IV. 'NECESSARY'

"But", it may be said, "you omit something essential. We may discern a necessity not in the meaning of the terms but in the nature of the subject-matter. We may discern a necessary relation between the characters mentioned, so that we know that they are always conjoined. Something additional to the mere meaning of the terms but belonging to the things they signify."

Such a position was inevitable. What the deductivist needs is a proposition necessarily true, but the necessity must on no account be 'logical' necessity, that of the implication of terms, for then the proposition would be merely analytic and could not be made the foundation of a deductive system revealing fact. Moreover, if it were analytic the necessity would have to be pointed out; otherwise it does not have to be pointed out, it can be 'discerned' or felt. Those who take this view can only, in each case they lay before us, appeal to us to discern it too. For them the truth of the proposition must be screwed down by necessity, but the necessity is not screwed down by anything. The proposition must not rest on mere individual belief, but the necessity, not being demonstrable, does rest on mere individual belief. What they are really feeling after is an implication that is not an implication – that has the advantage of being necessary without the disadvantage of being merely analytic. But what commonly happens is that they have hold of an analytic proposition without recognizing it.

As Hume showed us, there is no implication in Nature. No object or event implies any other. We can say on even broader ground: there is no necessity in Nature. That is clear from the meaning of the term. To say "You must do this" means "You will not be permitted not to do it" – alternatives are excluded. To say that something must be, or will necessarily be, means that nothing else is possible. But there is no possibility or impossibility in Nature; in Nature is only what *is*. The exclusion of alternatives is in the mind. There are no alternatives in Nature to be excluded. *Possibility* is a valid and indispensable term of thought to apply to matters where we do not yet know the outcome, but it is not an attribute residing *in* the object or event or physical relation itself. It is a proper part of our machinery of thought by which we deal with objects, events, relations.

If we are convinced by experience that there is a certain law of Nature, then anything contrary to this law will be for our thought impossible; that events will accord with the law will be necessary. Or if the definition of something includes a certain property, then anything to which that definition applies will of necessity have that property, because the definition would not apply unless it did. But neither of these cases means that there is any necessity in things.

Hence when a proposition asserts a relation that "from the very nature of the things mentioned", apart from the lessons of experience, is necessary, we shall always find if we look sharply enough that this necessity resides in the meaning or our terms. If on the other hand a relation can be denied without self-contradiction there is no reason to believe in it except experience. The question is not what is momentarily in the mind of the utterer, but what is in the meaning of the terms.

To be simply, and therefore irresponsibly, discerned as necessary is a dangerous situation for 'truth'. For it has a way of being mistakable. There is no better commentary on the situation than the history of Euclid's principles. But there are countless examples closer to us in time. Professor Blanshard, for instance, offers us a round dozen of necessary synthetic propositions, but eight of them turn out to be analytic, three not always true, and one of doubtful status.[2]

It is interesting that recent seekers-out of "synthetic judgments *a priori*" do not present among them any that could serve as a basis for induction.

The whole quest for a self-evident or necessary starting-point is not an endeavor to show deduction capable of proving fact – that is wholly out of the question – but an endeavor to supply it with a basic fact from another source, namely, a direct discernment of the mind.

We can not say "What a pity there is no clinching deductive proof that our conclusions from experience follow", we can not with Mr Bertrand Russell call it "profoundly unsatisfactory" that there is none, or intimate that the day may come when it will be found, for the reason that deduction as a process is by its whole nature irrelevant to the subject.[3]

V. GROUND, NOT SIGN

We must, of course, distinguish sharply between significance and mere sign, in the sense of token or signal or symbol, such as a word or a red light or a pointing arrow or the sounding of a dinner-gong. No one imagines that a mere sign or reminder contains in itself the evidence for the thing it stands for. Signs are a constant requisite for perception and for action. But they are not and are never pretended to be a proof or argument; we do not regard the sign as gathering up within it the justification for belief. But that is precisely what we regard our data as doing. To supply this justification in the case of a sign we have to recall the uniform coupling in the past of sign and thing signified. The sign does not contain in itself a uniformity of experience. But in just that uniformity evidence consists. Significance then does not mean for us here the function of a mere convenient mark or tag. It means, as we saw, a unique relation between facts and the probability of further facts. The data are a sign only in a deepened and completed sense of that term.

VI. THE CASE OF ERROR

It is the very nature of inference from experience to carry its own rule and corrective with it. It is an anticipation of the as yet unexperienced and it must correct itself by the experience when it comes. This, its own due correction, reminds it that it was only probable, however extremely so. The notion of mere probability of itself prepares us for an outcome other than the probable one. If the inference turns out unfortunate, if what was deemed probable does not appear, then we have for the future to supplement our inference from data by an inference from more data. It is the appearance of a uniformity in events that purports to render probable the continuance of uniformity; any departure from this that we discover is a new datum, changing the pattern of events, which is the whole basis of our reasoning; we may after a while be able to find an underlying uniformity which was there all the while and which explains the break that disappointed us. The extent of the uniformity is the extent of the probability. The conditions and qualifications of the uniformity are the conditions and qualifications of the probability.

Since our inference is only that the inferred event is probable, not certain, its failing us need not prove any error; it may still have been probable from the then point of view; the only possible error will have been in gauging the degree of probability. Just as in deduction there are hasty and false inferences, so there are in reasoning from experience. But they have no tendency to discredit the basis of all, the significance of data, which is uniformity's prophecy of its own continuance. On the contrary, our sense that errors are many and inference perilous is itself learned from experience and reaffirms the authority of that guide. Thus the sole standard of judgment arises out of the very nature of the whole process.

VII. THE RÔLE OF ASSOCIATION

But Hume says that reasoning from experience is just the association of ideas; it can be psychologically explained but not rationally justified. Well, but suppose it can be psychologically explained *and* rationally justified. All processes of thought, even deductive processes that no one doubts to be rationally justified, are due to the so-called association of ideas. Logic is not a propulsive force in the mind. And a propulsive force there has to be.

Was Hume perhaps half-consciously making here an unnoted assumption? Was he assuming that an expectation which was a valid inference would be *produced*, psychologically speaking, by the premises that justified it, and because they justified it? So that to show that it was produced by a mere association of ideas was to prove it invalid? At all events this is not the case. The idea of sequence in the mind and the idea of a ground that warrants a conclusion are ideas on different subjects, not rivals or alternatives. A probability appears not merely as succeeding but as based upon, conditional upon, the preceding data. They are its ground. Therefore what matters in Hume's argument respecting inference from experience is not that it can be explained by 'association' – all inference can – but that it is not rationally warranted on its own assigned ground; and this is where he was misled by his deductivism.

That there is a mental machinery that enables us, with voluntary care, to carry on justified inference, is a fortunate fact, not a disillusioning one.

To find that significance appears through the working of a law of association does not make it anything else than significance. For as such it does appear. It matters not what machinery it depends upon, it remains the first and last consideration for thought. The psychological law of association is not at the bottom of our logical world; it is a particular law of events – mental events – inferred by an inductive process. Significance *is* at the bottom of our logical world, and only by the use of it do we reach the discovery of the law of association. That discovery is no discovery, we have no reason to believe in the law of association, if data do not signify. The mind's outlook and its primary terms of thought can not be disqualified and dismissed by one of the discoveries that they alone render possible. The point is that *no logical inconsistency can be pointed out* between the discovery and the reasoning that establishes it, between the machinery of thinking as revealed by psychology and the reasons of thinking as they figure in inference. We are not asking that the manner and mechanism of mental sequence shall be the logical support of our conclusions from experience, we are only asking that they shall not be inconsistent with it. And in truth *they have no power to be inconsistent with it*. So that Hume's psychology and logical criticism can not effect the sabotage upon rationality in life that he imagined them to do.

Here is a world in which regular processes appear. Here is a mind fitted to be wound up by the regular processes so that it expects them. Thus the mind is made to reflect the regularities of the real world. Here is an inner discernment of significance which justifies that reflection from the mind's point of view. The three are in harmony. What Hume failed to see in this situation was the priority and ultimacy for thought of the essential terms of thought. And it was his ingrained deductivism, on which he never had any "sceptical doubts" at all, that made him miss it. A man of his time could not be expected to do otherwise. Let it be remembered that he took the great decisive step, and laid before us all that we require in order to make our escape from deductivism.

VIII. THE TRANSLATION

Thus far, for its great convenience, I have been using the term 'probability'. This expresses with exactness what is before the mind in empirical inference – except where absolute certainty is before the popular mind and has to be transformed into probability by any thoroughly circumspect thought. Such thought remembers that in empirical inference we have no absolute certainties but at best extremely high probabilities.

But now we must recognize that probability itself is only a conveniently simpler substitute for the objective real. There is no probability in nature, of course, any more than there is possibility, impossibility, or necessity. Probability is often defined as "degree of expectancy". But it does not appear before the mind as expectancy, but as something 'objective'. Expectancy is a psychological term. In thinking of something as probable, the mind is not psychologizing, not thinking of its own expectation as an expectation; its interest and attention are solely upon the object. When the object-matter of thought is not quite fixedly self-maintaining before the mind whenever we think of the subject (which it is in absolute belief) but only approaching to such fixity, we call it probable.

The reality for which probability stands is, of course, frequency. If certain events have uniformly been conjoined we expect that they will be conjoined in the future more frequently than not, and that an expectation of their conjunction will more frequently meet with the thing expected than any other expectation.

Thus the whole affair of probabilities can be translated into frequencies.

IX. FIRST PRINCIPLES

One can imagine a questioner saying: "You tell us that we may properly infer from the particulars of experience, but you really have not proved this principle. If it is a first principle, how do we know it to be correct?"

Yes, this might actually be said despite all that has foregone.

Significance, a relation given in experience, means real or true significance. The adjective adds nothing to the noun.

We do not take our start from a first principle. The notion that we must is simply the last gasp of deductivism. We begin with the concrete data, drawing our inferences directly from them. These are no first principles. It is the facts that are first. The general principle that such inference is justified, far from being the foundation, is itself a generalization from experience. The notion of first principles in philosophy is a creation of deductivism. It has led modern philosophy down the wrong path. Being 'first', there is nothing from which they can be derived, they can not be proved, consequently they have been the great sphere of irresponsibility. We have been told that the truth of first and fundamental propositions followed from the meaning of their own terms (as by Descartes and Spinoza in certain cases); that they are innate principles; that they are "intuitive certainties", "self-evident truths" (as by Locke); that they are perceived to be true by common sense; that they are necessary truths, reason being the faculty of perceiving them; that they are synthetic judgments *a priori* without which we can not experience an objective world; that they are voluntary postulates; that they are hypotheses upon which we act in order to put them to the test of experience (the assumption that experience will be a valid test being never rationally explained at all).

If we could deduce a body of knowledge from explicative, analytic,

merely verbal propositions, for instance, propositions in which the predicate only repeats an attribute of the subject, then knowledge might follow
by a tight deduction from first principles. But we can not, since from
explicative propositions no facts about the real world can ever be deduced
at all. This is the inexorable dilemma of first principles: either they are
analytic, and then they give us nothing about the real world, or they are
synthetic, and then there is nothing to guarantee that they are true.

No method of helping oneself to first principles is more curious or more
winsome than that of postulating them. The term gives to sheer assumption a sound of the highest intellectual respectability. What might puzzle
the novice in philosophy is why the postulator happens to posit the basis
of induction, for example, exactly as it is accepted and built upon in science and in life. The whole limitless field of conceivable hypotheses on the
subject lies equally open to him, and he is supposed to have no logical
ground for choice between them. Of course the answer is that he takes the
one he already knows to be the true one. Postulating is the ceremony in
which the deductivist, having pretended to surrender all the empirical
knowledge he has as a human being, takes comfortable possession of it
again – only as a pure venture of the intellect, you understand.

X. EMPIRICISM

By empiricism I mean the tenet that our knowledge is derived from experience; that, for instance, all generic truths are inferred from the data of
experience. It has been an expression in philosophy of the scientific
temper that in these centuries has been making its new and prodigious
conquests. It has been from the first a call to responsibility, responsibility
for thinking according to facts. It has said, Go to the facts of experience
as your only source, and at every stage grimly master your obstinate
impulses to give the rein to your own imagination, preferences, antipathies, – your favorite theories. But in philosophy it has been strangely
feeble, compared with its mighty advance outside, for the tradition of
deductivism and the "first principles" of which deductivism has been the
great fancier have weighed heavily upon it and kept it low. Deductivism
has abundantly patronized science but astonishingly delayed the real admission of scientific standards into philosophy.

How singularly unhappy have been the fortunes of empiricism! Did ever a salutary principle in philosophy have more luckless beginnings and early days! It was born under the bar sinister. Hume himself pronounced it an illegitimate child of philosophy, not fathered by reason. Its first great sponsor[4] sends it out into the world with the stigma of irrationality upon it.

Later in the same century it had to face the profoundly impressive and ingenious philosophy of Kant, with its unusually imposing machinery – all the more impressive because in emphasizing the distinction between the percepts we immediately experience and the objective world we construct he carried observation distinctly further than Hume, and because of something lovable in the personality of the author. But the peculiarity of Kant's system was that it made the mind itself in a certain manner give the law to experience. Here was an influence antithetic to the very essence of empiricism, which is that experience must give the law to the mind. Also Kant's philosophy affirmed the mind's right, for its own thinking, to give the law in a sense to "the supersensible world". Conceptions could hardly have been hatched more poisonous to the moral purpose which had its hope in empiricism. The new philosophy was in subtle conspiracy with the deep impulse of human nature to indulge its own congenial imaginations in the absence of corroborating evidence – the more insinuatingly so because, outside fundamental philosophy, Kant was himself so entirely in sympathy with science and modern intellect. The mind's shaping of the world, so far as that can go, is accomplished through action, whose first demand is that we shall learn from the world how *it* will act, a receptive learning with which our prepossessions tamper at our peril.

According to the well-worn quotion, Hume woke Kant from his dogmatic slumber – and the British idealist philosophy of the late nineteenth century seems to have regarded it as the former's whole function in history to 'call' Kant at the proper hour in the morning. But the fact seems to have been that Kant looked heavily at him a few moments, then turned over on the other side and went to sleep again. To be sure, he was not now on the same side, and his new and complex dreams were undoubtedly much affected by the interruption. Still, the last state of that thinker was, in ultimate character, dogmatic slumber. He had not thoroughly awakened, and philosophy had not thoroughly awakened, to the human mind's self-effacing quest for fact that had begun.

Midway in the next century (to pick out only a very few salient points in the history) came Mill, as the most prominent spokesman for the principle. He did very great service, but the best of it was not his fundamental rationale of the principle. In one vital respect he damaged its cause in the sight of philosophy by maintaining that the truths of mathematics are learned from experience – here relapsing from the teaching of Hume, who had made them "relations of ideas", not dependent for proof on "matters of fact". (As a logician a surprising inattention to Hume was one of Mill's chief failings). This and certain other features of his philosophy presented a sadly exposed front for empiricism to the idealist critics and the logicians of the remainder of his century, and the doctrine suffered accordingly.

Early in the present century empiricism fell into the hands of the pragmatists. Pragmatism is an excellent sermon but a confused philosophy. As a sermon it did not really require any new doctrine of its own about truth or meaning, any controversial paradoxes whatever. It could as well, yes, and better, have preached its practical gospel on the basis of the plain ideas of common intelligence; and its valuable amplifications of psychological truths already known need not have tried to turn into a philosophy. Instead of that, by introducing its very vulnerable paradoxes, it has gravely prejudiced the cause of empiricism, as also by strangely identifying itself in some chief quarters with the advocacy of "the will to believe", which is of course at deadly enmity with empiricism, and by confusing hypothesis with belief. The blurring of a distinction so elementary and broad at this last is deplorable.

Lastly, the established meaning of the term itself has been disregarded, it has been given various senses, the idea has fallen into confusion, and when anyone professes it who knows what he is professing?

XI. REASON

Deduction, we noted, has nothing to do with truth except the truth of implication, nothing to do except to follow out the scope of concepts and the meaning of terms. Now deductivism makes reason to be the deductive faculty, which is placing it in the same position. It has nothing to do with the real world. It has nothing to do with seeing things as they are. But adjustment to the real world is the whole business or struggle of life. We must know what we have to deal with. The human mind stretches out its rational faculty to clutch somehow at that world, but, if this long-established tradition be correct, can get no hold upon it, can not, by utmost reach, so much as touch it.

This consequence of deductivism has not been fully faced or seen – except by certain recent logicians who have set forth the nature of 'logic' with an explicitness that leaves nothing to be desired for complete exposure of the artificial narrowness of the conception.

Reason is the name we give to our recognition not only of implication but of indication. We see that certain facts indicate the probable coming of other facts. We see that this conclusion *follows* from the first facts. It is possible to define 'follows' as meaning simply that if the one is true the other is true. If that be our definition there is no difference between deductive and empirical following; the conclusion which is a probability and the conclusion which is an implicate equally 'follow'. But this definition does not really give us the whole idea of following in either case. We have the dead fact that where the one is true the other is true but this omits the vital idea that the one is a conclusion from the other, it omits the inner idea of consequence, it omits the fact that the one arises from the other. Now granting that by the definition just given the two cases are alike, in the other respect they are, of course, completely different. In both cases we write out the proposition called conclusion as separate from the premises, but in the deductive case it has been contained in those premises. In one true sense it does not have to 'follow' because it has gone on before; it has a place in the front rank. It is written out as a separate proposition, a conclusion, for the convenience of our slow grasp. Inductive following has a better right to the figure of speech. Here the conclusion truly comes after the premises, not having been present before. And the idea of following, the peculiar type of dependence or consequence, is a relation as elementary in nature as that of time, which we express by the words 'before' and 'after', a relation to which as presented in mental experience reason does not shut its eyes. For by reason we mean the power to perceive the justification for belief, be it of any sort whatever.

It is seldom that one is in the luxurious position of putting forth in this JOURNAL a thesis in which all readers will agree – I mean, in their capacity as human beings, whatever protestations their philosophy may raise. Such is the proposition that inference from experience is rational.

Our debt to Hume is immense, in that his disquieting result meant really nothing less than the downfall of deductivism. It has had a reign of extraordinary length and absoluteness, and great will be the fall of it.

NOTES

[1] I do not say "logical consequence", for logic is not all deductive, being the theory of proof, or of ground and consequent in general.

[2] *The Nature of Thought*, Vol. II, p. 407.

[3] Professor Reichenbach, whose deductivism is of the purest, gives us an attempt to justify the inductive procedure in spite of Hume. Accepting Hume's argument that no conclusions can be deduced from experience, he undertakes nevertheless to deduce (not from experience) that if we wish to predict at all, our "best bet" will be to proceed as if we were reasoning from experience in the approved scientific fashion. Thus all, practically, that Hume rejects, from the strictly deductive point of view, is brought back from that same point of view as our best venture if we are not to give up anticipating the future at all. But deduction breaks down in this ingenious approach just as utterly as under Hume's direct treatment. Professor Reichenbach appears to hold two propositions: (1) that *if* there is any uniformity in Nature continuing into the future, the inductive procedure will be a sound method of predicting it, and (2) that, such a uniformity being possible, no other procedure offers an equal advantage. It is the second proposition which is unfounded. In any one moment of time, standing isolated as we do between past and future, no method (if deduction is to be our only light) holds out any probability or any advantage whatever, not even that ghost of an advantage that he ascribes to the inductive procedure, hence no method is to be preferred to any other. He misses the broad fact that if Hume's analysis is right we can just as well predict on the basis of caprice, or dreams, or tossing up pennies, or the word of a fortune-telling gypsy or a 'clairvoyant' (to use an example he discusses) as on the basis of uniform data, because all exactly alike have no deductive bearing on the future. Conceivably any one of these might be a successful method of predicting. Nor can betting points, practical advice, or preference ever possibly be extracted from 'tautologies'. Were it not for the needless complication of his argument and its consequent elusiveness all this would leap to view. The moment the idea is stated in plain and brief language it goes to pieces. Alas, how often this happens in philosophy! Cf., e.g., Reichenbach, *Experience and Prediction*, Ch. V, and *Readings in Philosophical Analysis*, ed. by Feigl and Sellars, pp. 324ff.

[4] He may surely be so considered. Locke was not an empiricist though often called so; it was the 'materials' of our knowledge that he held we derive from experience, the idea-stuff – the terms, not the propositions. Hobbes desired to make experience the sole source but, owing to his period, had not recognized (nor had Locke) the conditions of the problem. The opportunity for Hume's insight was marvelously prepared by the convergence of Locke, Berkeley, and Malebranche. His greatness was that he saw what they, while helping him toward it, failed to see – the analysis of causation.

MORAL TRUTH

[Throughout his adult life Miller was persistently concerned with moral theory, with analysis of key concepts and principles in ethics, though other problems in philosophy were the center of his attention for longer periods and in his later years he was preoccupied with the application of morality. His second publication in 1893 was an analysis of the relation of 'ought' to 'is' as bearing on relativism. During his teaching at General Theological Seminary he wrote on the relation of rules to a "morality of results", and in 1929, after conversations with Ludwig Wittgenstein in Vienna, he published a brief analysis of how pleasure is conjoined with welfare. Now, in the following article from 1950, Miller is initially concerned with the problem of subjectivity and objectivity in moral judgments. He explores the relation of feelings and attitudes to statements of psychological fact and concludes that "moral truth" depends on the functional character of morality, its purpose to meet human needs, and ultimately on the facts in respect to consequences of action and man's nature.

Miller planned to devote chapters to the theme of this article and the one of 1929 in a book, started in 1941 but never completed, that would show "analysis at work" in ethics as well as on free will, the knowledge-problem, Hume and causality, and universals.]

(1) A classical story for the young represents a boy as saying of a younger one, "But he is such a nice little fellow". And a wise woman comments, "That is, you love him".

There is the key to the 'objectivity' and the 'subjectivity' of judgments of value. "It is good"; "That is, you like it". "It is morally good"; "That is, you feel moral esteem for it." Wherever the one can be sincerely said, with the staple meaning of the term behind it, the other is true.

(2) Nevertheless the purport of the one is not that of the other. The boy was not recognizing that he loved the younger one, he was not thinking of himself or his feelings; his attention and interest as he spoke were upon

the small boy. He may even be a little startled when attention is turned upon his own state of mind, a little unprepared for this sudden classification of it. That is decidedly, for him, introducing another topic. So it is when we think morally. We are thinking about what is good or bad, we are not thinking about our feelings.

(3) This is the reason behind the stout contention of G. E. Moore (in *Principia Ethica* and *Ethics*) and other writers that the statement that some person or persons have a certain feeling is never equivalent to an assertion of moral value and can never prove moral value. That contention is logically correct. The moral judgment takes an attitude toward the object of thought, embodies a feeling toward it. The psychological statement describes the attitude but does not take it.

(4) Value is the aspect that the object wears in the eyes of those who prize it. You cannot, by talking about the feelings of other people, demonstrate that the object you have your eye upon has value.

(5) You cannot do so even by talking about your own feelings. "It is morally good" does not mean "I approve of it", although when I say the former sincerely the latter is true. Even if I say the latter with earnestness and the intent to impress and influence others, still the proposition itself, taken in its actual import, introduces the foreign idea of self, says something about the speaker and nothing about the object, although it means that the speaker *regards* the object as good. The ethical statement says that the object *is* good. As a humorist might put it, the person in question, when saying this last, is approving of the object, but doing so strictly anonymously. "I approve of it" is a statement of fact, not of value. And the idea of value is not an idea of bare fact and cannot be extracted from any such.

(6) We cannot even say that "I approve of it" is "implicit" in "It is good", at least if implicit means implied. It is not implied but our knowledge of the situations in which particular words are used shows us that the speaker is approving.

(7) But though the ethical statement cannot be proved from the psychological statement it can be explained thereby. It can be understood thereby. The difference of import is an entirely natural matter, due to the difference between valuing an object oneself and describing someone else's valuation of it.

(8) This double aspect of value, the 'objective' and the 'psychological',

is of course a fundamental feature of the economy of life. Feelings expressed by the words 'good' and 'bad' are aroused by the object of our thought, are (ultimately at least) concerned with the effects of that object upon life, and (as is said of naval guns) are trained upon the object. From the practical point of view it would ordinarily be mere waste of consciousness to think of self as the possessor of the feelings or even to classify them as feelings at all. So far as we stop to think of that we are turning away from the concerns of life. Life calls upon us to take the front view, not to turn round upon ourselves.

(9) At last, however, it becomes advisable, for the best understanding and steering of life, to turn round upon ourselves. Eventually man discovers himself, just as the boy (with aid) discovered himself. Man discovers that value has its seat in his feelings, that the stuff of which the idea of value is composed in his reaction, that there is no such thing as intrinsic value in the object of his thought.

(10) This does not mean that he catches himself in an illusion, a superstition, which consists in an objectifying of what is a mere feeling. Mr Santayana wrote in an early book that beauty is "objectified pleasure". In the same vein it might be said that all value is objectified satisfaction or appreciation. This would be to say that, so far as its apparent objectivity is concerned, it is an illusion. But all he need have said, I think, was that beauty is pleasure not subjectified, not turned upon and classified as a state of mind, not subjected to psychology, but taken as it comes before us in experience, a glow, as it were, in which the object is bathed. There is no objectification and in that respect no illusion. There does not have to be. There is simple experience. We cannot begin by projecting our feelings out of the mind because we have never classed them as in the mind or as feelings at all. In the experience of value we have no call or occasion to do so. So long as the experience is not subjectified it appears as simply as the object appears, *it goes with the object*, it is not in any wise sundered from it.

(11) Pleasure indeed is not something that could be objectified – projected as a quale of the object. The pleasantness of pleasure is not an intrinsic quality of the sensations and other experiences we call pleasures, there is no intrinsic quality common to them all. The only attribute they all have in common, which makes us call them pleasures, is that they are attractive when absent and welcome when present; in other words, it is

an extrinsic attribute consisting of our reaction to them. The painful is the intolerable, that which we are so constituted as not to tolerate, and the pleasant is that which we are so constituted as to seek and prefer. Rather curiously, pleasure has been, even for much psychology, the last refuge and hiding place of the idea of intrinsic value. But there is no such thing. So what is called objectifying pleasure could be nothing else than uniformly regarding the object, for its own sake alone, with the same favorable re-action. And this, I think, is what regarding it as beautiful is. It is also, psychologically speaking, what regarding something as morally good is, except that the associations and the species of reaction are different, and that it is not thus regarded (in fully developed thought, which is rare) for its own sake alone but for its consequences.

(12) The ethical judgment "It is good" lays down this predicate un-conditionally. If you say it is not good, then from the point of view of the judgment you are wrong. Just as the person judging is not thinking of himself, not thinking of his feelings as such, so with equal innocence he is not thinking of the matter as an affair of other people's feelings – of any feelings at all. His sense of good arises in connection with some act, motive, or character he is considering, and *remains affixed* to it. He means simply that the act, motive, or character has the attribute expressed by the word 'good'. It is possible for a mind thus to think of something as morally good without qualification or condition; which means to think of it as something that "has the honor" expressed by the word (psychology knows its content to consist in the thinker's feeling) *as a matter of course – ohne Weiteres*. The mind stops there; and its stopping is the whole secret of the simple objectivity. The mind does not go on to class the feeling as such, to subjectify it. The act or motive simply presents itself in thought with a certain unquestioned favorable status. This is the fact expressed by saying (as Professor G. E. Moore originally said) that good appears in the judgment as a characteristic of the object. It does so appear. If we did not recognize this we should surely be doing less than delicate justice to the mental situation as it is.

(13) There is a possible thought here that might mislead us; namely, that the feeling remains in fact a mere feeling, whereas a judgment of truth refers beyond the mind to some independent object, so that the feeling unless falsely objectified, cannot serve as the meaning of a term in a proposition. But there is surely no such thing as consciously referring

any mental content whatever beyond the mind in the moment of experiencing or conceiving it, hence the supposed difference and discrepancy do not exist. But into this subject I cannot now go further.

(14) Thus to the mind in question the judgment when expressed in words is a proposition if ever there was one. What we have to say about it is not that it is no proposition but that if taken philosophically as a finality in this unconditioned form it is not true. Philosophically we must go on and recognize that the favorable status does not attach to the object as a matter of course; they can be disjoined; it is not an intrinsic attribute of the object.

(15) The moral word 'good' has of course many differences of association, suggestion, and use, as C. L. Stevenson has so forcibly illustrated in *Ethics and Language*. There are three stages in our use of it. First, it may have, and often has, no meaning at all in the mind except that this word is attached to, or is the word to use for, whatever is in question. Second, the word has, however, a staple meaning, taken as such and ready to be instantly recalled to mind. We must remember a chief characteristic of words, that they have a meaning *recognized* as *belonging* to them, which, however, does not always have to be recalled in full when the word is used. In this case it is the meaning made of our reaction. This staple meaning is not predictive, or imperative, or hortatory, or in any sense persuasive, merely because it is too simple, too bare, too unenlarged upon for all that; the mind does not linger to think of the future, or of other people to be influenced, not even of one's future self. Third, when we do use if for predictive, imperative, hortatory, or other persuasive purposes we are using the original simple reaction and emphasizing it for this further purpose – we are keeping it and adding something else.

(16) Upon this 'objective' and unconditional import of the moral judgment has been founded the philosophy which makes ethics a sphere of truth as independent of the affirmer's mind as the facts of history or natural science. At a large philosophical meeting in England some years ago, a British journal reported, most of the speakers took this view.

Now from the foregoing it is evident that their doctrine is thinkable; they were not in that respect deceiving themselves. To think it we have only to stop where the everyday mind stops in forming judgments of good and evil, right and wrong. We have only to leave the favorable or unfavorable moral status of the object-matter as it appears, not psychologized, not superseded, not taken up into a naturalistic world – we have only to stay where we are and thus keep the same background, instead of advancing or ascending and thus commanding an ulterior background. Their thought is definite, clear, and self-consistent. But is it true?

(17) Unfortunately for its truth it must on the same ground be extended to other cases to which they would not for a moment extend it. Not only to beauty, to which many of them do extend it, but to humor, for example. Our notion of a good jest or a bad jest, of a ludicrous incident or a 'delicious' remark, has precisely the same objectivity and subjectivity. The comic quality appears as imply attaching to the object-matter, but can be psychologized as the reaction of the person amused. So with the good or the bad in the taste of food, so with the horrible, the terrible, the eerie, the sepulchral, the foul, the vile, and many other phases of perceived things. These phases have their being in feeling but they do not label themselves as feeling or as subsisting in the mind. That is an afterthought.

Indeed, quite beyond the realm of value we find the same double aspect. If you must have an 'absolute' good and evil, then on just the same grounds you will have an absolute 'up' and 'down'. For us all in ordinary circumstances each of these words stands for an ultimate, unaltering standard direction. And so it was for the whole human race until they discovered that the earth was round and then (in their more reflective moments) saw that 'up' and 'down' were relative to the surface of the earth and to gravity, that what is here 'up' would on the other side of the earth be 'down'. Likewise it is entirely possible to conceive absolute rest, absolute motion, absolute location – without reducing them in thought to relativity – for that is what we do every day. Further instances abound. The believer in an ethical truth independent of the mind's feeling is merely doing the like in his sphere. He is clinging to the naive conception and resisting the insight that comes with the increase of the knowledge of nature, which includes human nature.

(18) Is there then no such thing as moral truth?

It is completely obvious that there is moral truth. Life forces the perception upon us. There is something strangely frivolous and shallow in the frame of mind that can deny it.

(19) The broadest fact about morality is that it arose and persisted to discharge a function, to enable men to live together satisfactorily, to protect and increase their welfare (which means what their nature demands)

in that social condition; and that it has never been aware of its function, and is not today (except in the minds of the tiniest minority). Hence the opportunity, dear to mankind, to forbid and denounce and punish has been taken advantage of in its name for all manner of fantastic and cruel purposes, and the diligent, single-minded study of what moral standards would best protect and increase welfare has hardly begun. Morality is an incomparably potent instrument that has never been finished in the making or fully used for its end.

(20) Thus morality exists to meet human need. It is entirely based on "the moral sentiments". There is a factor, namely human need itself and growing human knowledge of what will meet it, that works toward shaping the moral sentiments for the function for which they arose, and thus bringing them to a basis of agreement.

(21) In proportion as they are in agreement, in proportion as the moral sentiments are fundamentally shared, the simple objective statement of moral value has a true meaning. The favorable or unfavorable moral status that the naive mind has treated as going with the object unconditionally, as a matter of course, does go thus with it so long as we judge truly the object's effects upon life. Men react fundamentally alike to pain, cold, starvation, mutilation, robbery, insult, and much besides. The moral sentiments that arise from this tend to one type. Moral truth is based on the potential and inevitable ultimate agreement of reaction, the first or 'instinctive' and the second or moral reaction. In their tastes and fancies men are utterly different, but in their vital needs, including the need of liberty for their tastes and fancies so far as not seriously hurtful to others, they are in a certain true sense one.

When brothers and sisters speak of 'Father' or 'Mother', or even of 'the house', 'the dining room', 'the front door', their words would not tell a stranger to what persons or abode they referred. But within the family the reference is clear; they all stand in the same relation to what is spoken of. So when they say, "Well, we shall have to", or "That wouldn't do, of course", or "That would be the very thing", they may be speaking in relation to the family aims or interests, which they share and hence can all take for granted.

Value is the aspect that the object wears in the eyes of those who prize it. When the family of those who prize it are talking together they can refer to its value as something understood in common. Even when they differ about a particular value, they all know that there is for them, as soon as they see clearly the workings of the object, a value in the matter that all must ultimately perceive. And this is the situation for the human family. There is moral truth for them because they can say, "We are of one blood, you and I".

(22) Philosophy has only to add its illuminating insight that 'good' and 'evil' are not intrinsic attributes of the things so called, but attributes that necessarily pertain to them from the point of view of life. It is pure gain to see that they have this status and not an independent one. Morality as Max Otto has said, exists for life, not life for morality. All depends upon human necessities, and they upon the constitution of men *de facto*. Bad serves to mark the objectionableness, and good the acceptableness, of what is so called, in the light of human need.

(23) The effects of the object of our thought upon life, the consequences of the act, motive, or character we are considering, this is the one all-important theme. The end once settled, and it is settled by the requirements of human nature, all the rest is a question of cause and effect. And the question of cause and effect is so fateful, it so poignantly demands attention from ethics, as to throw every other topic of this article into triviality. Moral sentiments have conflicted and gone so disastrously astray, or fallen so short of the need, because they have not been adjusted to this standard.

RELIGION AND HUMAN WELFARE

WHAT RELIGION HAS TO DO WITH IT

[Throughout his life Dickinson Miller was concerned with the experience and interpretation of religion, specifically Christianity. His concern was such that he was ordained in the Episcopal Church, taught Christian Apologetics at General Theological Seminary from 1911 to 1924, and served as a 'supply' clergyman over many years. Like James, Miller saw religion as a reinforcement of life directed to human welfare, but he departed from James in regard to theism and the meaning of religious ideas. Above all, for Miller religion was centered on human welfare. This was the focus of its symbolical terms and statements, a focus apparent in his writings to follow on the defense of the faith, Matthew Arnold, conscience and morality.

'What Religion Has To Do With It' appeared while Miller was teaching philosophy at Columbia University in 1909 and was part of a course of reading in psychotherapy sponsored by the League of Right Living. Here Miller proceeds from the frictions and chaos of feelings and appetites to divine power, "personified Goodness", as a means of control and finally a presence sought for itself. Control and harmony in the higher portion of our stream of consciousness also brings strength to the body, and this becomes the ground of co-operation and mutual learning between clergymen and physicians as in the alliance begun by Dr Elwood Worcester. In the end Miller indicates that religion is concerned with another kind of truth than science, not the "bad science" of unproved metaphysical or theological propositions but "the truth of value, the truth of importance". In discussing the symbolical character of religious ideas in his 90th year, he remarked that he had been a 'naturalist' in his view of man and the world since the age of thirteen.]

It has been truly said by a German theologian that the sentiment of religion arises from the instinct of self-preservation. We now see why fear, disquietude, vague depression and oppression are enemies of life. They impair efficiency and this embarrass the labors that keep life safe and healthy. So much is obvious. But more than this, deeper than this, they poison the beckoning thought of life in a man's own mind. They weaken the strong spring of life within him. Then the vitality within him arises in desperation to shake off the oppression, to check and drive out the poison from his mind. If peradventure there is one overarching power it can trust, deliverance is within reach. Thus is the arrival of religion the arrival of reinforcements for human life.

And now comes a new and extraordinary phase. Man discovers that he has to struggle and contrive, not only against his outer environment, but against himself. There are impulses that in certain moments he would gladly make supreme over his life, gladly form into resolutions; but they are soon borne down by the impulses that other moments rouse. The spiritual weather within him is subject to change, heat giving place to cold and cold to a dull medium. There are indescribable times of moral paralysis. One could rule one's self if the same ruler were always there. Life is bewildering, memory short, circumstance fleeting, consistency difficult. Reason, habit, inertia, the appetites, the aspirations, are at friction with one another. He discovers the chaos of himself. Like the environment, he too has uncontrollable possibilities – unless here also there is controlling power with which, as it were, an understanding can be reached. If so, he may hope to attain some inward peace.

Inwardly now he makes submission to the divine power. He invokes its protection against the unruly forces in himself. He asks the divine power to take command in his soul, to save him from yielding to temptation, to pour in the reinforcements of its spiritual aid. Here is a notable proceeding – the typical proceeding of religion now carried into the penetralia of the soul. One moment tries to win security for all the moments – tries in one act to provide for all the unexpectednesses of life. Its act – its 'reaction' – is the religious reaction, the sacrifice and self-surrender to God, that he in his turn may invisibly safeguard what we hold dearest.

Only, in this innermost theater, the transaction tends to work its own fulfillment. To turn to personified Goodness and yield one's self, is by the very act to work upon one's self, to mellow in some degree the future disposition of the soul. The highest form of the religious act is to pray, no longer for God's gifts, but for his presence itself. And this very prayer is a potent force in transforming the inner man.

What relieves the soul relieves the body. The unrest that religion has power to cure is not only a mental unrest, but also a bodily unrest. So is man constructed. To relieve that bodily unrest is in itself to leave the nervous system and therefore the organism at large in a more healthy state. This is not wire-drawn logic; it is daily experience. More than this: the sense of divine presence which brings strength to the soul brings strength to the body. By the soul I mean no dubious entity, but only the higher portion of our stream of consciousness. This stream, and the tides of physical life, are far too intimately connected to admit of the rise of one without the other. Further still: the divine presence anywhere is the presence of Good, and steadily tends to the defeat of evil. The sense that God is in our whole being does make for the vitality of every organ and the cure of every ailment that the state of mind can affect at all.

Thus we see gradually a singular transformation. That which in its crude beginnings was but a guarantee of our own safety and success in dealing with our environment and securing what we care for, more and more becomes itself what we care for. At first we want it for its service, and at last we want it for itself. To the end the first need survives, for we have still to live in an environment. But the peace and harmony of spirit that religion comes to bring are drawn ever in greater measure from the presence and sympathy of God.

These considerations make clear how it is that religion, regarded scientifically and from without, is 'psychotherapy'. It is the relief of souls, and ministers through the soul to the whole vitality by allaying unrest and restoring confidence.

But – scepticism! "Religion may be efficacious", so the objectors reason, "but is it intellectually credible? It may be a potent sedative or stimulant, but the physician may scruple to use a drug for the heart that will weaken the brain. We may perfectly understand, as psychologists, that men find themselves chilled and bewildered by the vast intractableness of things, and crave the ability to strike a league with some single head of it all that will lend them security; yet, as logicians, we may see not a title of evidence that such a governing head of things exists. How do we know that there is any complete security in the world to be had? We may have to go without it, and merely learn, like the brutes, to confine our minds to the business in hand, and not to think of subjects that do not profit us. Scientific medicine is asked to welcome the aid of a new method. This method requires its practitioners to believe in certain extra-medical propositions which are in their nature highly questionable, and which many physicians regard as very amiable superstition. As scientific medicine it cannot do so. It can use and welcome only medical methods and propositions that can be put to scientific test."

Much of this reasoning is sound. It is not, to be sure, precisely in harmony with the doctrine so widely taught in the medical profession that veracity to patients is no virtue in a doctor where falsehood will do them good. Upon this doctrine 'superstition' should be a drug entirely welcome to the doctor's hand. It is to be hoped, however, that attention has been widely given to Dr Richard C. Cabot's admirable experimental study of truth and falsehood in medical practice. I fully share his carefully grounded conclusion that falsehood should be discarded altogether. Let us agree that no doctor should try to convince a patient of what the doctor does not believe, or in any but exceptional cases give silent co-operation to others, even if they are believers, in trying to produce such a conviction. It remains true that there are doctors enough who do believe to supply the need of the clergy for coadjutors. And to no conscientious or intelligent doctor is a proposition extra-medical which concerns the health, or means for the health, of his patient.

Note the position of the clergy in the matter. Religion by its innermost nature has something to say about peace, trust and the satisfying sense of divine presence; about the restoring and vivifying quality of this presence; about the love that casts out fear; about the regimen of the spirit; about the kinship of the divine with all sound and healthy things; about "the stream of tendency by which all things seek to fulfill the law of their being". Upon the ministers of all developed religions, and signally upon the ministers of Christian religion, rests the law of sympathy and service. Haunting the minds of the latter are the words and example of their Leader enjoining ministration to the sick and weak. When they find a form of vital ministration to which both their gospel and their appointed duty peculiarly call them, all the objections of professional etiquette and surrounding scepticism seem factitious and flimsy indeed. They will do their work and they will find expert work-fellows enough to assist and safeguard it.

The truth is that it would be difficult to imagine anything more healthful for the two professions than their working alliance in this broad social service which Dr Worcester and his medical coadjutors have so splendidly begun. Amongst other gains the clergyman will learn better to understand science at work. He will see in the end the value of that habit, nay, principle of scepticism which seems at first merely the deadly enemy of his life's cause.

The gain likely to accrue to the man of science from working to some extent side by side with the minister of religion corresponds to the gain on the other side; he is likely to have a growing perception that there is another kind of truth than that in which his studies have moved – another kind of truth than science. I do not mean metaphysical or theological propositions, which differ from his own sort mainly in not being proved, but only piously taken for granted. These would differ from his science mainly in being bad science. I mean the truth of value, the truth of importance, the truth that concerns the human will and mood.

THE DEFENSE OF THE FAITH TODAY

[Six years after joining the faculty of General Theological Seminary in New York and while still a full time teacher at Columbia University, Miller addressed a meeting of Pennsylvania clergymen in 1915 on 'The Defense of the Faith Today'. Extracts of major points in that address – the only form in which it is available – follow below and present key ideas in his philosophy of religion. He maintains that proof in religion rests on experience of results as with other forms of knowledge. It is not a matter of "beneficent illusions" because the truth in any idea is what makes it useful. Results are measured in terms of man's well-being, the very thing God requires for His good, and this involves satisfaction of all needs, bodily as well as religious. Results depend, however, on intelligence as well as motive, so we cannot be good without being wise. In many subsequent writings Miller defended the main thesis here, that Christian faith centers on human welfare in a morality of results.]

I

The real defense of the faith is the life. The substantial proof of religion is always the same, experience of results. Proving something to be real is testing its reality, putting it to the proof. Treat Christ as real, go to Him in prayer, ask to stay in His presence, try to feel His understanding sympathy His appreciation, and, as St. Francis would have said, His courtesy; call upon Him as one with the greatest power that can enter and surge up in the soul; and you have your reward. This reward is the awakening and the guiding of the nature. We find that He has the key to what Wordsworth called "the hiding-places of man's power". It cannot be too often said that such a prayer *requires* no previous belief. The man lost in the woods and calling for help need not believe that somebody is there; he may be trying to find out whether somebody is there. He calls in the most human personal appeal to a person as yet hypothetical. If any one calls genuinely to

Christ, he soon has reason to conclude, "From thence cometh my help". We have an antecedent *image* of Him whom we seek, derived if we are wise from the New Testament with the trustiest critical aid. No period has ever been so well equipped to understand the Christ of history in certain limited aspects, as ours. But of course the cries most speedily answered are not always the most critical cries. And the proof stands absolutely independent of any critical conclusions whatever. Happily no history of the New Testament can destroy the fact that the New Testament exists, can blot it out from religious literature. Christian apologetics does not primarily have to defend propositions about ancient history, but about present and living realities to which a distant drama in history was the mighty introduction. Present experience, if we attend to it, gradually brings out in clearness not only the proof but what it is that we are really proving.

All our knowledge of people, objects, and forces is of this nature, experience of results. They and their properties reveal themselves solely when we act as if they were real and note the results of so acting. I know that you exist, my hosts in this room, in this way only; not by a transcendental argument, but by what results if I act in a certain way, if I open my eyes, stretch out my hand, give the attention of my ears. If I got one glimpse of you, and, when I acted on that glimpse, no further results, I should think it an illusion. With unseen things it is the same. If I am finding my way through rocky places in the dark I go by results. If I stretch out for support and gain that support, coming on so far with security, I take it that I have so far formed a just idea of my unseen environment, the invisible reality in whose presence I stand. So far, be it noted. This principle of proof is also, fortunately, a principle of disproof and correction. As experience goes on, it proves and it also purifies. But it cannot, after a lengthened and searching test, deceive. It is surely a mistake to suppose that there are in the long run of human history any beneficent illusions. Our mental pictures of our environment do not help us to respond thereto by being false, and a fool's paradise is paradise but a little while, else he would be no fool. It is the truth in any idea that makes it useful.

Thus, be it said again, the truth is forced upon us that Christian apologetics is *primarily* concerned, not with a chapter of ancient history, not with propositions in archaeology, but with present realities, our actual spiritual environment, the Christ to whom we turn in prayer; to all which that ancient chapter is the historical introduction, and on all which it sheds an incomparable light. Indeed we may put in this way: Apologetics is the defense of the Church – the Church by its very nature and purport having to do with invisible, sovereign realities, being by its very nature and purport sacramental. And the conclusion to which we must come is that by its results the life of the Church is the true defense of the Church.

The real method of apologetics then is this: "Let your light so shine before men that they may see your good works and glorify your Father which is in heaven".

II

Our method, it is plain, will not let us go until we have seen what results are good and worthy, what are good works, what is the test.

Between the commandment to love God and the commandment to love our neighbor there is in the New Testament what may be called a mystical tie. If we see God as He truly is and love Him, then we are loving a character that loves men; our love, taken up into His, passes back to our neighbor. If a man says that he loves God and does not love his neighbor, he is a liar; – at best he is loving the wrong God. On the other hand, to do loving service for man is to do it for God; "Inasmuch as ye have done it unto one of the least of these my brethren ye have done it unto me". More than this, if we love man as he truly is, we love a being who needs God, who cannot reach well-being without that highest communion. If we go to God and arrive, we reach humanity. If we go to humanity and arrive, we reach God.

Here is the solving secret: that love must seek the well-being of its object. Our results must always be ultimately measured in terms of well-being. True love, in words that Bishop Rhinelander used in his lectures at the General Seminary last year, *loves people for their good.* In loving God we must seek what God requires for His good, for His satisfaction, the well-being of man. In loving man we must seek all that man requires for his real satisfaction, including his central need of God. But *all* that he requires, all his needs. We must have regard, as our Saviour on earth had regard, for his whole nature, as well for the body as the soul. His was a sympathy far too unstinted, far too humane, far too divinely large, to pass indifferently by any of the needs and clamors of our conscious life. He sympathized with all creatures that could feel and did not ignore any of their feelings. If every hair of man's head is numbered, then no feeling of his heart is too common and too creaturely to be noted. To think less than that would be to impoverish and shrivel the sympathy of divine insight. It would be to ignore the fact that man's nature is both spiritual and physical. It would be to ignore the Church's conception of the sacredness of the body and of its resurrection. It would be to ignore the eternal significance of the Body and Blood. It would be to forget that God is present in nature and natural joys, that, in the words of St. Thomas Aquinas, He is the good of all good. It would be to ignore Christ's singularly keen sense of physical need, – how he prizes the impulse to give but a cup of cold water to one of these little ones. He said, "I thirst". We may try to quench His very thirst ourselves, for "I was thirsty and ye gave me drink.... Inasmuch as ye have done it unto one of the least of these my brethren ye have done it unto me."

III

How can we make the real apologetic tell more convincingly amongst men today? Of course, by making our results more convincing. And the final question is, How can that be done?

The answer (for which the above has been a mere preparation) is this. Results depend on two things, motive and intelligence. The Church has indefatigably preached motive. The time has come, in the unfolding of her mission, to preach intelligence. She begins to do so. We are at the crest of the ridge that divides the waters.

We have preached holy motive and, being human, not always with discrimination. It has been said, "If some faithful and loving woman gives the wrong bottle of medicine to a patient, with fatal results, but in all innocence, I call hers a good act. Her motive was pure unselfish service". But why confuse a crystal-clear subject? Acts are one thing and motives are another. It was a good motive, but eternally not a good act, a bad act unwittingly committed. We approve the motive; we deplore the mistake. The motive may be good and the act bad, the act good and the motive bad; but (this is the main truth) the good motive *wants* the act to be good; the good motive itself is ignominiously frustrated, foiled in its own aim, if the act comes out bad. It is precisely a religion of loving motive which must become a religion of achievement.

Therefore it is, that, in the full sense of the word, we cannot be good without being wise. We cannot be good both in motive and in act. We can only be good by halves. The very intent of our goodness is exposed to defeat. A religion of achievement is a religion of intelligence.

In matters of faith we sometimes harbor suspicions against reason. Perhaps there is no good ground for such suspicions. Perhaps we should really suspect that a larger reason would dispel them. But when we turn from the Church's faith to the Church's work we perceive at once that she is destined to become again the champion and preacher of reason; of the God who is not only love, but wisdom, – unerring love.

HEART AND HEAD

[Key points in Miller's philosophy of religion and his commitment to the method of analysis are apparent in what follows, originally a mimeographed essay distributed to his classes at General Theological Seminary in 1915. It might well have been titled 'Emotions and Analysis', for it centrally argues, with a passing reference to Hume, that emotion or 'the heart' is the basis of value to be served, not created, by 'the head' or intellect. The head typically "analyzes while the heart realizes". All science, Miller insists, proceeds by analysis. Its very language is the language of analysis just as the language of common sense conveys an analysis in its reference to classes and causes. Analysis yields "truth of fact" to serve and be guided by "truth of value", and the special genius of Christianity in contrast to Greek philosophy is that it opened a new world of value. Thus Miller further explicates the point he had made earlier in 'What Religion Has To Do With It', namely: truth in religion is "the truth of value", not the "bad science" of unproved metaphysical or theological propositions.]

Nothing is more familiar to us than the distinction between the heart and a somewhat crasser term – the head. But what precisely do the terms mean? Consider the HEART. The word evidently conveys the idea of sympathy and compassion. We speak of the tender-hearted or kind-hearted man, a man of heart, a heartless man. This is perhaps the meaning that first comes to mind. But it is not all.

Secondly, the heart means also, quite apart from suffering and pity, the power of affection. Thus we speak of a warm-hearted person, or we say, he has no heart. Emerson describes the young Carlyle as "nourishing his mighty heart" in the Annandale Hills. He seems to refer to the young author's wide-embracing love for humankind and all high causes. These two meanings, though really different are kindred, for pity is akin to love.

But, thirdly, there is in literature and even in daily life a third sense of the term, different both from compassion and affection. It is used to signify the power of courage. Thus we have the name of Richard of the Lion-Heart, and Bunyan gives us Captain Greatheart. So in the Lay of Ancient Rome we read of Horatius, "But he was borne up bravely by the brave heart within". We say 'faint-hearted'. Mr Justice Holmes writes: "We have learned that whether a man accepts from Fortune a spade and will look downward and dig, or from Aspiration her axe and cord, and will scale the ice, the one and only success which it is his to command is to bring to his work a mighty heart". We feel that he means by 'heart' courage, and the persistence that belongs to courage. The word 'courage' itself means, as we may say, 'heartage'. 'Encouragement' illustrates this sense.

But we have not finished with this many-sided word. Close to the idea of courage lies a fourth meaning also frequent in life and literature. 'Light-hearted', 'down-hearted', 'heavy-hearted', a 'sad heart', – these point to a fourth sense which is simply high or low spirits, 'cheer' or depression of mood. "My heart leaps up when I behold a rainbow in the sky." Thus we have the magnificent words, "Lift up your hearts".

We cannot in any wise put these significations together and make one of them. A man may be 'heartless' and nevertheless 'stout-hearted'. He may be 'warm-hearted' yet he may have no heart for something that we propose to him, that is, no desire.

And besides, there is a fifth usage, broader but yet distinct and separate, in which 'heart' seems to mean simply feeling. We say, "with grateful hearts", "with a full heart", 'heart-felt'. Hence the adjective 'hearty'.

Then, sixthly, quite apart from these, the word means the organ of desire, as in the phrases, "his heart was set upon it", "an object that lay near his heart", "the desire of his heart". In the words of Pascal, "The heart has its reasons which the reason knows not", the term is used in this sense, taken together with the last. In the romantic movement, when the claims of the heart were opposed to those of the head, the heart meant the organ of all feeling and desire.

It is worth while to point out, however, that all these meanings have something in common. A compassionate mind *cares* whether another suffers or not. Another's happiness has a value for such a mind. A heartless man really sets no value on another's freedom from suffering, does not *care*, as we express it. So with affection. To have a warm heart means that other people have value in our eyes and are not a matter of indifference to us. So it is also, if we look closely, with *courage*. The man who presses forward against odds has a keener sense of the value of his object or of his duty than of his safety or comfort. Courage grows as the one value thrusts down the other. It is because his object or his duty glows hot with preciousness to him that he pushes on. So with *feeling* in general. It is always the goodness or badness that we feel in something, and this is just what we mean here by value. So most obviously with *desire*; for desire is exactly the sense of the alluring, the appealing value of its object.

Keeping, then, to the natural habits of speech, not departing from any meaning of the word, we may say that while the head deals with facts, the heart deals with values. The head is the organ of knowledge. The heart is the organ of appreciation. We know facts. We appreciate values.

By value, of course, I do not mean here what is meant by it in Political Economy or in Ethics or in conversation. I do not mean what we would give for a thing, nor the good that it may bring about. I mean the good *in it* that is directly felt – the quality a thing has for us when we like or want it. In this sense beauty has value, and so have pleasant tastes, the action of vigorous muscles, the rest of weary muscles, the sight of an old friend. Some psychologists would call it always pleasure. Whether they are right or superficial we need not linger here to ask. We need only note that value in this sense, is always *given to consciousness*, never a thing after which we must go out in quest; never a thing to be discovered only by investigation.

Value is not mere fact. It is a commonplace of philosophy that we can describe the facts in any case leaving none of them out and yet not mention any values; we could tell the story of a murder, the stealthy steps, the leap on the victim, the fatal dagger-stroke, the effusion of blood, the death; omit no circumstance, and yet use no words which implied that the deed was good or evil. That is, we could describe it but not judge it. What is true of moral values is true in art. We can give a full description of an oil-painting and drop no word committing us to the judgment that it was beautiful or ugly. We could tell the texture of the canvas, the composition of the pigments, the precise scene portrayed, yet always we should be telling a story of fact, and withholding any expression of esthetic value. The moment we have called a murder dastardly, the moment we have called a painting lovely we have added something new to the account of the bare facts.

This is equally true of the *fact that a man has* certain feelings. We can tell *about* feelings of love or disgust; but if we are simply playing the psychologist, if we merely say that the mind we are studying felt love or disgust, if we never permit any love or disgust of our own to enter into our language, then we are telling a story of bare fact and not of value. That hatred or desire was felt by somebody is mere fact. That it was a discreditable feeling or a noble one, that is a value. On the other hand, if a poet bodies forth some fine imagination, and does not say whether such a thing ever existed, then he is embodying a value and saying nothing about fact. Accordingly we may say that the head could, if it knew enough, give a complete account of the world, while the heart was silent. Or again the heart could give a complete account of its desire, while the head made no sign.

I

Now the first principle in this subject is that the head is the servant of the heart. Please notice that I am not saying, the head ought to be the servant of the heart. I am saying something more radical. The head is, and by the nature of things must be, the heart's servant. The head as we say is the organ for fact. Its business is to find out facts. It finds them out by perceiving or by inferring. The head is where the eyes and the brain are. The head can never find out a value. That is, you can never extract values from facts. The head can never give the law to the heart. Try, for instance, to prove by items of fact that something is good. You can prove by reasoning that it exists. You can easily prove that it has results, which when they have come, people find good. Those are facts. You cannot from facts prove how it ought to be regarded, what value attaches to it. You can prove that, if at all, only from principles of value. You cannot prove that the well-being of all mankind is a thing worth working for. *The heart discerns it to be so.* You cannot prove that anything is for its own sake worth while. The head can only tell how the heart's desire may be obtained; the facts, that we must grip and readjust to be at our object. The head is in charge of ways and means. If some end has value enough to be striven for, then I ask my head how 1 can get it. The heart's desire is referred to the head for execution.

We are only putting the same principle in another form, when we say that the head has no motive power. The motive power for human action comes solely from the heart. Why does the head ever go to work at all?

Because we want something. If no desire stirred within us, all the machinery of the head would stand stock-still. That portentous factory would be idle. It provides a supply to meet a demand. If the demand ceases, its occupation is gone. If we are thinking of some problem in science, it is because we *want* to solve it; because of some end that solution will enable us to attain, or because we want the solution itself, because we have come to love solutions. "To bring clearness out of obscurity", said Hume, "must always be delightful and rejoicing".

(It was always so for Hume in any case. When I say that, I am giving expression to a fact. It always is so for any sound mind. When I say this, I am adding the expression of a value.)

II

So far of course, we have been dealing in what has become a commonplace in philosophy. The second principle of the subject may be a commonplace or not; I do not know which you will call it. But it is not commonly taken to *heart*. It does not impel man as it should. It is this: The head analyzes while the heart realizes. All science is analysis. By analysis, I do not mean the opposite of synthesis. By analysis, I mean viewing a thing in its composition, viewing it as made up of parts, instead of simply accepting it as a whole. In this broad sense, analysis includes synthesis and also includes analysis in the narrower sense, in which it is opposed to synthesis. All science resolves things into their parts, or processes into their parts, or ideas into their parts. Science is a study of structure. In following the rules of investigation, for example, we separate one factor from another and experiment with it, to see whether it is the cause of the effect we are studying. But then the very language of science is the expression of analysis. Science, said Huxley truly, is common sense organized. Accordingly, the reasonings of common sense are in their informal way analysis too. The language of common sense is the product of analysis. Being sense, it is a matter of the head. Most of the nouns we use are common nouns, and *every common noun tells the story of an analysis*. For it is a name that applies to any one of a class of objects. The idea of a class is *made by analysis*. We have singled out one quality from all the mixture of qualities that anything possesses ignoring the rest, and formed the idea of *all the things that have that quality*. It does not matter what else they may have. This is an artifice, designed simply to serve a turn. Our distinction, for instance, between heart and head is an artifice. In life the class *facts* and the class *values* are almost inextricably mixed and blended. But it is a serviceable artifice. We must frame the idea of all the objects that have a certain property, because it concerns us to find out and remember what other properties all those objects may be expected to have. Then, if we recognize an object as belonging to the class, we already know what to expect of it. Water wets and fire burns. This is a type of all laws of science. Every law says, all objects that have one recognizable property, A, have another property, B; or, all A's are B's. This tells me how I am to behave towards A's, that is, I am to be on the watch, when I meet with them, for the other property. Where there is smoke there is fire.

Abstraction, that is, singling out one quality; classification, that is, ranging together in our mind all things that have that quality, simply because they have its; generalization, that is, discovering that all of a class have also other qualities; – all these are clearly matters of analysis, taking things to pieces, the refusal to accept them simply in their integrity as they come. The humblest activities of the head are of one kind with the most ambitious generalizations of science. They all have a motive, that is, a desire behind them, and always the head tries to gain the heart's end in the same manner. We could not live or move for an instant without knowing how objects were to behave, that is, what properties they were going to exhibit, what they were going to do to us. Even standing on the floor expresses a humble faith that one will not go through. That is, a surface which looks like that, (a) will behave like that, (b) and will not withdraw its support in the hour of stress. Getting about the world is a matter of reading signs. The appearance of the floor is a sign to me and the things signified is its competence to uphold me. *All* the industry of the head, that is, all inference, is passing from a sign to a thing signified.

It thus appears why the head does such violence to the fair face of things, why it divides and disintegrates, why the outcry of the heart is so often raised against it. The head wishes to abstract something, very much as we say that someone has abstracted our coat. It wants to carry away something for its own purposes from the object to which it belongs. It does not scruple in its thought to break a thing up, to get down to the very centre and lay hold of what it wants. The head is a ruthless character come with intent to break and enter. The more profound it becomes, the more penetrating, the more ruthlessly it must break and enter an object, throwing everything else aside in order to seize just what it seeks. We know a thing first of all and most naturally as a whole, an individual thing confronting us in our experience. It is in that form that it awakens our interest, that we like or dislike it, that it becomes an object for the heart, in the wide sense that we are using that term. When we want to express just the air a person has, just his special tone or flavor, we speak of his individuality, that is, his undividedness or indivisibility. For children, for primitive men, yes, for ourselves, a living thing, a scene, the woods at twilight, the mountains at daybreak have something all their own, have individuality. Analysis takes these things apart. It takes them apart in thought. This ideal dissolution of a thing is like a faint reflection of that real dissolution which is death. Analysis means indeed, while it lasts, the death of that first living interest that the thing had for us. Our valley of analysis is the valley of the *shadow* of death. Our first interest in life is chilled and shocked when these things are presented to us in pieces, in bundles of attributes, in sections, in molecules, in ions. Here the revolt of poets and men of soul raises its head. We have Wordsworth reproaching that science which "viewing all things unremittingly in disconnection, dull and spiritless breaks down all grandeur". In this matter psychology hurts us nearest the quick. It resolves our thinking, feeling, and seeing life itself into sensations and images, and measures in units mental content, mental intensity and the like. Life analyzed and atomized; that is as if some rich draught should grow dry in the very drinking and turn to sand between our teeth. Yet all the analysis of science springs from a desire of the heart, the deepest of its desires, the desire to live. We are in a deadly game of fence with our environment. It lunges and we must parry. It leaves an opening and we should seize our moment and advance. We must mark its slightest movement and know what it portends for us. If we were not quick to read the signs of what was in store for us, we should soon be butchered. This one desire of the heart to live and control, engages the head to override all the heart's other dearest interests. This one desire of the heart bids the head divide and conquer.

III

So the head has its vast industry and its army of agents, men of science and men of affairs. But there also is a business of the heart, a language and spokesmen. As there is a truth of fact, so there is a truth of value. As there is a just understanding, so there is a just appreciation. We know how in our awakened moments we meet what is good in every day, the fresh air in our faces as we leave the house, the sunlight as it streams into the room, the humour, the beauty, the striking traits about us, the refreshing individuality of things. They take hold of us. But in the dullness of routine the grip slackens, the glow fades. Our dullness is obtuse. It is unjust. We are so organized as to have a sense for these things. They are there in the economy of life for our spirit to feed upon. For the *normal* eye the flush of value is ready to suffuse them. Even where we have never caught the scarlet in the tissue, it lurks there, it may be pointed out; it leaps to view in the right light. To put it in this light the intellect is powerless. It can only unravel the tissue. Here is the power of the heart, which can speak to hearts and summon up the things of life in their native worth, in the integrity of their vital freshness. Imagination, not in the employ of reason, but in the heart's employ, knits up the ravelled robe and makes it whole. We sometimes say of one who joins in a game or enterprise that he does not catch "the spirit of the thing". Now the highest of all utterance is not the analyst's. It is that which imparts the spirit of the thing. In any subject it comes with such a spell that forthwith we "put our heart into it". This is not explanation, or dissection in the surgery of the mind. It has no affinity with dissolution. It is the giving of life. It is creation. It is the contagious vision of vitality in the world that makes the flame of passion leap.

This is why the language of our innermost vision is "vague and emotional". It is emotional because it is trying to render overwhelming values. It does not use the exact terms of science because it is not engaged in taking the frame of things apart. It is true to experience but makes no claim to be included amongst the manufactured mosaics of thought. It is training its vision into the dark. By its very confession and effort it is leaning over the brink and peering into the gulf of God. To a bounded mind a boundless source of benefit *is* vague and emotional; there is no help for it.

We touch here on a vice of the respectable intellect. It glides into a habit of assuming that all communication should be such stuff as science is made of. On the contrary, some of it should be such stuff as life is made of. It even stiffens its assumption into a tacit principle respecting man and society. Taking feelings always in the objective way, as other people's feelings, it calls them "the emotions", "the love-attachment between the sexes", "human nature", and the like, till it gradually takes for granted that they are a fairly well-measured quantity, a familiar property of the human object. They do not see emotion as a vision of value. They do not hear the note of creative appeal. Consequently they have lost their grip on religion. For what religion does is to reveal, *not merely facts*, but unsuspected values, within our reach, in life. What the respectable intellect does is to take an examining look at the asserted facts without regarding it as any part of its duty to realize the values. The flaw in their method is, (as I remarked last Monday), that you sometimes cannot read off the nature even of the 'facts', if you insist on stripping away the values.

The whole fallacy is easy to explain. The interest of the heart in these reflective men has gone to the things of the head and there abides. Analysis is not easy. It is an acquired taste. These trained minds, having triumphantly acquired it, rejoice in their hard-won accomplishment.

Their minds move more and more easily in the groove of analytical system and explanation. They acquire an admirable readiness to cross-question any asserted facts and demand their credentials. The possibility of discovering a new continent of values and making one's abode there is hidden from them. The profoundest error of these minds lies in their notion of rational life. What is rational life? It would seem that it must be life governed by the head. But there is no such thing as life governed by the head. Reason, as we saw, is a mere servant of the heart. The heart is the sole mover and inspirer of life. The head points out the way and the means to the heart's end. It is purely instrumental. But thousands of thinkers have spoken as though rationality could govern. If they were cross-examined, it would appear they meant that reason could at least find out what human desires normally were, and could provide for the most urgent and permanent of them. They miss the fact that something else than reason may come upon the scene and kindle desire, light up the scene with fresh value and keep a fire of worship burning there like a steadfast altar-lamp.

Let me illustrate. There was a species of philosophy amongst the Greeks which is clearly the finest flower of that mode of thinking that I ascribe to our intellectual class. Here is human nature, said the Greek thinker, the given fact. I have many wants. They cannot all be satisfied. Some conflict with others. Some the world will not gratify. I also have a deep desire for peace and harmony of mind. If I suffer all the pell mell of my other desires to struggle and be bruised with failure, this deep and lasting desire is always foiled. Let me, then, sternly gather myself together. Let me draw a line between what is within my control and what is beyond my control; what I must have to live, what I can do without. Let me do now all that in me lies to suppress a desire for all needless things that are beyond my control. Let me desire only those things that depend on myself alone and those other few things that are required for life. I shall forego many enjoyments. But then I shall be relieved of a thousand disappointments and I shall gain the great end of peace and quiet. The gratifications that depend solely on my self are the approval of my own conscience and my own reason.

There we have a classic product of Greek intelligence never surpassed or equalled in later times. But it is a false view of life. It did not know the keys that open new worlds of value.

Upon the scene of this philosophy came the Gospel. Let us not fail to mark that in a measure it has the same thought. It also called men away from the control of the appetites. It also says, rest your happiness on nothing but that which you can surely possess. It also offers peace and harmony. It also may, if you choose, be represented as a philosophy of life. But what is its great contrast with the Greek life-wisdom? The new world it opens. Remember, though there was a revelation of fact in the coming of our Lord it was not all a revelation of fact. It was a revelation of the satisfactions, the loyalties, the intimacy, the peace of the inward relation, the great companionship. It was a discovery in the region of the *heart*. I say, let us remember it was not merely the revelation that such a great companion there really was. Greek philosophy was not without the thought of one supreme deity. There might have been in the thought of Aristotle, there might have been in the Stoic thought, some opening of a door to that inward intimacy. But Greek thought tried to harmonize life and bring in peace by stern excisions. It cut away the rebellious and conflicting things. What it offered was a life cleared of conflict, but austere, not rich. We are tempted to exaggerate a little and say, it made a desert and called it peace. But straight into that austere, cleared plot of life, into that clean and calm vacancy came the generous riches of revelation.

Let me say it again, it was largely a revelation of unsuspected values, of satisfactions that had lain latent in the human soul. There is here, after all, only the great and simple problem of all full-grown life. If it is a moment for action, I am to do right and that is the end of it. But in the hours when no action presses, in the hours of consciousness, in the hours when I am in some sort alone with myself, what is to be my support? The sense, said the Greek, that I have done my duty, have acted fittingly. There he stopped. The sense, says the Christian, of communion, of understanding, of union with the highest, the presence of God, sublime presence, supreme good. The Gospel, considered on this side, opens in the depths of the human soul a door to a new world. It sees the problem of life, broadly speaking, as the Greek did, but it draws us away from unsatisfying appetites, not merely to calm our hearts but that our heart may truly there be fixed where true joys are to be found.

DEMOCRACY AND OUR INTELLECTUAL PLIGHT

[In his later years at General Theological Seminary Miller increasingly focussed his consequence-theory of morality, the morality of results in human welfare, on "the social idea". He became increasingly concerned with social welfare as the animating center of education, religion, and politics and gave expression to that concern in the article to follow, one of several with kindred themes that appeared from 1921 to 1925 in *The New Republic*, a periodical whose tendencies he shared.

Morality, Miller insists at the outset, is the scheme of ideas and rules existing "for the welfare of society and for that only". As it reinforces rules by making them sacred and inviolable, so must democracy make the participation of every citizen a sacred duty reinforced by education. The ideal of democracy as government by discussion is that the most reasonable proposal, not force, shall prevail. This requires general education in logic, in "elementary habits of the fair mind", now widely distorted by "that singular excrescence called a text-book of logic". The habit of relying on objective, public tests and rules of evidence must discipline "the will to believe", the willingness to believe on insufficient evidence because a belief is attractive. "The will to believe", Miller holds in continued but tacit criticism of James, obstructs the mobility of sound ideas and gives a handle to despots and political manipulators. Further, democracy cannot rely on the intellectual class for its progress because that class is not intellectual enough. It lacks the discipline of "honest thinking, the morals of the mind". Thus Miller sees democracy and social welfare as dependent on a redirection in education to fix in every citizen the habit of fair and honest thinking, what he subsequently and tirelessly in addresses and articles called for as "conscience of the mind".]

I. DEMOCRACY AND MORALITY

A certain deep-seated vice or weakness of democracy was pointed out long ago. It is that, for the individual democracy is uninteresting. Taken by himself alone, he has so little power that it seems to him unimportant whether he exercises it or not. To Frederick or Napoleon the business of government was interesting. It was creative work on a colossal scale. He could see his own strokes shaping a nation. His material, of course, was more or less intractable but still it again and again was fashioned to his purpose. To govern is, for a despot, an exciting occupation. To exercise the elective franchise of a single citizen under democracy is not exciting. Nothing can make the citizen believe that it is a vital matter whether he, as a single unit, casts his vote or not or even for whom he casts it.

It has often been said that this want of interest would be remedied under civic socialism; for there the government would be controlling interests so close and vital to every citizen that he would have to give his attention. No doubt the degree of attention would be increased, but the vice or weakness would still exist, for it would be yet more painfully evident to a citizen how little power he had by himself to control the affairs that concerned him. He would be but one of innumerable stock-holders. The obstacle is more deeply lodged in the nature of democracy than this suggestion realizes.

Now the curious thing is that there is a very similar vice or weakness in the scheme of morality. May it not be that the means by which this weakness has been met in morality is the very means required to meet it in democracy?

In morality what is in question is not the power of the individual but the power of the individual act. Morality exists for the welfare of society and for that only. But an individual cannot be made to believe that one particular lie or one unobserved petty theft or one small and unpunished breach of contract will do any great harm to society. He admits at once that if everybody did the like society would suffer. Indeed, he sees that if he on every occasion did the like society would suffer, not to mention himself. But that is not the case in question. The case in question is the single act. If he measures by consequences, his common sense tells him that what he does in such a particular case is often not very important.

Now what has morality done to meet the difficulty? I call it a difficulty because when the particular cases accumulate and we have many cases, lying, theft, breach of contract do injure society and it is important to suppress them. Morality introduces one of the most momentous of ideas, the idea of the sacred. It says truth is a sacred thing. It says honesty and contract are sacred things. It puts a peculiar stigma of discredit and disgrace, quite apart from the thought of consequences, on those who disregard the taboo. To make a moral law take effect and secure a volume of good consequences it is necessary to give it a certain prestige and majesty, to make it 'inviolable', to secure in its favor a dumb, uncalculating instinct of obedience. Unless people make up their minds to obey the rule always they will not obey it even enough for wholesale purposes. The rule must be sacred.

To be sure, this state of things is not fully realized in morality. The taboo is there but it is not always obeyed. It does not matter, however, for our argument, just how far it succeeds. The taboo does work powerfully toward getting the law more uniformly obeyed and obedience is sadly needed for the general welfare.

If we follow the same clue as to democracy we should endeavor to make the citizen's exercise of his elective franchise a sacred duty. Public opinion in a well constituted democracy would attach discredit and disgrace to the omission of civic duty or of anything that it involves. The organs of society most immediately charged with the office of teaching this civic morality and training conscience are the school and the church. The best available source of influence upon the school and the church is the college. At present there is on this point little or no public opinion that makes its pressure felt and its disapproval sting.

This is the first conclusion suggested; but it must be amplified a little. We may say that there are two groups, the enormous group consisting of all voting citizens and the small group consisting of elected officials, members of legislative bodies, etc. We may call them the inner group and the outer group. Now, strange to say, the vice or weakness that impairs the outer group as ultimate repositories of civic power impairs also the inner group as agents or instruments of that civic power. We find in the representatives the same vice or weakness that we find in the represented.

Anyone who has had to do with committees, boards, legislative bodies of any sort knows this. The power of the individual is small. He can do nothing except by convincing others. And the difficulty of moulding opinion by words becomes a too familiar fact. The etiquette and propriety of such a body calls for courtesy, modesty, reticence, caution, dignity, amiability, and the like. These obstruct the individual's standing out for the interest of those whom he represents. That is, the etiquette and

propriety of the occasion tend to be determined by the comfort and convenience of the inner group who are present, not by the interests of the
outer group who are not present but whom the inner group exists solely
to represent. Pages of *The New Republic* could be filled with examples,
taken from the procedure of "best citizens". It is often precisely the "best
citizens" who most feel the ethics of the inner group and forget their duty
to the outer group. The power of the individual being small, it seems not
worth while to make a great effort to exercise it.

What has been said of the larger group applies then to the smaller. The
duty of the representative to the represented could take to itself the emphasis of a "sacred duty". The alternative of a moral esteem or a moral
discredit could attach to it.

II. DEMOCRACY AND LOGIC

We have seen that the natural interest of the governor in government is
sadly reduced under democracy because one vote at the polls or one
voice in council accomplishes so little. Now this interest is reduced in
another way. Democracy is government not by force but by discussion.
The ideal of democracy is that the reasonable idea, the reasonable proposal,
should conquer by its reasonableness. According to this ideal there would
still be possible for strong minds and characters the interest of great
creative work. Whoever conceived or popularized the right ideas would
carry these ideas into law by influencing the fair minds of the electors.
The thinker or the popular leader would have power by the truth of his
ideas. He would become in a sense an effective governor in a new way, by
the power of right reason. Hence he would have incentive. Such is the
ideal of democracy. Instead of this we see the incentive of the thinker and
sound leader brought down to a minimum because truth is not mighty
and (for an indefinite length of time) does not prevail. There is no free
passage for ideas into the popular mind, but perpetual obstruction.

Now is there such a thing as logical education? Can citizens be trained
in the elementary habits of the fair mind? Can these elementary habits
be stated as a simple technique. I cannot help thinking that they can. Can
minds of average intelligence be drilled at school in this technique?
I believe so. Does any form of education now produce this result – or
aim at this result? I believe it does not. Would this teaching remove the

colossal mental obstruction to intelligent democracy? It would gradually and steadily reduce it.

"I don't know anything about logic", said an accomplished graduate of Cambridge University. Logic is a 'highbrow' subject, put in a historical scholar who was present. Unhappy fact, if fact it be; for logic is an indispensable basis of an efficient democracy. No manipulation of blind feelings and impulses will serve the purpose. No adjustment of 'interests' will do, for the evil is that voters will not vote according to their interests.

The actual nature and use of logic have been so distorted by that singular excrescence called a text-book of logic that we are put to it to see what they really are.

There is only one force that makes a bad mind out of a good one or a tolerable one, a force that has been able to accomplish this result in the majority of civilized minds. That force is "the will to believe"; more fully expressed, the willingness to believe on insufficient evidence, because the belief is attractive, or the opposite unattractive, or the labor of further thinking unattractive. To believe by attraction instead of believing on test, that is the temptation. To teach the tests, that is the business of logic. The effectual principles of logic are simple. The first principle of logic is the principle of objectivity; that is, that you do not carry the tests in yourself, that they are objective. The human mind has got upon firm ground just in proportion as it has escaped from its own plausibilities to objective tests. The will to believe takes the guise of certain fallacies that we are ever encountering, fallacies easily listed, easily exposed, the essence of which is that they beg the question of objective evidence and fall back on other recommendations to belief. The only difference between them lies in the nature of the other recommendation on which they fall back. The prevailing errors in reasoning, responsible for most of the harm of false conclusions, are *obvious* errors. We should all see and avoid them except that we are looking the other way. Fallacy, like the juggler, distracts our attention. To turn our heads round and make us look straight at the obvious principle we have ignored is the business of logic.

You will not make men thinkers, you will not make them thorough analysts; these arts are born of a temperamental bent; but you can make the growing mind learn to observe certain rules. They are not so difficult to learn as spelling. They are about as difficult as grammar. It must be remembered that *one* of the most important of the rules is mere caution in coming to a conclusion. Suspension of judgment till the tests are met requires to be inculcated and practised.

All this is abstract because it must be brief. Abstraction, as always, is shorthand.

Logic is not the correct reasoning process; it is not the way the mind moves when it moves rightly. There is not in the human mind a track or tramway called logic on which thought moves correctly and from which it should not be 'derailed'. Logic does not at all treat of the reasoning process; that is, the actual mental process by which we pass to new knowledge or opinion. Psychology does that. All minds pass in the same way to new knowledge or opinion. There is only one reasoning process. That is the association of ideas. One idea suggests another. All minds jump to conclusions or creep to conclusions by suggestion. "The method by which the fool arrives at his folly" is one with that by which the wise man reaches his wisdom. Logic is something quite different. It is an attempt to formulate the *tests* by which we discover whether our new idea is warranted, whether we have jumped to a safe conclusion. Logic has found, and found from human experience, that certain conditions are observable under which coming to a conclusion is safe and the conclusion will not have to be abandoned; and other conditions under which it is unsafe and untenable. Logic draws up these tests in certain rules. These rules never say, "Think thus and thus, put one foot before another thus and thus in your process of thought". That would be futile; we can only think in one way. They tell you how to test the conclusions of your thought after you have got it. They say, Observe whether the evidence, the data, fulfill certain conditions. If so, then go forward.

To draw up a list of prevalent fallacies, to give them suitable names, to gather instances of each, to show in each the presence of the will to believe, to point out the objective test that has been disregarded, this is the simple task of logical education. It is far simpler and more vital than the textbooks of logic. Logic is essentially "the fight against fallacy". Its life is in dealing with cases. It must teach us to define terms and remain true to our definitions. It must strengthen our faith in common sense when we judge of experiment and observation. It is indeed nothing but formulated common sense. It need not bother us with syllogism or the details of inductive methods – need not if its object be to arm the average citizen against fallacy. It is a brief and simple discipline in its maxims, but demands practice. It can never be imparted by lectures, only by drill.

Compare the expert with the average man. The expert knows by tests outside himself and has no desire but to abide by them. Anyone can sway his mind. If a child brings him a new fact that child can transform his judgment. His judgment is hung like scales to be delicately responsive to facts from without. The average judgment is caught in some obstruction and rendered immovable. It seems often to rejoice that nothing you can say, no fact you can bring, will affect it. Logic is a social bond. It forcibly opens our minds to each other when without it they would be closed and barred.

This social bond being largely absent, democracy miscarries; the community is not guided by its own real welfare; it is guided even at the best by spells and attractions. In 1893 Mr Shaw wrote as follows:

> The chief difficulty in dealing with Mr Gladstone as a statesman arises from the fact that his statesmanship, such as it is, has nothing to do with his popularity. A man must be a skilled citizen, so to speak, to appreciate statesmanship; and our electorate does not include one percent of voters who have skilled citizenship enough to know whether Mr Gladstone is a real statesman or not. It is as an artist, an unrivalled platform artist, that Mr Gladstone is popular. Jefferson's Rip Van Winkle never attained the vogue of Gladstone's Grand Old Man. Every touch of it delights the public. The tree-felling, the lesson-reading, the railway journeys punctuated with speeches, the feats of oratory and debate, the splendid courtesy and large style, the animated figure with the blanched complexion lighted by the great eyes, the encyclopaedic conversation, the elastic playing with an immense burden of years: all these bring rounds of applause louder and longer than any merely theatrical actor can hope for. Mr Irving in the Lyceum is but the microcosm: Mr Gladstone in England is the macrocosm. The parallel is close in every respect except that of magnitude. Mr Irving is deservedly so popular as an artist that it is unpopular to deny that he is a connoisseur in literature as well. And Mr Gladstone, too, is so popular as an artist that it is unpopular to deny that he is a great political thinker as well.

Just so, it may be added, Roosevelt's "Livest Man in America" had a phenomenally long run. He had undeniably some of the attributes of a sagacious statesman, but it was not his statesmanship, it was his fascination as a public figure that gave him, in the opinion of historians, the greatest following any individual in this country has had.

Again, everyone knows that the successful manager, whatever his office, is prone to resort to certain wiles in guiding other men in council, simply because they cannot be swayed by sound argument alone. He touches with a sure, light hand upon their self-interest, prejudice, vanity, dread of ridicule, indolence, etc.; he is thus able to bring about a good result which he cannot so surely or swiftly effect by reasoning. Mr Lloyd George has for the most part to deal with minds inflexible, unfair and blind to his situation; his amazing success is due to his acute study of these minds, not chiefly to the truth of his ideas. In general 'politicians' are produced by the mental state of the people who pour contempt upon them; at all events by a state of mind of which theirs is a fair specimen. Academic thinkers have little in their work to make them realize the parallelogram of the forces with which a statesman is in actual contact. Statesmanship, as Mr Ellis Barker has pointed out, is taught in no university. Statemanship in our present democracy is largely the thankless and baffled art of dealing with irrational forces.

Democracy, we say, wishes to substitute for the sway of despots the sway of true ideas. Nothing could be more remote from the actual state of democracy – or of human co-operation at large. "Those who govern", says Franklin in his *Autobiography*, "having much business on their hands, do not generally like to take the trouble to consider and carry into execution new projects. The best public measures are therefore seldom adopted from previous wisdom [that is, from previous reflection] but forced by the occasion". Unconsciously echoing Franklin, Mr Wells remarks that people in prominent positions cannot do any work, meaning any thorough reflective examination to find out what would be the true policy. The people do not demand or recognize such thorough insight into the means of securing their welfare. Disraeli's character Sybil "found to her surprise that great thoughts have very little to do with the business of the world; that human affairs even in an age of revolution are the subject of compromise". Bagehot remarks in his masterpiece, *Sir Robert Peel as a Statesman*, that the modern statesman is a man of common ideas though of uncommon abilities. The modern democratic community is not organized to give free passage to correct ideas, but is such as to obstruct their circulation. What we need, then, is free mobility for sound ideas such that the originator of formulator or preacher of them will have this incentive, that his ideas may prevail. Such a relation between minds can be secured by elementary logical education only, which is the abc-training of a fair and open mind. We are sufficiently remote from any such consummation. The teacher, however, sees his efforts begin to tell at once.

This conclusion seems doctrinaire, academic, remote from life, only as

long as we do not see a few guiding principles that can be disengaged from
the wilderness of mental detail.

III. LOGIC AND MORALITY

It appeared above that the citizen's governing function should be regarded,
for reasons given, as a sacred duty. We then saw that this duty could not
be performed to good purpose without an elementary training in logic, or
in other words, in fairness of mind. Very well, a part of the civic duty, a
part of the sacred thing, will be to observe the rules of a fair mind. To
serve the general welfare is what morality is for; the duty to observe the
plain rules of safe inference is not only a part of morality, it is the most
momentous part, for it has the greatest effect upon welfare. There is, in
fact, no more abject weakness in our intellectual state than its propensity
to forget that morality is not a mere blind taboo existing for its own sake,
but a means to an end, by which end it must be measured and shaped;
that its sole business is to avert misery and produce well-being. A state of
ideas in which this is not recognized remains primitive and barbarous;
when education recognizes it we take the step across into a civilization
aware of the possibility of controlling its own fate. Our present morals lay
stress on the control of self, but not on the control of events. The general
happiness, however, depends on the control of events. And this depends
upon intelligence. To be as intelligent as possible becomes a central part of
morality. We think of the acts of statesmen and of electors under the categories of opinion, which is free to all, of judgment, good sense, shrewd-
ness or their opposites. We must be taught to think of them also under the
categories of morality.

IV. DEMOCRACY AND THE INTELLECTUAL CLASS

The intellectual class is apt to feel somewhat thus: "Oh! If the populace
could only be like ourselves, if only we knew of some way of making them
intellectual!" "The thinking portion of society" laments its impotence to
spread its own standards amongst the multitude. But is it not possible
that the difficulty lies with that class itself? Is it not possible that the sound
standards of the intellectual class are – missing; that it is in that very class
that the abc-training of the fair mind must begin?

If we wish to employ a first-rate surgeon, civil engineer or sanitary engineer we know how to find him. We do not for this have to understand surgery or engineering. We can find the experts because people agree as to who they are. Such an agreement exists because, in a sufficient measure, the experts agree amongst themselves. And this because there are, within these several professions, definite tests by which achievement is measured. The case is typical. We find a large measure of consensus, we find recognized guides, in any subject in which the tests of achievement are recognized. If then you wish in a given subject to have recognized experts, secure within it the application of definite tests. This was the principle of John Stuart Mill. It follows that the intellectual portion of society would have authority and would lead, in things political and social, if it did its own work well enough, if it could develop that intellectual conscience which is mindful of the tests that alone protect us from arbitrary opinion and bring us to objective success.

In other words, the reason why the intellectual class does not possess a greater influence over affairs, the reason why it must so generally sit on a hill and watch the tide, is that it is not intellectual enough, that it lacks seriousness, self-criticism, a sense of responsibility, is self-indulgent and lets itself go in its thinking, that hence it is wanting in objective grip and lingers in a state of mental nonage. In a word, it lacks discipline. This is at once effect and cause of the fact that our education, including our higher education, does not impart such discipline. Nor does the world of printed discussion, "the republic of letters", give it. For example, there is a prejudice against detailed destructive criticism, such as Macaulay's review of Gladstone, or James Mill's of Mackintosh, or John Mill's of Sedgwick, Whewell, or Hamilton. But precisely so far as a subject, such as political and social science or ethical philosophy, is removed from experimental test, it requires that we shall be resolutely and persistently reminded of the obvious principles of common sense and caution, which, for all their obviousness, in our self-indulgence we persistently forget. A watchful and searching criticism becomes the chief means of applying the logical pressure which the immediate verdict of facts, the brute force of palpable refutation, no longer applies. Such criticism is but a form of that logical education the essence of which is the systematic exposure of fallacy. Speaking of Mill on Hamilton, an acute reader once remarked: "It wasn't that Hamilton was so bad, but that for once a book got reviewed." We have to be reminded by something outside ourselves, whether it be experiment or another and vigilant mind, of the dangers to which easy thinking is always exposed.

The conclusion is that the reforming efforts of the intellectual class should begin at home. The education to affect is first of all that given in universities. The persons to effect it are university teachers. The person to begin is – any teacher; provided he has had the requisite education himself, or is willing to give it to himself; to turn deliberate heed upon the humble principles of 'fair play' in coming to conclusions. What is most needed is a practical textbook. The first step toward making the simple technique of honest thinking, the morals of the mind, effective amongst the multitude, is a potent step; to set it at work at the points from which, according to the principle of Mill already stated, the most powerful radiations are capable of spreading.

MATTHEW ARNOLD, ON THE OCCASION OF
HIS CENTENARY

[Dickinson Miller was a man of wide intellectual interests and appreciation as revealed in what follows, a contribution to *The New Republic* of
December 27, 1922 assessing Matthew Arnold's views on religion and the
function of literature in relation to social welfare. Unlike those who see
Arnold as merely "a delicately gloved literary exquisite", Miller finds him
to be a great sharer, a proponent of "the social idea", viewing men of
culture as true apostles of equality and proposing dissolution of landed
estates and limitation of inheritance to achieve "the equality of all as the
true basis for a healthy civilization". Though Arnold well translated the
Christian faith into "the language of human experience and salutary consequence", he was, if anything, too moralistic and failed to take the point
of view of religion itself in dealing with God as personal. Further, Arnold
failed to see that literature, in addition to educating and forming men for
better living, also has the function of being a high and satisfying experience in itself.

Miller had already touched upon this double function of literature in a
brief essay on 'Beauty and Use', part of a symposium in *The New Republic*
of 1921 to which R. M. Lovett, H. L. Mencken, Morris Cohen, and Clive
Bell also contributed. Criticizing Emerson for being preoccupied in moral
judgment with behavior rather than service, Miller insisted that "all
moral judgment of actions, motives, ideas, institutions and men can have
but one standard or basis, their practical tendency to promote the collective welfare (except so far as certain ideas and feelings may be constituents of that welfare)".]

"For a spirit of any delicacy and dignity", says Arnold, writing of great
names that have passed away, "what a fate, if he could foresee it! To
be an oracle for one generation, and then of little or no account forever."
The fate on which he thus touches was not to be his own; the sensitive
care for truth, which was one with his own delicacy and dignity, preserved

him from it. To a deliberate view he is greater now than he seemed to his contemporaries; the content of his writing appears, upon the whole, more substantial and permanent. The poetry indeed, the best of it, still leaves the same exquisite and haunting impression upon a few; perhaps it will always be upon a few. It is the work in prose that takes to itself, the more we know it and see it in perspective, an added importance.

His greatness in his prose is double. First, he was the critic of our civilization; a critic of its literature (both produced and inherited), its education, its politics, its religion, its social structure and its manners. He saw that the most brilliant thing a critic can possibly be is – right. He has his limits, but there is a soundness that attends him even when he is signally incomplete. He is, though not the greatest, nor the richest, nor spiritually the deepest, yet the most intellectual of the Victorian literary figures, Tennyson, Browning, Carlyle, Emerson, Ruskin, Dickens, Thackeray and the rest; for intellect is understanding and meets its truest test in the broadest, the most decisive facts of life. The growth of human insight is marked, each step of it, by a new distinction; the felicity of his criticism is that in its exercise the distinctions he drew, the names by which he marked them, the classifications thus created, are (not only a few but many of them) of lasting, of far-reaching illumination. He left the finest instruments, with which his criticism can be carried on. And second, he was not satisfied with criticism, with just judgment, but made it the basis of a steady and sagacious effort toward amendment and a sound reconstruction. He "drove at practice". In particular, he saw, far in advance of his time, and indeed of our time, the modern task, and set about to perform it; the task of saving the treasures of the old order while frankly and absolutely accepting the new; the task of bringing them into living union. He was in the profound sense a conservative liberal.

Matthew Arnold lingers in the shadows of many a mind as a "superior person", a fastidious critic, a delicately gloved literary exquisite who called us Philistines and gently reprehended us for our crudity and commonness. But in truth he is humane and he is inclusive; there is nothing deeper in him than these instincts. He is inclusive: he is bent upon not overlooking any of the essentials of human life or conditions of human happiness. It is the essence of his work that he is trying, in the words he used of Sophocles in the sonnet – words that are perhaps too often quoted, but cannot be too often understood – to see life steadily and see it whole.

He perceives the merit of apparent opposites and tries so to put them in their places that the opposition turns into mutual help. He is not for waste; he will not wholly throw over what either the past or the enemy has to give. He is not only a conservative liberal but a Hebraical Hellenist, and he attempts to be a Christian rationalist. Again, he is humane: not only does he keep a steadfast hold on the rule that human intellect exists for human benefit but he will have the possessions of intellect itself, to the very utmost extent possible, a common possession of humanity. He is, in the words that Mrs Robinson has used of a very different person, her brother Theodore Roosevelt, "a great sharer"; he wishes to see the true idea shared, rendered social. "This", he says,

is the social idea; and the men of culture are the true apostles of equality. The great men of culture are those who have had a passion for diffusing, for making prevail, for carrying from one end of society to the other, the best knowledge, the best ideas of their time; who have labored to divest knowledge of all that was harsh, uncouth, difficult, abstract, professional, exclusive, to humanise it, to make it effective outside the clique of the cultivated and learned, yet still remaining the best knowledge and thought of the time.... Such a man was Abelard in the Middle Ages, in spite of all his imperfections.... Such were Lessing and Herder in Germany, at the end of the last century; and their services to Germany were in this way inestimably precious.... And why? Because they *humanized knowledge*; because they broadened the basis of life and intelligence, because they worked powerfully ... to make reason and the will of God prevail.

Such a man, in his measure, was Arnold himself, and the full fruit of his labors is yet to be seen.

To throw open every subject whatever to reason and humanity and to make them prevail and govern there (only making most cautiously sure that our light is not darkness), that was his constant aim. A hasty American economist and reformer has called him "a conservative literary man". A literary man in England who protests that we are seeing "a lower class brutalized" and "an upper class materialized", who pronounces for the equality of all as the true basis for a healthy civilization, who would see the British aristocracy, that "splendid piece of materialism", gradually dissolved, their great estates broken up, and laws limiting the amount of land or money that can be inherited, an Englishman who while favoring the notion of the establishment of religion would establish all of the large religious communions equally with the Anglican, who is so convinced that there is an ascertainable truth in political and social matters and that the nation in its collective and corporative character, as the state, can do so much more for civilization than now by carrying this truth into effect, is hardly a Tory. On the side of spirit and tone of life Arnold takes it as his own function to deal chiefly with the civilization of the middle class, but is entirely aware of the great problems that surround such a matter.

It is his interest in "the social idea", it is the instinctive need to share, that explains the simplicity of Arnold's style. He wishes to stand beside the reader and thus see the object "eye to eye" with him. If a certain fineness of vision is required he still has the faith that this is a latent possession of humanity and may be evoked; let us in any case evoke it wherever possible. "By our *best self* we are united, impersonal, at harmony". One of the cleverest of contemporary minds sees in these writings "thin-spun sermons for the general public", "Matthew Arnold's tracts for the times". Well, he certainly intended them to be thin-spun in the only sense in which they are so. His supply of thought is not thin. As Mr Brownell in an admirable essay has pointed out it is because in the interest of clarity Arnold resolutely takes but one thing at a time that we are tempted rashly to conclude that he has only a slender sheaf of ideas at his disposal. He is fertile of ideas. But he could not tolerate a dense and crowded growth of them in the same page or essay. He has a singular art of clearing out the undergrowth and permitting the tall and commanding thoughts to stand forth. The independent intelligence that he brings to bear tells him that "the easy writing that makes hard reading" is an almost universal fault in literature, that a true and important idea deserves an open approach, that it is only the fewest in our language who do justice to their own conceptions in the minds of others. Arnold is taking language as a means of communication; the task he sets the critic is "a disinterested endeavor to learn *and propagate* the best", etc. "Propaganda", writes Mr Santayana in his beautiful *Soliloquies in England,* "propaganda, that insult to human nature". If it is so, education must be an insult to human nature and I sometimes notice a tendency in the young to resent it as such. The Sermon on the Mount was no doubt a terrible reflection on existing human nature, but hardly because it was propaganda. We do not insult people by assuming that they are willing to learn or capable of learning. We do them honor. To be sure, pettish human nature is impatient of learning and of the supposition that any knowledge could profitably be added to it, but that is simply the most pitiful and indefensible of our weaknesses. Nothing gives the measure of the difference between

Arnold and Mr Santayana, of the want in the latter of a certain fundamental human seriousness – seriousness in one of its dimensions – a want that all the penetration of his acute and large-minded spectatorship can almost but not quite make us forget, better than the quoted words. The reach, the greatness and beauty of Mr Santayana's thought are not enough appreciated; if this trait were added they might be of the highest order.

The instinctive need to share is at the root of Arnold's view of criticism also. It is the business of criticism, he tells us, "to see the object as in itself it really is". Now clearly it is the business of criticism, for Arnold and for everybody, as the word implies, to judge, to pronounce good or bad. And at this saying of his both the common mind, with its maxim that there is no disputing about tastes, and the philosophic mind, with its remark that good and bad are not in the object but in the beholder's impression of the object – that "there's nothing either good or bad but thinking [that is, feeling] makes it so" – both the common mind and the philosophic mind demur or wonder. The truth is that Arnold is purposely oblivious of the philosophic subtlety; and the popular notion that there is no truth or standard in the subject of taste, that it is abandoned to individual caprice, is just what he is set upon correcting. He speaks as if good and bad were objective, meaning in effect that the sense of them is shared, common, social, reliable. The duty of the critic is "to get himself out of the way and let humanity judge". There is such a thing as the normal human impression. The economy of human life makes a certain impression helpful, and human nature is normal when it responds with this appropriate impression and no other. It cannot be said that from a man's arbitrary taste there is no appeal. There is an appeal, not to the majority, but to the normal, which means in the end an appeal to the type of taste most fruitful of human happiness or most consistent with it.

The depth of Arnold's social instinct is seen again in what he finds to be "the function of criticism at the present time". It is the function of purifying the wells from which creative literature is drawn. One thinks of the critic as judging the work after it appears; Arnold thinks of him also as gradually imparting his standard to the creative mind. Then in the struggle for existence between the various tentative imaginations that spontaneously spring up in that mind some will be promptly suppressed by the critical conditions that now reign there and only the fitter will survive. Criticism has thus the mission of raising the very starting-point of creation to a higher level, of cleansing the very atmosphere that the creative spirit breathes. The social function of criticism is the creation of taste, and of an instinctive wisdom.

As a critical leader Arnold with all his merits has two great inadequacies. The first is that he regards it as the office of creative literature itself to be in effect "a criticism of life"; to exhibit the things of life, that is, in such wise that their relative values stand forth in relief. Thus he ranges himself with those who hold it the business of literature to educate and form us for better living. How easy it is to turn in at this door and not see the larger one! True, literature often has a power to form us; let all use be made of that power. But literature has another reason for existence, namely, to be life instead of preparing for it; to be a high and satisfying experience, a worthy use of time, and an end and not a means, a form of happiness. "Art for art's sake", that is for beauty's sake, must have its place. To take this wider view would not a little have modified some of his judgments.

The other weakness has been besides a bad example. There must be in literature in any case an element of the criticism or estimate of the things of life. The critic cannot avoid pronouncing on questions of fact, of truth, as well as of aesthetic value. He must exercise not only taste but reason. Taste is an immediate verdict and Arnold, impatient of logical machinery, is too often tempted in large questions of truth to make his reason dispense with reasoning and issue an immediate verdict too, a prompt and easy 'intuition'. He will be a seer with the naked eye. This may be called the fallacy of the critic. The critic cannot always tell us with assurance what in life and literature does actually make for human happiness without taking a great deal of pains to find out. Through a cautious logic, through experiment and other tests, we escape from the plausibilities of our own minds, we make sure "that our light is not darkness". We do but follow Arnold's spirit further. He himself is too prone to forget his own lines and stop short of "the dragon-wardered fountains where the springs of knowledge are". Some of the examples of this Mr Stuart Sherman in his invaluable guide to Arnold, has analyzed. His sensitive care for truth is in this matter not always sensitive enough. The new world that is now "powerless to be born" awaits the development of intellectual conscience as the one absolute condition and means of arising.

Akin to this is his one defect as a moralist, a defect that is typically

Victorian. He lays it down that in morals the knowing is easy and it is only the doing that is hard. True within the field of established morality but quite forgetful of the morality that has yet to be established. We have a railway that as yet takes us but a part of the distance to our destination; at the end of it we must get off and make our way through the bush as best we can. He reminds us impressively that the fortunes of society depend upon morals, but not enough that it is the business of morals effectually to secure the well-being of society.

On religion, inspired by Spinoza's *Theological Political Treatise* and by Vinet, Arnold did some of his most momentous work. His early phase is one of scepticism and of sadness. He is private secretary to Lord Lansdowne and his writing is chiefly in verse. When he becomes a traveling inspector of schools, begins a long career full of work and tedium, meets the members of school boards and is a guest at middle-class tables, when in brief he comes close to English life, we see a new phase. Immersed in work and facing the defects that most repel him he becomes constructive and puts sadness away. Life gradually wrote out the equation: Critical and fastidious instincts plus deep humanity equal *reform*. This mood of statesmanship he carries into religion. He asks himself what are the elements of Christianity that no modern knowledge can shake, that rest verifiably upon experience, that the scientific sceptic himself must accept. The inadequacy of Arnold's answer must not blind us to the fact that no more fruitful and sagacious question has ever been asked. One after another he takes the conceptions of Christian faith and translates them into the language of human experience and salutary consequence. The points of view of science and of biblical research he supplements with that of humane history and letters. What he does not adequately take is the point of view of religion itself. He is moralistic, not sufficiently spiritual. There are sides of religious experience lighting up the whole problem of which he knows too little. He can even write of the idea that God is personal, "a being who thinks and loves", that the stress upon it is due to the Aryan love of metaphysics, not to Hebrew religion at all, that it has no deep value for human life. Still, his statement of the question of religion for our time, his setting of the conditions for the answer, are work of a statesmanlike courage and grasp that have not been sufficiently acknowledged. The truth is that because Arnold wrote on the most deep-reaching problems with a sustained simplicity of language and of touch academic scholars have at no time fully perceived his power as a philosopher.

CONSCIENCE AND THE BISHOPS

[Miller resigned his teaching position at General Theological Seminary in 1924, and the following article from *The New Republic* of that year indicates the event that occasioned his decision and the reasons behind it. The event was a pastoral letter from the Bishops of the Episcopal Church making a clergyman liable for trial for interpreting the words in the creed about Jesus' birth in any other than a literal sense.

In analyzing this historic step, Miller applies the view of religious truth he had defended since 1909 in 'What Religion Has To Do With It'. Religion does not have the function of science and does not aim to formulate a correct philosophical analysis. Rather it seeks to reveal aspects of reality that create impulse and transform life. Its symbolism is not something trivial but rather "a means to practical truth" centering on Christ as a person, a timeless presence embodying the "principle of love and benefit, which he declared to be the one basis of the whole moral law". This truth, however, must be freed in its own interest from literal misstatements of historical or cosmic fact and relieved of conflict with the discoveries of intelligence. Faithful pursuit of truth and intellectual honor must take precedence over loyalty to the clergy because it is the one hope of mankind for the solution of its problems.

Thus again Miller affirms the primacy of "conscience of the mind" as the indispensable means to the collective welfare of mankind. With such a commitment he could not but resign from the Seminary where he had been respected but never much understood. Nevertheless he retained his membership in the church, was fully ordained in 1935, and subsequently served as pastor from time to time.]

The House of Bishops of the Episcopal Church in an evening and a morning of last November created a new situation in that communion, not bringing order out of chaos, but something very like chaos out of what had been order. It was not fortunate that by an act so rapid and so slightly considered so profound an upheaval should have been occasioned; but since it was so, it would not be expedient to rest the matter until the question at issue has for practical purposes been settled. The question is of the right of individual clergymen to interpret certain articles of the creed in a symbolic, not a literal sense. And it would be neither expedient or honorable to rest the matter until it has been made clear to the public that the bishops' implied charge of dishonesty against some of their own number and many others is without basis. By that accusation (which had they paused to look into the state of opinion and into recent history and ecclesiastical rulings could hardly have been made) against some of the most respected men in the church, they secured a prompt and formidable revolt. As the matter stands at present, their act has in the short interval had results out of which has emerged a more incontestable basis for the liberties they condemned than has ever existed before. It is of capital importance that this result shall not be reversed.

The church is a deep-seated organ of society, powerful for good. It is the institute of the inner life, which is by nature weaker than the outer life and yet has the ultimate control over it. So long as man has an inner life, requiring to be developed, steadied and guided, there will be need of the church. It demands the best mind and soul of the community to lead it. Today there are crying tasks for moral influence and leadership (in no little part unnoted) which belong to its function and which it should perform. It is not forever limited to its present scope. Society should not encourage it to bar out the more enlightened and alert young spirits. Yet society is prone to forget its own stake in the matter, look on indifferently and merely say: "Every man has a right to his opinion, but if he doesn't believe what the church says he should go out of it". This is sound sense and truth, but it does not carry the conclusion fancied. The question is, What does the church really say? That is, what does it mean, or permit us to mean, by the words it uses? While historic and venerable words are retained, full of true symbolic force and fitness and holding the church in spirit together through the ages, is it forbidden that the mind and meaning behind them should grow in depth and enlightenment? That is what is being decided now and it is in the interest of society that it should be decided for the largest benefit.

It is a point that has to be decided. In any oath, vow or test the question may be raised, What do these words mean? And there is only one authority that can answer, the authority that imposes the oath, vow or test. If the church permits certain words of the creed to be accepted in a figurative or symbolic sense it is not dishonest to say them in that sense. If it refuses to permit this it will be dishonest. For that will not be within *the meaning of the words* as officially employed.

Religion involves worship, and this is an action in which many of the intellectual class have no desire to engage. "Only by bowing down before the higher", said Carlyle, "does man feel himself exalted". Those who do desire to engage in it know that the spirit of worship cannot express itself and give the measure of its depth without potent symbolism. When the worship is just, such symbolism is expressive of truth. Christianity is not the mere devotion to a principle but to a person as embodying that principle. Christ, by his principle of love and benefit, which he declared to be the one basis of the whole moral law, and by the identification of his whole personality, acts, teaching, death and spirit with the principle, becomes an object of the Christian's personal worship as an embodiment of the divine. There is no truer or higher object or worship. The historic dogmas that have gathered about him have this in common, that their purpose is to exalt and magnify Jesus Christ. To say in the creed that he was "conceived by the Holy Spirit, born of the Virgin Mary", that he was the Son of God and also of man, is, for many of us, to use a historic and poetic symbol to express the truth that while he had all the nature of the children of men he was divine in nature in that he was peculiarly one with the spirit of God.

Long ago at a university I had unexpectedly to take an oath. The dean placed a paper with the form of words before me. In doubt whether I could sincerely use certain expressions I asked him what they meant. He gave them a broad and nonliteral interpretation; to this I could subscribe and I took the oath. It was he who asked me to take it, he stood by to represent the imposing power, and it would have been idle and absurd to insist upon taking the language in a narrower sense when he authorized a wider one. The case is typical. When the meaning of the creed is in question the church alone can decide, the present church, for it is the present church that imposes it as a test and could cease to impose it. If instead I had at first said to the dean, "There is one sense in which I can say these words and I shall take the oath in that sense", and he had heard without demur, the case would have been precisely the same. The question of varacity depends wholly on the question, What are the permitted meanings? No one wishes to forbid the literal interpretation; the wish is that the non-literal shall be permitted also. Anyone who looks at history and the growth of a social organism will see that there is only one way in which wider meanings can begin to be permitted, namely by precedent; by the initiative of individuals, who find a larger sense possible for the words and let it be known that they take them in that sense. If the corporate church forbids this, or deems it ground for ejection from the ministry, the matter is settled – for the time at least. If the corporate church, knowing, does not condemn, it leaves the precedent standing; it is permitting the new interpretation. And when this fact is sufficiently clear others are entitled to regard the meaning as permitted. Individuals by their initiative are not merely deciding for themselves, they are playing a legitimate part toward forming the attitude of the church. Such growth and enlargement cannot be effected in the first instance by formal action of the whole church, for new interpretations must exist within the body before it is called upon to judge of them. It is in this respect properly a slow-moving body; it does not make up its mind quickly, having a wide range of mind to make up. Much consideration, warning experience, balancing of opposite forces, intellectual sympathy, charity, caution may go to the making of the church's ultimate will with regard to such a precedent.

The frequent indifference of society toward the individual who is fighting its battles within the ancient organization is seen not least in those who only too cordially agree with him in the negative or questioning part of his opinions; and this for the reason that they have little interest in the constructive and coöperative part. Their only aid is the casual advice to come and join them outside. It is therefore worth while to quote from John Stuart Mill, whom the late Lord Morley called "the wisest and most virtuous man whom I have ever known or am likely to know", some words uttered in the Inaugural address which he delivered as Rector to the students of St. Andrew's University:

Those of you who are destined for the clerical profession are, no doubt, so far held to a certain number of doctrines, that, if they ceased to believe them, they would not be justified in remaining in a position in which they would be required to teach insincerely. But use your influence to make those doctrines as few as possible. It is not right that men should be bribed to hold out against conviction – to shut their ears against objections, or, if the objections penetrate, to continue professing full and unfaltering belief when their confidence is already shaken. Neither is it right that, if men honestly profess to have changed some of their religious opinions, their honesty should as a matter of course exclude them from taking a part, for which they may be admirably qualified, in the spiritual instruction of the nation. The tendency of the age, on both sides of the ancient Border, is towards the relaxation of formularies, and a less rigid construction of articles. This very circumstance, by making the limits of orthodoxy less definite, and obliging everyone to draw the line for himself, is an embarrassment to consciences. But I hold entirely with those clergymen who elect to remain in the national church, so long as they are able to accept its articles and confessions in any sense or with any interpretation consistent with common honesty, whether it be the generally received interpretation or not. If all were to desert the church who put a large and liberal construction on its terms of communion, or who would wish to see those terms widened, the national provision for religious teaching and worship would be left utterly to those who take the narrowest, the most literal, and purely textual view of the formularies; who, though by no means necessarily bigots, are under the great disadvantage of having bigots for their allies, and who, however great their merits may be, – and they are often very great, – yet, if the church is improvable, are not the most likely persons to improve it. Therefore, if it were not an impertinence in me to tender advice in such a matter, I should say, let all who conscientiously can, remain in the church. A church is far more easily improved from within than from without. Almost all the illustrious reformers of religion began by being clergymen; but they did not think that their profession as clergymen was inconsistent with being reformers. They mostly indeed ended their days outside the churches in which they were born; but it was because the churches, in an evil hour for themselves, cast them out. They did not think it any business of theirs to withdraw. They thought they had a better right to remain in the fold, than those had who expelled them.

Apparently such members of the House of Bishops as voted on this matter in November did not hold that in these matters the church must act with cautious deliberation, on pain of discovering that it had not been the church that was acting but only an insufficiently informed portion of it. Summarily to condemn the precedents that had established freer interpretation was what they undertook. The House is for the most part a cautious, conciliatory, kindly body, for the individual bishops usually possess these qualities. But on this occasion it adopted and issued as a Pastoral Letter the report of a small committee which by implication finds well-known bishops, hundreds of the clergy, and thousands of the laity guilty of a position regarding the creeds inconsistent with "honesty in the use of language". In the same connection are used the words "dishonesty and unreality". The example given is the interpreting of the words "conceived by the Holy Ghost, born of the Virgin Mary" in any other than the literal sense. "For holding and teaching" such an interpretation "a clergyman is liable to be presented for trial". The subject had not been announced in the call for the meeting as coming up for action or discussion and many bishops were absent. It is credibly reported that some who were present were taken unawares and did not vote. The Letter was in response to a petition addressed to the House by Senator Pepper of Pennsylvania and other laymen asking some definite pronouncement on too free inter-pretations of doctrine in certain quarters. The report was adopted unani-mously.

A Pastoral Letter is merely a species of sermon addressed to the whole church; it has no binding authority. Only the decision of General Con-vention or of a court of final appeal created by General Convention could have that. None the less the action created instantly a new moral situation. So long as any fair-minded inquirer who asked himself, To what are the Episcopal clergy really committed? would find the true state of things and therein find the liberty that precedents had secured, the situation was tolerable. But when he would find these precedents declared null and void by a body so widely representative and so near the seat of legislative and judicial power this situation was gravely compromised. The wider interpretations had not yet by authority been forbidden but they had suffered a weighty challenge; they had become doubtful. The precedents must be reestablished; that is, they must be renewed in no uncertain manner and must remain uncondemned by any final authority. Any other course would have permitted the church to lock itself in a dark room and throw the key out of the window. Accordingly, numerous clergymen since the Pastoral Letter have been engaged in renewing the precedents. The Modern Churchman's Union and the faculty of the Episcopal Theological school of Cambridge, affiliated with Harvard, have issued protests. The rectors of the most prominent parishes, with few exceptions, in the largest city of the country have either by word or act expressed their disapproval. Not widespread controversy only but still more widespread acute distur-bance of private minds and feelings among devoted members of the church on both sides has ensued. The bishops had unwittingly thrown a torch into a somewhat inflammable building.

The question was now whether they would carry their opinion into action and bring non-literalists to trial. Almost immediately afterward the Rev. Lee W. Heaton in the diocese of Dallas, Texas, where the bishop's meeting had been held, was presented for trial. The Bishop Coadjutor of Texas announced however that, while the presentment was warranted, "as similar interpretations of the doctrine in question are held, taught and preached" by bishops, he was unwilling to consent to the trial, and waited until higher authority should point out the course of wisdom and justice. That is, Bishop Moore desisted on precisely what appeared above to be the natural ground, that the opinion was already too well intrenched in the church. The effect of the course he has taken is that the freer interpretation in his diocese is permitted; by an act whose deliberate and responsible character is notably enhanced by its coming directly after the bishops' pronouncement and under the aroused attention of the whole church. Unless Dr Lawrence or other bishops or priests are now not only proceeded against but condemned for their stand on the same doctrine, which is hardly likely, Bishop Moore's action, taken with what preceded it, remains a definitive and historic step.

To leave the subject here would be to leave a vital half of it unstated. What appears to be the public's impression of the whole matter is a caricature. This is not a simple struggle between modernists and conservatives, in which one party should conquer. To be sure the charge of dishonesty must be repelled and the poisonous suspicion of it removed by the light of day. For the rest, what is needed is not a triumph but a synthesis. The bishops in their instinct are right, though in their method wrong. They are springing to the defence of something vital. That something is the personal worship of Jesus Christ as an eternal presence, a being having not only goodness but power, a potent saviour. They regard this as essential to the faith and as imperilled by 'modernism', and they are right.

Incidentally, be it said that it is by no means only 'broad-churchmen' who take certain clauses of the creed in a non-literal sense. Many catholics or 'high churchmen', including some identified with the extreme and strictest school, do so too; while fully retaining their descent from "liberal protestantism".

Modernism! What an ominous party-name! An idea is not sound because it is modern. Not a few modern ideas and tendencies are bad and noxious. We should not be in quest of whatsoever things are modern but of what is true. If we are captivated by the fashions of thought of our own time one thing is tolerably certain, that we shall appear antiquated to succeeding ages. Modernism is provincialism in the realm of time. It is reasonable-ism, true-ism that should be our only concern. To say "The spirit of the age has changed; we moderns can't believe that sort of thing any more" is to trust to one of the most treacherous of guides, a contagious and prevailing mood or habit of mind. Education should enable man to reach out beyond the currents and eddies of opinion in which he lives and lay hold of something firm and unshaken, of principles of sound evidence, of those tests of truth that have nothing to do with fashion. An age gains no more than an individual from conceit of its ideas, and would do well to escape so far as it can from itself, its current impulses and easy assumptions, into a larger world, to detect its own blindnesses and learn how to cure them. Yet an age is no more disposed to do this than an individual.

The progress of the church's mind does not consist in discarding old Christianity or parts of it and substituting new ideas. Its business is not to adopt modern thoughts as patches on an old and ragged garment. Christianity has a logical development from within itself. The more conservative it is the more progressive it must be, if its conservatism is genuine, for it is conservative of a progressive thing. It is perpetually preaching "newness of life". A gospel of love is a gospel of ever-better service and therefore of ever-better intelligence. You cannot serve effectually without understanding your task, your beneficiary and his situation in the real world. "And this I pray, that your love may abound yet more and more in knowledge and in all judgment." There is no strife between realism and idealism, for you must know the world as it is to make it what it should be. Precisely in the interest of the service for which it exists the church must seek light from every quarter, "sitting in the midst of the doctors, both hearing them and asking them questions". Its maxim must be: "Prove all things, hold fast that which is good". I repeat, this comes out of its gospel and is not merely thrust upon it by modern enlightenment. In other words, the principle develops out of its gospel that it should take the fullest advantage of modern enlightenment.

The church is conservative because what it has to preserve is precious. It has to preserve religion. Its business is not to formulate a correct philosophical analysis but to reveal such aspects of reality as speak to the will and the mood, create impulse, transform life and satisfy or overwhelm contemplation. Christian religion is not merely ethics, else it could not be a powerful reinforcement to ethics. It is the worship of a person embodying a principle. It understands the secret of the heart and loves the principle in the person. We see the men and women of today; we cannot see Christ with our literal eyes; but the mind's eye seeks to perceive him across the centuries as a living being; or rather detaches him from his place in history and rests upon him as a timeless presence, the ever-accessible incarnation of the highest. There is indeed peril that much of this will be cleared ruthlessly away by levelling and modernizing habits of thought which criticize religion as if it had the function of science and neglect the needs of the inner life as if it were an impertinent and disturbing beggar, or by a complaisant religious modernism which yields too far to these habits. It is truth that for the soul the intervention of centuries is irrelevant and that Christ is a present and intimate saviour. For it was true that in intent his compassion and will to understand knew no limit and that he reserved a delicate sympathy for every soul that might come to him. That he asks men to repent, brings them forgiveness, gives them strength to amend, and is with them as consoler and support, has a truth far profounder than the barriers of historic time that divide him from us. It is true that simple souls (and in this all souls are simple) may cast their cares on him and feel relief. In this light, as the instantaneous deliverer of the spirit, an air of the transcendent and miraculous justly clings about him, – an air of one "supernatural, superrational, super-everything". To tamper with it seems to threaten his power and competence as a deliverer. The philosophy does not yet exist, nor the delicate justice to the facts, which would fully interpret and vindicate all this. In the interests of the soul during a difficult period of transition it may for some be far truer to surround the doctrine of the Virgin-birth with a wide and inviolate circle of reverence and caution, than to enter, as here, upon analysis. It is unpardonably wrong to teach something untrue because it will do good, but it may be right to refrain from teaching something true to certain persons because it will do harm; that is, because it would be asking too much to expect them to discern it without further intellectual experience, in its true perspective. No false word should be said, but – any word, in this sphere, paralyzing to the spiritual life is a false word. Few critics appear to grasp the whole function of symbolism. It is common to say "Oh that is symbolism, is it? Very well. But putting symbolism aside and speaking seriously," etc. It is not perceived that a symbol may be an instrument of knowledge, a means to practical truth, that its office is to exert forthwith the power upon life that philosophic truth *ought* to exert when at length secured and seen in all its true proportions.

Thus the bishops were hastening to the defence of a life, a habit of spiritual devotion, a source of power. Minds accustomed to an accepted body of ideas and not to its analysis must feel the whole threatened if rude hands are laid on any part. None the less the deep truth in Christian dogma must in its own interest be freed as soon as possible from literal misstatement of historical or cosmic fact and relieved from any conflict with the discoveries of intelligence. The gospel of intelligence must fully be joined to the gospel of the spirit. The task of complete synthesis is perhaps the most arduous that the human mind has ever attempted and it is but too easy for the advance-agents of enlightenment to "substitute a rude simplicity for the complexity of truth". Still, those who say, "This is a difficult time of intellectual transition" must not proceed, by a policy of persistent silence, to make that time as long as possible. Reserve within the church, which every mind of judgment and weight knows to be some-times indispensable, should have its limits and never be taken up as a permanent attitude; it should keep watch for the opportunities to carry the transition forward.

Still more firmly must it be said that to disregard Christian morals in the attempt to preserve Christian doctrine is of unhappy omen. The bishops address an emphatic admonition to conscience, declaring that a non-literal interpretation of the clause concerning Christ's birth is "plainly an abuse of language", implying that it is "to trifle with words and cannot but expose us to the suspicion and danger of dishonesty and unreality". Indeed they go further and appear to imply or suggest that it is flatly inconsistent with "honesty in the use of language". To conscience they ap-peal, let conscience speak. To bring such charges by plain implication against so many men of long service and honorable standing without taking up, or hinting at the existence of, the case for the defence, as stated above and in unnumerable other forms before, without considering the decisions of the Judicial Committee of the Privy Council in the mother-Church of England, without evincing any sense that such men must have something to say for themselves and that such a movement in history can hardly have been oblivious of moral considerations: this was to risk using their authority, as unhappily they have actually used it, to promulgate or suggest an injurious slander.

The bishops continue: "Objections to the doctrine of the Virgin-birth [meaning the literal doctrine]... have been abundantly dealt with by the best scholarship of the day". They have of course been "dealt with" by scholarship of various grades, but the bishops evidently mean, not merely dealt with, but effectually met. What a curious conception of the legitimate grounds of belief is betrayed by assuring us that all is well because "objections" "have been abundantly dealt with!" To prove an alleged historical fact what we need is sufficient evidence that it occurred: to controvert the objections that happen to have been made by this or that person or even to offer an explanation of the difficulties presented by the records, is not the primary requirement. That we are entitled to assume an alleged occurrence to have taken place until objections are made to it, which then have to be "dealt with", does indeed appear to be the impression of many minds but it receives no encouragement from logic. If the testimony of the church is invoked as the initial authority then that authority must first of all be validated from the ground up as adequate in respect of this particular event.

It would have been a more congenial task to write this article without a word to intimate that one position on the historical question was better intrenched than the other. But the bishops in an official document have undertaken to pronounce that the position they oppose is based on inferior scholarship. Once more, we have no right by our considerate reserves to prolong the period of precarious transition which they are intended to safeguard. The Pastoral Letter has precipitated a necessity for plain speaking under which we can no longer courteously cloak the fact that no thoroughly educated man believes in the literal Virgin-birth; – though many men do so whose spiritual life, ability and efficiency command our admiration. By education I do not mean learning, but the possession of a competent common-sense training in judging of ordinary matters of evidence. It by no means follows that all who do not believe are thoroughly educated. Loyalty to the clergy is a fine thing, so long as it is consistent with loyalty to the church and to humanity. It is sometimes said that the literal version of the doctrine is rendered so highly probable by certain presuppositions that it does not require such ample evidence as is supposed. But the presuppositions themselves rest upon the slenderest basis of evidence. It is not until we recognize that here too are stern matters of moral principle, that the faithful pursuit of truth by the path of sound method and intellectual honor – a well-marked path for those who sufficiently desire it – is the one hope of mankind for the solution of its problems that we shall escape from the welter of arbitrary opinion.

JAMES'S DOCTRINE OF 'THE RIGHT TO BELIEVE'

(*Revised*)

[Among Miller's articles and addresses occasioned by the James commemorations of 1942 was a further reckoning with "the will to believe",
published that year under the title above and presented as an address at
the banquet meeting of the Boston University Philosophical Club. It
consolidated and systematized his earlier criticisms, beginning in 1899, to
take account of controversies on the subject with James and F. C. S.
Schiller. In 1943–44 Miller revised and expanded his published article to
prepare it to serve as a chapter or appendix for "a book on religion" that
he never completed. Some of the revisions took account of considerations
that C. J. Ducasse had raised in correspondence about cases where
decision must be made solely by impulse. These revisions and additions
are included in what follows and thus provide Miller's fullest and maturest word on the subject.

Miller notes that James's doctrine was meant to apply particularly to
religious belief and finds its source in James's exceptional interest in
fullness of life and his sympathetic concern for the liberty of other minds.
Through close analysis of James's position, however, Miller finds it to be
confused at key points. James fails to make careful distinctions between
'probable' and 'valuable', between 'faith' and 'hypothesis', and between
'belief' and 'action'. Amidst these confusions lie James's loose extension
of the principle of empiricism and his inconsistent, indefensible thesis that
"there is no test of truth". His doctrine cannot be saved by his defenders –
Schiller, R. B. Perry, or even John Dewey – because their claims are not
supported by what he says and do not remove his momentous confusions.
"Putting subtleties aside", Miller basically objects to James's doctrine
because morality forbids it. Only by seeing things as they are, only through
intelligence controlled by fact and evidence, can we make ourselves better
and accomplish our ideals for humanity.]

James's thought on this subject, familiar to all of us, may be briefly recalled. It is that we have a good right to accept religious beliefs without evidence because they have value for our lives. Such a belief is, according to him, a working-hypothesis, – one might say, a living-hypothesis. We may live and act taking it for granted as true. It shall be true for us. But if we ask ourselves in a reflective moment, "Is this certain?", we have to answer, "No; it is a hypothesis that we choose to live by". We throw ourselves into it as a faith. But an inseparable part of the thought is that "the active faiths of individuals in such religious hypotheses, freely expressing themselves in life, are the experimental tests by which they are verified and the only means by which their truth or falsehood can be wrought out".

This doctrine, at the time the book was published, was more or less in the air. It was heard in James's lecture-room, but one could also go into a Boston church and hear Father Frisbie lay down the same doctrine. The same? Not precisely. Preachers would lay it down as a duty, the duty to embrace the faith; James put it forth not at all as a duty but as a liberty. We are *free* to choose belief. It was not "You should" but "You may". And we ought "delicately and profoundly to respect"[1] the liberty of others in the matter, a liberty both as to what they should postulate and whether they should voluntarily postulate on this subject at all. Another difference was that the church set forth the faith to be accepted as a certain and absolute truth, whereas for James a true philosophy "is contented to regard its most assured conclusions concerning matters of fact as hypotheses liable to modification in the course of future experience". Since the affirmation is to be "true for me", is there perhaps to be a certain difference between the daily religious attitude of faith (as much faith as possible) and the occasional philosophical acknowledgment of uncertainty? In any case James does not say this.

Having entitled his book *The Will to Believe* he subsequently felt that *The Right to Believe* would have been more fitting, since the former title suggested too much a deliberate highly conscious intent to imprint a belief on one's mind, whereas what he chiefly contemplated was gradual mental processes of tendency, inclination, preference, 'instinctive' attraction or repulsion, naturally engendering more or less belief. What he was maintaining as to life and religion might perhaps in considerable part be expressed (for the class of cases specified just below to which alone he would have applied it) in Burke's phrase, "the latent wisdom of prejudice".

The particular class of cases in which we have "a right to believe" was

that in which the option before our mind was (1) 'living', (2) 'forced', and
(3) 'momentous'. That is, in which the proposition accepted was 'alive'
not dead, in other words made a real appeal to the mind as a possible
belief; in which there were only the two alternatives, Yes and No; and in
which the decision was of high consequence for life. He accordingly views
his principle as applying by no means only to religion, but to morals,
enterprise, personal relations, etc. James's essays on the subject, however,
were written to apply it to religion.

His doctrine can hardly be understood without a proposition that he
often repeats: "There is no test of truth". The intellect has "no infallible
signal" for knowing whether a proposition be truth or no. "No bell in us
tolls to let us know for certain when truth is in our grasp"; so "it seems
a piece of idle fantasticality to preach so solemnly our duty of waiting for
the bell". We cannot tell that any positive belief is true nor that the denial
of it is true nor yet that judgment should be suspended.

What we do is to seize upon one standpoint or the other. Every belief
is or depends on some affirmation which is voluntary. The unbeliever is
choosing his attitude as truly as the positive believer. He must decide by
his voluntary nature, seeing that there is no other way, in the absence of a
test of truth, to reach a conclusion of any sort. This applies even to the
foundations. Even the proposition that "there is truth" is a "postulate"
that "we are deliberately resolving to make, though the sceptic will not
make it".

In this situation it is evidently wiser, he holds, in the interest of life to
choose the attitude that will most enhance life. It is better to die in a belief
that is the noblest possible even if it should in reality be false.

But (and this is the final consideration) that a belief enhances life is, as
we have alredy seen, the experimental test by which it is verified. "The
truest scientific hypothesis is that which, as we say, 'works' best; and it can
be no otherwise with religious hypotheses".

But let us not forget that in his doctrine there was always another element, even before the process of 'verification', besides the choice exercised
by our voluntary nature. There was what may be called a secret persuasion that the faith was probably true; a divination, a perception of the
mind, not based on any argument that could be formulated, but none the
less a sense of real plausibility, the consciousness of inexpressible tokens
of likelihood. The two things co-existed in the mind: the adoption of the

working-hypothesis and the deep realization that this working-hypothesis was probably true. 'Probable' was not James's word, but it seems fairly to interpret his meaning. "I can, of course, put myself into the sectarian scientist's attitude and imagine vividly that the world of sensations and of scientific laws and objects may be all. But whenever I do this I hear that inward monitor of which W. K. Clifford once wrote whispering the word 'bosh'! Humbug is humbug even though it bear the scientific name, and *the total expression of human experience* [the emphasis is the present writer's] as I view it objectively, invincibly urges me beyond the narrow 'scientific' bounds. ...So my objective [perceptive] and my subjective [voluntary] conscience both hold me to the over-belief which I express".[2] But it appears to have been always to him a high probability only, not a certainty.

This was one phase of the reason he perceived for belief. At another time he answers a questionnaire as follows:

QUESTION. Why do you believe in God? Is it from some argument?
ANSWER. Emphatically, no.
Q. Or because you have experienced His presence?
A. No, but rather because I need it, so that it 'must' be true.[3]

FROM WHAT DID IT ARISE?

Out of what elements in James's mind and outlook did this doctrine arise? It naturally arose from his powerful bent toward religion, together with his disbelief in the philosophical arguments offered for theism, and his tendency as a psychologist to think of belief in terms of will. He rejected the arguments all. By their very form and nature they lacked appeal for him. His doctrine sprang then chiefly from his scepticism, his profound religious interest, and his psychological voluntarism.

Bound up with the bent toward religion was his immense stress on character, on the strenuous mood, on will and fortitude, on "the heroic life". The impulse to these is not sufficiently stirred, he deliberately says, by any humanitarianism.

The capacity for the strenuous mood probably lies slumbering in every man, but it has more difficulty in some than in others in waking up. It needs the wilder passions to arouse it, the big fears, loves, and indignations; or else the deeply penetrating appeal of some one of the higher fidelities, like justice, truth, or freedom. Strong belief is a necessity of its vision; and a world where all the mountains are brought down and all the valleys are exalted is no congenial place for its habitation. ... This ... is why, in a merely human world without a God, the appeal to our moral energy falls short of its maximal stimulating power. ... When, however, we believe that a God is there, and that he is one of the claimants, the infinite perspective opens out. The scale of the symphony is incalculably prolonged. The more imperative ideals now begin to speak with an altogether new objectivity and significance, and to utter the penetrating, shattering, tragically challenging note of appeal. ... All through history ... we see the antagonism of the strenuous and genial moods, and the contrast between the ethics of infinite and mysterious obligation from on high, and those of prudence and the satisfaction of merely finite need.[4]

The scientific philosophy of the time, while challenging the existing faiths, had provided nothing to take their place. It had left the inward life without the support and inspiration of anything comparable in its power and spell to those faiths. James saw this want and he would not submit to it. With his exceptional interest in fulness of life, depth of feeling, the richer colors of experience, he saw sceptical criticism without religious reconstruction as simply impoverishing life, robbing it of its noblest possessions. What the scientific philosopher (he thought) callously and pedantically passed by was *the requirement of the human spirit*.

Apart from the three factors mentioned, which are chief, there was also the passion for freedom. Cold lawgivers of logic must not be permitted to "put a stopper on our heart", to "put an extinguisher on my nature", in order to maintain their fancied proprieties. His doctrine has in it the note of revolt, the snapping of irksome bonds, a break for liberty from all this.

Further, the benefit and liberty of other minds than our own, his quick sympathetic sense of what cherished faiths mean to numberless men and women who may in their tenets differ from us but who find their guidance and support in them, played a greater part in his motives than has commonly been seen. The liberty of others to believe, and to believe perhaps otherwise than we do, to derive all the solace and encouragement that they could from their private faiths, was, I think, all but as much a factor with him as his own need of belief.

Next to be mentioned is the conception of 'empiricism' as James entertained it. Strictly empiricism has meant the view that our knowledge of laws of nature and general propositions of every sort comes from experience, depends upon the evidence that experience offers. But he meant by the term 'experience' something more inclusive and less definite than it signifies in inductive logic. Our beliefs were sustained not only if experience offered evidence for them as evidence is commonly conceived but if they were and remained emotionally satisfying and productive of satisfactory living. If our beliefs "worked well" in that wider sense, then they were 'empirically' justified.

Lastly, among the traits and tendencies that led him to the doctrine must be noticed a basic fact: the place he gave in his world to irresponsible perception, divination, intuition (in the popular sense of that term), the spontaneities of our mental nature. 'Wisdom' was not for him a thing largely charted, largely based on definite principles of thinking. It was an *aperçu*, a piercing glance of insight, a thing unique in each case, which often, and especially in the highest cases, could not be brought to book or turned into argument.

CONFUSIONS BY THE WAY

Before general comment on the truth of the doctrine as a whole, let me try to point out certain particular confusions that surely vitiate its exposition and argument.

First, there is the confusion between *probable* and *valuable*. We saw above that besides the factor of choice in our believings there was in James's mind the element of a sense of probability not susceptible of analysis or formal statement. Now though these elements are two, not one, though they are distinct in nature, James does not distinguish them or does not keep them distinguished. The evidential support given to theism by "the total expression of human experience" is evidently in his eyes a matter of probability pure and simple. But elsewhere he declines to discriminate this case in kind from such inducements to belief as attractions, values, appeals to desire. Probability and desirability alike he calls "liveliness". Confronting this very point he writes: "I can find nothing sharp (or susceptible of schoolmaster's codification) in the different degrees of 'liveliness' in hypotheses concerning the universe, or distinguish *a priori* between legitimate and illegitimate cravings".[5] Here he is shutting his eyes to the distinction that underlies all intelligence and is part of its essential foundation, between allurement (of whatever sort) and evidence, between a ground for thinking something real and a ground for finding it, in idea, attractive. As long as he insists that amongst the inducements to belief we cannot separate probability from desirability, he is saying in effect that we cannot think as rational beings, and hence cannot find our way safely amidst the baits and snares of this world. The distinction he declines to recognize is the beginning of wisdom, the basis of sanity. But he himself does after all come to recognize it, when in a passage quoted above he separates his objective (that is, cognitive) conscience from his subjective (that is, volitional or elective) conscience.

Second, there is the confusion between faith and hypothesis. "Faith is synonymous with working-hypothesis". But faith or belief means regarding a thing as real or probably real, regarding a proposition as true or probably true. (The probability is of course susceptible of degree, and thus we may speak of degrees of belief. We may believe partially or fully; that is, believe something as a probability, strong or faint, or as a certainty.) A hypothesis, on the other hand, is a mere temporary supposition, a tentative conception of the matter, deliberately made up for the sake of experiment. That is, it is to be acted upon in investigation only in order to see whether the consequences will confirm it. A hypothesis may be thus provisionally adopted because we think it probably true; its adoption may be based upon some degree of belief. Or it may be adopted because it alone suggests itself or is one of two or three which alone do so and which we decided to try in succession. In the latter case there would be no belief. A hypothesis as such does not require any belief; by its nature it excludes belief, so far as it is strictly hypothesis; we do not take up an idea to try except because we are uncertain whether it is true or not. In so far as it is already regarded as true there is no reason to try it. In so far as it requires trial it is evidently not yet regarded as true. In proportion, then, as it is literally a hypothesis it is not a belief. In proportion as it is actually a belief it is not a hypothesis. So far from faith being synonymous with working-hypothesis the two ideas are mutually exclusive. It does not follow, of course, that the same man may not be entertaining a proposition at once as a partial belief (that is, as a probability greater or less) and as a hypothesis. Where his belief stops his working-hypothesis can start and go on. That is, so far as the probability in his eyes falls short of certainty he may take the idea as a hypothesis. Prompted by his partial unbelief he recognizes that the idea must be put to trial; prompted by his partial belief he has chosen it as the one to try. But the confusion of these two leads to James's never quite clearing up the question, What would be your 'believer's' real state of mind; how far would it be merely a course of action, imagination, devout attitude, etc? How far is it comparable in degree of assurance to the prayer, "O God, if there is a God, save my soul, if I have a soul"?

Had James argued simply that we are logically free to take any doctrine as a hypothesis and live accordingly, fully recognizing that it is only a hypothesis, and watching to see if life supplies any confirmation of it, then he would not have raised the question of "the will to believe" at all. There would be no departure from ordinary logical principles as to belief. And there could be no objection to his advocacy unless on the ground of some want of sufficient initial probability in the particular doctrine to justify conforming one's life to it, or on the ground that life could not supply confirmation.

Indeed can we be certain that this is not the position that James himself (at least sometimes) is actually taking? To be sure, he speaks of "the will to believe" and "the right to believe", he fixes attention, so far as words go, on belief; but he keeps telling us that we are to take the attitude he recommends *at our own risk* and nowhere hints that we should cease to be conscious of that risk. And to be conscious of it would be to have a sense of uncertainty, not of plain fact. Indeed he lets us infer that he finds zest in "a certain amount of uncertainty" in his faith. But exactly in the measure in which we are conscious of a risk of error we are not believing. This cannot be too definitely said: In so far as one believes one is not envisaging any risk of error. You cannot have it both ways: You cannot believe and yet in the heart of that very belief be heroically facing the uncertainty of your whole position. Your state of mind would not be belief, which is regarding something as fact, not as uncertain. And of any degree of incomplete belief the same holds good. *In so far* as you believe there is for you no risk. James's language suggests that in point of fact he was thinking of a case where a mind would seek to believe as much as possible and yet would at the outset, in entering upon that intention and again occasionally later when in a philosophic frame of mind, be fully aware of the uncertainty – that is, for the moment, be doubting – in consequence, be alternately believing and doubting. But he does not anywhere say this; he does not recognize any alternation of inward attitude as required by his teaching. So it may be that he meant we should all along be fully conscious of the uncertainty, which would mean that he was advocating not a will to believe but a will to entertain a working hypothesis involving a habit of religious imagination (which was accompanied in his own case by a degree of belief consisting in that antecedent sense of probability that we noted above).

Taking the doctrine as it is laid down in his text, we are bound then to note three elements: (1) his initial sense of probability that his theism as he conceives it is fact, a probability never mounting to certainty, (2) a set purpose to believe in this theism *as much as possible* and to live in accordance with it; (3) a refusal to deceive oneself, an unflinching awareness of just how uncertain it all is (characteristic of James's thoroughgoing intellectual candor and forthrightness); this third element being flatly inconsistent with the second, for I cannot throw my whole mind without reserve upon the side of belief, acceptance, contemplation of the idea as fact, and yet intend to remain fully cognizant of its uncertainty.

We shall have to leave this question of James's own attitude in the unsettled state in which his own words leave it, and simply consider hereafter each for itself the propositions to which that text commits him.

Religious belief or faith, we see, is not hypothesis; equally true is it that a working-hypothesis could never constitute religion in its thoroughgoing form. The soul of religion involves a sense of security in the divine. It must feel an unfailing and unthreatened support. It involves an escape from insecurity, a refuge from the changes and chances, the dissatisfactions and disappointments of life. It rises into a region above all these. (This does not in the least mean that it may not send the believer straight out into life to cope with these very chances and difficulties, it means only that at the heart of religion there is a rapport with something profound and unshakable from which such inspiration comes.) The object of mature religion is in some sense an object of utter trust. God's being, however conceived, is not precarious like ours, exposed to dangers, *contretemps*, uncertainties. Whatever He is, *eine feste Burg ist unser Gott*. A mood that relishes "a certain amount of uncertainty" in its belief is akin to the spirit of adventure, the romantic spirit, it marks a deeply interesting human temperament, but it is not the distinctive mood of religion. Such a temper may approximate religion, may have in it a potent tincture of religion, but in just so far as it welcomes uncertainty in its faith, religion is not consummated in it, does not reach its profoundest form.

James's undiscriminating use of the two distinct ideas of hypothesis and belief, causes us to feel more or less adrift to the end, as we read his arguments, in a strange element of ambiguity and elusiveness.

That life is a trying, a failing, a succeeding and a learning; that its ideas should be in great measure provisional, tentative; that they should grow, even if slowly, in adequacy; that the mind should be open and experimental: this is James's special realization. Our wishes should keep making us try and our tryings should be such as to keep making us learn. But there is nothing in this broad fact that is bound up with voluntary belief. Properly understood, it urges against voluntary belief. It urges in favor of voluntary hypothesis and voluntary inquiry and against voluntary belief.

Third. It is only enlarging the last distinction, rendering it more comprehensive, when we speak of the conclusion between belief and action. Nothing is more important in the logical aspect of James's view. From his taking cases of mere action as if they were cases of belief a great part of its plausibility has arisen. The confusion has seemed to supply him with an argument from life that has in fact been the means of winning over not a few to his position. Let me quote a casual passage from Professor Charles Morris, whose final position on the matter I do not know:

> James was impressed by the essentially dramatic and adventurous character of men and by the need for choices which ran beyond available scientific evidence. ... We are forced to recognize again what James so clearly recognized: that life demands decisions and commitments in situations where full scientific knowledge is not at hand....

Yes, but choices, decisions, commitments are not belief. That we so often have to *act* without certainty or any approach to it, that "probability is the guide of life", that again and again we have to decide without delay, hastily estimating the probability to guide us – what can be more familiar? But these are questions of action, not of belief. Or rather, the only belief required is that in our ignorance what we choose is on the showing of the moment the best course or as good as any. There is no reason why when we act at a venture we should view our course as certainly the most expedient when its actual expediency is utterly uncertain. We can act firmly in the manner that seems best at the time, but why should we shut the eye of intelligence to the position as it really is, that is, to the absence of adequate knowledge? The proprieties of action and the proprieties of belief in the matter are not the same. Circumstances outside oneself call for prompt action. The needs of life at large as manifest from the mind's point of view within oneself call for sedulously preserving unblinded intelligence. But James speaks as if in such cases belief had to go with action. It is precisely the practical man who is fully aware of the hazard, who does not permit his mind and judgment to be rash, however promptly he must act.

Fourth, there is the deep confusion between belief and will. A belief (the regarding something as real or probably real) is not a voluntary conception; it is precisely an involuntary conception. We believe; that is to say, when we think of the objects in question they group and arrange themselves in our mind in a certain configuration of their own accord, without any interference from our will. That is the form in which the world presents itself when we think of the subject. We are not thinking "This shall be so", we are thinking "This is so – of itself – in itself" – not by my decree, not subject to my volition. If *we* arrange them according to our wish, that is not belief but imagination. Belief is a recognition, not a creation. To suppose that it is an act is to confuse it with assertion, which is an act of speech or writing. So decisive is this distinction that as long and as far as we are saying, "This shall be true for me", we are not believing it. Both the "shall be" and the "for me" are inimical to belief. Such a fiat, if it is to have any effect, must be repeated and acted upon till by the psychological working of the repetition the idea at length stays in the mind of itself and the willer of belief can "let go". I am speaking just here of the psychology of the subject, the nature of the mental state we call belief, while it is actually present, not of how we should reach belief, not of any logical or moral question whatsoever.

Belief, of course, produces action or shapes it, and any man's belief can to a great extent be ascertained and measured by this effect. But the mental fact of belief is not in itself an action, any more than sense-perception is; it is (what seems to be) the appearance of an existent thing before the mind, though the thing may appear in a fragmentary or obscured form or only by token. It may instantly suggest action but it is not action.

Of course all belief, when it comes to mind, has connection with our voluntary nature. Our calling a belief to mind is ordinarily incident to some purpose. Not however the purpose to believe, but some end the attainment of which calls for attention to the facts as we believe them to be. We are thinking of certain facts as facts because they have to be considered and tackled in attaining our end. The end is a matter of desire;

292   RELIGION AND HUMAN WELFARE

the facts are cold facts, which we must not get wrong if we are to succeed in our purpose.

Fifth, there is the confusion of reason as a whole with formal reason, which is but a part, – with formal logic, formal science, explicit reasoning. Rationalism he supposes to approve nothing but these.

Rationalism insists that all our beliefs ought ultimately to find for themselves articulate grounds. Such grounds, for rationalism, must consist of four things: (1) definitely statable abstract principles; (2) definite facts of sensation; (3) definite hypotheses based on such facts; and (4) definite inferences logically drawn.[6]

But reason and rationalism (in the true and comprehensive sense of that term) are not bound up with formal statement. By reason we mean the perception of cogency, the perception that a conclusion follows from our premises, whether deductively or empirically. Rationalism is the doctrine that our knowledge has completely rational foundations. It is the doctrine that reason can and should rule in the affairs of the mind. It does not at all say, it could not say, that we must always insist, even 'ultimately', upon formal and explicit ground for a conclusion, for we may not be able to secure such grounds. In an emergency where there is no leisure for reflection and we judge with one glance what it is best to do, reason may be prevailing as much as anywhere. It would be irrational to pause for formulation when pausing would be fatal. The most rational mental conduct may sometimes be that which abridges the process of reason, snatches at the most likely expedient, knowing it to be no more than likely, and proceeds with it as the best resort that the moment affords; as when we are crossing a brook by leaping precipitately from stone to stone without being able to pause and consider at each venture which stone is the best to leap for. This is reason doing the most rational thing upon a rational gauging of the exigency. Likewise, if a mind has the genuine sense that a certain religious idea is probable, it cannot clearly tell why, then that mind in acting upon it is from its own point of view acting rationally. It is a dangerous position, in relation to truth; experience bids us look twice and thrice very critically. But if then we still retain the persuasion, we are warranted in acting accordingly. James's drawing a line of alienation between rationalism and all informal, impromptu, spontaneous glimpses and descryings of the mind, claiming all the latter as on his own side, opposed to rationalism, this encouraged him to rise in revolt against reason and call himself an 'irrationalist'.

Incidentally James opposes empiricism to rationalism, as is usual. This, I submit, is a false antithesis. Learning from experience is of the essence of rationality. To oppose it to reason makes for misguidance and confusion.

'THERE IS NO TEST OF TRUTH'

Again before general comment on the doctrine, a word as to the pronouncement that "there is no test of truth". Is not the whole of logic, deductive and inductive, a body of tests of truth? Is not that just the purpose that logic is there to serve? A physical theory is tested by experiment. Many a proposition can be tested at once by comparing it with accessible fact. Deductive logic can test an opinion first of all by examining into its consistency with itself; then into its consistency with conclusions substantially established by experience; further still, into its consistency with probabilities established by experience. Where logic is not a test of certain truth, it is very frequently a signal test of probability. No, there is no ever-present mental test, equivalent to a perfectly informed secretary who accompanies us everywhere and instantly pronounces true or false any assertion referred to him. The individual reason is not equipped with an infallible detector. We are human; it is by the more laborious processes of experience, including observation and experiment, also of a close study of the import and consequence of ideas, that we can put to the proof the appealing suggestions that enter our minds. But because, once for all, we do not possess the magical and invariable test that James calls by that name, we have no reason to forget or leave unused the humbler and care-requiring tests at our disposal. While saying that there is no test of truth, James elsewhere speaks of "the experimental tests" by which religious hypotheses "are verified", "which are the only means by which their truth or falsehood can be wrought out". Just how *these* tests, which are "the active faiths of individuals... freely expressing themselves in life", *are* tests of truth, how they are experimental, how they prove the point, how far they prove it, and how long they take to prove it, are questions he never answers with precision. He conceives an ideal criterion that does not exist, and then a loose, vague, and easygoing substitute that exists but does not seem to be a criterion; while sweeping impatiently aside, for the subject of religion, those slowly gathered and painstaking processes that have evinced themselves the surest reliance of our race.

Since *The Will to Believe* was published, the book has had, it seems, between twenty and thirty reprintings. No wonder; it contains many insights, the expression of a great personality, and some of the noblest pages of English prose. It could not fail to have influence. Had the case been otherwise this would not have been written.

There has been no human being of whom I should like so much to be a disciple as William James. His marvellously large, human, candid, invariably meliorist outlook, his eye for the concrete, the breadth of his understanding of temperaments, of humanity, are incomparable. On some momentous topics I *am* his disciple. One philosophical conviction in particular which to me has been fundamental (and, as just implied, it does not stand alone) I simply learned and took over from him. I cannot take over "the right to believe". Here the bold sallies of his thought have brought him upon ground that happens to be simply the most crucial ground of all for civilization, education, human safety and well-being. He would not, were he alive, have wished any writer to refrain from speaking his mind about it; in any case I cannot do so. It was hard to assail his view thus while he lived; it is harder now. But he and his deserved repute can very well stand anything we say about him.

There are indeed through it all three fundamental respects in which James was assuredly right.

(1) He would not let religion go by the board. He perceived its place in life and, steeped in science as he was, educated in medicine, schooled in chemistry, physics, physiology, which last he taught, devouring the sceptical literature of his time, seeing no force in the traditional arguments for religion, he yet stubbornly refused to be carried away by the negative intellectual fashions, he insisted upon some basis for its free influence. This was one of James's essential intuitions and through and through it was surely sound. If we say that it resulted in a somewhat violent mode of keeping religion, we have to remember that for him there was no other alternative: either let religion go or keep it by main force.

(2) He was on equally firm ground in maintaining that it was in

experience that religion had to approve itself and could do so. He never entered sufficiently into the closer questions respecting the verification by experience, in what it logically consisted, how it proved, what it proved, how far it proved; he was never very definite even about what must in his view be proved; but the perception that on the whole or in the main guided him as to the ultimate dependence of it all upon experience was surely the true one. He is even in some passages momentarily tempted to the view that fruits and possible fruits in experience are all that it deals with, the whole meaning of its language – a point I mention only to illustrate what his general tendency was.

(3) And, as already implied, the benefit of religion in which from first to last he was essentially interested was a benefit in experience, a benefit in this present life. This was where his attention was fixed.

None the less his advocacy of his chief thesis seems to me one tissue of ingenious sophistry from outset to end – though no mind could have by nature less kinship or bent to sophistry than his. He was driven to his ingenuities by the peculiar position that we have noted earlier. He took the worst weakness of the human mind, the bribery of the intelligence, and set it up as a kind of ideal. It is the worst weakness because the most hurtful; producing not only private miseries but war, destruction, torture, the ruin of lives, communities, civilizations. Wisdom truly says, in the *Book of Proverbs*, "They that hate me love death"; – in effect their own or the death of others – and the one saving fidelity of wisdom is to fact, as distinguished from enticement of any sort. The intervention of "our passional nature", of which James approves, is that which chiefly interferes, in all human beings, with good and trustworthy judgment. It is the magnetism in the human mind that keeps tampering with the compass by which alone we can safely steer. There is a deep kinship and connection between the tragedy of sophistical reasoning – the mind's miscarriage – and the tragedy of human affairs.

As for "I need it, so that it 'must' be true", he who feels that because we need something we shall have it has not learned the first lesson of philosophy, even the first lesson of life. It is just because our desires and preferences do not of themselves magically control reality, and because our fate depends on steering aright with reference to reality, and not to dreams, that we must learn in framing our conception of things, as in our grade of civilization we have not yet learned, to keep our eyes on fact alone. "The will to believe" is the will to deceive oneself; it is the will to regard something as true which is doubtful.

Perhaps the most illuminating instance to adduce in which James's reasoning on this subject goes astray is his essay on 'Reflex Action and Theism'. There are the three departments of our reactive nature, he reminds us, the sensory, which brings in impressions from without, the central, in which we form ideas and the voluntary in which we act, choose, prefer. Now the first two of these, says James, exist for the sake of the third. They are there to shape our voluntary life. Their purpose will be best served if this third part of our reactive nature acts in the way most healthy and satisfying. Now if the second, the thinking function, adopts a belief that gives the third, the voluntary nature, practically the most healthful stimulus it is possible to conceive, then the second is performing its function in the proper and best manner.

With what unconscious perversity of skill does he contrive to miss the real relation that stands out here! Of course the sensory and the reflective functions do exist for the sake of the active function (so to express ourselves for convenience). Of course, then, our power to form ideas is there primarily to subserve action. But to subserve it how? By supplying true and undeceiving ideas of the environment in and upon which we have to act, in relation to which we have in everything to adjust ourselves. Our wishes and our goals are one thing; the stubborn necessities of the world in which we have to attain them by action are another. If you represent a state of things as existing merely because desirable for the purpose of rousing and inspiring us, you are dangerously misrepresenting the actual, so far as we know it, and thus sinning against the life-subserving function of the mind.

It is easy to imagine that, because we are availing ourselves of "the right to believe" only in the supernal region of religion, of something behind the scenes and higher than the affairs of daily life, these considerations do not apply, that we are escaping from the sphere in which we have to be careful as to fact; that here we are at a place where our assumptions can do us good but cannot do us harm. How remote from the truth! It is just because religious faith is to affect our action that James would have us accept it. *How* is it to affect our action? That depends wholly on the particular belief we form.

ARGUMENT II: DOUBT AMOUNTS PRACTICALLY TO DENIAL

There is another argument by which James sets special store. In the absence of sufficient evidence to provide knowledge we might as well believe what is precious to believe, for a suspension of judgment on grounds of logical scruple is practically tantamount to disbelief. In matters of religion the doubter is as truly deprived of belief, with its inspiration and solace, as if he were a dogmatic denier. Practically there are only two alternatives, having and not having, and if you suspend judgment you go without the object of belief just as if you denied it.

This appears forcible. But what are the facts? For full belief, the object (for instance, the existence of benign and world-governing deity) is *there*; for disbelief it is *not there*; for suspension of judgment it is *there or not there*. For each of these the reaction is different, intellectually, emotionally, and practically. Practically, in disbelief I drop the matter; but in suspension of judgment I seek to find out whether the object is there or not, and watch for every indication. I have regard in my course of action to both possibilities. It would be unwise, would it not, to assume that the object was there when this was doubtful; that is, for instance, the typical rash assumption of the dupe when somebody tricks and makes a fool of him. But it would also be unwise to assume that it was not there; that is the typical lazy assumption of the pessimist when effort might enable him to secure knowledge that it is there and to profit thereby. Moreover, as I pointed out, if, in case further knowledge does not seem procurable, we proceed on the cautious hypothesis that the object is there, candidly recognizing that it is only a hypothesis, our course cannot on ordinary logical grounds be impugned and does not involve (it excludes) "the will to believe". Working-hypothesis is the resource and the peculiar mark of the doubter's position, it being irrelevant to that of either the believer or the disbeliever.

(James here is disparaging the attitude of suspending judgment, yet, strange to say, working-hypothesis, which is characteristic of suspended judgment alone, is the very thing he identifies with his own position.)

There is indeed this resemblance between doubt and disbelief: that in neither is the object given to us. But there is a corresponding resemblance between doubt and belief; in neither is the object denied to us. In belief we have it, in doubt we may have it. And doubt, being a matter of degree, may range between closeness to belief on the one hand and closeness to disbelief on the other.

It is unfortunate that James would belittle the distinction between disbelief and the unbelief that does not see its way to a positive conclusion. Popular thought and talk confuse the two and hardly any distinction is seen at all; so undeveloped in society at large is that spirit of critical caution and judicial poise of mind which is simply realism – the demand for realities instead of hasty illusions; so easy and natural to us all is it to yield to the temptations of plausibility and partiality and hasten to conclusions. "I don't believe it" is the established expression for "I disbelieve it". The capacity to suspend judgment is a mark of maturity. James belittles the clear distinction that enables the mind to grow up.

ARGUMENT III: OUR FUNDAMENTAL BELIEFS MUST BE VOLUNTARY

Another major argument for the doctrine is that all belief is and has to be a voluntary matter, so we need not draw a line at religious belief. In science, etc., we choose to believe cautiously and upon evidence, but the very basis of science, the first principles of all thinking, have for us no rational basis. We simply choose to believe them without evidence. Since that is the case, he thinks it shallow affectation to refuse similar decisions in religion.

But in our fundamental belief we feel the thing to be true; the reality is before us. That is how it seems and this seeming constitutes our belief. We do not decide or decree or enact that things shall be so; when our mind looks out at things, it finds them so. Thus I say the matter appears to us. How our faith is justified or rational I do not now discuss. It is enough here that from the fact that in the case of first principles there is no proof or prior evidence it does not follow that our faith is a matter of choice, a preference of our voluntary nature.

Equipped with the first principle that experience instructs us, we are in a position to learn from it. And one thing we learn is the peril of making up our minds without careful attention to the evidence that experience offers; the peril of gliding to conclusions that please us instead of looking sharply to find just what conclusions are warranted.

In passing let me pause upon James's example of fundamental faiths. "The postulate that there is truth, and that it is the destiny of our minds to attain it, we are deliberately resolving to make, though the sceptic will not surely make it." The sceptic does make it; cannot be a sceptic without making it. To doubt is to doubt whether something is true, and this admits and affirms that there is a truth in the matter. What he is admitting and affirming is that the category of truth is a valid category, for he is using it with full confidence.

That "there is truth" – what does James himself mean by these words? Truth is the characteristic of a proposition which affirms something to be the case when it actually is the case, or of a belief which regards something as real when it actually is real. That "there is truth" might mean that there *are* such propositions and such beliefs (not saying how many) and perhaps further that we ourselves actually possess some. "That it is the destiny of our minds to attain it", that is surely not a first principle. It is a hope, it is certainly not originally known as a destiny or sure consummation. But I cannot help fancying that James meant something even more funda- mental than what I have suggested, that he meant the postulate that there is reality, a real world, a universe about which true propositions could conceivably be framed, and that it is the destiny of our minds in some degree to know it.

Now that there is reality, that it makes sense to allege that things exist, that there are real existences, is not a postulate, is not a first pronounce- ment of our thought that we might conceivably refrain from making; it is an immediate unquestionable gift of experience to us. Our own sensa- tions are cases of existence; we directly know that they exist in that they are what we mean by existents; and the meaning and intelligibility (I do not say the correctness, which is another question) of belief beyond the limits of our own immediate consciousness is something supplied for the mind by automatic memory, which provides instances of such belief. A remembrance is a belief. Thought in its very beginning is out beyond the question whether there is in this deeper sense a truth. (This I repeat is quite distinct from the question what beyond consciousness does exist.)

The questions that scepticism canvasses do not arise until after the fact that "there is truth" in this sense is made manifest.

Nor is it really helpful to call a first principle "a postulate". A postulate is an assumption that we demand, that we deliberately announce and proceed with. Employed in geometry, it has been a recognized procedure in discussion. What has that to do with the question whether in a particular case it is true? The interest of philosophy is in whether and why we are justified in so assuming or thinking, and how we know we are justified. We are not concerned with the permissions and proprieties of a kind of parliamentary law, with modes of procedure that it sanctions, with motions that are in order or not in order, but solely with truth or untruth, basis or baselessness. Why do we choose to 'postulate'? Because we believe. So it seems better to call our first principles not postulates, which only diverts our attention from the point and is confusing, but beliefs.

ARGUMENT IV: BELIEF OFTEN MAKES ITSELF TRUE

Amongst James's striking and subtle arguments for his position is this: that when we heartily believe, our very doing so often makes the belief true; that this may be the case in some real sense with religion. He does not do much, so far as I can perceive, to render the second half of this statement plausible; he does not do much to show us how our believing that the deity as conceived by him exists could make it true. That seems to remain a not over-probably "may be". However, as the second part depends upon the first part that many beliefs make themselves come true, I devote attention to that. It presents itself in effect as a reason for believing without evidence.

Consider one of the examples he cites.

A man who in the company of gentlemen made no advances, asked a warrant for every concession, and believed no one's word without proof, would cut himself off by such churlishness from all the social rewards that a more trusting spirit would earn....

He goes on further with this

class of questions of fact, questions concerning personal relation, states of mind between one man and another. *Do you like me or not?* – for example. Whether you do or not depends, in countless instances, on whether I meet you half way, am willing to assume that you must like me, and show your trust and expectation. The previous faith on my part in your liking's existence is in such cases what makes your liking come. But if I stand aloof, and refuse to budge an inch until I have objective evidence, until you shall have done something apt, as the absolutists say, *ad extorquendum assensum meum*, ten to one your liking never comes.

Should not this be a matter of working-hypothesis rather than of belief; a matter of good-natured action, of amenity and courtesy and friendly overture rather than the out-and-out belief that friendly interest on the other side is already there? A conviction in advance that the other party desires friendship is surely a fatuity to avoid. And it is part of courtesy itself to avoid it. Everything that pertains to action and disposition may be gracious, without hasty assumptions, without any violence done to cautious intelligence or to respect for the preferences of another, whatever they may prove to be.

Or consider this impressive example.

Often enough our faith beforehand in an uncertified result *is the only thing that makes the result come true.* Suppose, for instance, that you were climbing a mountain and have worked yourself into a position from which the only escape is by a terrible leap. Have faith that you can successfully make it and your feet are nerved to its accomplishment. But mistrust yourself, and think of all the sweet things you have heard the scientists say of *maybes*, and you will hesitate so long that at last all unstrung and trembling, and launching yourself in a moment of despair, you roll in the abyss. In such a case (and it belongs to an enormous class), the part of wisdom as well as of courage is to *believe what is in the line of your needs*, for only by such belief is the need fulfilled. Refuse to believe, and you shall indeed be right, for you shall irretrievably perish. But believe, and again you shall be right, for you shall save yourself. You make one or the other of two possible universes true by your trust or mistrust, – both universes having been only *maybes*, in this particular, before you contributed your act.

We have also to be intently regardful of the danger of falling short; we have to put every faculty upon the need of aiming aright and mobilizing all our force; we must be as alive to the exact demands of the position as to the hopeful fact of our own energy and our very probable competence to meet them. To behave intelligently toward the situation as it is will be to see that thoughts of fatal failure and its horror have unmanning effects and to avoid them, fixing our minds firmly on the thought of doing our utmost and triumphantly succeeding. It is mainly a purpose, not a belief. If we simply believe that we shall in fact succeed, we tend to lose the intense alertness that the danger sternly demands. No use to adjourn intelligence or close even partly its open eyes; to turn away attention from disturbing facts or possibilities at the moment is not to tamper with rational belief.

Perhaps the most specious of all the examples that could be cited for belief making itself true is that of the religions of healing. "Only believe", we are told, "believe that you are well, believe that the principle of life and health is all-powerful and will prevail, and you will find it really does so". Now if we look closely a curious fact soon discloses itself: that nobody does believe it without reserve, that nobody is intended to do so, and that it would not conduce to his health or safety if he did. He must still observe the ordinary prudences of all mankind as to poison, indigestibility, bruises and injuries, physical perils of all sorts. He must in short wink at himself and accept the principle only in a highly discreet sense. In other words, what he is really doing is trying to believe something for which there is real evidence and refraining from a more whole-sale belief (though his words imply it) for which there is manifestly none. He is recognizing, and fixing his attention upon, the wholesome energies of the body and mind, he is rejoicing in them, and turning his attention away from the unwholesome, – an altogether excellent thing to do. Thus we see that the case is really parallel to the two just examined. There must be caution as well as belief and the belief is to be accorded because there is good reason.

If you say to somebody, "Only believe and it will come true", you are really offering your auditor a reason for believing. And if, as a natural accompaniment, you add that in many cases this has come to pass, you are adding to that reason.

The invaluable principle of mental health-making is grounded upon fact; however it may express itself, that is its real warrant and appeal.

In all these three cases what we see is, not an arbitrary belief, but a reasonable one, attention being given in the first instance to the whole situation and governing the attitude accordingly. So that they cannot be counted in support of a will to believe without evidence.

ARGUMENT V: GRASPING AT POSSIBLE TRUTH OR SHUNNING ERROR

We now come to another point to which James attaches much importance.

There are two ways of looking at our duty in the matter of opinion, – ways entirely different, and yet ways about whose difference the theory of knowledge seems hitherto to have shown very little concern. *We must know the truth*; and *we must avoid error, –*

these are our first and great commandments as would-be knowers; but they are not two ways of stating an identical commandment, they are two separable laws. Although it may indeed happen that when we believe the truth A we escape as an incidental consequence from believing the falsehood B, it hardly ever happens that by merely disbelieving B we necessarily believe A. We may in escaping B fall into believing other falsehoods, C or D, just as bad as B; or we may escape B by not believing anything at all, not even A.

Believe truth! Shun error! – these, we see, are two materially different laws; and by choosing between them we may end by coloring differently our whole intellectual life. We may regard the chase for truth as paramount, and the avoidance of error as secondary; or we may, on the other hand, treat the avoidance of error as more imperative, and let truth take its chance.... We must remember that these feelings about either truth or error are in any case only expressions of our passional life... he who says, "better go without belief forever than believe a lie!" merely shows his own preponderant private horror of becoming a dupe... It is like a general informing his soldiers that it is better to keep out of battle forever than to risk a single wound... Our errors are surely not such awfully solemn things.

All this for James helps to the conclusion that we do well to believe the more inspiring thing, for we *may* be right and it is better not to lose that chance of being right in a precious faith even if in clutching at it we also incur the danger of being wrong.

All this resetting of a familiar scene is rendered possible by his forgetting that the attainment of truth and the avoidance of error are secured, both of them, by identically the same method, the method of accepting only that for which we have evidence and accepting it only so far as the evidence goes. Anything that steps beyond that method into arbitrary assumption steps into untruth: the untruth of looking upon something as fact when it is doubtful. James's proposed method is that of throwing over the care for evidence and jumping at one alternative in the question before him because for high reasons he likes it, wants it to be true, and is willing to cling to the mere possibility that it is so, as his only hold upon truth in the matter. We are to abandon the 'nervousness' about evidence, and this is to abandon the nervousness about truth, for it is ceasing to bother ourselves about the indications of truth and just how far they go, it is helping ourselves to one alternative at once and merely hoping that it is true. We are not to secure the truth by cautious inquiry, that is too slow, patient, and sacrificial a process; we are to gamble for it. If a thinker cares for truth, however, he will find only one means of getting it: not impulsively to shut his eyes and believe at once but *to believe the evidence*. This will at one and the same time avoid error and reach truth so far as it can be done. Essentially, I say, there is and can be no differ-ence between the process of avoiding error and that of getting at truth. That a certain opinion is an error is itself a truth; while on the other hand regarding a certain idea as true when it is doubtful is itself an error. Once more, what James does is to throw over our clues to truth and adopt an opinion because we value it in the devout hope that it may be true. And this he calls caring more about gaining truth than about avoiding error. I do not think his foremost motive here can be to secure truth; I think it is to gain a satisfying and uplifting faith; and that he adds this particular piece of ingenuity in order to parry a reproach from the logical 'purists'. Indeed the concern for truth cannot be first with him; for he regards it as better to die in a high faith even if it is baseless.

It is a great argument with James, to which he often comes back, that something *may be*. For instance: "Is it not sheer dogmatic folly to say that our inner interests can have no real connection with the forces that the hidden world may contain?" That is, our desire that something should be true may be a sign that it really is so. Our wishes may have a real connection with the objective realities for which they long. Why, yes, certainly it is dogmatic folly; our inner interests might have such an connection. If they did and we knew it, we could infer from our having these interests that the things in which they would fondly believe veritably exist. Yes, there might conceivably be such a connection. But we do not know that there is; we see no token that there is.

The inner need of believing that this world of nature is a sign of something more spiritual and eternal than itself is just as strong and authoritative in those who feel it as the inner need for uniform laws of causation ever can be in a professionally scientific head. The toil of many generations has proved the latter need prophetic. Why *may* not the former one be prophetic, too?

Certainly it may, though we cannot say in advance of evidence that it is; and we have every right to try to verify such a preconception as science tries to verify its hypotheses. (But do not take for granted that it has never been tried before, that no results on the subject have ever been reached. It is curious how James would have us set out to verify things as if it were a virgin subject and the attempt to do so had never been made.)

Incidentally be it said, "the inner need of uniform laws of causation" does not seem to be the only occasion of the quest for them. Experience shows us such laws of causation as really existent, and thus we naturally look for them in other cases.

At the end of the longer passage above cited was one of the most arresting sentences in the book. "Our errors are surely not such awfully solemn things." He goes on: "in a world where we are so certain to incur them in spite of all our caution, a certain lightness of heart seems healthier than this excessive nervousness on their behalf". We need not, he feels, be so solicitous to avoid them by rational caution. For one of the least academic of all professors that have ever lived, this is a strangely academic remark. He is evidently thinking mainly of private reflection and of discourse removed from action; of conversation, the dining-room, the drawing-room, the class-room, and the lecture-hall; he is thinking mainly of speculative opinions and discussion, for which there is no ready or formidable test. But there is another and a larger region, in which errors have consequences. There is nothing more solemn or tragic in life than its chapter of errors. A mistake may wreck a hope, an enterprise, a business, a life, an institution, a government, and, for the time being, a nation. The consequence of a mistake in British policy, a palpable and undeniable mistake having its most vital center in the year 1934, devastated great parts of the world and created a volume of human misery that we shrink back from contemplating. Even in small affairs everyone from children up knows what it is bitterly to rue a mistake. And it is just because a delusion about the government of the world means a false conception of how best to act and order our lives, just because it too misleads life, with profound far-reaching consequences, that it is not to be described as a light matter.

If I sought a single compact expression that gathers up the detriment to life that lies in the gospel of the will to believe, I think I should simply quote this one sentence: "Our errors are surely not such awfully solemn things". The whole call upon us to be faithful to the elementary principles of intelligence, a call which in education has never been clearly heard and in public thought has never been fully recognized, arises from the unsparing consequences of our errors.

PUTTING SUBTLETIES ASIDE

Finally, putting aside all special ingenuities of argument, we must face a broad question that really does remain. If it would do us good, make us more moral beings, keep us up better to our own ideals and purposes, to hold a certain faith, why should we not try to hold it? Why should we not use any psychological means we can bring to bear upon ourselves to implant that faith within us? So to put the matter, I say, waives all the fine-spun reasonings and comes back to common ground. Once more, if it would do us good and make us do more good in the world, why not? Is it not in the interest of morality that we should do so?

Such is the question which still rises in some minds after all the special apparatus of controversy has been cleared away.

The answer must be: It is morals that forbid. You do not become by such means a more moral being. Morals have an object, the guarding and benefit of human life, and it is this object itself at which you strike. Do not ignore the need of seeing things as they are and our situation in the midst of them as it is. Do not seek to uplift morality by indulging and encouraging the most mischief-making and misery-making force in the human world, the force of arbitrary opinion, which is the force of unintelligence. Do not tamper with our native wits, such as they are. At the present stage of history we discover that the most momentous of all duties is the duty of being as intelligent as we can; the most momentous because it has the most momentous consequences. Falling back on the will to believe will not make us truly better; it will reinforce the tendencies of mind that make the misunderstandings, the blunders, the blindnesses, the inextricable confusions that tend to keep life wretched. It will dull the perceptions that we sorely need to make keener and finer.

All idealism by its nature requires realism as its means. To accomplish our ideals for humanity in any measure, to make things as they should be, we must know things as they are, that we may lay hold of them accurately and mend them as they need.

It is no service to morality to maintain that it requires, for a motive to sustain it, a fond imagination that may have no solidity at all. Moral conduct needs for motive a true sense of what it is for and what depends upon it, in other words, of the poignant need for it; and of the depth of just approbation and disapprobation that respond to it.

And now lastly let me say that I do not think this doctrine of believing things because we want to do so is even at the outset very plausible to a steady mind, or naturally requires such a long and scrutinizing reply. But

James was a spirit of such a glowing manhood and genius, so right and inspiriting in his sympathies and ends, much of his utterance was such a breath of fresh air in American philosophy, that he has given the doctrine a hold upon many that it would not have otherwise had. And of that hold we must take account.

DEFENDERS OF THE DOCTRINE

As we saw, James wished he had christened his book *The Right to Believe*. He felt that critics' objections had been provoked chiefly by the title, by the emphasis on the will, by the interpretation that we were by a fiat of volition deliberately to create belief where there had been none. "What I meant by the title was the state of mind of the man who finds an impulse in him toward a believing attitude and who resolves not to quench it simply because doubts of its truth are possible."[7] The 'will' that he meant was the "passional nature". Thus, too, Schiller commented that James's principle was misconstrued, being in reality "an analysis of the psychological process of acquiring belief".[8] In other words, critics were supposed to have overlooked the difference between consciously sitting down to produce in one's self a belief and the slow natural drift of belief-formation through the processes and appetencies of the whole nature.

Now it is this reply, and not the criticism, which misses the point. There was no misapprehension. It is of the essence of James's view that at some stage or other our conscious decision or choice may rightfully intervene. We may encourage a tendency to believe, we may discourage doubts. Instead of vigilantly looking for evidence and refusing to glide to conclusions without it, we may turn away from such doubts and scruples. We may voluntarily direct our attention one way rather than the other. We are not to give watchful heed to freeing our ideas of fact from the bribery of desire, we are to say Godspeed to that same bribery. If there is no point at which we are thus to influence the drift of our minds, his doctrine, which is essentially an advisory doctrine, a preaching, has no meaning at all. He wants us to do something, or at least to persuade us that we have a perfect right to do it. If there is nothing to do, no question of any step on our part or deliberate abstention from a step, he is discoursing for nothing. This fully appears not only throughout the exposition but also at the very moment of making the reply quoted above to his critics. "...The man who finds an impulse in him toward a believing attitude, and who *resolves* not to quench it...." He resolves; that is the point where his volition enters.

To substitute for the "will to believe" the "right to believe" would in no wise avoid this implication. As Miss Stettheimer has pointed out, "the right to believe" means the right to will to believe. It means the right to do something; and James, as we have just seen, indicates what is to be done. On the most passive interpretation it means that a mind is not to be blamed for consciously *letting* partialities or antipathies determine its belief, when in greater or lesser degree it might check them for critical reasons. And this *letting* is a volitional decision. If it were not, I repeat, James by his teaching could not influence it as he seeks to do.

His meaning on this topic could not well be 'misconstrued'. He had made it too clear. "Voluntarily adopted faith", "the liberty of believing", "freedom to believe", an "action of our willing nature", "a passional decision", "a passionate affirmation of desire", "believing by our volition", – such are the phrases he finds it natural to use.

Having these considerations in the front of my mind I wrote long ago describing the will to believe as a procedure of hypnotizing one's self into a belief; that is, deliberately employing processes of a non-rational nature to produce the state of mind desired. I wrote thus, confident that the reader would perceive that, whatever the process, the logical attitude of one's voluntary self toward it was the same as if one had deliberately arranged it all to bring about the result; that one is by initiative or by consent using psychological forces to work upon one's own credulities. This confidence was misplaced. The point was not seen by all and the objection was raised that James's doctrine had been misinterpreted. Professor Dewey in particular has more than once appeared to raise this objection.[9]

If one wants a perfect illustration of hypnotizing one's mind into belief, here it is in the process that James subsequently described and called "the faith-ladder".

A conception of the world arises in you somehow, no matter how. Is it true or not? you ask.
    It *might* be true somewhere, you say, for it is not self-contradictory.
    It *may* be true, you continue, even here and now.
    It is *fit* to be true, it would be *well if it were true*, it *ought* to be true, you presently feel.

It *must* be true, something persuasive in you whispers next, and then – as a final result –

It shall be *held for true*, you decide; it *shall be* as if true for *you*.[10]

In his monumental and invaluable biography of James Professor Perry writes:

> He was accused of encouraging *wilfulness* or *wantonness* of belief or of advocating belief for belief's sake, whereas his whole purpose had been to *justify* belief.

His purpose had been to justify belief morally and practically in cases where it was not justified intellectually. Wilfulness of belief was exactly what James, upon one side, encouraged.

> He had affirmed that belief was voluntary but had naturally assumed that in this as in other cases volition would be governed by motives and illuminated by reasons.

Of course it would be governed by motives; but James's whole point was that it need not be illuminated by reasons for the belief. To be sure he himself felt in a degree inexpressible reasons for the belief. But he indicates many times that his "subjective conscience" would approve his religious faith even had he not this sense of inexpressible evidence – so long as the hypothesis is a 'living' one, that is, appeals to the individual as a possible belief, which appeal, in James's instances, is often one purely of desirability.

> His critics had accused him of advocating *license* in belief whereas on the contrary his aim had been to form rules for belief.

The rules Professor Perry has in mind are perhaps the specified requirement of "living, forced and momentous" options. If this is the meaning James did formulate a rule for belief but a rule permitting and encouraging license in an enormous class of cases. To encourage what Professor Perry calls license and James himself calls liberty was, as we have seen, his chief design in writing.

If we look back and ask ourselves who and how many of all those we have known have cared conscientiously for fact in their thinking, and not permitted their partialities and antipathies, their preference for mental ease, their taste for novelty, their pride or their pretensions, to have a stronger hold upon them; if we really push this question and review the figures in the gallery of memory, what a sobering answer is forced upon us! Here is the one trusty lifeline of the race, this conscience of the mind, here is a scruple easy to notice in talk and to miss when wanting, easy to awaken in the young and most easy to teach by examples of its presence or absence, – the point of carefulness and sound sense practically more important and telling than all the formulas of logic, – and what do we find? That it is sadly rare – with consequences. Of all those whom I have been privileged to know as teachers or other mental aiders James in this respect stood first. He was utterly candid, utterly unpretending, utterly open-minded, utterly truthseeking. And yet by an unhappy fatality it had to be just he who was eloquently to defend wilful opinion! There is no more impressive argument I can adduce against "the will to believe" than the living and daily example, in all matters of inquiry and converse, of William James.

NOTES

[1] *The Will to Believe*, 30.
[2] *The Varieties of Religious Experience*, 519.
[3] *Letters*, II, 213.
[4] *The Will to Believe*, 75.
[5] R. B. Perry, *The Thought and Character of William James* II, 240.
[6] *The Varieties of Religious Experience*, 73.
[7] Perry, *The Thought and Character of William James* II, 244–5.
[8] *Op. cit.*, II, 241. The expression "the will to believe" though a correct name for the process James defends, would not be an accurate name for the usual drift of the human mind in believing from desire. The mind thus drifting in all too human fashion toward a belief from what he calls a "passional motive" is surely not setting before itself as the object of desire its own future belief. That would mean that it was a mental state, a future mental attitude of its own, that was beckoning and alluring it as a good thing. Now this occurs, and this is what James, under certain conditions, commends. There are cases in which people are desiring to be happier or better themselves through a more comforting or uplifting state of belief. But it seems comparatively rare. In the ordinary case of such human credulity the mind is thinking of the subject itself, that is, of the facts, imagining them in a certain form and liking so to imagine them, but not considering itself, not thinking about its own future opinions. This lingering on a welcome representation of the facts tends to establish that representation as a belief. The person's state would not be expressed by the words "He wishes to believe", but by "He wishes the facts to be thus and thus"; it is this wanting the fact to assume a certain form and constitution that is influencing the mind's belief. To repeat, a belief produced by desire is not ordinarily produced by the desire to be in a certain mental state, one's attention is not given to one's own coming mentality, it is given to the facts of the matter, and the presence of the desire leads to their assuming a certain form in the mind other than that which evidence alone would give them there.
[9] It is not wholly clear why Professor Dewey is concerned to sustain "the will to believe". I find him saying that "perhaps the part of his James's teaching which is most precious for us today is connected with" "those ideas to which he gave the name of 'the will to believe'", though deeming it "that aspect of his teaching which superficially

is most open to legitimate criticism". Professor Dewey does not appear in any wise to use it in religion, which was the object of James's great interest in its advocacy. That advocacy was an apology for arbitrary opinion, something, one would have supposed, of which Professor Dewey would especially wish the world to be rid.

10 *A Pluralistic Universe*, 328–9.

MORALS, INTELLIGENCE, AND WELFARE

[In the mid-1940s Miller addressed the Clericus Club of Boston on 'Morals in School and Parish'. The text of his address follows, its first publication, but with a title more revealing of its central themes. Though Miller links religion and morality as he persistently did in other writings and addresses, his main concern is the use of intelligence in morality and the application of what he had long defended as the consequence-theory of morality, "the morality of results". Utilizing the "case method", he introduces vivid autobiographical illustrations – including James's vigorous repudiation of anti-semitism – to show failures of intelligence in applying the rules of morality we already have, rules firmly established by their service to human welfare. Further, he analyzes the failure of intelligence to perceive the standard and aim of morality in welfare because we are blinded by "the tradition of passivity". To be sure, welfare and satisfaction of human needs are not themselves moral conceptions. Only acts are right or wrong, but their rightness or wrongness depends on results, on actual service or disservice to human welfare, the main point of the Gospel of love.

In pattern and content this address summarized the book on which Miller was at work up to the last year of his life and variously thought of titling 'Revolution In Ethics', 'Principles of Practical Intelligence', or 'Intelligence, How and Why It Has Not Been Taught'.]

In the nineteenth century Matthew Arnold wrote that morals are the subject in which the knowing is easy and it is only the doing that is hard. The Church has a tendency to proceed on the same assumption: to take for granted that we know and simply inspire us to do. This paper is written to question the assumption. The subject is twofold: first, the forgetfulness of moral standards that we have known, the failure to remind ourselves of them and mark them out clearly; and, second, moral standards that remain unknown. The thesis is that morals need to be specifically taught in school and parish. 'School' is meant to include Sunday School, week-day school, and university.

I hope you will not deny me the aid of unsparing criticism. This remark preceding a paper is often taken as a sort of ritual incantation that means nothing in particular. But the most definite experience of gain from criticism makes me ask it. Moreover, I can't help thinking that anyone who reads or publishes a paper should tolerate criticism, and not only tolerate it but welcome it, and not only welcome it but seek it, and not only seek it but extract from it every grain of truth that may be in it. What he is undertaking is to get hold of the fact on his subject, if he can, and present it. That is the aim. Then anyone who corrects him is helping him toward his own aim. I repeat, he is not trying to make an idea accepted, unless it is fact. This, to be sure, is pious platitude; but it may be regarded as new until it can be counted upon in practice. I have known a professor in a theological school (far away from here, and, let me add, far away from New York) turn white with annoyance and resentment at a criticism, purely factual and impersonal. I have known a distinguished professor of philosophy to stay away from a meeting because his system of philosophy was to be criticized there. I have known another distinguished professor of philosophy who all his life made it a rule never to reply to criticism, thus setting what he conceived to be his dignity above the interest of the inquiring public in hearing both sides, in knowing whether to a plausible objection there is any answer. And I remember from Carlyle's *Reminiscences* how he burnt a copy of a weekly paper lent him by a neighbor because it contained a criticism of his work that he did not like, destroying the property of another and marring that other's complete set of the journal, which he prized. Gladstone said he had known few men who could "put their minds into the common stock". It is of course no easy task, but to try to do so seems to me the one business of people who discuss. So turn me white without hesitation.

I

Now to my subject. Please allow me to begin with cases in the border-land, cases of half-remembrance, of half-recognition, of not turning full attention upon a vital principle, and let me pass gradually over to cases in which the forgetfulness is more complete.

Mr George Biddle in his autobiography tells that a teacher at Groton School shouted at him before the whole school: "Biddle, I am not accustomed to be called unfair and dishonest". I think the teacher might suitably have said with a smile and without a shout, "I don't think I need discuss with you whether I am dishonest; but (and here the smile might cease) you say I was unfair. Please tell me what was unfair. If you show me I'll set it right". How that form of expression, "I am not accustomed to being called unfair", brings back to us the attitude, natural enough of the teacher. The teacher should be treated with respect, but let him not put respect before justice. Justice comes before respect. It seems to me that if a boy appeals for justice he is appealing for a sacred thing, and here is an opportunity, by giving earnest heed to his appeal, to deepen in him the feeling for justice, so profoundly needed, and the sense that decent people care about it. The truth is, they don't care enough. Should not the teacher care so instantly that he can postpone the point of disrespect (that is, of bad manners) until afterwards? In fact, he failed to see his opportunity; he failed to recognize a vital principle when to recognize it was everything; he put his own bruised feelings first. Justice was too dim in him, and he may have left it ill satisfied in the boy.

The state, the Church, and society at large have an insufficient sense for justice. The Church has a great feeling for love and loving kindness, above all praise, but an insufficient sense for justice. As for schools, if you teach boys and girls that respect and decorum come first (invaluable as these are) you tend to breed that type of mind which abounds in important affairs and in diplomacy, public and private, that cares more about avoiding present disturbance and what it calls a furor, avoiding decisions that may be adversely commented upon, than about avoiding injustice or eventual suffering. And we have never in history had a better example of the practical fatality of this type than in the last fourteen years. It has made the tragedy of the world.

I did not go to a boarding school; I went to the Episcopal Academy in Philadelphia.

(In this friendly circle perhaps you will not mind if I digress enough to say that great things as I owe to that school, the *best* fact for me about it was the building opposite. Face to face with it across Locust street was the Philadelphia Library, a private library like the Athenaeum, but admitting to its well-proportioned, finely designed, sunny reading-room the general public, if it cared to enter. I use to go in very, very often after school even though it postponed for an hour or so my lunch, which I got when I reached home. In that high reading-room near the entrance was a pillar with bookshelves round it on which were ranged new books and – thank heaven! – new editions of old books, which any comer could take down, carry off to a table and comfortably read. There were books at home, but in the main not those particular books. When I recall what I got there in my school days, when I recall the wine-colored editions of certain authors who have stood by me all my days, whom I read now, even this month, as I read them then, I cannot but hold that pillar a principal pillar of my life. I could not wish to have gone to any school, not to Eton College, if it did not offer conspicuous shelves of choice books – not too many – such that the curious boy might notice them, take them down and look in. From the School I got indispensable training. From the Library I got ideas. They did not grow in the School.)

Coming back from the digression, what I was about to tell was a particular piece of silliness. When I was in about the third or fourth form, I think it was, I noticed that the principal teacher of Latin and Greek, a quiet, good teacher who later became headmaster, beamed upon a particular boy when he was reciting and spoke pleasantly to him in a way that he did not quite with anyone else in the class. He was a good-looking boy and belonged to a well-known family. I wrote on a bit of paper, "Dr. X is partial to Y", and then folded the paper again and again, writing new remarks to the same effect on each small square surface made by the folding, without signing my name. I then threw it in through the open door on the floor of Dr. X's classroom in his absense, so that he could not help seeing it when he came back to his room. Of course I thought he would not know who it was; he had nothing to do with our handwriting. From some internal evidence he guessed it. Presently I received a summons to his room. As I looked through the door in approaching, he was not at his desk. In fact, he was standing in the corner just alongside the open door out of sight. As I came in he stepped forward suddenly, holding out the paper, and said, "Why did you write that?" Of course I gave the regular boy-performance: I didn't know what to say, I was silent. He then went on to the effect: "You know that every boy who comes into this classroom is absolutely on an equality with every other, that no one is favored". I made no defense, I was still silent. I had had no real jealousy of the boy, had just curiously observed Dr. X's manner with him, and in the usual schoolboy spirit of mischief had tried to thrust it down the teacher's throat without being caught.

Later that day, or next day, I was sent for by the headmaster, who looked extremely grave and said little. I got "ten notes"; each of which meant a reduction of one in the total ten, so that for that week I had a cypher in conduct.

This was just. As I look back, however, what is striking is that no stress was laid on the bit of writing being anonymous; I can't remember that it was mentioned at all. Great stress was laid at home, but none at school. What was mentioned by the headmaster was the gross disrespect, and by the teacher mainly the injustice, as he saw it. I had not meant that he favored the boy in marks, I knew nothing about that. Was it not their opportunity to point out how mean is an anonymous charge against anyone? Not merely to say that it is contemptible, that it is generally deemed so, but to point out why? That surely is education. Could it not be put thus? In writing anonymously against anyone you give him no chance to show that you were wrong. You don't let him ask, "Where is your evidence?" It is unjust. You may be disseminating the charge, and you don't let him get at the source of it, namely yourself. If your charge is false or exaggerated you are yourself a wrongdoer. You pronounce judgment upon him while you take cover from all judgment yourself. Since it is wrong to make a false charge, it is wrong to make an irresponsible charge, even if true, for in such a case the accuser might be wrong and there is need of a standard of conduct in the matter to protect all cases. Did not the teacher and the headmaster lose an opportunity to point this out to a boy so that he would not forget it? What he had written was true, though of no importance whatever; but *this* point was of importance: that he had happened to do something worse than he had accused his teacher of.

In each of two parishes of which I had very temporary charge, I received anonymous letters venomously denouncing someone, in each case I think a woman, in the parish. In each case I thought I knew the writer, a woman.

The following example is obviously not characteristic of the clergy – its connection with them is accident. It happened that during Hitler's ascendency I heard very little talk about things in Germany from fellow-clergymen. But I remember one, not now in this neighborhood, saying in a small gathering of the clergy that whatever we might think of the treatment of the Jews in Germany (he seemed to regard it as an open question), it was certainly a great relief in crossing the ocean in a North German Lloyd steamer to have no Jews on board. Now the prejudice against Jews seems to me one of the lowest, meanest, shabbiest of prejudices. If some or many Jews have bad qualities they should be disparaged because they have bad qualities, not because they are Jews. The statistics of population would suggest that there are many more people with bad qualities outside the Jewry than in it. This clergyman did not have to consort with Jews, had they been aboard; it was apparently just the lighting of his eyes upon their features that was offensive to him. He took a certain satisfaction in their exclusion from the steamship line, and could mention it without being moved to remark on any other side of the matter. He could speak thus of the race of Louis Brandeis, of Felix Adler, I will add, of David Niles and Reuben Lurie.

There was a hotel high up in the Adirondack Mountains which William James found a great convenience in his annual trip thither. There was no other near it. One spring the hotel put into its circular the notice that no Jews would be admitted. James at once wrote to them that in that case his visits would have to cease, and he wrote to a friend suggesting that he should do likewise.

Mr Ellis, in notifying me long ago of my turn tonight, suggested reminiscences of James with whom I studied and to whom I owe a great deal. I will mention one more recollection of him. At the baths of Nauheim there was a spot out of doors where medicinal salt waters poured down the side of a long sloping screen. Patients were recommended to sit close to it. One black night James was sitting there, and I, who was also taking the baths, sat with him. The moment lent itself to unreserve, and in the course of the conversation he said that there was one type of person to which he had always given his highest admiration, one who could esteem, admire and have regard for others without reference to their attitude toward *him*, one capable of perceiving their qualities independently of his share in their friendship, enmity or indifference. There was in James in the manliest form what Emerson calls "romance of character". I can say it measuring my words: he was of as rare an eminence in character as in genius. What he praised was really justice of appreciation.

In like manner a person is surely admirable who can estimate an idea independently of his partialities, antipathies and habits of mind.

At a meeting of a Sunday School where I was taking the place of the absent rector for the day, I raised the question what the Catechism meant, in the words "evil speaking, lying and slandering", by "evil speaking". No one knew, none of the scholars, none of the teachers. They suggested meanings, but none were right. And yet speaking evil of people behind their backs is a thing that goes on plenteously in many a parish, especially by women about women. It happens to be one of the things about which St. Paul was particularly concerned.

After a service one day I talk with a young woman teacher in the Sunday School. Going away, I remember in a moment that I have left behind on a chair a private notebook. I hasten back, to find her reading it. She says that she is trying to find out to whom it belongs. It is tolerably obvious to whom it belongs. And to read the notes is not first aid in finding out.

Another young woman, regular attendant at church and regular attendant once a year at a religious conference which she values, makes a very definite appointment for a bit of church work and without notice breaks her promise, afterwards saying only with a pleasant little laugh, "I promised to come and then I didn't". An unimpeachable statement of fact. But the fact evidently did not in the least trouble her.

Now in these cases, I say, people's minds are more or less blurred, or the writing upon them is faint; if they see any standard in the matter, the degree of its claim is not definite. It is charmingly flexible. There is nothing pedantic about it. The notion of honor in especial is a vague one, which they don't pry into. It is not more arresting than the distant tinkle of a cowbell. They were attached to religion, these people: they did not see that it involves anything particular about toeing the line of a tiresome rule.

I asked a diocesan director of education whether there was any teaching of morals in the Sunday Schools of his diocese. He answered, "No, we don't undertake that". I am not able to say in how many cases the preparation for Confirmation includes specific teaching on this topic.

I have heard in my life a good many sermons, but I have happened never to hear one setting forth a principle of conduct, elucidating it, offering guidance.

However, can we not at least say that respected laymen of refinement and mature years, occupying positions of responsibility, have a set of moral ideas that are substantially right, that "the knowing", in Arnold's phrase, the knowing of right from wrong, is theirs?

Case I. A man of this type, an editor and ambassador, also an excellent fellow, is asked his opinion on the origin of the first World War, on the responsibility of certain statesmen. He answers in effect that he doesn't think it right, when a great misfortune has occurred, to go back on the record and try to fasten the responsibility on particular persons. It is too unsparing. The thing is done, can't be undone; let us go on to other matters.

This does honor to his feelings, which of course, so far as he took cognizance of the matter, were wholly good and fine. But there is another side. The one and only clue to the future is the past. The one and only means of meeting circumstances, of mastering life, is the light of experience. Besides, could it not be called on the statesman's part unsparing to bring about the death or suffering of millions? Is it certain that the pain of the few statesmen in question at criticism of their responsible acts tips the scales so decidedly against the vast suffering and slaughter that war would bring? The man was considering only one side, a friendly social side near to him; forgetting the preponderance of human fates. If we take all the facts in our view, his position reveals itself as moral imbecility. If taken as guidance for the mind, it was the precise opposite of what we need to learn and do.

Case II. Another excellent man, with strong philanthropic interests, a respected lawyer, a vestryman, gives the following opinion. A statesman, X, feels that a certain policy in wartime is disastrous, not safe for the country. He urges his argument against it, and in consequence statesman Y, who stands for the policy, has to resign, and statesman X is put in his place. "Ah!" says our respected man, "I can't stand that. Disloyalty on X's part. Y was his friend and his chief. He has driven him out of office and taken his place."

That is, X should have put his personal relation to Y above his official loyalty and also his patriotic loyalty to his country, his duty to save her from what he deemed great danger. Again, morally looked at, this turns things upside down, making the lesser consideration (real and poignant as it was) greater than the overwhelming consideration.

Case III. A respected Dean of a college, a worthy and impressive man, is consulted about a public attack on a friend of his. The person consulting shows him a letter he means to publish in *The New York Times* supplying the facts that exonerate the accused person. The Dean heartily approves of the letter and gives an explicit pledge that he will speak of it to no one till it is published. He then goes to the house of the man accused and tells his wife about the letter. Afterward he states to the person who had consulted him that on reflection he was "not content" to leave her uninformed. Before speaking to her he has not consulted by telephone, letter or telegram the person to whom the pledge had been given. He has most deliberately broken a most deliberate pledge, and he evidently thought he did right. This was a Dean in a position of authority, moral decision and counsel to a whole college.

Case IV. An instructor at a university is compelled by an emergency in the lives of others to ask of the president a brief leave of absence. He tells the president the facts, asks and receives an explicit promise of silence. The president, during the instructor's absence, meets a professor who has heard a false version of the reason. The president tells him the true version. He does not at any time let the instructor know this, but he feels he acted rightly. Evidently he could have said to the professor, "I happen to know the facts, though I am not free to tell them. What you have heard is not correct, quite unfounded". Observe, his motive was a good one. Had he taken his pledge seriously he would have seen that there was another way to give effect to the good motive. But as he took his pledge lightly, he did not take the trouble to bethink himself of any other way, but simply broke his word. This president was eminently respected and in my opinion deserved, on the whole, the respect he got.

In view of the position, responsibilities, connections and known character of these two men, one might conclude that there is no such thing as a safe confidential communication. These are only two cases. Plenty of others could be cited. One person said, "Mr So-and-so has been so kind that I felt that I owed it to him to tell him". He felt he owed it to him to tell what he antecedently owed to his informant not to tell, – promises being soap-bubbles. Another man explains: "This is confidential, but I can tell *you.*" Indeed, in some quarters it is said, "If you want a report to spread quickly and far, give it as something strictly confidential." But I do not draw the conclusion that there is no such thing. I have known, and I know, persons who would not betray a confidence, persons with a sense of honor to be trusted. The elder Pitt said to an inquisitive admiral, "Can you keep a secret?" Yes, said the admiral, delighted at the coming revelation. "So can I", said Pitt.

Case V. A well-known artist in New York, another respected and excellent fellow, talks to me about President Wilson repeating at length and with zest as true the stories of his relations with a woman, of which so much use was made against him politically by telephone that no suit for libel could be brought. These charges were false. Wilson's bitterest opponents at Princeton never believed them. The facts are known. And here a man reckoned as good repeats them for truth because he has heard them. And he thinks that warranted.

Case VI. Sitting at lunch, a professor at a university, discussing a bitter attack in a newspaper against a certain man, says to another professor, "What would you do if an attack like that appeared against you?" "That editor", said the other, very seriously, "would find himself attacked by thugs as he went home at night through a dark street". That is, the speaker would remain safely aloof himself, but would hire what he called 'thugs' to break the law and assault the editor for him. He was a scholar, a man "internationally known", as the newspapers say, belonging to a long-respected family, a professor who lectured to hundreds of students.

These are but a few examples. In view of such, can it be said that the moral ideas of respected citizens are of a sort to be surely relied upon?

Arnold's saying was that morals are the subject in which the knowing is easy, and it is only the doing that is hard. Thus far what we have noticed is that the forgetting is easy, and the knowing by no means sure.

II

The second part of my topic is, moral standards that remain unknown – unknown, that is, to society in general.

Now the staggering thing is that *the* standard remains unknown. Morality has two stages: the blind stage and the stage that has received its sight. We have to recognize that society as a whole, nearly all of it, remains in the blind stage. It is blind to the main fact about the subject: that morality exists, not for its own sake but for a purpose, that it is there to accomplish something. To this conclusion every reputable philosophy of our day known to me subscribes. Rules of right and wrong are not only taboos that we are to regard as sacred, but means to an end, they are there to guard the life and welfare of those affected by our acts, to guard their life and welfare and if possible to increase their welfare. Just as traffic regulations, and harbour regulations, and hospital regulations etc. guard the common welfare, so in a far higher and more pervasive degree moral regulations guard it.

Now this, that the particular moral laws exist for a beneficent purpose beyond ourselves, is the principle of Christ. In the two commandments of love hangs all the laws. It is in the nature of love to desire the welfare of those who are loved, to desire to help and not to hurt. And out of this proceed all the duties. St. Paul sees this. "Love worketh no ill to his neighbor." This for him is the principle of all the specific commandments. And of course he would have said with equal fervor, "Love worketh good to his neighbor".

But educated people, even most of those we call cultivated people, are not aware that morality has an object. Instances could be given from conversation. But look for instance at the novelists. Who would dare to call Henry James uncultivated? Yet what decides for him is moral taste in conduct. We might go on, were there time, to a variety of other novelists with whom moral sentiments of one sort or another are decisive. But consider the moralists. Emerson, by common consent our greatest American author, has not seen the point. Phillip Brooks denies the point. And consider biography. Perhaps in the last chapter we have set out for us the specific fine qualities of the man, and, it may be, some unfortunate qualities. But what came of his life? What good or evil fruits came out of it? What were the consequences of the man? Well, for the most part, this does not occur to the biographer as an inquiry that pertains to his task, though he may incidentally hazard a remark or two on particular results. Happy man! Imagine the biographer of Stanley Baldwin, of Neville Chamberlain, of Daladier. It is not, broadly speaking, in the frame of mind of our age to trace the consequences of acts. And they are just as fateful in private life as on the stage of the world. To trace them and understand them is the whole secret of mastering life. If a man does not know the object of what he does, nor that it has any object, should you expect him to be efficient in securing it? Do you then expect the moral standards and vision of our age to be equal to the tremendous evils they confront, which have arisen from their own abject insufficiency?

Underlying the state of mind and naturally giving rise to it is the tradition of our stage of civilization, *the Tradition of Passivity*, the fatalism of the multitude. Events come and we cannot control them. It is intelligence half-awake. War comes, youths are forced into it by the draft, and more than nine thousand graves are in the cemetery near the Anzio beachhead. Well, war is an understood thing, we know they come sometime; let us hope that there will not be another. Hope.

If a student in college chooses a course of instruction that includes ethics he becomes acquainted with the fact that morality has an object. But (what a symptom of our frame of mind!) even in college he learns it in accord with the Tradition of Passivity. Here is morality as a great given fact, and philosophy too often comes forward simply to explain it, to furnish the rationale for it – an interesting intellectual topic, that trains the mind. Whether as a means to an end our morality *accomplishes* its end, how far it does so, what requires to be added unto it in order that the end may be accomplished, the benefit delivered, the service take effect – that is apt to remain out of sight. Even in the presence of the tragedies of this age.

Here have stood in men's minds two things that seemed to have nothing to do with one another: goodness on the one hand, and achievement on the other. The awakening to what morals are for brings them together. Their separation it is that has made morals look to many a young mind so washed-out and uninspiring. The refrainer, the abstrainer, the conformer, the good boy, even the saint seem so colorless and 'unexciting', as the phrase is. Could there be any better jest to call forth the Devil's ironic laughter than that morals have nothing to do with achievement? The whole essence of morals is achievement, not of self-control only – that is a mere preliminary – but the control of events. It is the confirmed idea that morals are a set of taboos, with no purpose to gain beyond themselves, that makes the task of writing a paper such as this somewhat repellent to the writer, a piece of moralizing, sour moralism, with a task of moralic acid.

Now out of this fact of a moral end to be intelligently secured arises a new moral force that has in it the promise and potency of a new age: *the conscience of the mind*. This points us not to efforts of difficult reasoning, not to intellect but to intelligence, not to science but to sense. The phrase 'common sense' reminds us that sense is truly a common possession; yes, but it has to be evoked and trained. Its conscience has to be awakened and kept awake. And what the conscience does is first of all to make us face the obvious, to stop our turning away from the obvious at the behest of our feelings and habits. I have known a student's life to be wrecked, brought down to degradation and misery (having seen the whole remainder of his life), because the parents would not face the obvious. The war came on us because statesmen would not face the obvious. The peace negotiations have been lamed because statesmen did not face the obvious. The obvious becomes all overlaid by the immediate conventions, customs and pressures. It is to this that the conscience of the mind has first of all to put us on our guard.

The word 'school' in this paper includes even theological schools. My respected and more than respected colleague, Dr Hall, who some years ago was professor of Systematic Theology at the General Theological Seminary held a highly definite theory of Christian ethics. He denied with indignation that duty had for its object the compassing of human welfare. The whole object of morals was character. We are to aim at character in order to be acceptable to God, fit to be admitted to His presence in Heaven. How do we know what character is good? Why, certain modes of action are manifestly right and holy, *we see that*, our conscience tells us so, and moreover they are ordained of God in Holy Scripture. To be true in action to what we thus know to be right and holy is to obtain a right and holy character. That is what God would have of us.

Curiously, the late Dr Richard Cabot of Boston, brought up in a Unitarian family, and taking to philosophy some time after he left college, stood with Dr Hall to this extent, that for him character was the true object of all conduct. Like Hall, he was indignant at the notion of happiness as the object.

Now following Dr Hall's point, this confirms the ordinary notion of morals. Certain things are to be done for their own sake. The consequences, even the consequences to others, even the consequences to humanity at large, even worldwide war and agonies, are not in our hands, they are in the hands of God. We are to be kindly, where the occasion for it arises within our individual sphere, because kindliness happens to be one of those right and holy things which God enjoined upon us. But this did not mean for Dr Hall at all that we must carry this kindliness into

organized management of human affairs, into statesmanship and steers-
manship for humanity. Kindliness, on the recognized occasions for it,
was simply one of the virtues, by exercising which we attain good character and thus are qualified for Heaven.

This is a natural carrying up into theology of the Tradition of Passivity
and the blind stage of morals.

If this truly is Christianity, then I reject Christianity with all my soul.

III

It is sometimes commented, "Yes, the object of morals is the welfare of
human beings, *their true welfare*". It is as if the speaker wished to make it
manifest that he had missed the point. "True welfare" means virtuous
welfare, a welfare consistent with morality, a welfare that morality can
approve. This is making morality the object of morality. It is missing the
point, namely, that this entire system of acts and approbations that we call
morals has an aim outside itself, that it is a means and not an ultimate
end. Here is someone confounding means and ends, setting up the means
as an end. He is so drenched with morality that he cannot call anything
an end until he has mixed it up with morals. You have heard perhaps of
the sailor who was trying for the first time to ride on horseback. The
stirrups were hung rather low, he lost one of them, it swung to and fro,
the horse was kicking and unhappily caught his hoof in the stirrup. The
sailor shook his head and said, "If you're going to get on I'll get off".
The question is, what is morality to carry? It can't carry and at the same
time get on and be what is carried; that doesn't make sense. Its function
is to sustain and carry forward something distinct from itself – namely,
the common life and the common weal.

Welfare is of course not a moral conception at all. Welfare is just a
condition. What constitutes it is determined by the law of our being, what
a man's nature in the last resort cries out for. And sympathy, humanity,
fellow-feeling prompt us minister to these needs. The needs themselves,
of course, are not a matter of right and wrong. Right and wrong are
determined by the requirements of our common life. Suffering in itself is
not a matter of right and wrong. It is not an act. But whether or not you
help the sufferer is a matter of right and wrong. Happiness, relief from
misery, deliverance, joy – these are not matters of right and wrong,

but whether or not you create them is a matter of right and wrong.

I am only saying in other words that a Gospel of love is a gospel of service to human need. Goodness is not just a matter of behavior, but of service. 'Behavior' is a word that makes no reference to an end, 'service' does make reference to an end.

As I try to gather together the meaning of all this for a Christian, the words of Dante come back to me: "In His will is our peace". These words may be taken in two quite different senses. They may mean that in resignation to His will, as we see it in irrevocable events outside ourselves, is our peace; and that is a true meaning. But they may also mean that in accepting His will *for us, for our action*, His good will toward men, in discerning its purpose of securing their welfare, and *carrying its purpose into effect*, so far as we can, is our peace. This latter mood will not be in love with blindness. It will pray, "Lord, that I may receive my sight". It will try to unite realism with its idealism, to see things exactly as they are, in order to make them what they should be. It will address God as in the Psalm: "Thou God of truth", and ask Him to graft in our hearts a love of the truth, that we may not turn away from obvious stern facts. We know that the Holy Spirit may be invoked to work His will through us, "looking through our eyes, using our hands", to create order in the world, or in our little corner of the world, where there is chaos, to bring relief and well-being where there is misery. This is the true union with God. It is in the very centre of our faith, it also happens to be in the center of the Ordination-Office, in the words: "Come, Creator Spirit".

PUBLISHED WRITINGS OF DICKINSON S. MILLER

1893   *Das Wesen der Erkenntnis und des Irrthums*, Kaemmerer and Company, Halle, 1893. [Miller's Doctoral Dissertation.]

'The Meaning of Truth and Error', *Philosophical Review* **2** (1893), 408–25. [Most of the above Dissertation, translated by Miller.]

'The Relations of "Ought" and "Is"', *International Journal of Ethics* **4** (1893–4), 499–512.

1895   'Professor Watson on Professor Fullerton's Translation of Spinoza', *Philosophical Review* **4** (1895), 641–42.

'Confusion of Function and Content in Mental Analysis', *Psychological Review* **2** (1895), 535–50.

1897   *Notice*: William James, 'The Will to Believe and Other Essays', *International Journal of Ethics* **8** (1897–98), 254–55.

1898   'The Will to Believe and Duty to Doubt', *International Journal of Ethics* **9** (1898–99), 169–95.

Review: Henry Rutgers Marshall, 'Instinct and Reason', *International Journal of Ethics* **9** (1898–99), 511–16.

1899   'Professor James on Philosophical Method', *Philosophical Review* **8** (1899), 166–70.

1905   'Matthew Arnold on the "Powers of Life"', *International Journal of Ethics* **16** (1905–6), 352–58.

1908   'Naive Realism: What is It?', in *Essays Psychological and Philosophical in Honor of William James*, by his colleagues at Columbia University, Longmans, Green and Company, New York, 1908, pp. 233–61.

1909   'Roosevelt's Opportunity as President of a University', *Popular Science* **74** (January, 1909), 62–69.

'What Religion has to Do With It', *Good Housekeeping* **48** (January, 1909), 116–18.

1910   'Some of the Tendencies of Professor James's Work', *Journal of Philosophy* **7** (1910), 645–64.

'Is Consciousness "A Type of Behavior"?', *Journal of Philosophy* **8** (1911), 322–27.

1912   Letters on Woodrow Wilson's Application for a Carnegie Foundation Pension, *New York Times*, 17 June 1912, 25 June 1912.

1915   'The Defense of the Faith Today', *Bulletin of the General Theological Seminary*, New York City, **1** (1915), 25–30.

Review: W. E. Hocking, 'The Meaning of God in Human Experience', *Bulletin of the General Theological Seminary* **1** (1915), 46.

Review: Hardy, 'The Religious Instinct', *Bulletin of the General Theological Seminary* **1** (1915), 76–77.

Review: T. A. Lacey, 'Catholicity; Conciones ad Clerum', *Bulletin of the General Theological Seminary* **1** (1915), 111–13.

1916   *Review*: C. A. Ellwood, 'The Social Problem', *Journal of Philosophy* **8** (1916), 81–82.

      'An Ordination Sermon', *Bulletin of the General Theological Seminary* **2** (1916), 75–85.

1917   Autobiographical Notes, *Reports of Harvard College Class of 1892* (Plimpton Press, Norwood, Mass., 1917, 1922, 1928), alphabetical listings.

      Review: Galloway, 'Philosophy of Religion', *Bulletin of the General Theological Seminary* **3** (1917), 145.

      Review: William Temple, 'Mens Creatrix', *Bulletin of the General Theological Seminary* **3** (1917), 33–35.

      Review: Sanday and Williams, 'Form and Content in the Christian Tradition', *Bulletin of the General Theological Seminary* **3** (1917), 172–75.

      Review: H. G. Wells, 'God the Invisible King', *The Churchman* **115** (June 16, 1917), 710–11.

1918   'The Problem of Evil in the Present State of the World', *Anglican Theological Review* **1** (1918), 3–23.

      'Another Problem of Evil', *Anglican Theological Review* **1** (1918), 191–213.

      'Education of the Clergy: the Root Question', *The Churchman* **117** (May 4, 1918), 583–84.

1919   'Dr. Temple and Anglican Thought', *Anglican Theological Review* **1** (1919), 407–25.

      Review: Lyman, 'The Experience of God in Modern Life', *Anglican Theological Review* **2** (1919), 77–80.

      Review: Felix Adler, 'Outlines', *Anglican Theological Review* **2** (1919), 237–42.

      'The Shaping of Seminary Education', *The Churchman* **119** (May 24, 1919), 12–13.

1920   'Impressions of William James as Teacher', in Henry James (ed.), *Letters of William James*, Atlantic Monthly Press, Boston, 1920, Vol. II, pp. 11–17. [Reprinted in *Great Teachers*, ed. by Houston Peterson, (Rutgers University Press, New Brunswick, 1956), 221–30.]

      Letter on 'Dr. Grant and *The Churchman*', *The Churchman* **121** (Jan. 30, 1920), 7–8.

      Review: Lord Fisher, 'Memories and Records', *New Republic* (Aug. 4, 1920), 285–86.

1921   'Mr. Santayana and William James', *Harvard Graduates' Magazine* **29** (1921), 348–64. [Answered by Santayana, anonymously, in 'Professor Miller and Mr. Santayana', *Harvard Graduates' Magazine* **30** (1921), 32-36.]

      'M. Bergson's Theories', *New Republic* **26** (April 20, 1921), 242–46.

      'The Great College Illusion', *New Republic* **27** (June 22, 1921), 101–105.

      'The Strange Case of Mr. Chesterton and Mr. Shaw', *New Republic* **28** (August 31, 1921), 10–13.

      'The Antioch Idea', *Nation* **113** (September 7, 1921), 263.

      'Beauty and Use', *New Republic* **28** (October 26, 1921), 255-57.

1922   'Democracy and Our Intellectual Plight', *New Republic* **31** (June 21, 1922), 93–97.

      'New Life, A Commencement Address', *Bulletin of the General Theological Seminary* **9** (1922), 3–14.

      Review: John Haynes Holmes, 'New Churches for Old', *New Republic* **33** (December 13, 1922), 72-3.

'Matthew Arnold on Occasion of his Centenary', *New Republic* 33 (December 27, 1922), 113–16.

1923 'Resignation from General Theological Seminary', *School and Society* **18** (December 29, 1923), 767.

1924 'Conscience and the Bishops', *New Republic* **38** (March 5, 1924), 35–39.

1925 'Fullerton and Philosophy', *New Republic* **42** (May 13, 1925), 310-12.
'Intelligence in Our Time', *New Republic* **44** (Oct. 21, 1925), 221–24.

1927 *Review*: Whitehead, 'Religion in the Making', *New Republic* **49** (Feb. 16, 1927), 362–63.
Review: J. S. Bixler, 'Religion in the Philosophy of William James', *Journal of Philosophy* **24** (1927), 203–10.
'Dr. Schiller and Analysis', *Journal of Philosophy* **24** (1927), 617–24.

1928 'A Bird's-Eye View', *Journal of Philosophy* **25** (1928), 378–83.

1929 'The Pleasure-quality and the Pain-quality Analysable, Not Ultimate', *Mind* **38** (1929), 215–18.

1930 'Hume Without Scepticism', *Mind* **39** (1930), 273–301 and 409–25 (under the name R. E. Hobart).

1931 'Life of Harvard's Greatest President', *New Republic* **66** (March 4, 1931) 77–78.

1934 'Freewill as Involving Determination and Inconceivable Without It', *Mind* **43** (1934), 1–27 (under the name R. E. Hobart). [Reprinted in part in William Alston and Richard Brandt (eds.), *Problems of Philosophy*, Allyn and Bacon, Boston, 1967, and in John Hospers, (ed.), *Readings in Introductory Philosophical Analysis*, Prentice-Hall, Englewood Cliffs, N.J., 1968.]

1936 'James's Philosophical Development: Professor Perry's Biography', *Journal of Philosophy* **33** (1936), 309–18.

1937 'Is There Not A Clear Solution of the Knowledge Problem?', *Journal of Philosophy* **34** (1937), 701–12; **35** (1938), 561–72.

1940 *Mrs. Glendower Evans, Two Memorial Addresses*, Boston, 1940.

1942 'A Debt to James', in Blanshard, Brand, and H. W. Schneider (eds.), *In Commemoration of William James*, Columbia University Press, New York, 1942, pp. 24–33.
'William James, Man and Philosopher', in Otto, M. C. *et al.*, *William James, The Man and Thinker*, University of Wisconsin Press, Madison, 1942, pp. 31–51.
'James's Doctrine of "The Right to Believe"', *Philosophical Review* **51** (1942), 541–58; **52** (1943), 70.

1945 'An Event in Modern Philosophy', *Philosophical Review* **54** (1945), 593–606.

1947 'Professor Donald Williams versus David Hume', *Journal of Philosophy* **44** (1947), 673–84. [Reprinted in M. Martin and M. Foster (eds.), *Probability, Confirmation, and Simplicity*, Odyssey Press, New York, 1966.]

1949 'Hume's Deathblow to Deductivism', *Journal of Philosophy* **46** (1949), 745–62.

1950 'Moral Truth', *Philosophical Studies* **1** (April 1950), 40–46.

1951 'Descartes' Myth and Professor Ryle's Fallacy', *Journal of Philosophy* **48** (1951), 270–80.

1952 'Is Philosophy a Good Training for the Mind?', *Philosophical Forum* **11** (1952), 3–10.

PUBLICATIONS ABOUT DICKINSON S. MILLER

Eastman, Max, *Enjoyment of Living*, Harper and Brothers, New York, 1948, pp. 269–70, 281, 288–9.

Feigl, Herbert, 'Dickinson S. Miller', *The Encyclopedia of Philosophy*, ed. by Paul Edwards, The Macmillan Co. and The Free Press, New York, 1967, Vol. V, pp. 323–24.

Hare, Peter H. and Edward H. Madden, 'William James, Dickinson Miller, and C. J. Ducasse on the Ethics of Belief', *Transactions of the Charles S. Peirce Society* **4** (1968, No. 3), 115–29.

Hatch, William H. P. [Professor of New Testament, General Theological Seminary], 'Dickinson Sergeant Miller 1868–1963', *Proceedings and Addresses of the American Philosophical Association* 1963–64, Antioch Press, Yellow Springs, Ohio, 1964, pp. 121–22.

INDEX

Analysis, method of 1–3, 14, 26, 32, 39–43, 53–54, 59–60, 106, 175, 192, 201, 204–07, 241, 245–47
Arnold, Matthew 19–20, 62, 263–69, 312, 319

Balfour, Arthur 93–95
Belief 3–6, 27, 35, 133–35, 140–41, 208, 281–85, 298–302
  and action 290–92
  and hypothesis 23, 61, 201, 217, 282, 287–90
  see also Faith, Will to believe
Bell, Clive 20, 263
Bergson, Henri 15
Berkeley, George 2, 9, 30, 42, 60, 62n, 81, 133, 157–61, 177–78, 182, 219n
Blanshard, Brand 30, 184, 190–91, 195, 200n
Bradley, F. H. 153–54
Brightman, Edgar S. 27–28

Carlyle, Thomas 241, 264, 272, 313
Carnap, Rudolph 75, 79–80
Causality 24, 30–31, 58–59, 201–02, 205
  and necessity 31, 117, 184–88, 195–98
  and power 112–16
Clifford, W. K. 147, 284
Cognition, *see* Knowledge
Cohen, Morris 20, 263
Conscience of the mind 2, 14, 18, 32–33, 39, 46, 75, 252, 270, 309, 323–24
Consciousness 10–12, 28, 48, 57, 135–39, 146–55, 231, 233
  and unconscious mind 146–48, 151

Democracy 12, 19, 252–55, 258–61

Descartes, René 3, 78, 80, 153
Determinism, *see* Free Will
Dewey, John 2, 13, 16, 36n, 45, 281, 308, 310–11n
Ducasse, Curt J. 29, 31, 34, 184, 281

Eastman, Max 13, 29
Education 18–19, 32–33, 255–62, 266, 277, 280, 314–16
Emerson, Ralph Waldo 20, 241, 263–64, 317, 322
Empiricism 5, 11, 14, 21–22, 34, 182n, 201, 215–17, 285–86
  vs. deductivism 24, 30, 132, 187–90, 198–203, 208–10, 214–15
  radical 7–11, 146
  and religion 36n, 236–38, 269, 294–95
  and rationality 24, 26–27, 30–31, 42–43, 198–204, 212, 217–19, 292–93
  and significance 201, 207, 210–13
  See also Induction

Faith 16, 282, 285, 287–90, 298–99, 304, 309
Feigl, Herbert 21, 23
Free Will 15, 23, 26, 42, 56–60, 104–31, 205–07
  and fatalism 119–21, 206
  and prediction 119
  and moral judgment 121–31
Fullerton, George S. 1–2, 21, 26, 39–46, 52, 62n, 147

Gladstone, William E. 258, 261, 313

Hobart, R. E., Pseudonym of D.S. Miller 1, 25, 104, 184

Hobbes, Thomas 60, 80
Hodder, Alfred 35n, 50, 145n
Hodgson, Shadworth 5, 26, 60,
    62n, 97
Hume, David 2, 5, 21, 24–27, 30–31,
    34, 42–43, 60, 132-33, 150–51,
    177, 184–205, 209, 212–13,
    216–19, 241, 245
Husserl, Edmund 30, 156, 170,
    174–75, 177–81

Induction 24, 26–27, 132
    rationality of 27, 203, 217–19
    see also Empiricism

James, William 1–12, 22–23, 26,
    28–33, 43, 47–62, 64–68,
    146–54, 156, 168, 190, 201, 231,
    252, 281–311, 317–18
    see also Pragmatism, Will to
    believe
Joseph, H. W. B. 24, 184
Justice 128–31

Kant, Immanuel 24, 30, 35, 66,
    102–03n, 138, 141, 143, 184,
    189–90, 194–98, 201, 205, 216
Knowledge 3–7, 9–11, 35, 91,
    149–52, 302–05
    identity of indiscernibles in 27,
    132, 136–37
    James-Miller theory of 7, 33, 35
    and panpsychism 28, 146, 154
    presentation of object in 27–28,
    136–37
    reference in 3, 9, 26–28, 132–38
    see also Belief, Perception

Language 12, 34, 43, 131, 142–44,
    157, 164–66, 224, 241, 245–46,
    248, 278–79
    see also Propositions
Leibniz, G. W. 49, 80
Liberalism 31–32, 63, 72–73,
    264–65
Locke, John 2, 5, 26, 42, 60, 102n,
    153, 157, 219n
Lovejoy, Arthur O. 13, 145n
Lovett, R. M. 20, 263

Meaning 21–22, 26, 60, 75, 79–81,
    159–60, 178–82
Mencken, H. L. 20, 263
Mill, John Stuart 28, 71, 104, 146,
    217, 261–62, 273–74
Moore, G. E. 131n, 221, 223
Morality 17–20, 252–55, 268–69,
    281, 306, 312–26
    consequence theory of 17–20, 32,
    46, 252, 312, 322
    and free will 121–31, 206
    imperatives in 95–96
    intelligence in 18–19, 239–40,
    312, 322–24
    objectivity of judgments in 32, 98,
    220–25
    and oughtness 17, 94–102, 128,
    220–27
    and rules 17–19, 32, 252–54, 312,
    318–22
    and welfare 18–20, 220, 225–27,
    252, 260, 263, 269, 312, 321–26
    see also Justice, Punishment

Natural realism 9–11, 28, 146, 183n

Ontological argument 174

Peirce, Charles S. 53–54
Perception 9–12, 23, 27–28, 135–37,
    139–41, 151–54, 157–63, 166–69,
    197–98
Perry, Ralph Barton 13, 22, 26, 52,
    55, 281, 309
Personality 26, 52, 56–57, 173,
    231–32, 263, 269
    see also Self
Plato 92, 100
Pragmatism 3–4, 6, 9, 27, 31, 33,
    54, 59, 61, 91, 132, 135, 156,
    201, 203, 217
Probability 211, 213–14, 283–89
Propositions 24, 92, 95–96, 100–02,
    139–44, 174, 184, 189, 197–99,
    202, 205, 224, 231, 235, 283
    and necessity 208–10, 214–15
Punishment 127–30

Reform, social 18–20, 31, 73,
    264–66, 269

see also Democracy, Education, Liberalism
Reichenbach, Hans 219n
Religion 14–17, 23, 204–05, 231–35, 270–80, 282–85, 289, 294–96
  divine presence in 231–34, 251, 270, 276, 278
  and health 231–34, 302
  and morality 18, 20, 32, 232, 239–40, 312, 322
  and problem of evil 16–17
  symbols in 16, 20, 36n, 231, 270–73, 278
  and truth of value 14, 16, 20–21, 36n, 231, 235, 241, 249–51
  and welfare 231, 236, 238, 263, 269
  see also Faith, Ontological argument
Renouvier, Charles 60, 62n
Roosevelt, Theodore 66, 258, 265
Royce, Josiah 2–4, 7, 47, 51, 68, 71, 75, 81–83, 145n, 156
  on absolute mind 4, 82, 91
Ryle, Gilbert 12, 28, 84, 146
Russell, Bertrand 24, 85, 156, 165, 184, 210

Santayana, George 2, 7–8, 19, 21, 30–32, 42, 50, 55, 63–74, 169–70, 222, 266–67
Schiller, F. C. S. 29, 307
Self 43, 57–58, 105–11, 121–22, 135, 151–53, 205
  see also Personality
Sidgwick, Henry 47–48, 96, 113–14
Singer, E. A. 11, 146
Socrates 2, 39–40

Spinoza, Benedict 78, 80, 269
Stout, G. F. 27, 132, 139–41, 143–44
Street, Charles 14–15, 36n
Strong, Charles A. 7, 13, 22–24

Teaching 40–41, 47–51, 86–87, 255–58
  see also Education

Universals 24, 27, 134–35, 137, 142–44, 156–83
  concrete 30, 156, 168–69
  and essence 30, 156, 169–70
  as functions 30, 156, 160–64, 175–77
  and intentionality 178–81
  nominalism and 5, 175
  and psychologism 170–71, 180–81
  and subsistence 30, 156, 170–74

Value 220–27, 243–46, 248–51, 267–68, 286–87
  see also Religion

Welfare 8, 15–22, 32, 39, 44, 46, 52, 231, 236, 258–60
  and beauty 20
  and morality 18–20, 220, 225–27, 252, 260, 263, 269, 312, 321–26
  and pleasure 22, 220
Whitehead, Alfred North 24, 184
Will to believe 4–6, 19, 23, 28–29, 201, 217, 252–55, 281–311
  and morality 281, 306
Wilson, Woodrow 3, 321
Wittgenstein, Ludwig 22, 220
Worcester, Elwood 231, 235